# THE PROPHET PUZZLE

---

## INTERPRETIVE ESSAYS ON JOSEPH SMITH

ESSAYS ON MORMONISM SERIES
[to date]

Line Upon Line:
Essays on Mormon Doctrine
*Gary James Bergera, ed.*

The Word of God:
Essays on Mormon Scripture
*Dan Vogel, ed.*

The New Mormon History:
Revisionist Essays on the Past
*D. Michael Quinn, ed.*

Faithful History:
Essays on Writing Mormon History
*George D. Smith, ed.*

The Search for Harmony:
Essays on Science and Mormonism
*Gene A. Sessions* and *Craig J. Oberg, eds.*

Multiply and Replenish:
Mormon Essays on Sex and Family
*Brent Corcoran, ed.*

Tending the Garden:
Essays on Mormon Literature
*Eugene England* and *Lavina Fielding Anderson, eds.*

# THE PROPHET PUZZLE

## INTERPRETIVE ESSAYS ON JOSEPH SMITH

Edited by
*Bryan Waterman*

Signature Books Salt Lake City

COVER ILLUSTRATION: *JOSEPH SMITH*–FROM THE SERIES 12 FAMOUS MORMONS, BY LANE TWITCHELL, 1997, LATEX ON PANEL, 12" x 14", PRIVATE COLLECTION

COVER DESIGN: JULIE EASTON

∞*The Prophet Puzzle: Interpretive Essays on Joseph Smith* was printed on acid-free paper and composed, printed, and bound in the United States of America.

©1999 Signature Books. Signature Books is a registered trademark of Signature Books, Inc.

03 02 01 00 99 6 5 4 3 2 1

*Library of Congress Cataloging-in-Publication Data*
The prophet puzzle : interpretive essays on Joseph Smith /
edited by Bryan Waterman.
p. cm.
Includes bibliographical references.
ISBN 1-56085-121-X (pbk.)
1. Smith, Joseph, 1805-1844. I. Waterman, Bryan
BX8695.S6P77 1999
289.3'092
[B]–DC21 98-47222
CIP

# CONTENTS

# EDITOR'S INTRODUCTION

TO SUGGEST A PARALLEL BETWEEN JOSEPH SMITH, MORMONISM'S founder, and nineteenth-century American writer Nathaniel Hawthorne may seem far-fetched. The two men, though only a year different in age, inhabited largely different worlds–Smith on the "frontier" in New York, Ohio, Missouri, and Illinois; Hawthorne in the urban hub of Boston and vicinity. On closer look, however, their stories (Smith's continually retold story of his own life, Hawthorne's published tales) carry similar elements: markings, perhaps, of a cultural moment they shared after all. Historian Paul E. Johnson, reviewing John Brooke's 1994 book, *The Refiner's Fire: The Making of Mormon Cosmology, 1644-1844*, offered this succinct description of the antebellum culture in which both Smith and Hawthorne lived: "Americans after 1820," he writes, "suspected that confidence men, seducers, hucksters, counterfeiters, sneak-thieves, and impostures were everywhere. They lived in a new free-market society, a bank-note world that promised rationality and justice, but that many suspected was rigged by insiders. They depended on paper money that was usually authentic, sometimes untrustworthy and too often counterfeit. They worshipped their republic but distrusted every politician. They read cheap fiction and thronged to stage melodramas that portrayed a dark world of deceit and cruelty beneath placid appearances–a world in which heroes used evil means to fight for the greater good."[1] Themes of secrecy and exposure, authenticity and imposture are common in Hawthorne's tales and in Smith's life. But another link exists–specifically with Hawthorne's novel *The Scarlet Letter* (1850): a fascination not only with authenticity and fraud, or religion and sexuality, but also with ambiguity and interpretation.

"No man knows my history," Smith told his followers in 1844.[2]

The phrase was made famous a hundred years later as the title of Fawn McKay Brodie's seminal biography—a book that earned its author excommunication from the church Smith founded.[3] The memorable sentence forms the same sort of challenge Hawthorne presents in *The Scarlet Letter*: just as Smith refused to pin down his history, Hawthorne left the "A" word conspicuously out of his text and, furthermore, rendered the book's attitude toward its own protagonist ambiguous as well.

According to literary critic Sacvan Bercovitch, Hawthorne's ambiguity forces readers to interpret for themselves the symbolic letter and acts as "a function of prescriptiveness" that eventually "eliminate[s] possible divisions" in the culture we inhabit. Hawthorne's novel "impresses upon us," Bercovitch writes, "the need for personal interpretation; the inevitably partial nature of such interpretations; the richly varied experiential bases of interpretation; the tendency of these partial and shifting interpretations to polarize into symbolic oppositions, such as rumor and event, metaphor and fact, natural and supernatural, good and evil, head and heart, concealment and revelation, fusion and fragmentation; the need to recognize that these polarities, because symbolic, are never an inherent source of conflict, but instead they are always entwined in symbiotic antagonism and therefore mutually sustaining; and, as the key to it all, the clavis symbolistica, the need for faith both in the value of experience (shifting, private, and partial though it is) and in some ultimate hermeneutical complementarity, as in an ideal prospect that impels us toward an ever-larger truth." Ambiguity allows for such contraries, but eventually points to "some larger, truer interpretation."[4]

To some degree, Joseph Smith used ambiguity—especially regarding his own life—in similar ways. Taking into consideration the "deeply suspicious world" into which the Mormon prophet "introduced his Adamic restoration," writes Paul Johnson, "we must conclude that Joseph Smith expected to arouse accusations of fraud" by leaving many details about his story unanswered. Throughout his life Smith said very little, for example, about the translation process that resulted in the Book of Mormon, and he offered multiple versions of his "first vision" experience.[5] Indeed, Smith at some points knowingly fostered an "aura of ambiguity" around himself: such a cloak of secrecy made possible the institution in Illinois of rituals designed to protect the political and sexual peculiarities being introduced by Smith and others. Smith's legacy, Johnson concludes, is a "game," an "enigma that demands (as is demanded of no other major American religious figure) that we guess at the authenticity or fraudulence of the founder and the visionary," even a century and a half after his death.[6] In Bercovitch's terms, Smith uses ambiguity to demand "faith" in an "ideal prospect that impels us toward an ever-larger truth"—the truth of his own prophetic calling.

The essays in this volume take up Smith's legacy of enigma. Using tools from disciplines as diverse as history, psychology, literary studies, sociology, and theology, the selections here represent thirty years of writing about Joseph Smith. Many of the contributions contain arguments that have become familiar to those working in Mormon studies; others point to new directions, such as exercises in textual criticism and gender studies. The collection's purpose is to make a variety of interpretations of Joseph Smith, both previously published and new, accessible to a larger audience. They serve as reminders that the interpretive process, like Smith's own retelling of his life story, is always ongoing, always incomplete, always historically bound.

A number of recent interpretations of Joseph Smith deserve notice here, although their formats did not lend themselves to easy inclusion in this volume. The most significant treatment of Smith to emerge from within the Mormon studies sector during the last fifteen years is D. Michael Quinn's *Early Mormonism and the Magic World View* (1987), a landmark attempt to make sense of the connections between Mormon origins and early American and European cultures of magic.[7] While the Mark Hofmann forgeries, which had initially helped fuel Quinn's research,[8] left complicated questions about Smith and magic unresolved within Mormon circles, more recent developments, including Dan Vogel's ongoing compilation of hundreds of early Mormon documents[9] and Richard L. Bushman's plans for a new biography of Joseph Smith, will set the stage for another round of examinations.

Important recent interpretations from outside the Mormon community include historian Nathan Hatch's *The Democratization of American Christianity* (1989). Hatch framed Smith and early Mormonism against other populist religious movements in antebellum America to illustrate his argument that American religion in this period witnessed shifts in cultural authority from elite control to mass movements led by common people. His reading of the Book of Mormon as a populist text and treatment of Smith's and other Mormon leaders' early lives not only helped explain Smith's inner dynamics but examined him in a comparative focus. The next important interpretation was literary critic Harold Bloom's *The American Religion: The Emergence of a Post-Christian Nation* (1992), which embraced the Mormon prophet as a "religious genius" on the level of Ralph Waldo Emerson.[10] In the above-mentioned *The Refiner's Fire*, John L. Brooke surveyed much of the same material examined by Michael Quinn as well as the social histories and genealogies of early Mormon converts. He argued that Smith, via "memory" over "milieu," derived much of his cosmology from European hermetic traditions integral to the Radical Reformation of Christianity in Europe.[11] Paul E. Johnson saw the Mormon founder as reacting conservatively to a liberalizing American culture in which an eroding patriarchal authority was yielding to new religious and domestic authority for women.[12]

Several of the essays in this compilation treat similar topics and interpretations. Alan Taylor examines the "supernatural economy" that provided context for Joseph Smith's interest in magic.[13] Bloom's book is a departure point for Newell G. Bringhurst and Lance S. Owens. Other selections–Thomas G. Alexander's review essay in particular–offer broader historiographical surveys of work on Joseph Smith.[14]

The essays collected here represent, for the most part, established traditions of interpreting Joseph Smith. Jan Shipps's important contribution includes the admonition that "the mystery of Mormonism cannot be solved until we solve the mystery of Joseph Smith." She and Dan Vogel, who writes over two decades later in response, take up Smith's guessing game–his own cultivation of the prophet/fraud dichotomy. Steven C. Walker and Richard S. Van Wagoner focus on the translation of the Book of Mormon, a process that Richard L. Bushman examines in terms of Smith's sense of personal identity. Eugene England writes as believer, theologian, and literary critic, examining Smith's doctrinal innovations in the context of American Romanticism. The selections from Lawrence Foster, Robert D. Anderson, and Gary James Bergera work in various ways from psychological perspectives, a tradition that extends backward through Fawn Brodie to turn-of-the-twentieth-century psychologists such as I. Woodbridge Riley and William James. The final three essays by Ronald V. Huggins, Susan Staker, and Karl C. Sandberg demonstrate a variety of relatively unexplored ways–including Staker's ground-breaking feminist reading–in which textual criticism may be employed to gain insight into Joseph Smith's world. For believing Mormons, Smith's revelations and translations are best understood literally, and are not typically treated as windows into his own mind. Many of the essays collected here, however, illustrate ways in which such readings may be useful.[15]

Like the comparison between Smith's and Hawthorne's uses of ambiguity, the painting used on the cover of this compilation, from artist Lane Twitchell's series Twelve Famous Mormons (1997), also foregrounds the issue of interpretation. Twitchell's *Joseph Smith* is intentionally distorted, filtered it seems through television static, a reminder that we inhabit a world different from the one Smith was born into almost two hundred years ago. We do not, Twitchell's painting seems to say, know Smith's history, though we are better off for continually venturing new interpretations. While some readers may disagree with some of what they read in the essays that follow, such points of disagreement should serve to inform the continued conversation about Joseph Smith that has taken place since his own lifetime, a conversation he seemed to enjoy himself.

Appreciation is extended to the following authors and publications for permission to reproduce, sometimes in a slightly different format, the essays appearing here: to *Dialogue: A Journal of Mormon Thought* for the essays by Robert D. Anderson, Lawrence Foster, Ronald V. Huggins, Karl C. Sandberg, Alan Taylor, Richard S. Van Wagoner and Steven C. Walker, and Dan Vogel; to *Gnosis* magazine for the essay by Lance S. Owens; to the *Journal of the John Whitmer Historical Association* for the essays by Gary James Bergera and Newell G. Bringhurst; and to the *Journal of Mormon History* for the essays by Thomas G. Alexander and Jan Shipps. The essays by Richard L. Bushman, Eugene England, and Susan Staker are published here for the first time.

*NOTES*

1. Paul E. Johnson, "The Alchemist," *The New Republic*, 12 June 1995, 48.

2. Stan Larson, ed., "The King Follett Discourse: A Newly Amalgamated Text," *BYU Studies* 18 (Winter 1978): 193-208; reprinted in *The Essential Joseph Smith* (Salt Lake City: Signature Books, 1995), 232-45, quote on 245.

3. Fawn M. Brodie, *No Man Knows My History: The Life of Joseph Smith* (New York: Alfred A. Knopf, 1945).

4. Sacvan Bercovitch, *The Office of the Scarlet Letter* (Baltimore: Johns Hopkins University Press, 1991), 22-23.

5. On the Book of Mormon translation, see the essays by Bushman and Van Wagoner and Walker in this volume. On the first vision story, see the important essay by James B. Allen, "The Significance of Joseph Smith's 'First Vision' in Mormon Thought," in D. Michael Quinn, ed., *The New Mormon History: Revisionist Essays on the Past* (Salt Lake City: Signature Books, 1992).

6. Johnson, "The Alchemist," 48.

7. D. Michael Quinn, *Early Mormonism and the Magic World View* (Salt Lake City: Signature Books, 1987; 2nd ed. rev. 1998). Quinn's book influenced the treatment of Joseph Smith in the widely read book by American historian Jon Butler, *Awash in a Sea of Faith: Christianizing the American People* (Cambridge, MA: Harvard University Press, 1990).

8. See Lance Owens's essay in this volume, and Linda Silltoe and Allen Roberts, *Salamander: The Story of the Mormon Forgery Murders* (Salt Lake City: Signature Books, 1989).

9. Dan Vogel, ed., *Early Mormon Documents*, 2+ vols. (Salt Lake City: Signature Books, 1996).

10. Harold Bloom, *The American Religion: The Emergence of the Post-Christian Nation* (New York: Touchstone, 1992), 105.

11. Brooke, *The Refiner's Fire*, quotes from xvi.

12. See Johnson, "The Alchemist"; also "Democracy, Patriarchy, and American Revivals," *Journal of Social History* 24 (1991): 603-10. For Johnson's other treatments of Smith, see his book, co-authored with Sean Wilentz, *The Kingdom of Matthias: A Story of Sex and Salvation in 19th-Century America* (New York: Oxford University Press, 1994), esp. 3-11, and Johnson's portion of a standard college American history text, John M. Murrin, Johnson, et al., *Liberty, Equality, Power: A History of the American People*, 2 vols. (Fort Worth, TX: Harcourt Brace, 1996), esp. 349-50.

13. The term "supernatural economy" is taken from another of Taylor's essays, "The Early Republic's Supernatural Economy: Treasure Seeking in the American Northeast, 1780-1830," *American Quarterly* 38 (Spring 1986): 6-34.

14. Alexander covers material published through the late 1970s. For more up-to-date historiographical essays, see Bushman, *Joseph Smith and the Beginnings of Mormonism* (Urbana: University of Illinois Press, 1984), 189-92, and James Allen and Glen M. Leonard, *The Story of the Latter-day Saints*, 2nd ed.

rev. (Salt Lake City: Deseret Book Co., 1992), 687-89, 696-70, 703-20.

15. For a more devotional collection of historical essays, see Larry C. Porter and Susan Easton Black, eds., *The Prophet Joseph: Essays on the Life and Mission of Joseph Smith* (Salt Lake City: Deseret Book Co., 1988).

# 1.

# The Place of Joseph Smith in the Development of American Religion: A Historiographical Inquiry

*Thomas G. Alexander*

*[Author's note: In one of his monologues, that perceptive commentator on the human condition, George Carlin, said that an event he had just experienced left him with a sense of* vu ja-dé. *That is, that nothing like this had ever happened before. That's how I felt when I received the proofs for this essay. Published in 1978, the essay attempted to categorize and interpret examples of literature on the Mormon prophet Joseph Smith through about 1977. More than twenty years later, the essay seems almost like an artifact that I had never seen before.*

*My beliefs about historical methodology have undergone some changes in the past twenty years. I am less convinced that structural functionalism is a valid technique for historical analysis, and I believe more than ever that historians must try to understand their subjects in times past as they understood themselves. I say this with a sure knowledge that since my graduate school days I have believed that objectivity is possible–a noble dream, as Charles Beard called it. Still, in spite of the postmodern critique of historical methodology by scholars like Jacques Derrida and Michel Foucault in France, Theodor Adorno and Jürgen Habermas in Germany, and Hayden White and Simon Schama in the United States, I firmly believe that attempting to rethink the thoughts of past people is the only legitimate basis for historical understanding. (For a cogent discussion of these arguments from the point of view of an informed historiographer, see Georg G. Iggers,* Historiography in the Twentieth Century: From Scientific Objectivity to the Postmodern Challenge *[Hanover, NH: Wesleyan University Press, 1997].)*

*As the act of a thoughtful faith and a rejection of certain aspects of the postmodern critique, I reaffirm the imperative to study and understand the context in which people create texts. I affirm also that texts are the only legitimate sources from which historians can reconstruct the past. Whether historians tell stories or use analysis, they must study all that they can about the historical conditions in which the texts appeared.*

*Moreover, I reaffirm that historians must try to understand people in times past as they understood themselves. For Joseph Smith, this means that whatever else we see in his life, we must accept him as a religious figure and a prophet since that is how he and those who remained closest to him saw him. This means that we must understand his revelations and practices such as seer stones, magic, communitarian economics, polygamy, and bloc voting as aspects of religion not as secular or fraudulent phenomena.*

*Finally, historians have written a great many essays and books since 1977 which this essay does not consider. Were I to rewrite the essay, I would undoubtedly try to interpret and categorize those works, and I would undoubtedly adopt a different point of view on many of them. In view of the problems associated with rethinking the historiography of the past twenty-plus years, I was relieved when the editor suggested that I not do so.]*

SINCE 1830 HUNDREDS OF GALLONS OF PRINTER'S INK HAVE FILLED thousands of reams of paper with millions of words on the relationship between Joseph Smith and the development of religion in America. Many writers working independently have come to similar conclusions, but most have tended to fall into several categories ranging somewhere between two extremes. On the one hand, Mormons have argued that their church was the restored church of Christ—a unique creation—and that other religious organizations were either corrupt or precursors. At the other extreme, those antagonistic to the church have tended to see Mormonism and Joseph Smith as frauds or delusions. Other positions have ranged between these extremes, some viewing Mormonism as Joseph Smith's creation but as authentic religious experience, others seeing it as growing from the religious interests of early nineteenth-century America. This essay explores the views of various writers and offers some suggestions for future research.

## LITERATURE DURING JOSEPH SMITH'S LIFETIME

Any work on Joseph Smith and the development of American religion must take into account–indeed must begin with–the Book of Mormon (Palmyra: Joseph Smith, Jr., 1830). The title page states the official view of the book and of the relationship between Mormonism and other religions. Written to the Lamanite, Jew, and gentile "by the spirit of Prophesy and of Revelation," it was to show "the remnant of the House of Israel how great things the Lord hath done for their fathers; ... and also to the convincing of the Jew and Gentile that Jesus is the Christ, the Eternal God, manifesting Himself unto all nations."

The Book of Mormon became both a source and a target. One attack was Alexander Campbell's *Delusions: An Analysis of the Book of Mormon ...* (Boston: Benjamin H. Greene, 1832; originally published in *Millennial Harbinger,* 7 Feb. 1831). Campbell lumped Mormonism and Joseph Smith with the false Christs of previous ages and millennialist sects of his time. Campbell concluded that Joseph Smith was an atheist influenced by contemporary Protestantism. Campbell's major criticisms centered on what he viewed as anachronisms. "The Nephites," he wrote, "were good Christians, believers in the doctrines of the Calvinists and Methodists, and preaching baptism and other Christian usages hundreds of years before Jesus Christ was born!" Though Campbell considered Joseph Smith a fraud, he recognized that Mormonism dealt with the issues important to contemporary religionists.

Eber D. Howe's *Mormonism Unvailed; or, a Faithful Account of that Singular Imposition and Delusion* (Painesville, OH: Author, 1834) also began with a discussion of false messiahs, millennialist sects, and personal revelation. In a statement which could as well have been written by a recent biographer, Howe said that though Joseph Smith was poorly educated "it is obvious that all those deficiencies are fully supplied by a natural genius, strong inventive powers of mind, a deep study, and an unusually correct estimate of the human passions and feelings." Using themes which were to reappear again and again in the literature, Howe compared Smith to Muhammad and emphasized his belief in magic.

Two features of this book separated it from Campbell's work and formed the basis for some anti-Mormon studies as late as 1977.[1] In Howe's view, Sidney Rigdon was "the *Iago,* the prime mover, of the whole conspiracy." Admitting that he had "no positive proof," he argued that the Book of Mormon was really a novel written by the Reverend Solomon Spaulding which Rigdon stole from a printing shop in Pittsburgh.

Collaborating with Howe was Dr. Philastus Hurlbut, a Mormon excommunicant, who provided the Spaulding story and supplied a set of character-defaming affidavits from a large group of Joseph Smith's New York neighbors. Charges included money digging, use of peep-stones, drinking, ignorance, and poverty. The Howe-Hurlbut work became the basis for a phalanx of anti-Mormon writers like Henry Caswell *(The Prophet of the Nineteenth Century* [London: J. G. F. & J. Rivington, 1843]); and Jonathan Baldwin Turner *(Mormonism in All Ages* [New York: Plat and Peters, 1842]), whose commitment to traditional Protestantism led him to reject Mormonism as a deviant and irrational millennialist sect.

The Mormons themselves were not silent on this topic. Parley P. Pratt outlined the church's position on the question in *Mormonism Unveiled: Zion's Watchman Unmasked, and Its Editor, Mr. L. R. Sunderland, Exposed,* 3rd ed. (New York: Orson Pratt and Elijah Fordham, 1838). He pointed out that it was he who presented the Book of Mormon to Sidney Rigdon, and he reiterated the position that his church was the restored church of Christ. Pratt also differentiated between Mormon and Protestant doctrine on such questions as trinitarianism, the source of authority, baptism, gifts of the spirit, and millennialism.

Pratt's views were reinforced in 1839 by John Corrill's *Brief History of the Church of Christ of Latter Day Saints* (St. Louis: Author, 1839) which rejected the changes which had taken place in the church in Missouri. Corrill placed the church squarely in the Christian primitivist tradition and argued that the doctrines preached in the Book of Mormon coincided with those of the Bible. Most of the other pro-Mormon works written during Joseph Smith's lifetime likewise reinforced Pratt's position.[2]

In 1842 John C. Bennett, in *The History of the Saints* (Boston: Leland and Whiting, 1842), introduced a new element into the discussion by urging that Mormons attempted "to destroy the sacred institutions of Christianity, and substitute, instead of its powerful restraints upon the unholy passions of the human heart, a frightfully-corrupt system that would enable them to give free course to their lust, ambition, and cruelty." Thus the church was not a religion at all, but a cult, designed for the expression of base instincts. His examples included a bizarre form of elitist complex marriage and the Missouri Danites.

By Joseph Smith's death, many positions taken since that time on Mormonism and American religion had been outlined. For Mormons, it was *sui generis*—a religion for all the world designed to restore pristine Christianity. For some critics like Alexander Campbell, it was a sect, developed in the Protestant tradition of English and American millennialists and Christian primitivists with claims like the rest to new revelation and special authority. For those in the Hurlbut-Howe tradition, it was fraudulent—developed by a facile, creative, but unscrupulous mind, and in part the creation of Sidney Rigdon or Parley P. Pratt. The oft-used comparison with Muhammad[3] and the idea of a cult also developed before 1844.

## FROM THE DEATH OF JOSEPH SMITH THROUGH 1902

In the fifty-eight years between the death of Joseph Smith and the publication of William A. Linn's *Story of the Mormons: From the Date of Their Origin to the Year 1901* (New York: Macmillan, 1902), works on Joseph Smith and American religious development became essentially commentaries on themes already developed before 1844.[4]

Of the works written in the 1850s, perhaps the most useful was Lucy Mack Smith's *Biographical Sketches of Joseph Smith the Prophet and His Progenitors for Many Generations* (Liverpool, Eng., 1853; reprint, Independence, MO: Herald House, 1969), which provided considerable insight into Mormonism's religious and cultural background. More than half of this book is devoted to the period prior to 1830 and about two-fifths to the Smith family background. Clearly a lower-class family ravaged by modernization, the Smiths experienced poverty throughout the period of their residence and moves in Vermont, New

Hampshire, and New York. Joseph Smith, Sr., was a seeker influenced by universalism, and was a man given to dreams to which he attributed mystical significance. Lucy was also deeply religious, though she belonged to no denomination until she joined the Presbyterians in Palmyra. Thus, for Lucy, Mormonism grew out of special revelation from a background of Evangelical Protestantism and seekerism.

Perhaps second only to Lucy's *Biographical Sketches* was Parley P. Pratt's *Autobiography* (1888; Salt Lake City: Deseret Book, 1968), principally because of the insight into contemporary religious life and the attraction of Joseph Smith and Mormonism to the religiously aware. Pratt was converted because of the emphasis on biblical literalism, authority, millennialism, Christian primitivism, and gifts of the Spirit. The Pentecostal experience of the confirmation of the Spirit convinced Pratt that Mormonism was a restoration of primitive Christianity.

Mormonism changed over time as John Corrill had indicated, and some of those changes were outlined in David Whitmer's *An Address to All Believers in Christ* (Richmond, MO: David Whitmer, 1887). Whitmer affirmed his testimony of the Book of Mormon and said that the church had been functioning at least eight months before the formal organization on 6 April 1830. However, he left the church when new doctrines and offices not to his liking were introduced.

Significant views of the relationship between Joseph Smith and American religion were found in two works written by non-Mormons.[5] One of these was Jules Remy and Julius Brenchley's *A Journey to the Great Salt Lake City, with a Sketch of the History, Religion, and Customs of the Mormons,* 2 vols. (London: W. Jeffs, 1861). The authors considered the revelations of Joseph Smith to be pure speculation and the church to be "the coarsest form of mysticism"—a church that could not have grown in more settled and stable regions.

For them, however, Mormonism was *sui generis.* Joseph Smith, they argued, was a man of ability, and the secret of his success was his knowledge of the masses. He knew that "we must never make a complete breach with the past, and that the human mind never passes abruptly from one order of ideas to another and a different one, still less to an order that is completely antagonistic." Connection to traditional Christianity came through the Bible and Jesus Christ. In addition, the doctrines are "a sort of universal bazaar, with wares for every taste, and all comers." Joseph Smith and Mormonism could be seen as "a syncretic system, often of gross aspect when seen from a metaphysical and theological point of view," but attractive to people and "far from deserving those anathemas of which it has been subject." They saw that Joseph Smith's teachings were thoroughly Christian, "the spirit of equality and charity circulates through it, as it were, even to overflowing." They admired Joseph Smith's flexibility in various doctrines. Thus Mormonism for Remy and Brenchley became a curious mixture of Christianity, magic, mysticism, and pragmatism. Moreover, they were convinced that Joseph Smith had found sets of inscribed plates while digging for money.

Perhaps most striking, given the vilification he received from the Mormon community in the nineteenth century, was T. B. H. Stenhouse's *The Rocky Mountain Saints: A Full and Complete History of the Mormons, from the First Vision of Joseph Smith to the Last Courtship of Brigham Young* (New York: D. Appleton and Company, 1873). Mormonism, he argued, was a culturally derived religion of the heart. Only after mystical experiences had captured his soul did Joseph Smith and others turn to the Bible to find justification for the church. Stenhouse pointed out that it was impossible to invalidate Joseph Smith's experiences, because they were personal. Additionally, Stenhouse believed "that Joseph had at one time in his possession metallic plates of some kind, with engraved characters upon them, ... but where and how he got the plates which he exhibited to a number of persons, and whether the Book of Mormon is a veritable interpretation of the characters on those plates, and whether or not the narrative presented is true and of any importance to the world, are subjects purely of faith."

By 1902 new light had been shed on Mormonism by Lucy Smith, Parley P. Pratt, and David Whitmer. Remy and Brenchley had shown that scholars could gain some insight from disinterested study. Still, there was little basis for rational discussion of Mormonism and American religion because of the failure of writers even to agree on basic factual information. For instance, Linn's book, perhaps the best known work on Mormonism during the period, accepted the Spaulding theory which scholarly writers like Remy and Brenchley and virtually all Mormon writers had rejected as unsubstantiated.

## THE EARLY TWENTIETH CENTURY

From 1902 to 1949 the historiography changed somewhat as national publishers began to market books written about Mormonism by practicing Mormons. Nevertheless, most of the works published within the Mormon community did little more than add detail to the evidence of restoration and to the uniqueness of Joseph Smith. Among these were Brigham H. Roberts's *New Witness for God,* 3 vols. (Salt Lake City: Deseret News, 1895-1909);[6] Mary Audentia Smith Anderson's *Ancestry and Posterity of Joseph Smith and Emma Hale* (Independence, MO: Herald House, 1929), which provided extensive biographical information on the Smith family; and Francis W. Kirkham's *A New Witness for Christ in America,* 2 vols. (Independence, MO: Zion's Printing and Publishing Co., 1942-51), a collection of data on the Book of Mormon.

A major exception is Daryl Chase's *Joseph the Prophet as He Lives in the Hearts of His People* (Salt Lake City: Deseret Book, 1944). Because of his training in religious studies, Chase recognized that many of the features of the church which had been considered unique, such as baptism for the dead, apostles and prophets, the Apostasy, personal revelation, and the inefficacy of the Reformation, were in fact shared with other movements.

At the same time, a large group of anti-Mormon writers continued to trot out the same old themes such as the Spaulding theory.[7] Perhaps the one worthwhile contribution from that group was S. H. Goodwin's *Additional Studies in Mormonism and Masonry* (Salt Lake City: n.p., 1927), which pointed to the anti-Masonic background in upstate New York from 1826 to 1831 and the anti-Masonic themes in the Book of Mormon.

Perhaps no book written in the twentieth century offers such a mixed bag of insight and absurdity as I. Woodbridge Riley's *The Founder of Mormonism: A Psychological Study of Joseph Smith, Jr.* (New York: Dodd, Mead, 1902). Many of the important points in the book had already been made by Remy and Brenchley–and by Lucy Mack Smith. Imposing a psychological interpretation on this material, however, Riley arrived at the dubious conclusion that Joseph Smith was an epileptic.[8] Most significant, however, was his willingness to take the Book of Mormon seriously. This became necessary because of his view that "its contents will serve as an analysis of the prophet's mind, an intimate means of judging his early mental ability." He concluded that Joseph Smith was a person of extraordinary imagination and creativity. He argued that Smith picked up the idea of Hebrew origins for the Indians from the surrounding culture, and saw many religious ideas as coming from Evangelical Protestantism. Joseph Smith was, nevertheless, an authentic religious leader because he believed his gifts came from God and had convinced others of that belief. Riley believed that Joseph Smith was a "mystic rather than a materialist," and that the materialistic aspects of Mormon theology were engrafted by Orson Pratt. For Riley, Mormonism was a Protestant sect molded by the unique character of Joseph Smith and influenced by the theology of other converts.

Another scholarly study was Eduard Meyer's *Ursprung und Geschichte der Mormonen ...* (Halle: Max Niemeyer, 1912), now available in English: *The Origin and History of the Mormons, with Reflections on the Beginnings of Islam and Christianity,* trans. Heinz F. Rahde and Eugene Search (Salt Lake City: University of Utah, 1961). For Meyer, as for Remy and Riley, the relationship between Mormonism and American religion was to be found in Joseph Smith's cultural traditions. Joseph was a product of a belief in biblical literalism, continuous revelation, spiritual gifts, and the rejection of the Protestant belief that the canon of scripture was complete. He shared many of these things with the Catholics, Anabaptists, Quakers, and Christian primitivists.

In the scholarly tradition of Remy, Riley, and Meyer was Fawn M. Brodie's *No Man Knows My History: The Life of Joseph Smith, the Mormon Prophet* (New York: Alfred A. Knopf, 1945; 2nd ed., New York: Knopf, 1971). Although this book has been regarded as a significant scholarly breakthrough on the question of the relationship of Joseph Smith to American religion, Brodie essentially selected from and added detailed evidence to previous authors' views. Her views are perhaps most like Riley's, whose position on the background of Joseph Smith's ideas she accepts. Unlike Riley, however, she discounts the first vision as "probably the elaboration of some half-remembered dream stimulated by the early revival excitement and reinforced by the rich folklore of visions circulating in his neighborhood. Or it may have been sheer invention." Thus, though Mormonism for her is culturally derived, she seems uncertain whether Joseph Smith was a sincere, brilliant, and charismatic leader, or a brilliant and charismatic fraud. Nevertheless, she later sees Joseph "rapidly acquiring the language and even the accent of sincere faith."[9]

Brodie's principal drawback is that while she recognizes Joseph Smith's tremendous creativity, her views require ambivalence about the religion he created. Her narrative makes it plain that Mormonism was attractive and religiously satisfying to thousands of people during Smith's lifetime and afterward, but in the end she sees the stark granite shaft in Vermont as symbolizing "the barrenness of his spiritual legacy. ... he could not create a truly spiritual content for that religion." At the same time, she argues, "Joseph in his own person provided a symbol of nearness to God and a finality of interpretation that made the ordinary frontier evangelist seem by comparison all sound and fury."

By the early 1920s Mormons had begun to add scholarly insights to studies from outside. Ephraim Edward Ericksen's *The Psychological and Ethical Aspects of Mormon Group Life* (Chicago: University of Chicago Press, 1922; reprint ed., Salt Lake City: University of Utah Press, 1975) argues that though Mormonism grew out of the frontier and revivalist environment, it reacted against these influences by emphasizing the idea of restoration. Erickson argued that Smith developed a unique religion from origins which it shared in common with other less successful movements.

In some ways John Henry Evans's *Joseph Smith: An American Prophet* (New York: The Macmillan Co., 1933) is the most satisfactory work yet done on Joseph Smith. Its main drawbacks are the lack of notes, its organization by topics, and its dated research. Nevertheless, Evans recognized Smith's creative ability and religious insights; and his comparison of Joseph Smith and Alexander Campbell is insightful. For him, Campbell was a theologian and Smith an intuitionalist. "Joseph Smith," he wrote, "was a mystic, as a close examination of his teachings will show ... in that he saw the eternal in the temporal. His mind penetrates the shell and lays secure hold on the kernel." Withall, Evans realized that Joseph Smith was "a product of his times. No idea came to him till, apparently, there was a need for it; and there never was a need, it seems, but was satisfied immediately out of the capacious resources of the Mormon prophet. If he ran upon an idea–the communistic Family in Kirtland, for instance–he presently brought out of his ample reservoir of wisdom what appeared to him and his disciples 'a more perfect' plan." Moreover, the attraction of Joseph's spiritual and intellectual power was great.

By 1950 Mormonism had been subjected to searching investigation. With the exception of scholars like Ericksen, Evans, and Chase, however, Mormons seemed unwilling to confront the issues of their origins. Non-Mormon scholars, on the other hand, wrote copiously of origins but failed generally to confront Mormonism as an uplifting religious experience. Thus we find a contradictory Brodie, an interested but flawed study by Riley, and a Meyer who could not bring himself to read the Book of Mormon.

## FROM 1950 TO THE PRESENT

A new era in scholarly studies of Mormonism dawned with the publication in 1950 of Whitney R. Cross's *Burned-over District: The Social and Intellectual History of Enthusiastic Religion in Western New York, 1800-1850* (Ithaca, NY: Cornell University Press). Cross placed Mormonism in the larger context not only of millennialist sects but also of the development of Arminianism, free will, and perfectionism in previously Calvinist churches by Charles G. Finney and others and the reemphasis by Samuel Hopkins and Joseph Bellamy of traditional Calvinist doctrines like the sovereignty of God and the absolute powerlessness of man.

Cross's analysis of the cultural background of Mormonism is insightful. Palmyra, he argued, was not a frontier, but a rural area experiencing rapid growth. He accepted the evidence for gold digging, but pointed out that it was culturally based. He rejected the Howe-Hurlbut testimonials as self-serving and vague, pointed to the evangelical background of the family, and rejected the hypothesis of imposture together with the Spaulding story as "too transparently simple to explain the broad appeal of the new church. Such myths not only destroy Joseph's character but also breed serious misconceptions of how any religious novelty is likely to arise." Joseph Smith, Cross argued, combined appeals to reason, self-interest, and emotion. The church was egalitarian but approached doctrine with argument rather than excitement. Though Mormonism stressed the doctrines which revivalism had made most important, it approached them with a combination of rational and emotional fervor which the anti-intellectualism of evangelical religion could not comprehend. Above all, Cross recognized, as Brodie did not, that Mormonism's religious heritage was rich and varied rather than "sterile," since it was based on authentic religious experience rather than half-disguised fraud.

After Cross's insightful study came Thomas F. O'Dea's *The Mormons* (Chicago: University of Chicago Press, 1957). Perhaps O'Dea's most important contributions were his recognition of the importance of the Book of Mormon as a source for Joseph Smith's 1830 views on religious questions and his application of sociological insights to the study of Mormonism. In the Book of Mormon, O'Dea argued, the fundamental problem is the nature of good and evil. The book considers prophecy and revelation as a means of leading people. O'Dea saw Mormon emphasis as authoritarian rather than antinomian with no trace of perfectionism. The point of view of the Book of Mormon is democratic, Arminian, and mildly millennial while rejecting revivalism. It is, according to O'Dea, "an ideal projection of left-wing Protestantism."

Following the work of Cross and O'Dea came Mario S. DePillis's "The Quest for Religious Authority and the Rise of Mormonism," *Dialogue: A Journal of Mormon Thought* 1 (Spring 1966): 68-88. For DePillis, "Joseph Smith was a facile syncretist who took his ideas where he found them." In contrast to Cross, DePillis believes that western New York was indeed a frontier of New England in a cultural–if not a Turnerian–sense. For an understanding of Mormonism, it is in DePillis's view insufficient simply to discuss the relationship of the idiosyncratic features of Mormonism to the history of the time as Cross does. This approach, DePillis says, transforms Mormonism into "a kind of religious Grahamism." On the other hand, he takes Mormon historians to task for not relating "the doctrines of this new body of revelation to the historical and *theological* time and place of the Book of Mormon and the Doctrine and Covenants." Thus, though Mormons shared much with Campbellism, their central and most important doctrine was the authority which they found in the restoration of the priesthood. Campbell also believed in the idea of authority, but he found his authority in the consent of the congregation.

For DePillis, the central problem in understanding Mormonism is in understanding Joseph Smith. Sidney Rigdon, Parley P. Pratt, and others may have been important, but the elaboration of Mormon doctrine and practice between 1831 and 1844 was Smith's work. For DePillis, Mormonism is *sui generis.* The triad of Catholicism, Judaism, Protestantism ought to be a quadrad, including Mormonism.

A similar perspective, that Mormonism ought to be treated as a separate Judaeo-Christian religion, has infused the work of Jan Shipps ("The Prophet Puzzle: Suggestions Leading toward a More Comprehensive Interpretation of Joseph Smith," *Journal of Mormon History* 1 [1974]: 2-20; and "The Mormons: Looking Forward and Outward," *Christian Century*, 16-23 Aug. 1978, 761-66). Shipps opines that, even though Mormonism shares much of its value structure with middle-class Protestantism, Mormons have refused absorption into Protestantism.

In spite of the fact that there are now more Mormons than Presbyterians, as Shipps points out, the tendency in the general histories of American religion is to treat Mormonism as a Protestant sect or as an undefinable anomaly. William A. Clebsch ("Each Sect, the Sect to End All Sects," *Dialogue: A Journal of Mormon Thought* 1 [Summer 1966]: 84-89), writing in answer to DePillis and following the lead of Jerald C. Brauer and Winthrop S. Hudson, is an example of the first. Sydney E. Ahlstrom, *A Religious History of the American People,* 2 vols. (Garden City, NY: Doubleday, 1975), 1:613, discusses it with offbeat Jacksonian communitarianism but admits he is not sure whether it "is a sect, a mystery cult, a new religion, a church, a people, a nation, or an American subculture."

In recent years the question of Joseph Smith's alleged frauds has been revived by a number of studies. In general, they have dealt with the question of the first vision,[10] Joseph Smith's Palmyra reputation,[11] the use of magic and the occult,[12] and Joseph Smith's translation ability–particularly the Book of Abraham.[13] Except as they bear on the question of fraud as a means of understanding Mormonism, these studies have been helpful principally in revealing details about Mormonism and about the culture in which it developed.

Some of the most important recent research bearing on Mormonism and American religion has been done on Mormon doctrinal development and its millennialism. In addition to works like Ernest Lee Tuveson's *Redeemer Nation: The Idea of America's Millennial Role* (Chicago: University of Chicago Press, 1968), those dealing with the temporal aspects of theological millennialism like Klaus J. Hansen's *Quest for Empire: The Political Kingdom of God and the Council of Fifty in Mormon History* (East Lansing: Michigan State University Press, 1967) have been important. Arguing that Mormonism is in the tradition of the Anabaptists, British Fifth Monarchy men, and millenarian New England Puritans, Hansen places Mormonism with the premillennialists in their expectation of an imminent return of Christ. The Book of Mormon provided Mormons with a usable historical past which placed them in a dual Anglo-European and Hebraic tradition. Hansen also sees Mormon millennialism as imperialistic.

Another view of Mormon millennialism is presented in Marvin S. Hill's "Quest for Refuge: An Hypothesis as to the Social Origins and Nature of the Mormon Political Kingdom," *Journal of Mormon History* 2 (1975): 3-20. For Hill, Mormons were seeking refuge from a pluralistic society in which they felt uncomfortable; and he argues that the idea of the Kingdom of God as an aspect of Mormon millennialism ought to be seen as a way to escape rather than dominate the existing society.

Other doctrinal questions recently considered include Christian Primitivism, communitarianism, plural marriage,[14] and the nature of salvation. These doctrines took decidedly different twists in Mormonism than in other contemporary religions. Marvin S. Hill in "The Shaping of the Mormon Mind in New England and New York," *BYU Studies* 9 (Spring 1969): 351-72, drawing upon material used in part in his doctoral dissertation, points to the restorationist and Christian primitivist elements in Mormonism. As Gordon Irving has shown, the concept of salvation through families developed over a long period of time and in fact Joseph Smith's ideas in 1830 were close to traditional Protestant views of a heaven for the righteous and a hell for the wicked (Gordon Irving, "The Law of Adoption: One Phase of the Development of the Mormon Concept of Salvation, 1830-1900," *BYU Studies* 14 [Spring 1974]: 291-314).

## THE CURRENT STATE OF HISTORIOGRAPHY AND SUGGESTIONS FOR FUTURE WORK

The position of recent quasi-official studies on the relationship between Joseph Smith and the development of religion in America differs little from that taken in the early nineteenth century.[15] Though they often deal with background influences and are much more detailed and often better researched, they emphasize the church as restorationist and thus as *sui generis*.

Perhaps the logical successor to the scholarly studies of Ericksen and Evans is Donna Hill's biography, *Joseph Smith: The First Mormon* (Garden City, NY: Doubleday, 1977). A sympathetic Mormon, Hill has undertaken extensive and searching investigation into the presently available primary and secondary sources on the life of Joseph Smith. She recognized Joseph Smith's work as authentic religious experience, but sees also that the use of magic, seer stones, and divining rods was not inconsistent with early nineteenth-century religious faith. Most importantly, perhaps, she accepts Joseph Smith on his own terms. Recognizing, with writers like T. B. H. Stenhouse in the nineteenth century, that it is impossible to prove or disprove religious experience, she accepts religious motivation, deals with the mystical and supernatural events, and cites evidence of the practical results of those experiences. She also deals with such problematic areas as the kingdom of God and plural marriage.

Hill's biography seems to be the best yet written, but it too has some drawbacks. In the first place, she fails to develop a clear thesis on the relationship between Mormonism and other religions. In some cases she allows detail to substitute for analysis and, unfortunately, in many cases contradictory evidence is not reconciled. Many of the difficulties could probably have been avoided through the use of a larger conceptual framework. Writers on complex topics like this need to realize that evidence does not speak for itself.

Scholars like Klaus J. Hansen and Marvin S. Hill have emphasized the cultural circumstances in which Mormonism grew by analyzing the religious currents of the time and their relationship to Mormon doctrine and practice (see Hansen, "Mormonism and American Culture: Some Tentative Hypotheses," in F. Mark McKiernan, Alma R. Blair, and Paul M. Edwards, eds., *The Restoration Movement: Essays in Mormon History* [Lawrence, KS: Coronado Press, 1973], 1-25). Though Hansen tends to view Mormonism as revolutionary in the nineteenth-century context and Hill sees it as escapist, they both emphasize that it was millennialist and Christian primitivist and trace many doctrines to other denominations.

A recent scholarly view which sees Mormonism as unique, but differs from others in its view of the nature of that uniqueness, is Paul M. Edwards's "The Secular Smiths," *Journal of Mormon History* 4 (1977):3-17. Edwards argues that Joseph Smith was a mystic, but of the Eastern rather than Western tradition. For him, the church organization and theology are the products not only of Joseph Smith, but of Hyrum Smith and Parley P. Pratt. His argument is that Hyrum created the church on the Masonic model by historicizing Joseph's mystical and thus ahistorical experiences. Thus, for Edwards, Mormonism becomes a combination of ahistorical mystical experience and secular Masonic religion.

It should be pointed out that scholars will undoubtedly find much that is controversial in Edwards's views. As numerous writers like O'Dea and Goodwin have argued, many anti-Masonic elements are present in the Book of Mormon and in the church's origins. On the other hand, Reed Durham, in an unpublished Mormon History Association presidential address, pointed to many similarities in Masonic and Mormon mythology, but these seem to date from the Nauvoo period.

Edwards's views on the relationship between Joseph Smith and the development of the church organization are also problematic. If one feature separates the New Testament and the Book of Mormon accounts of Christ's ministry, it is that the organization and ritual of the church are much more explicit in the Book of Mormon than in the Gospels. If the Book of Mormon is to be used as a source for Joseph Smith's views, acceptance of Edwards's position will require the explaining away of the explicit organizational features of the Book of Mormon.

DePillis and Shipps, while recognizing the similarities in doctrines and practice with other contemporary religious movements, have both argued that Mormonism must be viewed as a unique part of the Judaeo-Christian tradition. Interestingly, this view is quite compatible with that held by orthodox Mormons that the church is the restoration of primitive Christianity. Even though DePillis and Shipps use naturalistic explanations, they see Joseph Smith's work as authentically religious.

In this their views differ from a broad range of writers taking various positions assuming Mormonism is better understood as fraud than as religious movement. These range from the somewhat equivocal views of Fawn Brodie to the rather more clear-cut position of Wesley Walters.

Those writing from within the Protestant tradition like Clebsch and Ahlstrom have tended to see Joseph Smith and Mormonism somewhat equivocally as a Protestant sect or as a communitarian curiosity.

As scholars have delved into the background of Mormonism in order to place Joseph Smith into perspective, there has been a tendency to rely, often unconsciously, upon the variant of structural functionalism called loose structuralism. Both of these techniques analyze the structure of a major culture and a subculture and the relationship between the two. In structural functionalism, however, care is given to probing and systematic analysis of both the major culture and the subculture. Loose structuralism, on the other hand, generally assumes a particular structure for one of the two cultures then analyzes the other in depth. Studies using loose structuralism have developed both among the defenders and the critics of Joseph Smith. Often within the Mormon community loose structuralism has been used to prove that the Book of Mormon or the Book of Abraham derives from Hebraic or Egyptian sources.[16]

As the background of Mormonism in western New York has been studied, the methodology of loose structuralism has been used quite often. A recent study using this technique is Richard L. Bushman's "The Book of Mormon and the American Revolution," *BYU Studies* 16 (Autumn 1976): 3-20, which defends the Book of Mormon by arguing that, by Jacksonian American standards, Nephite government was not democratic, and thus that the ideas of the Book of Mormon are not nineteenth-century American in origin.

Loose structuralism has been used since the time of Alexander Campbell to question the authenticity of the Book of Mormon. This is the case with the unpublished paper by William D. Russell, "The Historicity of the Book of Mormon: The Thought of Pre-exilic Israel and I & II Nephi Compared" (1977 presidential address of the John Whitmer Historical Association).

The major problems in both the Russell and Bushman studies are similar. Russell outlines in detail the cultural milieu of pre-exilic Israel but assumes a particular structure for Nephite America. In Bushman's study, the Book of Mormon society is explicitly outlined, but undocumented assumptions are made that Joseph Smith shared the cultural attitudes of dominant Jacksonian America. It seems clear that in the case of the Nephites, and of the Mormons during the life of Joseph Smith, we are dealing with subcultures or deviant cultures. This is obvious in part because most Hebrews did not leave Israel before the exile and polite early nineteenth-century American society did not believe in personal revelation or the occult. Both papers assume too much and prove too little about the unity of dominant and subcultural groups.

Structural functionalism is, of course, a valid technique which can be used in the analysis of the interrelationships between cultures. Scholars using this methodology must, however, be certain that their analysis does not stray into the realm of loose structuralism in which they assume rather than demonstrate particular cultural traits for either a sub- or major culture.

The points made with regard to loose structuralism are valid also for those who use psychohistorical techniques. If, for instance, an author asserts that Joseph Smith was an impostor (in the psychological sense) or an epileptic, it must be shown that he exhibited the various aspects of that syndrome. The use of glib analogy or parallel will not suffice.

One method which promises a great deal in furthering our understanding of Joseph Smith and Mormonism is what Robert Berkhofer has called "behavioralism."[17] This is the technique of analyzing a particular set of experiences by looking at them through the eyes of the actors. This has been used in several recent studies of Mormonism including Richard Bushman's "Joseph Smith and the Palmyra Magicians" (presented at the annual meeting of the Organization of American Historians, 13 Apr. 1978). Since scholars using this technique must try to understand experiences in the way in which the actors themselves understood them, the analysis, while rigorous, must judge the participants by their own standards.

The use of this method would immediately reduce the range of disagreement among scholars by eliminating at least two categories into which writers have previously placed Mormonism. No longer could Mormonism be considered as a Protestant sect or as anti-Christian. Realistically, however, there is little hope that the technique will be adopted and that either of these views will be overthrown.

Nevertheless, as the literature of the relationship of Joseph Smith and Mormonism to the history of American religion unfolds, scholars must be certain that they clearly understand the scope and limitations of the methodology they use. Discussions of the culture in which Mormonism grew must take into consideration the obvious cultural disunity of early nineteenth-century America. Even the evidence of the 1826 Bainbridge trial, used by many to attack the Mormons, makes clear the acceptance of the occult by many of Joseph Smith's contemporaries. The application of twentieth-century standards or even the standards of contemporaries who did not share a belief in magic and the occult help little in understanding Joseph Smith.

It seems improbable at this point that various views on Joseph Smith and Mormonism will soon be reconciled. We have a right to expect, however, proponents of various positions will work for more precision of research and definition. It is far past that time when scholars can be satisfied with vague categories and glib generalizations. Writers on complex topics like the development of important religious movements must be clear in their demonstration of causal connections between events. The similarities and differences must be analyzed and these must be played against a background of Joseph's experiences. Above all, careful cultural analysis must precede interpretations, since readers have a right to expect the most painstaking and sophisticated efforts.

*NOTES*

1. Lester E. Bush, Jr., "The Spaulding Theory Then and Now," *Dialogue: A Journal of Mormon Thought* 10 (Autumn 1977): 40-69.

2. See, for instance, Benjamin Winchester's *Plain Facts, Showing the Origins of the Spaulding Story* (Bedford, [Eng.]: C. B. Merry, 1841), which attacked the Howe-Hurlbut affidavits. Other defenders of Mormonism included Parley P. Pratt's *A Reply to Mr. Thomas Taylor* (Manchester, [Eng.]: W. R. Thomas, 1840); Orson Pratt's *An Interesting Account of Several Remarkable Visions ...* (New York: Joseph W. Harrison, 1841); and Joseph Smith's story in *Times and Seasons*, 1 Mar. 1842, and in *Correspondence Between Joseph Smith, the Prophet, and Col. John Wentworth* (New York: John E. Page and L. R. Foster, 1844).

3. Arnold H. Green and Lawrence P. Goldrup, "Joseph Smith, an American Muhammad?: An Essay on the Perils of Historical Analogy," *Dialogue: A Journal of Mormon Thought* 6 (Spring 1971): 46-58.

4. John Thomas's *Sketch of the Rise, Progress, and Dispersion of the Mormons* (London: Arthur Hall, 1847) compared Mormonism to Islam; George Sexton's *Portraiture of Mormonism* (London: W. Strange, 1849) viewed it as one of a series of "false Anti-Christian Isms"; Thomas Ford's *A History of Illinois ...* (Chicago: S. C. Griggs, 1854) sees it as Rigdonite fraud and communitarian sect; T. W. P. Taylder's *The Mormon's Own Book* (new ed., London: Partridge and Co., 1857) views it as cult and accepts the Spaulding theory; Pomeroy Tucker's *Origin, Rise, and Progress of Mormonism* (New York: D. Appleton and Co., 1867) accepts the Howe-Hurlbut stories; An Apostle's Wife, *The Mysteries of Mormonism: A Full Exposure of Its Secret Practices and Hidden Crimes, Fully Illustrated* (New York: Richard K. Fox for the Police Gazette, 1882), is designed to titillate repressed Victorians; W. Wyl's [Wilhelm Ritter von Wymetal], *Joseph Smith, the Prophet, His Family and His Friends ...* vol. 1 of a projected series called *Mormon Portraits; or, The Truth about the Mormon Leaders from 1830 to 1886* (Salt Lake City: Tribune Printing and Publishing Co., 1886), emphasizes the mystery cult; James H. Kennedy's *Early Days of Mormonism Palmyra, Kirtland, and Nauvoo* (New York: Charles Scribner's Sons, 1888) argues the fraudulent nature and millennialist sect position; Thomas Gregg's *The Prophet of Palmyra* (New York: John B. Alden, 1890), citing long quotations from contemporaries, sees Mormonism as "miserable fraud"; and Orsamus Turner, *History of the Pioneer Settlement of the Phelps and Gorham's Purchase* (Rochester: William Alling, 1852).

Lu B. Cake's *Peepstone Joe and the Peck Manuscript* (New York: Lu B. Cake, 1899) credits the fraud to Reed Peck. The Spaulding theory received new fuel from Robert Patterson's *Who Wrote the Book of Mormon* (Philadelphia: L. H. Everts, 1882); and was reinforced by Linn's *Story of the Mormons from the Date of Their Origin to the Year 1901,* which also emphasizes the occult.

On the Mormon side, we find the argument of a *sui generis* restoration in Edward W. Tullidge's *Life of Joseph the Prophet* (New York: n.p., 1878); George Q. Cannon's *Life of Joseph Smith, the Prophet* (Salt Lake City: Juvenile Instructor Office, 1888), which deals with the Reformation, but shows no causal connection with the Mormons. The relevant passages in Joseph Smith III and Heman C. Smith's *History of the Reorganized Church of Jesus Christ of Latter Day Saints,* 4 vols. (1897-1908; Independence, MO: Herald House, 1967), might as well have been written by Cannon.

The Spaulding theory received some shocks by E. E. Kelley's edition of Spaulding's *Manuscript Found or Manuscript Story ...* (Lamoni, IA: Reorganized Church of Jesus Christ of Latter Day Saints, 1885); and the Hurlbut-Howe affidavits were brought into question by William H. Kelley's "The Hill Cumorah and the Book of Mormon," *Saints Herald* 28 (1 June 1881): 161-68.

William W. Blair's *Joseph the Seer* (Plano, IL: Reorganized Church of Jesus Christ of Latter Day Saints, 1887) defends Joseph Smith against detractors by denying the inerrancy of the Book of Mormon and allowing for Joseph Smith's mistakes of grammar.

5. Two of these works, Richard F. Burton's *City of the Saints* (New York: Harper and Brothers, 1862) and Josiah Quincy's *Figures from the Past: From the Leaves of Old Journals* (Boston: Roberts Brothers, 1888), while admiring Joseph Smith and presenting a favorable image add little new. Burton considered Mormonism an evangelical sect and Quincy thought Joseph a charismatic leader.

6. Roberts is also significant for his work on the method of translation of the Book of Mormon which rejected the mechanical theory and took the view consistent with that which W. W. Blair had earlier proposed, that the words and phrases were worked out in Smith's mind by inspiration rather than appearing magically in the Urim and Thummim. Also significant was G. Homer Durham's *Joseph Smith: Prophet Statesman* (Salt Lake City: Bookcraft, 1944) for its explication of Joseph Smith's political views.

Works like Joseph Fielding Smith's *Essentials in Church History* (Salt Lake City: Church of Jesus Christ of Latter-day Saints, 1922) and William E. Berrett's *The Restored Church,* 4th ed. (Salt Lake City: LDS Department of Education, 1944) essentially reinforced previously held views, though Berrett emphasized also the frontier influence, as did Milton R. Hunter's *The Mormons and the American Frontier* (Salt Lake City: LDS Department of Education, 1940).

7. See the critique of this theory in Walter Franklin Prince, "Psychological Tests for the Authorship of the Book of Mormon," *American Journal of Psychology* 28 (July 1917): 373-89; the rebuttal by A. Theodore Schroeder, "Authorship of the Book of Mormon," ibid., 30 (Jan. 1919): 66-72; and Prince's reply, ibid., 30 (Oct. 1919): 427-28.

See also Charles A. Shook's *Cumorah Revisited* (Cincinnati: The Standard Publishing Co., 1919) and *The True Origin of the Book of Mormon* (Cincinnati, OH: Standard, 1914), which falls back on the Hurlbut affidavits; and Harry M. Beardsley, *Joseph Smith and His Mormon Empire* (Boston: Houghton Mifflin, 1931), which has to be one of the most confusing books on Mormonism produced by a major publisher in the twentieth century. Don Carlos Seitz's *Uncommon Americans: Pencil Portraits of Men and Women Who Have Broken the Rules* (Indianapolis: Bobbs-Merrill, 1925) emphasizes the bizarre. George B. Arbaugh's *Revelation in Mormonism: Its Character and Changing Forms* (Chicago: University of Chicago Press, 1932) accepts the Spaulding-Rigdon story and sees Joseph Smith as a pretended mystic. F. S. Spaulding's *Joseph Smith Jr. as a Translator: An Inquiry* (Salt Lake City: Arrow Press, 1912) attacks the Book of Abraham.

Alice Felt Tyler's *Freedom's Ferment: Phases of American Social History to*

*1860* (Minneapolis: University of Minnesota Press, 1944) is essentially based on secondary sources and provides no particularly useful insights.

8. This had already been suggested in M. Etourneau's *Les Mormons* (Paris: Bestel, 1856), as cited in Green and Goldrup, "Joseph Smith, an American Muhammad?" 49. Joseph Smith's psychological state was subjected to scrutiny and pronounced normal by T. L. Brink in "Joseph Smith: The Verdict of Depth Psychology," *Journal of Mormon History* 3 (1976): 73-78.

9. Perhaps no book in recent years has evinced more comment. See the rather outrageous Hugh Nibley's *No Ma'am That's Not History* (Salt Lake City: Bookcraft, 1946) and the scholarly Marvin S. Hill, "Brodie Revisited: A Reappraisal," *Dialogue: A Journal of Mormon Thought* 7 (Winter 1972): 72-87, and "Secular or Sectarian History? A Critique of 'No Man Knows My History,'" *Church History* 43 (Mar. 1974): 78-96.

10. Wesley P. Walters, "New Eight on Mormon Origins from the Palmyra Revival," *Dialogue: A Journal of Mormon Thought* 4 (Spring 1969): 60-81 (originally published in *Evangelical Theological Society Bulletin* 10 [Fall 1967]); Richard L. Bushman, "The First Vision Story Revived," *Dialogue: A Journal of Mormon Thought* 4 (Spring 1969): 82-93; Walters, "A Reply to Dr. Bushman," ibid., 94-100; Richard L. Anderson, "Circumstantial Confirmation of the First Vision through Reminiscences," *BYU Studies* 9 (Spring 1969): 373-404; Milton V. Backman, Jr., "Awakenings in the Burned-over District: New Light on the Historical Setting of the First Vision," ibid., 301-20; Backman, *Joseph Smith's First Vision* (Salt Lake City: Bookcraft, 1971); James B. Allen, "The Significance of Joseph Smith's First Vision in Mormon Thought," *Dialogue: A Journal of Mormon Thought* 1 (Autumn 1966): 29-45; and Dean C. Jesse, "Early Accounts of Joseph Smith's First Vision," *BYU Studies* 9 (Spring 1969): 275-96.

11. Richard L. Anderson, "The Reliability of the Early History of Lucy and Joseph Smith," *Dialogue: A Journal of Mormon Thought* 4 (Summer 1969): 13-28; "Joseph Smith's New York Reputation Reappraised," *BYU Studies* 10 (Spring 1970): 283-314; and *Joseph Smith's New England Heritage: Influences of Grandfathers Solomon Mack and Asael Smith* (Salt Lake City: Deseret Book, 1971). It should be noted that this is hardly an issue in the scholarly literature any longer, since at least from the time of Brodie scholars have generally treated the Hurlbut-Howe affidavits as unspecific and probably unreliable.

12. Hugh Nibley, *The Myth Makers* (Salt Lake City: Bookcraft, 1961); Jerald and Sandra Tanner, *Joseph Smith's 1826 Trial* (Salt Lake City: Modern Microfilm, 1971); Marvin S. Hill, "Joseph Smith and the 1826 Trial: New Evidence and New Difficulties," *BYU Studies* 12 (Winter 1972): 223-33; and Wesley Walters, "From Occult to Cult with Joseph Smith, Jr.," *The Journal of Pastoral Practice* 1 (Summer 1977): 121-37.

13. Klaus Baer, "The Breathing Permit of Hor: Translation of the Apparent Source of the Book of Abraham," *Dialogue: A Journal of Mormon Thought* 3 (Autumn 1968): 109-34; Richard P. Howard, "A Tentative Approach to the

Book of Abraham," ibid., 88-92; Hugh Nibley, *The Message of the Joseph Smith Papyri: An Egyptian Endowment* (Salt Lake City: Deseret Book, 1975); Michael Dennis Rhodes, "A Translation and Commentary of the Joseph Smith Hypocephalus," *BYU Studies* 17 (Spring 1977): 259-74; Wesley Walters, "Joseph Smith among the Egyptians: An Examination of the Sources of Joseph Smith's Book of Abraham," *Journal of the Evangelical Theological Society* 16 (Winter 1973):25-45.

14. Raymond Lee Muncy, *Sex and Marriage in Utopian Communities: Nineteenth Century America* (Bloomington: Indiana University Press, 1973); Leonard J. Arrington, Feramorz Y. Fox, and Dean L. May, *Building the City of God: Community and Cooperation among the Mormons* (Salt Lake City: Deseret Book, 1976).

15. John A. Widtsoe, *Joseph Smith: Seeker after Truth, Prophet of God* (Salt Lake City: Deseret News Press, 1951); Hyrum L. Andrus, *Joseph Smith, the Man and the Seer* (Salt Lake City: Deseret Book, 1962); Ivan J. Barrett, *Joseph Smith and the Restoration: A History of the Church to 1846* (Provo, UT: Young House, 1973); James B. Allen and Glen M. Leonard, *The Story of the Latter-day Saints* (Salt Lake City: Deseret Book, 1976); and Francis M. Gibbons, *Joseph Smith: Martyr, Prophet of God* (Salt Lake City: Deseret Book, 1977).

16. See above, n12, and also Hugh Nibley, *Lehi in the Desert and the World of the Jaredites* (Salt Lake City: Bookcraft, 1952); and *An Approach to the Book of Mormon* (Salt Lake City: Deseret News Press, 1957); John A.Tvedtnes, "Hebraisms in the Book of Mormon: A Preliminary Survey," *BYU Studies* 11 (Autumn 1970): 50-60.

17. Robert F. Berkhofer, Jr., *A Behavioral Approach to Historical Analysis* (New York: Free Press, 1969), 48-168; Mark P. Leone, "Comment on Joseph Smith's Temples: A Study in the Creation of Sacred Space," presented at Kirtland, Ohio, 22 Apr. 1977.

# 2.

# The Prophet Puzzle: Suggestions Leading toward a More Comprehensive Interpretation of Joseph Smith

*Jan Shipps*

JOSEPH SMITH WAS JUST ONE OF A PROLIFERATION OF PREACHERS AND prophets who found God along the stony ridges and narrow lakes of western New York in the first half of the nineteenth century. It was a place and a time of intense interest in religion: pathways to paradise ran in all directions. Prospective pilgrims had a choice, and many a wanderer journeyed a little way down first one path and then another, testing alternate routes to heaven. The story of the strange systems and unusual faiths that resulted is essentially a record of unsuccessful experiments with religion. Some survived for a season, but most of the cults and sects disappeared at the death of their leaders–if they lasted that long. Of all the unorthodox theological systems introduced in the New York hinterland between 1800 and 1850, the only one that has become an important American religion is the Church of Jesus Christ of Latter-day Saints.

The Mormon church found scant support in New York state, however. Within a year after the formal organization of the church, the Mormons had started their celebrated westward hegira by moving to Ohio. Because the phenomenal growth of the organization began after this initial move from New York state, the successful development of the church has generally been predicated on evidence found in the subsequent history of the sect. Tendentious histories–whether pro or con–almost invariably begin with the events that preceded the founding of the church in 1830, but for a long time the *objective* historiography of Mormonism was largely made up of studies which explained how Mormons built the Kingdom of the Saints following the removal of that realm from western New York.

In the mid-1960s the "Case of the Missing Information about Mormon Origins," as Truman G. Madsen once styled the problem posed by the paucity of information on the New England-New York background, can be said to have reopened. James B. Allen's article on "The Significance of Joseph Smith's 'First Vision' in Mormon Thought" was published in *Dialogue: A Journal of Mormon Thought* 1966, and the following year an intensive reexamination of Mormon beginnings was spurred headlong by the challenge to the integrity of Joseph Smith represented in the outcome of the Reverend Wesley P. Walters's investigation of the religious situation in and around Palmyra, New York, in the 1820s.[1] So much research has been carried out since then that a steady stream of articles, essays, and books on the early period in Mormon history is pouring forth.[2]

While some of these new works are little more than arguments with the Reverend Walters and LDS chronology, or with Philastus Hurlbut and Eber D. Howe about valid interviewing techniques, much of it is interesting–and extremely significant. Richard L. Bushman's description of what one can learn from a close reading of the rhetoric of the Book of Mormon, for example, is not only intrinsically useful, but methodologically important. Mario S. De Pillis, with his analysis of dream accounts, is also making a methodological contribution while adding to our understanding of the initial appeal of Mormonism.[3] At a less theoretical level, Dean Jessee's work with holograph writings provides precise information about who wrote what when, and, at the same time, demonstrates the procedures employed in the original production of such basic works as the Book of Mormon and Joseph Smith's history.[4]

Nevertheless, complacency is not in order. It is true that many major points have been clarified and many minor issues settled, but there are still loose ends not neatly tied up between the covers of *BYU Studies* and *Dialogue*; inconsistencies still exist that must be resolved before the case can be considered closed. In the meantime, all that can be said is that while a great deal is known about the methods used in building up this extraordinary religious society, its creation is still surrounded by mystery.

Throughout the nineteenth century, when the church was regarded as a threat to the social and political fabric of the nation, those who wrote about it were less concerned with the mysterious nature of Mormon origins than with their perceptions of present dangers. For a very long time the mystery connected with Mormonism appeared to be corporate—and criminal—and its solution was seen, therefore, less as a matter of understanding Mormon origins and theological beliefs than discovering the secrets of the temple and penetrating the plottings of the "sinister" hierarchy.[5] When polygamy and the political Kingdom were shorn away, the mystery for a time seemed to dissipate. Emphasis on the radical and revolutionary elements in Mormonism diminished, and the Saints seemed destined to fade unobtrusively into the American religious landscape. From the outside it even looked as if, in their search for acceptance and respectability, they might find a place, if not in the fold, then certainly along the fringes of American Protestantism.

In an essay Klaus J. Hansen speculates that something of this sort has, in fact, happened. After reviewing the reasons that explain Mormonism's failure to fit into the pluralistic, voluntaristic pattern of nineteenth-century American religion, he points out that, in the twentieth century, these reasons no longer function as boundaries marking Mormon peculiarity, and suggests that, as a result, Mormonism as a "distinct cultural unit" has more or less ceased to exist.[6] As is usually the case, Professor Hansen's elegant argument is extremely persuasive. Here, however, agreement must be made contingent on a clear understanding of the difference between a "cultural entity" and a religio-theological unit. While the homogeneous character of Mormondom is plainly giving way, the Saints are still set apart—certainly in their own self-consciousness—as a "community of the faithful." Despite a value structure and belief in Jesus Christ which Mormons share with middle-class American Protestants, the Saints have not been absorbed into Protestantism. A chosen people living in the new dispensation of the fullness of times cannot be a party to the denominational contract; they retain an identity as separate and distinct from American Protestantism as either Roman Catholicism or Judaism.[7] For that reason the "mysteries" of Mormonism, particularly the early years, remain matters of concern not only for Latter-day Saints who wish a deeper understanding of their faith but also for historians who would fully comprehend American religion.

Now that the nineteenth-century bias toward Brigham Young as the "real" genius of Mormonism is clearing away, it is obvious that the logical place to begin is with the study of Joseph Smith's life. That is not an easy task, however. As is so often the case with controversial figures, the prophet's adherents and detractors built up public images which they have been at pains to protect, leaving apparently irreconcilable interpretations of the Mormon leader's life. As a result the historian must cope with the contradictory accounts found on the one hand in memoirs penned by apostates and in affidavits collected from Smith's neighbors and on the other in the official *History of the Church*, a reconstruction of events compiled by diverse people including the prophet himself, which was commenced in 1838 with the express purpose of countering the reports that were circulated by "evil-disposed" persons clearly designed to militate against the character of the church and its prophet. The situation is further complicated by the need to establish the extent to which the contents of the Book of Mormon, the Pearl of Great Price, and the revelations of the prophet—works purportedly produced with the aid of deity—can be utilized as primary source material.

All these difficulties notwithstanding, a continuing effort must be made to solve the mystery of Mormonism by coming to understand the enigma at its core. The image that now exists is fragmented and incomplete. The perspective must be lengthened through a consideration of the prophet in the context of the social, political, economic, and theological milieu from which he came; the range of resources must be expanded to utilize the information and the insight that can be found in the Mormon canon; and the entire project must be approached with an open mind, a generous spirit, and a determination to follow the evidence that appeals to reason from whatever source it comes, wherever it leads. Only then will the outcome be a picture of the prophet and an account of the foundations of the Mormon faith which will be convincing to both *tough* minds, which demand empirical facts, and *tender* minds, comfortable in the presence of leaps of faith. What follows here are some suggestions leading in that direction.

In the first quarter of the nineteenth century, western New York was in effect the New England frontier. As they crossed the Adirondacks, emigrants from New England left behind the Half-way Covenant that had allowed church membership to be handed down from generation to generation. On the frontier the social satisfactions that had accompanied full standing in the Congregational churches of the older regions all but disappeared. Even long after the frontier character of this area had passed away, religion ministered primarily to the emotional rather than social needs of the populace. The unfolding economic opportunity that attended the building of the Erie Canal seemed to make everyone an heir to fortune; status came with success, and society no longer gave church members special social or religious privilege.

This fluid economic and social environment made an anachronism of the theological doctrine of divine election, and yet the Protestant community was still too close to the Reformation to alter the balance between faith and works in favor of the latter. As a result, the way of conventional Christianity throughout the district was the way marked out by George Whitefield and Gilbert Tennent during the Great Awakening in New England in the 1740s. Beyond the mountains, doctrinal distinctions denoting denominationalism were blurred by a stylized evangelism that forced the wide thoroughfare of Protestant Christianity into the confines of the sawdust trail. Whether the ecclesiastical connection of the minister made the service a Baptist gathering or a Methodist meeting, the sermon followed the predicted pattern of its "New Light" Presbyterian prototype.

With jeremiads that were painstaking catalogues of sins that would lead to destruction–and they were legion–Charles Finney and his fellows cautioned the unregenerate to beware the day of judgment. While penitents approached the sinner's benches, these lamentations were extended into compelling crescendos of exhortation designed to disturb the indifferent and terrify the wicked with speculation about the fate of unrepentant sinners abandoned to the wrath of an angry

God. As fear and guilt pulled heartstrings taut, the preacher watched with practiced eye for signs that the limits of emotional stress were near. Sounds of weeping and audible appeals for mercy were the prelude to skillful modulation from admonition to invitation and promise. When a contrite soul accepted the pledges of forgiveness and love and yielded absolute trust in God, release and rejoicing–sometimes verging on ecstacy–followed. Another Christian had been born again.

As unquestionably effective as such techniques were, their often transitory results reflected the limitations of a theology that attempted a compromise between the uncertainty inherent in the doctrines of predestination and divine election and the ineffable assurance of the interior religious experience. Using conversion as a catalyst, the Puritan theologian Jonathan Edwards had sought to merge mystic rapture and Calvinistic logic into a stable compound, but the subtleties of the speculations of this great philosophic intellect were lost when lesser minds proved unable to keep conversion at the center of Christian life where it had been placed by the Northampton divine. One result was the development of an emotional evangelism that made conversion the capstone of religious experience.

The good Master Edwards had kindled such a fire as has never yet been put out, but seldom has the flame blazed so brightly or for so long as it did beside the banks of the Erie Canal during the youth of Joseph Smith, the Mormon prophet. Revivalistic fervor swept through western New York state with such regularity that Orthodoxy back across the Adirondacks looked on the region as the "Burned-over District." The religious holocaust predicted by use of this derogatory designation failed to occur, however, and in 1825 it was clear that the fire that raged over the area was like the fire in the midst of the bush that burned and was not consumed. As if increase of appetite had grown by what it fed on, the spiritual longings of the people had created one of those spheres of genuine religious exploration that have served from time to time throughout human history as the seedbed for new theological systems.

Within a span of twenty-five years after the frontier gave way to the settled community life that paralleled the building of De Witt Clinton's canal, this "burnt" district sheltered a multitude of small bands and large congregations that had turned aside from traditional faiths to travel toward eternity along unmarked trails. As guides, contemporaries might follow Andrew Jackson Davis, the "Poughkeepsie Seer," and the amazing Fox Sisters into Spiritualism, or William Miller into Millennialism; they could make a more total commitment and move to Oneida to search for Perfection with John Humphrey Noyes; they could join the Shakers at New Lebanon or the Community of the Publik Universal Friend at Jerusalem in Yates County—or any of a host of lesser known groups that sought God with creeds embracing vegetarianism, sexual abstinence, communism, complex marriage, or some other equally esoteric doctrine.

But man has a way of packing the past among his personal possessions when he moved from place to place, and most of those who settled in the area had come with Protestant traditions so firmly fixed that no alternative was acceptable. The overwhelming majority of western New Yorkers looked for religious assurance in the old familiar places, and Presbyterians (and Congregationalists under the Plan of Union), Baptists, and Methodists all hastened to provide ministers to preach the gospel to the community beyond the Catskills. Unfortunately, these virtually simultaneous home missionary efforts of the several Protestant denominations sometimes brought religious chaos not spiritual comfort, for when conversion rather than spiritual guidance and pastoral care was made the primary purpose of the Protestant ministry, success became a matter of numbers. And since this quantitative criterion was not limited by the sum of uncommitted souls, the successful evangelist often had to build his church by tearing others down. There was a buyer's market in salvation, and in the confusion of contested credentials and conflicting claims, it was not at all unusual for a single soul to have been saved several times.

Although the Mormon prophet emerged from this volatile psychic ground, no evidence exists to indicate that religious tensions there caused him to move—as many other incipient religious leaders did—through a succession of affiliations with different religious groups, searching for satisfactory answers to spiritual questions. Like his father, Joseph Smith stood aside and refused to join any of the churches in the Palmyra region.

According to a biographical sketch written by his mother, Joseph Smith's father, Joseph Sr., did not become a member of any of the churches that were already established because he interpreted a dream (or vision) which he had had in 1811–the elder Smith like the father of Nephi in the Book of Mormon regarded dream and vision as synonymous–as a warning that these churches were the outposts of Babylon.[8] Joseph Jr. came to the same conclusion in a not altogether different fashion. When he dictated the explanatory prologue to the official *History* in 1838, the prophet described the way that the bewildering religious landscape had confused him. He said that in 1820 he had made prayerful inquiry about which church he should join and that the prayer had been answered in a vision wherein he saw two "personages" and was told that he should join none of the established churches as they were all wrong.[9]

Since the account of the first vision published in the *History of Joseph Smith, the Prophet* (the official history, Period One) seems to tie it chronologically to a revival that was going on in 1824 and 1825, since the prophet apparently mentioned this vision rarely if at all before 1830, and since no description of it seems to have been written down until almost a dozen years after it is said to have happened, Fawn Brodie, Jerald and Sandra Tanner, Wesley P. Walters, and others take the position that the first vision never occurred–that the prophet invented it in order to defend himself when his credibility was under attack.[10]

These critics may be right, of course. Certainly the Reverend Walters's reconstruction of the events surrounding the 1824 revival, his argument that this was the "war of words and the tumult of opinions" the prophet spoke of, is more convincing than the counter-argument that Smith was referring to an awakening that took place, not in the immediate Palmyra-Manchester area, but nearby, around 1820.[11] But using the confused chronology presented in the official *History* as the basis for assuming that an early vision–one which led Joseph Smith to stay away from organized religion–never occurred is less persuasive. And, considering all the available evidence, it is an exercise in unsound logic to use the same confused chronology to question the reliability of Smith's reports of subsequent visions and to conclude that his descriptions of most, or all, of the spiritual events in his life during the 1820s are *ex post facto* inventions designed to validate the story of the discovery of the metal plates which became the basis for the Book of Mormon.

As for considering all the available evidence: In addition to

William Smith's earliest known recollection of his brother Joseph's conversion, which does not connect the first vision to the 1824 revival, and in addition to the general tenor of the prophet's personal diaries, from which an attitude of piety and devoutness can be read back,[12] the evidence which has not been adequately brought to bear on this question is the Book of Mormon itself. Although this work has been considered—often at length—in general histories of Mormonism, it has by and large been neglected as a source which might facilitate a better understanding of Joseph Smith's early career. The reasons for this center on the answers that have usually been given to questions about who wrote the Book of Mormon and what its intrinsic merit is. Most Mormons have taken the position that Joseph Smith was the translator of the book, not its author, which means of course that since they believe the prophet did not write the book, they could not regard it as a potential source of insight into his early life. Throughout the nineteenth and much of the twentieth century, many non-Mormons were led to a similar conclusion, not because they thought the substance of the Book of Mormon had been taken from the plates of Nephi et al. but because the work was widely believed to have been plagiarized from a manuscript which had been lost by the Reverend Solomon Spaulding. Even if this notion was wrong and Joseph Smith had written the book, taking the work into account in explaining his career seemed foolish; after all, what could an amateurish historical novel masquerading as scripture reveal about a man's spiritual history?

The situation is changed now. In 1945 Fawn Brodie completely demolished the Spaulding manuscript myth and made it absolutely clear that anyone who wanted to fully understand Joseph Smith would have to come to terms with his "golden bible."[13] A dozen years later, in a critical explication included in his 1957 sociological study of Latter-day Saints, Thomas F. O'Dea made it just as clear that scholars would be mistaken to accept Mark Twain's assessment of the Book of Mormon as "chloroform in print" and in taking at face value Judge Cradlebaugh's description of the book as "a conglomeration of illy cemented creeds from other religions."[14] As a result, historians have reconsidered the Book of Mormon. And it is becoming increasingly obvious that whatever its source—whether it was translated from engravings on metal plates or dictated directly from Joseph Smith's extraordinary mind—this book functions as a powerful and provocative synthesis of biblical experience and the American dream, and it occupies a position of importance in both the religious and intellectual history of the United States.

It is likewise evident that beneath its crude exterior, the Book of Mormon reflects knowledge of the Bible, familiarity with theological currents, perception of the problems posed by Protestant denominationalism, and experience with extra-rational religious phenomena that simply are not consistent with the theory that its religious framework was an afterthought.[15] Since it posits a Book of Mormon produced by an essentially irreligious young man, adopting such a position requires a greater leap of faith than accepting a naturalistic explanation which holds (1) that Joseph grew up in a family fascinated with religion; (2) that, as he said, he thoroughly searched the scriptures and came to know them well; (3) that around 1820 he probably did have a vision or go through some other nonrational experience, which at least left him convinced that his father's dream about the organized churches all being in error was true; (4) that in the throes of revivalistic excitement he could well have come to doubt his earlier conclusion about the Protestant churches, leading him to inquire about the matter a second time, thereby stimulating a second vision around 1824; (5) that (as will be discussed below) in connection with his money-digging activities, he actually found some Indian artifacts, or hoped to do so, which inspired the writing of the Book of Mormon. Which, leaving aside the question of whether the book has captured eternal truths, plainly reflects the religious experiences and concerns that had been an important part of his life until that time.

Because Smith's history—so misleadingly alleged to have been written "by himself"—was, at once, a defensive reconstruction of events and a proselytizing treatise, and because, as Joseph grew in spiritual stature and theological sophistication, he seems to have reinterpreted some of the things that occurred in his early life, the confused accounts of the spiritual episodes of the 1820s will never be reconciled entirely. Yet the effort to learn more must be continued, for the greater our knowledge of the prophet's history in the decade prior to 1830, the more likely we are to comprehend the meaning of events which occurred after the founding of the church.

If the foregoing conceptualization of the events of Joseph Smith's youth which includes the visions as an integral part of his life is not completely congruent with what really happened, it does nevertheless assist us in understanding his complex personality. Reports of visions not unlike those described by this gregarious and handsome, albeit somewhat strange young man were by no means unknown in western New York in the 1820s, but these experiences were sufficiently singular to convince Joseph Smith that he was set apart from his peers. His subjective recognition of separateness may well account for the apparently compulsive need for acceptance that led him into "vices and follies" after he had been rejected "by those who ought," he said, "to have been my friends and to have treated me kindly." He wanted to belong but could not; he did not fit the pattern of men whose worlds were limited by scant schooling, mortgaged homesteads, and revivalist religion. He was different; he knew it, and the knowledge made him abnormally sensitive to the opinions of others. Although it was camouflaged in later years by his self-confident, almost cocksure, personality, this sensitivity persisted throughout his life. It caused him to place an unwarranted value on flattery and praise, and it made him react to criticism with an intensity that at times approached paranoia in his transformation of slight censure into "bitter persecution."

It was not his propensity to prophetic vision that first made Joseph Smith's difference distinct and introduced him to condemnation, however, for he was also gifted with what his contemporaries called "second sight." Using a "peepstone" (a luminous semi-precious gemstone which served as a screen for mental images) as a kind of psychic Geiger counter, Smith attempted to supplement the meager farm income of his family by assisting in the location of lost articles and buried "treasure." Because ventures of this nature which proved unsuccessful left the "peeper" vulnerable to charges of dishonesty and fraud, Smith was brought to trial in 1826 after he had failed to locate a silver mine he had promised to find, and he was charged with being a disorderly person and a fraud.

A year or so following the conclusion of that trial, Smith reported that he had in his possession a book, "written upon gold plates, [containing] an account of the former inhabitants of this continent and the sources from which they sprang." The existence of the plates, Smith said, had been revealed by an angel; they were instruments of divine revelation, which would, after translation, be the occasion of the ushering in of the new dispensation of the fullness of times. When the translation of the plates was completed and published to the world, the juxtaposition of these two apparently antithetical activities–digging for money and translating holy scripture–was used to bring the prophet's integrity into question and to cast doubt on the validity of his claims.

Testimony was collected in 1833 from almost a hundred people who had lived in the same general area where the prophet grew up, and their affidavits almost uniformly maligned the reputation of the Smith family and featured reports of the prophet's youthful search for buried treasure. Mormon apologists have sought to discredit these affidavits by charging muckraking and demonstrating how the information the witnesses supplied was contaminated by the attitude of the investigators. They are probably right on both counts. But attempts to discredit the information gathered by Philastus Hurlbut and Eber D. Howe can never prove that the attitudes reflected in the affidavits were not current or that the information in them is necessarily wrong, because newspaper articles and first-hand accounts written by Obadiah Dogberry, the Reverend Diedrich Willers, and James Gordon Bennett, which contain precisely the same information were published in 1831–a full two years before the preparation of *Mormonism Unvailed.*

The fact that so many of Smith's neighbors and acquaintances used the reputation of the Smith family (an important issue, but one which will not be dealt with here) and the "money-digging" to demonstrate the incongruity between the man they knew and a man of God is not surprising if the extraordinary difference between their perception of jovial Joseph and their Old Testament notions of appropriate prophets is kept in mind.

The situation can perhaps be compared to one occasionally encountered in today's world. A "model" devout church-going teenaged boy suddenly kills his father, and neighbors and acquaintances—finding it difficult to immediately alter their perception of the boy—explain over and over again that the young man had been a perfect child. Just as these explanations are crucial in developing a psychic profile which will facilitate an understanding of the patricidal act, so the Dogberry, Bennett, and Hurlbut and Howe reports of the way the people of Palmyra perceived the prophet are crucial to the development of a complete religious profile of Joseph Smith.[16]

Although Professor Hill is right in his assertion that magic and religious faith were not incompatible in nineteenth-century America,[17] it is nevertheless clear that the prophet and those who participated with him in the compilation of the official *History of the Church* were anxious not to emphasize the prophet's early connection with the divining art. It seems reasonable to conclude that the motive for playing down this part of the prophet's background was the knowledge that it could be used as the basis for charges that might endanger his reputation. But by sliding over that part of his life in the preparation of his history, Smith left himself vulnerable to the charges that have been used from that day to this as Exhibit A to prove at best his insincerity, at worst outright fraud.

If the prophet's preference for leaving the money-digging part of his career out of the picture is ignored, and the events of that part of his life are placed alongside the clearly defined spiritual events of his early years, a pattern emerges which leaves little room for doubting that Smith's use of the seerstone was an important indication of his early and continued interest in extra-rational phenomena and that it played an important role in his spiritual development.

| | |
|---|---|
| ca. 1820 | first vision |
| 1822 | peepstone discovered while digging a well |
| 1823-24 | angel said to have revealed the existence of the plates |
| 1824-26 | most intense period of money-digging activity |
| 1826 | trial at Bainbridge |
| 1827 | Smith reports having possession of the plates |
| 1828-29 | engraving on the plates is "translated" by means of the "Urim and Thummim," an instrument which operated on same principle as the peepstone |

Integrated in this fashion, the early events of Smith's life add up to a coherent whole that makes more sense than the charlatan-true prophet dichotomy which has plagued Mormon history from the beginning.

Historians who deal with Joseph Smith's post-1830 career are also faced with disparate interpretive models, but since the fruits of the prophet's labors after the church was established are more amenable to assessment, these models do not represent the same sort of polar opposites that have been developed to explain the Book of Mormon. The building up of Kirtland, Far West, and Nauvoo, the formation of an efficient and effective organizational structure for the church, and the overall development and remarkable growth of Mormonism were substantial achievements which can hardly be credited to a ne'er-do-well, practiced in the magic arts and proficient at deception and trickery or for that matter to a prophet intoxicated with divinity. Some students of the Mormon past have denied Smith's crucial role as the leader of the church–suggesting that he was a dreamer, a visionary, or a madman, who was fortunate enough to have Brigham Young around to handle practical things, and who managed to be martyred, as Bernard DeVoto said, "at precisely the right time" to allow his blood to become "the seed of the church." But this view, like the notion that someone other than Smith wrote the Book of Mormon, has not survived in the wake of Fawn Brodie's *No Man Knows My History*. Historians are now generally agreed that the prophet's influence was the decisive factor in almost every phase of the construction of the Mormon Kingdom, though they do not agree on the reasons why this is so. Devotional interpretations explain almost everything in terms of the "Will of the Lord," but historical interpretations of Smith's later career are variations on two themes: Joseph Smith as charismatic personality and Joseph Smith as pragmatic prophet.

These two themes are not diametrically opposed; as categories they are not mutually exclusive; each depends on the other. Biographical treatments of that part of Smith's life which follows the founding of the church, therefore, betray less anti-Mormon/pro-Mormon bias than the portrayals of his youth. The images remain distressingly different even so. Difficult questions are not adequately answered either with the explanation that the prophet was an effective leader because he was ultimately taken in by his own deception or with the reminder that the prophet was a prophet only when he was acting as such.

Perhaps the situation will be clarified if the problem is approached from another direction. Joseph Smith was a dynamic personality, it is true; and there was undoubtedly a charismatic quality to his leadership. If his charisma is seen not as a function of his personality but as an integral part of his role as prophet, seer, and revelator, the reasons for the reactions to his leadership of both Mormons and non-Mormons will be more intelligible. While the distinction being made here was not important for the large portion of the Saints who perceived his personality and his prophet's role as one, it is important in fathoming the behavior of those Saints who made Smith's ability to carry everything before him contingent on their ideas about the authenticity of his prophetic position. When his pronouncements and actions led certain Saints to conclude that Smith was a fallen prophet, his charisma, for them, evaporated.

The prophet, seer, and revelator *role,* then, is central to an understanding of the prophet's life. Because this role grew out of and was defined by the Book of Mormon and the circumstances surrounding its "translation," it is there that we must look to get a glimpse of how the prophet's role was perceived by Smith and by his followers. There too we must turn if we would begin to analyze the importance of the *role* of the prophet as a factor in early Mormonism's appeal.

The Book of Mormon claimed to be the history of the Western Hemisphere between 600 B.C. and 400 A.D., but its account of that millennium was interspersed with such an astonishing variety of philosophical notions and theological speculations that it was immediately apparent that this was no ordinary history. The work recounted stories of voyages and battles and tales of intrigue and treason. Yet the most striking passages in the Book of Mormon are those which are essentially explications of ideas that had also been a part of the visions of Joseph Smith's youth. Allusions to the ideas which, according to Smith's own account, were conceived in the course of his extraordinary experiences, were particularly clear in the second section of the book. This section, 2 Nephi, included a series of chapters which detailed the state of society existing when the plates of gold would be opened to the man chosen of God. These prophetic predictions returned again and again to the themes of the visions; that churches already current were corrupt and that a book containing a "revelation from God from the beginning of the world to the ending thereof" would be delivered into the hands of a "seer" whom the Lord would bless, whose name like that of his father would be Joseph, who would bring the people who loved the Lord to salvation.[18]

Since a far greater portion of the book was concerned with a fanciful history of the western hemisphere, it stands to reason that its initial appeal was not entirely religious. This was a time when the people of the United States were busily engaged in the manufacture of instant heritage, substituting inspiration for antiquity with regard to the Constitution and producing a veritable hagiography of popular biography designed to turn America's political leaders into national heroes in the shortest possible time. Joseph Smith's visionary account of the American past was therefore not entirely out of place.[19] The passages which referred to the United States as the "land of promise" and as "a land which is choice above all other lands" appealed to (and reflected) the nationalistic sentiment of the age in overt fashion. And in addition Smith's golden book was a fascinating expression of the prevalent American desire to declare cultural independence from Europe. In a pseudo-Elizabethan prose style that recalled the King James version of the Bible, the Book of Mormon maintained that the American Indians were remnants of the twelve tribes of Israel and that Jesus Christ had appeared on this continent in 34 A.D. Thus the book provided a link between the history of the United States and the Judeo-Christian tradition that by-passed the European culture filter altogether.

Nevertheless, this unconventional pre-Columbian history of the western hemisphere must in large measure be regarded as suits and trappings for the prophetic device that reiterated the errors of established churches and promised that the seer who read the record found on the golden plates would be the agency through which the ancient church in all its purity should be restored.

> And it shall come to pass that my people ... shall be gathered home unto the lands of their possessions. ... (2 Ne. 19:14).
>
> If they will repent and hearken unto my words, and not harden their hearts, I will establish my church among them, and they shall come into the covenant and be numbered among his remnant of Jacob, unto whom I have given this land for their inheritance ... that they may build a city which shall be called the New Jerusalem (3 Ne. 21:22-23).
>
> And blessed are they who shall seek to bring forth Zion (1 Ne. 13:37).

Joseph Smith said that the "miracle" of translation was accomplished by means of a "curious instrument which the ancients called

'Urim and Thummim,' ... two transparent stones set in the rim of a bow fastened to a breastplate," that somehow allowed him to read the "reformed Egyptian" engraving as if it were English.[20] As news of his unusual project spread across the countryside, a small band of followers including Martin Harris, Oliver Cowdery, Joseph Knight, several members of the family of Peter Whitmer, and most of Smith's own immediate family gathered round. They watched the progress of the work as Smith dictated it from behind a makeshift curtain to be written out on foolscap paper by Cowdery or Harris or his new bride Emma, and they were convinced that Joseph Smith had a divine calling.

Martin Harris's wife, Lucy, was convinced otherwise, and so after a portion of the manuscript had been completed, Harris persuaded the translator to let him take those pages home in order to prove to Lucy that the work was inspired of God. But Lucy Harris was not impressed. She had never liked Smith, and she heartily disapproved of her husband's association with him. She feared, not without reason, that Harris intended to use his modest fortune to make publication of Smith's golden Bible possible; and consequently when she got her hands on the manuscript, she destroyed it.

The crisis that resulted profoundly affected the new religion. Joseph Smith prayed for guidance and received two revelations directing that the lost section should not be retranslated. Lest the devil arrange publication of the missing section, God would provide another set of plates which would summarize the account contained in the missing chapters.[21] Thus did Joseph Smith don the prophet's mantle.

Thomas F. O'Dea has suggested that the exigency of the situation with which Smith was faced simply proved to be the necessary occasion for the introduction of contemporary revelation; he says that a belief in continuing revelation was vital to the secure establishment of the new religion and that it should probably have come in any case.[22] Fawn Brodie failed to credit the translator with so much foresight; she concluded that the revelations were a ruse—perhaps an unconscious one—to conceal the fact that the story of the golden plates was false and that Smith merely capitalized on their effect among his followers.[23] Yet Fawn Brodie and Thomas O'Dea agree that this event was decisive in Mormon history, and most students of Mormonism concur, so that accounts of the origins of the Church of Jesus Christ of

Latter-day Saints usually trace the doctrine of continuing revelation to this juncture in Joseph Smith's career.

Notwithstanding the importance of the doctrine of continuing revelation in the development of the faith, few serious attempts have been made to delineate the difference between these revelations and Smith's earlier esoteric activities. Church doctrine makes no distinction between the divine character of the Book of Mormon and the prophet's revelations. From the outside all the reports of visions and revelations and the writing of golden Bibles and the pursuit of treasure with a peepstone tend to become so confusing that it is entirely understandable that historians often dismiss the problem by saying that it is all a matter of faith. And indeed it is. But just as Vernon Louis Parrington and Perry Miller were obliged to go to theological polemics to fully comprehend the social and economic and political developments in Puritan New England, so the student of Mormon history must seek the explanation of many of the significant events in Joseph Smith's life in the subtle distinction between vision and revelation.

In the eyes of the Latter-day Saints, Joseph Smith's early visions and his later revelations are both dialogues between God and humanity. The difference turns on who initiated the conversation. Whether it is regarded as a metaphysical event or a psychic phenomenon, a religiously-oriented vision is an intensely realistic subjective experience which leaves the individual who has experienced it with a definite sense of having been in direct communion with God. Like other spiritual manifestations, the hearing of transcendental voices, infused meditation, illumination, and so on, visions are spontaneous occurrences apparently independent of the conscious human mind.

Although it is true that many of the prophet's revelations–particularly the ones having to do with theology or the organization of the restored church–were accompanied by visions, voices, or some other metaphysical phenomena, much of the revelation in Mormonism proceeds from a more prosaic but more dependable method of communicating with God. As it worked out in Mormon history, this process of revelation involves asking for divine instructions and receiving an "impression" of the will of the Lord in return. In theological terms, God initiates the vision and humanity responds; men and women ask for revelation and God responds.[24]

The difference was clear even to the prophet. The visions left him with no doubts about the reality of what he had seen and heard. When William James said that persons who have undergone traumatic religious experiences "remain quite unmoved by criticism from whatever quarter it may come, [because] they have had their vision and they *know*," he could have been referring directly to Joseph Smith who wrote, "Why does the world think to make me deny what I have actually seen? For I had seen a vision; I knew it and I knew God knew it, and I could not deny it."[25]

This same confidence did not always extend to the revelations, however. David Whitmer wrote that Smith himself said "some revelations are of the devil."[26] Historians who deal with the prophet's life and the history of the church must take note of the implications of that statement and weigh the possibility of considering the revelations according to some classification scheme. This does not mean—*must not mean*—that a dash through the Doctrine and Covenants identifying revelations of a first, second, and third order is necessary. It means rather coming to realize and consciously accept what Robert Flanders's *Nauvoo: Kingdom on the Mississippi* and Leonard Arrington's *Great Basin Kingdom* demonstrate implicitly, a recognition of the fact that a continuum on which the revelations can be placed *exists*. At its highest terminal point are the revelations which came during those moments when a higher reality erupted into the prophet's everyday world; at its opposite are the revelations which can perhaps best be marked not, as Smith said, "of the devil" but as wishful thinking.

Taxonomical exercises in history are always dangerous, frightfully so when the subject is the history of religion. But in view of Mormon history's double interpretative strand of Joseph Smith as man of God and Joseph Smith as fraud who exploited his followers for his own purposes—lately summed up as a religious versus a rational being—it is possible that drawing distinctions between the character of the different parts of the Mormon canon will allow us to see the prophet's mature life as more coherent than is now possible. I am not an expert on Joseph Smith. But I do know that the mystery of Mormonism cannot be solved until we solve the mystery of Joseph Smith.

In a biography I once heard described as the best biography ever written of an American historical figure, Carl Van Doren described Benjamin Franklin as a "harmonious human multitude." We do not have a comparable biography of the prophet. Joseph Smith was also a "human multitude," an extraordinarily talented individual, but our picture of him is anything but harmonious. What we have in Mormon historiography are variations on two Josephs: the one who started out digging for money and when he was unsuccessful, turned to propheteering; and the one who had visions and dreamed dreams, restored the church, and revealed the will of the Lord to a sinful world. While the shading was varied, the portraits have pretty much remained constant; the differences are differences of degree, not kind.

The approach I am suggesting at least has the virtue of providing a different perspective from which to view the prophet's life. The result cannot be harmony, because Joseph himself had difficulty integrating the many facets of his complex career. But it might allow us to reconcile enough of the inconsistency to reveal, not a split personality, but a splendid, gifted–pressured, sometimes opportunistic, often troubled–yet, for all of that, a larger-than-life *whole* man.

*NOTES*

1. James B. Allen, "The Significance of Joseph Smith's 'First Vision' in Mormon Thought," *Dialogue: A Journal of Mormon Thought* 1 (Autumn 1966): 29-45. Madsen's remarks were made at the 1968 Edwardsville Conference on the Mormons in Illinois. Walters's article, "New Light on Mormon Origins from the Palmyra Revival," was first published in 1967 as an Evangelical Theological Society tract and was reprinted in *Dialogue: A Journal of Mormon Thought* 4 (Spring 1969): 60-81.

2. Concentrated research in the available records relevant to Mormon history in New York was carried out under the direction of a committee of Mormon historians and scholars headed by Madsen. The first fruits of this project were presented in the spring 1969 issue of *BYU Studies* (vol. 9), which included the following articles: James B. Allen and Leonard J. Arrington, "Mormon Origins in New York: An Introductory Analysis"; Dean C. Jessee, "The Early Accounts of Joseph Smith's First Vision"; Milton V. Backman, Jr., "Awakenings in the Burned-over District: New Light on the Historical Setting of the First Vision"; Larry C. Porter, "Reverend George Lane–Good 'Gifts,' Much 'Grace,' and Marked 'Usefulness'"; T. Edgar Lyon, "How Authentic Are Mormon Historic Sites in Vermont and New York?"; Marvin S. Hill, "The Shaping of the Mormon Mind in New England and New York"; Richard L. Anderson, "Circumstantial Confirmation of the First Vision through Reminiscences." The 1970 spring issue of the same journal was also devoted to the

New York period. It included two articles by Russell R. Rich, "Where Were the Moroni Visits?" and "The Dogberry Papers and the Book of Mormon," as well as Dean C. Jessee, "The Original Book of Mormon Manuscript"; Richard L. Anderson, "Joseph Smith's New York Reputation Reappraised"; Stanley B. Kimball, "The Anthon Transcript: People, Primary Sources, and Problems"; Leonard J. Arrington, "James Gordon Bennett's 1831 Report on 'The Mormonites'"; and Larry C. Porter, "The Colesville Branch and the Coming Forth of the Book of Mormon." A chapter on "The Church in New York and Pennsylvania, 1816-1831," in *The Restoration Movement: Essays in Mormon History,* ed. F. Mark McKiernan, Alma R. Blair, and Paul M. Edwards (Lawrence, KS: Coronado Press, 1973), 27-61, was also written by Mr. Porter. In addition, see Marvin S. Hill, "Joseph Smith and the 1826 Trial: New Evidence and New Difficulties," *BYU Studies* 12 (Winter 1972): 223-33; and "Brodie Revisited: A Reappraisal," *Dialogue: A Journal of Mormon Thought* 7 (Winter 1972): 72-85; Milton V. Backman, Jr., *Joseph Smith's First Vision* (Salt Lake City: Bookcraft, 1971); and Richard L. Bushman, "The First Vision Story Revived," *Dialogue: A Journal of Mormon Thought* 4 (Spring 1969): 82-93; and Reverend Walters's reply to same, 94-100.

3. Doctors Bushman and De Pillis read papers reporting the results of their research at a session on "Early Mormonism in Its American Setting" at the annual meeting of the Western Historical Association in New Haven, Connecticut, 13 Oct. 1972.

4. In addition to the articles noted above, see "The Writing of Joseph Smith's History," *BYU Studies* 11 (Summer 1971): 439-73.

5. In a chronologically stratified representative sample of articles on Mormons and Mormonism published between 1860 and 1895, 74 percent contained references to Mormonism as a threat to the American political system, 66 percent contained pejorative references to the internal control church leaders exercised over the LDS community, but only 57 percent contained references which were coded as "unflattering descriptions of Joseph Smith, of the origins of Mormonism, or of the religion itself." Jan Shipps, "From Satyr to Saint: American Attitudes Toward the Mormons," a paper presented to the annual meeting of the Organization of American Historians, Chicago, Mar. 1973.

6. "Mormonism and American Culture: Some Tentative Hypotheses," in *The Restoration Movement,* 1-25. The complexity of the ideas put forth in this essay make summary difficult. The essay should be read in its entirety.

7. This conclusion agrees with the characterization of Mormonism as the fourth major religion generally accepted in American society found in Mario S. De Pillis, "The Quest for Religious Authority and the Rise of Mormonism," *Dialogue: A Journal of Mormon Thought* 1 (Spring 1966): 78. The full effect of the abandonment of the policy of the "literal gathering" is more apparent today than it was in 1966. While cultural distinctiveness is disappearing–an

inevitable consequence, in any case, of the international outreach of both major branches of Mormonism–it is possible that the dispersal of LDS "communities of the faithful" throughout the nation and the world has resulted in a heightened consciousness of Mormon peculiarity, both from within and from without.

8. Lucy Mack Smith, *History of the Prophet Joseph* (Salt Lake City: *Improvement Era,* 1902, 54. The 1908 edition of this work has been reprinted by Arno Press, New York.

9. Joseph Smith, Jr., *History of the Church of Jesus Christ of Latter-day Saints: Period I, History of Joseph Smith the Prophet,* ed. B. H. Roberts, 6 vols., 2nd ed. rev. (Salt Lake City: Church of Jesus Christ of Latter-day Saints, 1955), 1:4-6; hereafter cited as HC. (An official publication of the Mormon church.)

10. See Fawn M[cKay] Brodie, *No Man Knows My History: The Life of Joseph Smith, the Mormon Prophet* (New York: Alfred A. Knopf, 1945), 25; Jerald and Sandra Tanner, *Joseph Smith's Strange Account of the First Vision* (Salt Lake City: Modern Microfilm, n.d.), 3; Walters, "New Light on Mormon Origins," 71-73.

11. See Bushman, "The First Vision Story Revived"; Larry C. Porter, "Reverend George Lane"; Porter, "The Church in New York and Pennsylvania, 1816-1831," chap. 1 in *Restoration Movement*; and Backman, *Joseph Smith's First Vision.*

12. Hill, "Brodie Revisited," 76, 78-81.

13. Mrs. Brodie categorized the Mormon Bible as merely one of several ostensibly inspired sacred books made up of "an obscure compound of folklore, moral platitude, mysticism, and millennialism" (67). Readers of *No Man Knows My History* come away convinced, however, that the "compound" is Joseph Smith's own.

14. See chap. 2 of O'Dea's *The Mormons* (Chicago: University of Chicago Press, 1957). Mark Twain's sally is in the appendix to *Roughing It.* Judge Cradlebaugh's description was given in his testimony before Congress in 1863. It is reprinted in Andrew J. Hanson, "Utah and the Mormon Problem," *Methodist Quarterly Review* 64 (Apr. 1882): 213. The description is of course not unique: it is a variation of Alexander Campbell's 1832 charge that the book contained answers to every conceivable theological question. Nineteenth- and early twentieth-century anti-Mormon literature, especially that portion of it published in religious periodicals, is shot through with similar charges that the Book of Mormon is made up of wholesale borrowings from other religions. It is likely that Sterling McMurrin's *Theological Foundations of the Mormon Religion* (Salt Lake City: University of Utah Press, 1965) was also a factor in the reappraisal of the Book of Mormon.

15. Reverend Walters summarizes this position in the concluding section of "New Light on Mormon Origins." With reference to this same point, Brodie states: "What had been originally conceived as a mere money-making history

of the Indians had been transformed at some point early in the writing, or possibly even before the book was begun, into a religious saga" (83).

16. The Dogberry editorials and selections from affidavits collected by Hurlbut and Howe are reprinted in the appendix to *No Man Knows My History*. Bennett's articles are reprinted in Arrington, "James Gordon Bennett's 1831 Report on the 'Mormonites,'" 353-64.

17. Hill, "Brodie Revisited," 78.

18. Specific references to the errors of already established churches are found in 2 Ne. 26:20-21; 28:3-20. The content of the records engraved on the plates of gold are described in 2 Ne. 27:6-11; 28:2. The prophecy about the seer to be called Joseph is in 2 Ne. 3:1-19.

19. The German historian Peter Meinhold has commented at length on the way in which the Book of Mormon provided America with a usable past. See "Die Anfaenge des Amerikanischen Geschichtsbewusstseins," *Saeculum* 5 (1954): 65-86. This work is discussed in Klaus J. Hansen's chapter on "Mormonism and the American Dream," *Quest for Empire* (East Lansing: Michigan State University Press, 1970).

20. In his 1974 Mormon History Association Presidential Address, "'Is There No Help for the Widow's Son': Mormonism and Masonry," Reed C. Durham alluded to a Masonic legend which utilized many of the same elements–metal plates, stones called Urim and Thummim, and Egyptian hieroglyphics–found in Smith's account of the origin of the Book of Mormon. The quotation is from the Wentworth letter, HC, 4:537.

21. HC, 1:22-28.

22. O'Dea, *The Mormons*, 19-20.

23. Brodie, *No Man Knows My History*, 55-57.

24. The two categories, vision and revelation, which are being put forth here are not intended to be mutually exclusive; they are rather semantic symbols intended to encompass *process* (the means by which communications between God and the Mormon prophet were initiated) as well as the extra-rational phenomena themselves.

25. HC, 1:7-8. While this quotation is taken from the official history, which account has been called into question, the reality of the prophet's perception of his having been made responsible for translating the plates is substantiated in chaps. 2, 4, and 9 of the Book of Commandments (1833; reprt., Independence, MO: Herald House, 1972), 8-13, 22-27.

26. David Whitmer, "An Address to All Believers ...," reprinted in Keith Huntress, *Murder of an American Prophet: Events and Prejudice Surrounding the Killings of Joseph and Hyrum Smith; Carthage, Illinois, June 27, 1844* (San Francisco: Chandler Publishing Co., 1960), 23. This point must not be confused with Smith's clear distinction between his actions as a prophet and his actions as a "mere man."

# 3. "The Prophet Puzzle" Revisited

*Dan Vogel*

IN HER ESSAY "THE PROPHET PUZZLE: SUGGESTIONS LEADING TOWARD a More Comprehensive Interpretation of Joseph Smith," first published in 1974 and reprinted in the present compilation, Jan Shipps confronted the anomalies in the historical record concerning Smith, noting: "What we have in Mormon historiography is two Josephs: the one who started out digging for money and when he was unsuccessful, turned to propheteering, and the one who had visions and dreamed dreams, restored the church, and revealed the will of the Lord to a sinful world."[1] To resolve this "schizophrenic state of Mormon history, with its double interpretive strand of Joseph Smith as a man of God and Joseph Smith as a kind of fraud who exploited his followers for his own purposes," Shipps called for a more fully integrated view of Smith, one that allows for the complexities of human personality. More than twenty years later, Smith remains an enigma for historians, believer and skeptic alike.

My intent is not to rehash evidence on both sides of the prophet/fraud issue, but to suggest a possible solution to Shipps's "prophet puzzle." Unraveling the complexities of Smith's character and motives is difficult, but before the puzzle can be solved, all the pieces, or at least the most significant ones, must be gathered and correctly interpreted. Some of these, in my opinion, have been overlooked, ignored, or mishandled–pieces which I believe reveal previously hidden features of Smith's complex, conflicted, and gifted personality. Throughout, however, one would do well to bear in mind Marvin S. Hill's warning that those who attempt such endeavors "must write with courage, for no matter what they say many will disagree strongly."[2]

I

The most obvious solution to Shipps's puzzle is to suggest that Smith was a "pious deceiver" or "sincere fraud," someone who deceives to achieve holy objectives. Admittedly, the terms "pious deceiver," "sincere fraud," and the like are not wholly satisfying. Nevertheless, "pious" connotes a sincere religious conviction, and my use of "fraud" or "deceiver" is limited to describing *some* of Smith's activities–the possible construction of plates from tin as well as his claim that the Book of Mormon is a translation of an anciently engraved record, for example–not to Smith's perception of himself. In other words, Smith may have engaged in fraudulent activities while at the same time believing that he had been called of God to preach repentance in the most effective way possible. In fact, this was the thesis of Lutheran minister Robert N. Hullinger's 1980 book, *Mormon Answer to Skepticism: Why Joseph Smith Wrote the Book of Mormon.*[3] Responding to Shipps's complaint that the Book of Mormon "has by and large been neglected as a source which might facilitate a better understanding of Joseph Smith's early career,"[4] Hullinger attempted to discover Smith's motives for writing the book by examining the book's rhetoric, and concluded: "Joseph Smith ... regarded himself as [a] defender of God."[5] "Even if one believes that Joseph Smith was at best a scoundrel," he observed, "one still must account for the Book of Mormon."[6] Indeed, the book's religious appeal–its defense of God, Jesus Christ, and spiritual gifts, and its call to repentance–argues strongly against presuming that Smith's motives were malicious or completely self-serving.[7]

Marvin S. Hill has similarly cautioned against seeing Smith in eith- er/or terms, insisting that one balance the implications of Smith's 1826 trial with his private and genuine expressions of religious concern.[8] In his 1972 review of Fawn Brodie's influential biography of Smith, *No Man Knows My History,* Hill criticized her for ignoring the religious side of Smith's personality and portraying him as essentially irreligious. "[Brodie] says little about the rationalizations Joseph would have had to go through where his religious role was imposed upon him," Hill observed. "Brodie was never able to take us inside the mind of the prophet, to understand how he thought and why. A reason for that may be that the sources she would have had to use were Joseph's religious writings, and her Smith was supposed to be irreligious."[9]

Among the first lines Smith wrote in his new journal, which he began keeping in November 1832, was: "Oh my God grant that I may be directed in all my thoughts Oh bless thy Servant Amen." A few days later he wrote: "Oh Lord deliver thy servant out of temptations and fill his heart with wisdom and understanding."[10] Such passages, which Brodie either ignored or was unaware of, reveal Smith's inner, spiritual world, and those who disregard this, who fail to recognize a deeply spiritual dimension to Smith's character, or who count his profession of religion as contrived, throw away a major piece of the prophet puzzle. I am convinced that those who wish to understand Smith on his own terms must escape the confinement of Brodie's paradigm.

At the same time, one cannot turn a blind eye to Smith's willingness to deceive. One of the clearest indications of this is his public denials of teaching and practicing polygamy while privately doing so.[11] But perhaps of more relevance is his activity as a treasure seer. This is one of those pieces of the puzzle that, I believe, has been mishandled, or at least not fully appreciated by Mormon scholars generally. Some wish to compartmentalize Smith's treasure-seeing activity as irrelevant to his prophetic career, or to view it as some kind of psychic training-ground for the developing prophet.[12] If these perspectives are not entirely inaccurate, they are at least incomplete.

Despite an attempt to minimize his early involvement in treasure searching, Smith was in reality an aggressive and ambitious leader among the competing treasure seers of Manchester, New York. It was in fact his unparalleled reputation as a treasure seer that drew Josiah Stowell to hire Smith, not as a digger, but as a seer to locate treasure.[13] From November 1825 until his arrest and court hearing in South Bainbridge in March 1826, Smith was employed by Stowell and others to locate treasure not only in Harmony, Pennsylvania, but also at various locations in the southern New York counties of Broome and Chenango.[14] During the 1826 proceeding, Smith admitted under oath that he had been actively engaged as a treasure seer for the past three years and that he had recently decided to abandon the practice because it was straining his eyes.[15] It was not without reason that Smith tried to conceal these facts in his history: if he did not consider them at odds with his role as prophet, he at least found them easier to omit than to explain.

It is when we examine specific examples of Smith's treasure seeing that apologetic or traditionalist explanations run aground. Jonathan Thompson, for instance, testifying in Smith's defense at the court hearing, reported that on one occasion Smith located a treasure chest with his seer stone. After digging several feet, the men struck something sounding like a board or plank. Excitedly they asked Smith to look into his stone again, probably to verify the source of the sound as there was apparently some doubt. But, as Thompson reported, Smith "would not look again pretending that he was alarmed ... on account of the circumstances relating to the trunk being buried [which] came all fresh to his mind, that the last time that he looked, he discovered distinctly, the two Indians who buried the trunk, that a quarrel ensued between them and that one of said Indians was killed by the other and thrown into the hole beside of the truck, to guard it as he supposed." Despite failing to uncover the trunk, Thompson remained a believer in Smith's "professed skill," explaining to the court that "on account of an enchantment, the trunk kept settling away from under them while digging."

Those who believe Smith literally translated the Book of Mormon from anciently engraved plates or who attempt to dismiss his previous treasure-seeing activities as irrelevant have difficulty with Thompson's testimony. Central to their conundrum is the knowledge that Smith used the same stone later to translate the Book of Mormon. The implications are obvious: if Smith *actually* translated and received revelations with his stone, as Mormon apologists maintain, didn't he also locate *real* buried treasure by the same means? Specifically, in the instance that Thompson reported, was there an actual trunk and did Smith really see the two Indians who had fought over it?

Any explanation of Joseph Smith must account for the details provided by Thompson's friendly testimony if it is to be taken seriously. As I view it, there are three possible interpretations, none of which fits comfortably with traditionalist views of Smith and his subsequent work as a translator: (1) Smith saw a treasure chest in his stone that was not really there; in other words, his visions and revelations were the product of his imagination; (2) Smith saw nothing in his stone but only pretended that he did; and (3) Smith saw a real treasure chest in his stone which, no matter the explanation, was never recovered. Thus, to be consistent, apologists must either accept the treasure-seeking lore of Smith's day as reality–including belief in seer stones, mineral rods, guardian spirits, bleeding ghosts, enchanted treasures that slip through the earth, and the like–as D. Michael Quinn has done,[16] and thereby reject rationalist categories of historical investigation, or come face-to-face with a Joseph Smith who either consciously or unconsciously deceived.

The fact that Smith allowed family and friends–even those hostile to his claims such as Lucy Harris and Isaac Hale–to handle the plates while covered with a cloth or concealed in a box excludes the possibility of an unconscious fraud. Likewise, a detailed examination of Smith's activities as a treasure seer presents examples not easily explained as Smith's self-deception. Josiah Stowell, another believer in Smith's gift, testified at the same court hearing that Smith said that he saw in his stone a treasure "on a certain Root of a stump 5 feet from [the] surface of the earth, and with it would be found a tail feather." After digging, Stowell said that they "found a tail feather, but the money was gone, that he supposed that [the] money moved down." The discovery of an object not normally found underground becomes either proof of Smith's true gift or evidence of his fraudulent activity, for the deluded do not accomplish such feats. In this instance, rather than accept Stowell's explanation for the treasure's disappearance, it seems easier to suggest that Smith planted the tail feather during a previous visit to the area or, more likely, during the process of digging. It may have been this kind of activity that gave Smith an edge over his competitors, perhaps also explaining how he excelled them in reputation.

Despite the apparent evidence of conscious fraud, I would caution against viewing Smith's activity as a treasure seer in either/or terms, for it is possible that Smith was both deluded and deceptive in his operations. In other words, Smith may have been sincere in his claims about seeing treasures and guardian spirits in his stone but was sometimes tempted to provide proof through fraudulent means, either to satisfy his followers or silence his enemies. Although the evidence for fraud is more easily demonstrated, nevertheless Smith's complaint about being persecuted for his gift, if not pure rhetoric, may have been sincere after all.

In the Book of Mormon, Smith does not deny the treasure-seer's world view but integrates it with his subsequent religious beliefs, describing cursed and slippery treasures (Hel. 12:18-19; 13:17-22, 31; Morm. 1:18-19) while restricting the use of the seer stone to translating (Mosiah 8:13-18). The fact that Smith's claimed interviews with the heavenly messenger were concurrent with his treasure seeing and that he later used the same stone to translate the Book of Mormon excludes any explanation that attempts to separate the two roles.[17] If Mormon historians remain unpersuaded by the preceding analysis, as I suspect they will, they will at least better understand the dilemma of which Shipps speaks.

## II

Hullinger's devout-fraud thesis has the advantage of harmonizing many disparities in the historical record concerning Joseph Smith, and explains much of his motives and character that otherwise remains elusive. But Hullinger, in my opinion, did not go far enough, for—like Brodie—he never attempted to explore the underlying assumption of his thesis. In other words, what were the rationalizations or, more precisely, the inner moral conflicts of an individual who deceives in God's name while also holding sincere religious beliefs?

In rejecting Brodie's paradigm, one need not confuse Smith's inner, spiritual world with the prophet-image that he projected to his followers. Those close to Smith eventually discovered the disparity between the mantle and the man, between the persona and the person. Historians too must distinguish between the public and private Joseph Smith, between the myth and the man, and peel back the layers of Smith's public image, created to satisfy the demands of his followers, to reveal the "real" Joseph Smith, or at least his true beliefs and assumptions. We must seek to discover the emotional, spiritual, and intellectual "reality" from which he operated. It is not enough to know that Smith was religious, or had a spiritual dimension to his character, one must know what those beliefs were—for what is privately believed, as opposed to publicly taught, makes all the difference.

Sometimes private beliefs can be clearly stated but withheld from the public, as with plural marriage. But often privately held beliefs and assumptions are unconsciously or unintentionally revealed in the implied or connotative meaning of texts. The remainder of this essay examines the texts of the Book of Mormon and Smith's early revelations, highlighting instances in which he articulated the ideas and philosophies of an apparent religious pretender, even the very principles upon which a pious deception could be founded.

A revelation dictated by Smith in March 1830—the very month that the Book of Mormon came off the press—is most revealing of Smith's early state of mind. Directed at Martin Harris, the revelation defends Universalist doctrine, a seeming reversal of Book of Mormon teaching,[18] and advances an unorthodox version of Jesus' atonement.[19] A close examination of this revelation reveals not only Smith's private belief in Universalism but also an unintentional glimpse into his pious rationalizations.

Despite scriptural references to the torment and suffering of the wicked, the revelation declares "it is not written that there shall be no end to this torment" (D&C 19:6), explaining that the terms "eternal punishment" and "endless punishment" simply mean "God's punishment," that "eternal" and "endless" are synonyms for God's name (vv. 10-12). In other words, "endless" and "eternal" have reference to the nature or quality of the punishment, not to its duration.[20]

While one might wish to conclude that Smith was simply placating Harris, whose Universalist beliefs may have caused him some misgivings about the book he had promised to sponsor financially, I suggest that the Restorationist tone of the revelation reflects Smith's true theological leanings—leanings he would develop further in his 1832 vision of three heavens (D&C 76). The revelation itself suggests a reason for the conflicting doctrines, stating that God has purposely used misleading language in order "that it might work upon the hearts of the children of men" (D&C 19:7). In other words, God sometimes deceives humankind for their own good. This is exactly the kind of rationalization one expects of a pious deceiver or religious pretender.

Not surprisingly the revelation invokes secrecy concerning its contents. Fearing that its teaching of a temporary hell would encourage sinners to remain unrepentant, the revelation instructs its recipients to "preach nought but repentance; *and show not these things, neither speak these things unto the world,* for they can not bear meat, but milk they must receive: Wherefore, *they must not know these things lest they perish*" (BofC 16:22-23, emphasis added; compare D&C 19:21-22).[21] Despite publicly posing as a believer in the traditional heaven and hell, Smith was privately a Universalist and therefore did not fear an eternal, never-ending hell that would have troubled most pious deceivers.

Like previous religious pretenders, Smith may have taken comfort in such biblical examples as Abraham and Jacob. Fearing for his life, Abraham instructed his wife Sarah to withhold their true marital status from the Egyptians and present him instead as her brother (Gen. 12:10-20; 20:12). This was a half-truth, certainly, but a deliberate deception nonetheless.

Perhaps responding to those who found it difficult to excuse Abraham's behavior,[22] Smith included in his Book of Abraham a predictable variation on the already troubling story. Instead of Abraham telling his wife to lie about their marital status, Smith has God instruct Abraham to tell Sarah to lie (Abr. 2:22-25/Gen. 12:11-13).[23] Thus in excusing Abraham, Smith introduced the more troubling proposition that God is sometimes the author of deception. This assertion would have outraged orthodox believers, that is, had they been paying sufficient attention to Smith's teachings.[24] It was nevertheless a concept that fit with Smith's personal and private theology.

Jacob's deception of Isaac is perhaps the most striking example from the Bible (Gen. 27). At the instigation of his mother Rebekah, who agreed to receive the curse should Isaac discover the deception (v. 13), Jacob extracted the first-born's blessing from his blind father by pretending to be his older twin brother, Esau. Of course, the deception is justified on the grounds that Esau had incorrectly left the womb first and that deception was necessary to fulfill God's will. In the popular commentary of Smith's day, Methodist Adam Clarke dismissed the suggestion of some that Rebekah was acting under "Divine inspiration," but nevertheless quoted one ancient Chaldaic Targum that renders Rebekah's words differently from the Hebrew or Septuagint versions: "It has been revealed to me by prophecy that the curses will not come upon thee, my son." Seemingly aware of the story's possible misuse, Clarke warned that the author of Genesis "nowhere says that God would have any man to copy this conduct."[25]

Despite such biblical precedent, Universalism remains a major element in Smith's ability to rationalize his fraudulent activities, both as a treasure seer and later as a prophet. When the Book of Mormon and March 1830 revelation worry that Universalism leads to laxity towards God's commandments, we find an explanation for Smith's own tendency to fall into "divers temptations to the gratification of many appetites offensive in the sight of God."[26] Combined with a belief that God sometimes deceives in order to save his children, Universalism helps explain how Smith could perpetrate a religious deception while at the same time having the appearance of a deep and sincere faith. Those who continue to overlook this aspect of his private belief system will never understand his evolution as a prophet.

III

The opening portion of the Book of Mormon includes the story of Nephi obtaining the brass plates through deception and murder (1 Ne. 4). Despite the Spirit's command, Nephi is hesitant to kill the drunken and defenseless Laban. "Never at any time have I shed the blood of man," Nephi protests (v. 10). This is not unlike the moral dilemma that Abraham faced when commanded to sacrifice his son Isaac, only that Nephi actually carries out the directive (Gen. 22:1-14; cf. D&C 132:36, 50-51). The Spirit reissues the command and reasons with Nephi: "Slay him, for the Lord hath delivered him into thy hands; behold the Lord slayeth the wicked to bring forth his righteous purposes. It is better that one man should perish than that a nation should dwindle and perish in unbelief" (1 Ne. 4:12-13; cf. John 11:50). Overcoming his aversion to murder, Nephi cuts Laban's head off with his own sword. Dressed in Laban's armor, Nephi–like biblical Jacob–deceives Laban's servant into giving him the brass plates. Thus by crossing moral lines Nephi accomplished the Lord's errand and thereby preserved the Hebrew scriptures for future Nephite generations.

I suggest that on the evening of 21-22 September 1823 seventeen-year-old Joseph Smith spent a sleepless night struggling with his own moral dilemma, whether or not to proceed with his story of finding gold plates. On the following morning, as the story goes, while returning from the field an angelic messenger appeared to him and—similar to the exchange between the Spirit and Nephi—chastised him for not telling his father about the plates as previously instructed. Smith had hesitated, fearing that he would not be believed. But the angel commanded him to tell his father and promised that he would "believe every word."[27] This was a decisive moment in Smith's career, although the story takes on a different cast if one views Smith as a pious pretender. In this instance, the event becomes the moment of Smith's resolve to cross moral lines, perhaps with the Spirit's urging, to invent the existence of the plates for a good cause. While Nephi pretended to be the evil Laban to gain access to the brass plates, Smith would pretend to be Mormon, the ancient editor of the plates.

The Book of Mormon's version of Adam's fall also lends itself to pious rationalizations. A radical departure from orthodox Christianity, the Book of Mormon declares that the Fall was part of God's plan, that it would ultimately produce more good than evil: "Adam fell that men might be; and men are, that they might have joy" (2 Ne. 2:25). Similar to Nephi, Joseph's Adam found it necessary to violate God's commandment not to eat of the tree of knowledge in order to fulfill a higher law and bring about a greater good. Smith was not the originator of what is sometimes called the "fortunate Fall," but for more than obvious reasons he was attracted to an otherwise obscure idea.

The essence of what probably attracted the would-be prophet to the fortunate Fall is clearly set forth in the words of fifth-century theologian St. Augustine: "The works of God are so wisely and exquisitely contrived that, when an angelic and human creature sins ... it fulfills what He willed."[28] English poet John Milton portrayed Adam as uncertain if he should even repent of his sin, since by it God had produced so much good that otherwise would have remained undone: "O goodness infinite, goodness immense!/ That all this good of evil shall produce,/ And evil turn to good; more wonderful/ Than that which by creation first brought forth ..." In order that "much more good ... shall spring" from his sin, Milton's Adam decides to delay repentance trusting in God's mercy.[29] Thus, unlike Eve, Adam had willfully sinned and knowingly brought both spiritual and physical death upon himself—all for the good of humankind. The advantages of the fortunate Fall for the pious deceiver are obvious, and Smith was perhaps attracted to it because it seemed to justify the ethically contradictory actions of his own mission.

## IV

Assuming Joseph Smith a pious deceiver, did he—like the Targum's Rebekah or even his own Abraham—believe his deception was inspired of God? Specifically, did Smith believe the Book of Mormon was inspired although he knew it was not ancient history?[30] Despite Smith's claims that the Book of Mormon resulted from a purely mechanical process of translation (one in which Smith simply read the translation from the seer stone),[31] he seems to have actually operated from a liberal view of revelation, one that rationalizes the production of fraudulent scripture.

Early in the work of translation, Oliver Cowdery expressed a desire to translate and received permission through a revelation Smith dictated (D&C 8). However, without use of the translator's stone, Cowdery did not know how to proceed. A subsequent revelation explained his failure: "Behold you have not understood, you have supposed that I would give it unto you, when you took no thought save it was to ask me. But, behold, I say unto you, that you must study it out in your mind; then you must ask me if it be right, and if it is right I will cause that your bosom shall burn within you: therefore, you shall feel that it is right. But if it be not right you shall have no such feelings, but you shall have a stupor of thought that shall cause you to forget the thing which is wrong; therefore, you cannot write that which is sacred save it be given you from me. Now, if you had known this you could have translated" (D&C 9:7-10).

As an experienced rod worker and clairvoyant, Cowdery naturally expected the "translation" to be revealed to him from an outside source. In the previous revelation, God had promised him: "I will tell you in your mind and in your heart, by the Holy Ghost" (D&C 8:2). Now he is being told that "you must study it out in your mind"—that the translation would come from his own thoughts. Thoughts about what? What is there to work out in one's mind if there is nothing there to begin with? If the thoughts come from his own mind, is not that the same as writing the book himself? It is doubtful that Cowdery found such a definition of translation useful—at least, he never returned to the subject although "other records" awaited his attention (D&C 9:2).

Regardless of the outcome, the revelation hints that Smith privately held a definition of translation and revelation that was more liberal than that of many of his followers, one which is so internal that the seer stone and the plates become mere props. Of course, Smith encouraged the view that he was simply reading the God-given translation from his stone when actually he was working the words out in his mind, dictating the words he felt good about and forgetting those not worth remembering. In Smith's view, the words were inspired regardless of their true origin.

Near the close of the Book of Mormon, Moroni writes that "every thing which inviteth and enticeth to do good, and to love God, and to serve him, is inspired of God" (Moro. 7:13). And again, "every thing which inviteth to do good, and to persuade to believe in Christ, is sent forth by the power and gift of Christ; wherefore ye may know with a perfect knowledge it is of God" (v. 16). In another place Christ is made to reason: "These things are true; for it persuadeth men to do good. And whatsoever thing persuadeth men to do good is of me; for good cometh of none save it be of me. I am the same that leadeth men to all good" (Eth. 4:11-12). Thus even if Smith wrote the Book of Mormon himself, under this definition it was inspired of God because it attempts to persuade humankind to do good and to believe in Christ.

Smith's reasoning was simple, the Book of Mormon is of God because "all things which are good cometh of Christ" (Eth. 4:24), for the devil "persuadeth no man to do good, no, not one; neither do his angels; neither do they who subject themselves unto him" (v. 17). Thus he would have extended the principle to include himself: his desire to save others, even if by deception, was a good thing and therefore inspired of God, not Satan, and evil men do not perform good deeds.

Early in his career Smith probably conceived his prophetic role much the same as the Book of Mormon prophets, who for the most part write according to their best knowledge rather than by direct revelation. Mormon, whose early life parallels Smith's—including being "visited of the Lord" at age fifteen—became the editor by "commandment" and records the things he has "both seen and heard" (Morm. 1:1, 5). He was chosen to write the final chapter of his people's history because he is "sober" and "quick to observe" (v. 2). His son

Moroni later confesses that he and his father made their records "according to our knowledge" (9:32). Nephi also made his record by "commandment of the Lord" and "according to my knowledge" (1 Ne. 1:3; 9:3, 5; 19:2, 3), and is qualified for the work because he is "highly favored of the Lord" and possesses "a great knowledge of the goodness and the mysteries of God" (1:1). Perhaps Smith, too, believed that he was specially qualified to write scripture, that God had called upon him because of his talent as a story teller and considerable powers of persuasion, that he was inspired by God in the general but not in every particular.

V

In pursuing the prophet puzzle, I have sought to understand Joseph Smith, not condemn him. Smith, to be sure, presents historians with a formidable puzzle, but, as Shipps said, "The mystery of Mormonism cannot be solved until we solve the mystery of Joseph Smith."[32] The paradigm explored in this essay attempts not only to bring Shipps's two Joseph's together but to search out his motives, inner conflicts, and rationalizations, as suggested by Hill. Because this model has the advantage of explaining the historical record more fully than previous attempts, either pro or con, I believe it may be destined to replace Brodie's, at least as far as non-Mormon historians are concerned.

In refining Hullinger's thesis, I suggest that Smith really believed he was called of God to preach repentance to a sinful world but that he felt justified in using deception to accomplish his mission more fully. Like the faith healer who uses confederates to create a faith-promoting atmosphere in which true miracles can occur, Smith assumed the role of prophet, produced the Book of Mormon, and issued revelations to create a setting in which true conversion experiences could take place. It is the true healings and conversions that not only justify deception but convince the pious frauds that they are perhaps after all real healers or real prophets.

What did Smith hope to accomplish by his pious deception? One goal, as the March 1830 revelation shows, was to bring humankind to repentance. Initially, Smith hoped to frighten his fellow humans into repentance and therefore help them avoid the torments of even a temporary hell. Later he used the incentive of higher rewards. Meanwhile, if humankind were saved by incorrectly believing in an eternal hell, to that end Smith believed his method was justified. Whatever the means, he believed his followers would be saved as long as their repentance and faith in Christ were sincere.

What did he believe his own fate would be? Perhaps he believed that with God's sanction he would escape punishment, but there is another possibility, one that takes us to the core of his private world. The March 1830 revelation declares that the unrepentant would suffer for their own sins: "For behold, I, God, have suffered these things for all, that they might not suffer if they would repent; But if they would not repent they must suffer even as I" (D&C 19:16-17). Of course, the idea that humans can suffer as Jesus did for their own sins is viewed by orthodox Christians as an infringement on Jesus' infinite atonement. But in Smith's day it was a concept held by many Restorationists in one form or another. Applied to Smith's pious deception, his reasoning perhaps went something like the following: those who believe the Book of Mormon and repent, regardless of the book's true origin, will be saved or, perhaps of more immediate concern, will not be destroyed at Jesus' appearance. For this act, Smith–like Jesus–would suffer in a temporary hell and become a savior to his followers.[33]

Smith's March 1830 revelation, the Book of Abraham, the story of Nephi and Laban, and the fortunate Fall demonstrate that Smith believed that God sometimes inspires deception, that some sins are according to his will, or that occasionally it is necessary to break one commandment in order to fulfill a higher law. Smith likened the command to take plural wives to Abraham's moral conundrum (D&C 132:29-37), and in attempting to coax twenty-year-old Nancy Rigdon into secretly becoming a plural wife in 1842 Smith argued that "That which is wrong under one circumstance, may be and often is, right under another. ... Whatever God requires is right, no matter what it is, although we may not see the reason thereof till long after the events transpire."[34] We may never know exactly Smith's reasoning, but we can at least say that if he wrote the Book of Mormon, became a prophet, and founded the church as a pious deception, it is evident he had the psychological means of justifying such acts.

*NOTES*

1. Jan Shipps, "The Prophet Puzzle: Suggestions Leading Toward a More Comprehensive Interpretation of Joseph Smith," *Journal of Mormon History* (1974): 19. Shipps's essay was reprinted in D. Michael Quinn, *The New Mormon History: Revisionist Essays on the Past* (Salt Lake City: Signature Books, 1992), 53-74; it is also reprinted in the present compilation. Citations in this essay are to the first printing.

2. Marvin S. Hill, "Brodie Revisited: A Reappraisal," *Dialogue: A Journal of Mormon Thought* 7 (Winter 1972): 85.

3. Robert N. Hullinger, *Mormon Answer to Skepticism: Why Joseph Smith Wrote the Book of Mormon* (St. Louis: Clayton Publishing House, 1980); reprinted as *Joseph Smith's Response to Skepticism* (Salt Lake City: Signature Books, 1992). For convenience, I have used the second edition.

4. Shipps, 10.

5. Hullinger, xv.

6. Ibid., xvi.

7. In assuming the role of prophet, Smith was not necessarily acting maliciously or selfishly. In this regard, Smith's comment to Oliver B. Huntington is most interesting. Huntington recalled: "Joseph Smith said that some people entirely denounce the principle of self-aggrandizement as wrong. 'It is a correct principle,' he said, 'and may be indulged upon only one rule or plan–and that is to elevate, benefit and bless others first. If you will elevate others, the very work itself will exalt you. Upon no other plan can a man justly and permanently aggrandize himself'" (quoted in Hyrum L. Andrus and Helen Mae Andrus, comps., *They Knew the Prophet* [Salt Lake City: Bookcraft, 1974], 61).

8. Marvin S. Hill, "Joseph Smith and the 1826 Trial: New Evidence and New Difficulties," *Brigham Young University Studies* 12 (Winter 1972): 232.

9. Hill, "Brodie Revisited," 74-75.

10. See Dean C. Jessee, ed., *The Personal Writings of Joseph Smith* (Salt Lake City: Deseret Book Co., 1984), 16, 17; and Dean C. Jessee, ed., *The Pap- ers of Joseph Smith: Volume 2, Journal, 1832-1842* (Salt Lake City: Deseret Book Co., 1992), 2, 5.

11. See Richard S. Van Wagoner, *Mormon Polygamy: A History* (Salt Lake City: Signature Books, 1986), 61. On 26 May 1844 Joseph Smith countered those who were accusing him of practicing polygamy, stating: "What a thing it is for a man to be accused of committing adultery, and having seven wives, when I can only find one" (Joseph Smith, Jr., et al., *History of the Church of Jesus Christ of Latter-day Saints,* ed. B. H. Roberts, 7 vols. [2nd ed. rev.; Salt Lake City: Deseret Book Co., 1948 printing], 6:411). Such statements from the pulpit succeeded in misleading many of the Saints who remained unaware that Smith

was privately practicing polygamy until the church made a formal statement in 1852.

12. Richard Bushman, who concludes that "[t]he Smith family at first was no more able to distinguish true religion from superstition than their neighbors" and "were as susceptible to the neighbors' belief in magic as they were to the teachings of orthodox ministers," believes Smith's treasure-seeking activities were irrelevant to his subsequent career as a prophet (*Joseph Smith and the Beginnings of Mormonism* [Urbana: University of Illinois Press, 1984], 72). Whereas Michael Quinn attempts to demolish the barriers between magic and religion and, in accepting Smith's activities as a treasure seer as "real," sees Smith's activities as a treasure seer as part of his development as a prophet (*Early Mormonism and the Magic World View* [Salt Lake City: Signature Books, 1987], 46). See also Richard L. Anderson, "The Mature Joseph Smith and Treasure Searching," *Brigham Young University Studies* 24 (Fall 1984): 489-560, which attempts to combine both perspectives.

13. Besides not telling about his procurement of a seer stone from the Chase family in 1822, Smith concealed the major role he played in Stowell's treasure-digging venture in Harmony, Pennsylvania, by portraying himself as merely a hired hand (Smith, *History of the Church,* 1:17; see also Dan Vogel, ed., *Early Mormon Documents* [Salt Lake City: Signature Books, 1996], 1:67-68).

14. See Dan Vogel, "The Locations of Joseph Smith's Early Treasure Quests," *Dialogue: A Journal of Mormon Thought* 27 (Fall 1994): 213-27.

15. The trial transcript was published in "A Document Discovered," *Utah Christian Advocate* (Salt Lake City) 3 (Jan. 1886): 1. Concerning Smith's confession, Justice Albert Neely recorded in his docket: "[Smith] has occasionally been in the habit of looking through this stone to find lost property for 3 years, but of late had pretty much given it up on account of injuring his Health, especially his eyes, made them sore–that he did not solicit business of this kind, and had always rather declined having anything to do with this business."

16. "Unfortunately," Quinn states, "Mormon apologists have in the past accepted rationalist categories of superstition and fraud rather than Smith's and his supporters' affirmations of supernatural powers from the perspective of folk magic" (Quinn, *Early Mormonism and the Magic World View,* 46).

17. Marvin S. Hill has similarly argued that "there was certainly more continuity between the money-digging religious culture and the early Mormon movement than some historians have recognized. Joseph Smith began receiving revelations as a prophet in 1823, and thus began assuming the role central to his religious movement long before he abandoned his money digging in 1827" (*Quest for Refuge: The Mormon Flight from American Pluralism* [Salt Lake City: Signature Books, 1989], 20).

18. Dan Vogel, "Anti-Universalist Rhetoric in the Book of Mormon," in Brent Lee Metcalfe, ed., *New Approaches to the Book of Mormon: Explorations in Critical Methodology* (Salt Lake City: Signature Books, 1992), 21-52. Actually,

the Book of Mormon's attack on Universalism seems to focus on those who believe in no punishment after death. Only in one instance does the Book of Mormon attack Restorationists (2 Ne. 28:8). However, in this passage the Book of Mormon does not attack their belief directly but rather their attitude of taking the punishment for sin too lightly. Regardless, Alma speaks of the "punishment, which also was eternal as the life of the soul" (Alma 42:16). The revelation's concept of atonement is also at odds with the Book of Mormon's teachings about the necessity of an "infinite" atonement (2 Ne. 9:7; Alma 34:10, 12), a concept Universalists rejected.

19. By 1830 the Universalist denomination was overwhelmingly Unitarian, denying the deity of Jesus and rejecting orthodox concepts of the Atonement. Of course, there was the odd Universalist church like the one in Charleston, South Carolina, that declared in 1829 its belief in trinitarianism (see *The Evangelists' Manual: or a Guide to Trinitarian Universalists* [Charleston, S.C., 1829]). On an individual level the matter was fluid, as is illustrated in a letter from M. Wing to his brother living in Montpelier, Vermont, dated 10 March 1827. The orthodox brother writes: "You should not blame me David, for not correctly representing the sentiments of the Universalists for there are hardly two societies that agree in every thing. Those in this neighborhood, & a majority, I believe, elsewhere, believe there is no other punishment than what takes place in this world. But that which gave me most pain, was your denial of the Divinity of the Son of God. It is not necessarily connected with Universalism, & I did not suppose you had embraced it. ..." (as quoted in Rick Grunder, *Mormon List 23,* Mar. 1987, [15]).

20. This is not unlike the argument of Unitarian-Universalist Hosea Ballou (see *A Treatise on Atonement* [Randolph, VT: Sereno Wright, 1805], 161-62).

21. When published in the 1835 Doctrine and Covenants, this passage was altered to explain why its stipulated secrecy had been violated by publication: "show not these things unto the world *until it is wisdom in me*. For they cannot bear meat *now*" (D&C 19:21-22). And the phrase "neither speak these things" was deleted. Publication of this revelation in 1833 and 1835 was to Smith's advantage as it improved his position with those having difficulty accepting his 1832 vision of three heavens, because it provided the needed transition between the Book of Mormon and the vision.

22. Commenting on Abraham's defense in Genesis 20:12 that he had not lied but only suppressed part of the truth, Methodist Adam Clarke, for example, said: "*What is a lie?* It is any action done or word spoken, whether true or false in itself, which the doer or speaker wishes the observer or hearer to take in a *contrary* sense to that which he knows to be true. It is, in a word, any action done or speech delivered with *the intention to deceive,* though both may be absolutely true and right in themselves" (*The Holy Bible ... With a Commentary and Critical Notes* [New York, 1810], s.v., Gen. 20:12). Making no excuses for Abraham, Clarke criticized the ancient patriarch and concluded:

"Had Abraham possessed more charity for man and confidence in God at this time, he had not fallen into that snare from which he barely escaped."

23. This portion of the Book of Abraham, absent from all extant manuscript copies, was probably written in Nauvoo shortly before publication in the *Times and Seasons* in 1842 (see "The Book of Abraham," *Times and Seasons* 3 [15 Mar. 1842]: 719). Susan Staker has suggested that Smith's alteration of Genesis should be understood in the context of the prophet's secret polygynous and polyandrous marriages in Nauvoo. She argues that Smith's Book of Abraham version seemed to justify the secrecy and deception he requested of his wives. See Susan Staker, "'The Lord Said, Thy Wife Is a Very Fair Woman to Look Upon': The Book of Abraham, Secrets, and Lying for the Lord," 17 Aug. 1996, Sunstone Theological Symposium, Salt Lake City, copy in my possession, and reprinted in the present compilation.

24. In this regard one might consider the reaction of Warren Parrish to a similar situation involving Sidney Rigdon, a counselor in the First Presidency. Among other things Parrish, who was in May 1837 quickly becoming disenchanted with Mormonism, accused Rigdon of "lying & declaring that God required it at his hands" (Warren Parrish to Bishop Newel K. Whitney, 29 May 1837, Newel K. Whitney Papers, Special Collections, Harold B. Lee Library, Brigham Young University, Provo, Utah).

25. Clarke, *The Holy Bible,* s.v., Gen. 27:13.

26. Joseph Smith, Manuscript History of the Church, Book A-1, 5, Joseph Smith Papers, archives, Historical Department, Church of Jesus Christ of Latter-day Saints, Salt Lake City, Utah, hereafter LDS archives (Vogel, *Early Mormon Documents,* 1:63). The phrase "to the gratification of many appetites" was subsequently stricken from Smith's History.

27. Lucy Smith, "Preliminary Manuscript," 81, LDS archives (Vogel, *Early Mormon Documents,* 1:291).

28. As quoted in Sterling M. McMurrin, *The Theological Foundations of the Mormon Religion* (Salt Lake City: University of Utah Press, 1965), 73.

29. Ibid.

30. Some may wish to retain their belief that the Book of Mormon is ancient history despite the possibility that Smith lied about the plates, or that despite his construction of fake plates Smith nevertheless believed he was dictating ancient history. While this is possible, the awkwardness with which he handled Harris's loss of the translation manuscript, particularly his subsequent creation of the "small" and "large" plates of Nephi and the clumsy addition of the explanatory bridge between the two records called "The Words of Mormon," not to mention the convenient revelations issuing therefrom (D&C 3 and 10), suggest conscious fabrication (see Quinn Brewster, "The Structure of the Book of Mormon: A Theory of Evolutionary Development," *Dialogue: A Journal of Mormon Thought* 29 [Summer 1996]: 109-40; and Brent

Lee Metcalfe, "The Priority of Mosiah: A Prelude to Book of Mormon Exegesis," in *New Approaches to the Book of Mormon,* 395-437).

31. Those close to Smith during the translation–Emma Smith, Martin Harris, and David Whitmer–all describe a mechanical process of translation. For a discussion of this testimony, see Richard Van Wagoner and Steven Walker, "Joseph Smith: The Gift of Seeing," *Dialogue: A Journal of Mormon Thought* 15 (Summer 1982): 48-68, reprinted in this compilation; and James E. Lancaster, "The Translation of the Book of Mormon," Dan Vogel, ed., *The Word of God: Essays on Mormon Scripture* (Salt Lake City: Signature Books, 1990), 97-112. Smith's inability to translate when Harris secretly switched stones demonstrates that the stone was essential to the translation process, not incidental as some apologists have asserted–at least as Smith explained his gift to his followers (see, e.g., Edward Stevenson to the Editor, 30 Nov. 1881, *Deseret Evening News* 15 [13 Dec. 1881]).

32. Shipps, 19.

33. That Smith's mission of saving souls went beyond the usual calling of sinners to repentance is hinted at when the Book of Mormon applies Old Testament scripture, traditionally interpreted as messianic prophecy, to Joseph Smith. Jesus, for instance, is made to declare concerning the coming forth of the Book of Mormon: "there shall be among them those who will not believe it, although *a man* shall declare it unto them [Acts 13:41]. But behold, the life of my *servant* shall be in my hand; therefore they shall not hurt him, although he shall be marred because of them. Yet I will heal him [Isa. 52:13-14], for I will show unto them that my wisdom is greater than the cunning of the devil" (3 Ne. 21:9-10; emphasis added). Here Jesus alludes to Isaiah's suffering servant (previously quoted in 20:43-44), traditionally interpreted as a messianic prophecy fulfilled in Jesus (compare John 12:37-38; Mark 9:12), and applies it to Joseph Smith. On a deeper psychological level, one might view Smith's death as an inevitable extension of a messiah complex. The *Broome County Courier* for 29 December 1831 may have picked up on this theme when it called Smith a "second Messiah."

34. Joseph Smith to Nancy Rigdon, Apr. 1842, *Sangamo Journal,* 19 Aug. 1842, as cited in Jessee, *Personal Writings of Joseph Smith,* 508; cf. Smith, *History of the Church,* 5:134-36.

# 4.
# Joseph Smith as Translator

*Richard L. Bushman*

THE BOOKS AND ESSAYS ON JOSEPH SMITH'S TRANSLATIONS, MANY OF them by skeptics who doubt he translated at all, overlook one large question: how did Joseph Smith come to think of himself as a translator? Laying aside the accuracy of the translations, the preceding question is where did the idea of a translation of any kind originate? No other religious young man in nineteenth-century New York–or anyone else for that matter–offered a volume of translated reformed Egyptian as his initial claim on the public's attention. What inspired Joseph Smith to think of himself as a translator? Ethan Smith, author of *View of the Hebrews,* did not translate ancient records to justify his speculations about Native American origins; Joseph Smith did, and historians who think of the Book of Mormon as a nineteenth-century production need to explain why.

The closest precedent is Solomon Spaulding's "Manuscript Story," the work of a sometime preacher and ironmaster who migrated from Connecticut to New York to Ohio and wrote a purported translation of a supposed Latin document telling about a Roman voyage to the New World. For a time Eber D. Howe, the hostile Ohio newspaper editor who published *Mormonism Unvailed* in 1834, claimed Spaulding's story was a source for the Book of Mormon.[1] When the manuscript was eventually located and published in 1885, that theory collapsed, but was Spaulding a precedent for the idea of translation?[2] The faint similarities notwithstanding, Spaulding's translated story no more serves as a precedent for Joseph Smith than renowned translations such as Alexander Pope's rendition of *The Iliad*. Spaulding and Pope were learned men who understood the language they translated. A Dartmouth College graduate who knew Latin, Spaulding made no claim to inspiration. The question is not the idea of translation itself–the learned world was filled with translators and translations–but translation without prior training. Why would Joseph Smith think that he could translate when he lacked all the necessary qualifications?

Joseph Smith's enthusiasm for translation deepens the problem of historical explanation. The role of translator did not spin off from the larger task of writing the Book of Mormon and then disappear once the book was finished. Within a few months of its publication, Joseph began to translate the Bible, and after that the books of Abraham and Joseph. His enthusiasm for translation carried over into a passion for Hebrew. He seemed to embrace translation as a fixed element of his religious identity. An early revelation said he was to be called "a seer, a translator, a prophet" in the records of the church.[3] Why did he find the role of translator so congenial when it was so foreign to his education and background?

Other religious young men of that time did not think of themselves as budding translators of scripture. The conventional path for young people with a religious calling led from personal conversion to preaching. Charles Grandison Finney, a contemporary of Joseph Smith and a revivalist in Joseph's area during the time when the Book of Mormon was published, went through experiences much like Joseph's up to a point. Born in Connecticut in 1792, Finney was studying law in Adams, New York, when he became convinced of his utter sinfulness. In the summer of 1821, desperate for relief from his guilt, he stole into the woods for a private prayer. Like Joseph Smith, he had his prayer answered and, again like Joseph, had a vision of Jesus Christ. The Savior appeared while Finney was praying in his law office that night. "It seemed as if I met the Lord Jesus Christ face to face." Later in life he decided the vision was "a mental state," but at the time, he said, "it seemed to me that I saw him as I would see any other man." "It seemed to me a reality, that he stood before me, and I fell down at his feet and poured out my soul to him."[4]

The desire for forgiveness, the prayer in the woods, the vision of Christ put Joseph Smith and Charles Finney on parallel tracks until

1821 when they abruptly diverged. Finney went on to become the foremost revivalist of his age, converting thousands in towns along the Erie Canal, the famous "burned-over district" that included Palmyra, New York. Later he was installed as president of Oberlin College. Joseph Smith was not particularly notable for his preaching as a young man, did not attract followers that way, and never conducted a revival of the kind Finney would recognize. Instead at age twenty-three, Joseph translated a lengthy book, virtually another Bible, and made it the foundation of his new religion.

Joseph Smith always subordinated his role as translator to the more encompassing office of prophet. He chose the larger title when he had an opportunity to define himself in February 1831 upon first arriving in Kirtland, Ohio, to meet a new group of followers. In the legendary account, when Joseph jumped from his sleigh after the journey from Palymra, he grasped storekeeper Newell K. Whitney by the hand and said, "I am Joseph the Prophet"; and so he was to the Saints from then on.[5] But what stood out about his prophethood in 1831 was the translation. The first vision was scarcely ever mentioned in those years and received only the most glancing reference in the revelations.[6] During the first months in Kirtland, a little more was made of the restoration of the Aaronic priesthood and the revelation about the New Jerusalem, but these revelations had not been published yet. The tangible evidence of Joseph's divine calling was the Book of Mormon and the miraculous translation of the hieroglyphs. A few years later in 1834 and 1835 when Oliver Cowdery wrote down his memories of Joseph Smith, Oliver still summed up his account by saying that "the translator of the book of Mormon is worthy [of] the appelation of a seer and a prophet of the Lord."[7]

Outsiders saw Joseph in the same light in the early years. The improbability of a translation struck newspapers as being nearly as strange as the gold plates of the Book of Mormon themselves. The first paper to report the "pretended discovery" said the record was "written in ancient characters impossible to be interpreted by any to whom the special gift has not been imparted by inspiration."[8] Two months later in August 1829, a Rochester paper gave as much space to the translation process as to the plates. The editor said the "blindly enthusiastic" Martin Harris "went in search of some one, besides the interpreter, who was learned enough to English [translate] them."

Finding no one, the article went on, "Harris returned and set Smith to work at interpreting the Bible."[9] Rather than talk about the contents of the Book of Mormon, the editor of the *Painesville Telegraph* in Ohio noted that "it contains about 510 octavo pages, which is said to be translated from Egyptian hieroglyphics, on metal plates, by one Smith, who was enabled to read the characters by instruction from angels." The curious fact, doubtless passed along by believers, was that "the said Smith, though a man so illiterate that he cannot write, was by divine inspiration, enabled to give the true interpretation."[10] In newspapers the translation of the Book of Mormon was Joseph's chief claim to notoriety.

Unfazed by the editors' skepticism, Joseph Smith kept on translating even after the Book of Mormon was published. The role of translator of many records evolved out of experiences with the Book of Mormon. A revelation received in April 1829 while the Book of Mormon was still in process broached the possibility of more records yet to come. The additional records were mentioned in a revelation to Oliver Cowdery who himself had asked for the privilege of translating. Oliver had watched Joseph turn out page after page of Book of Mormon translation, and then settle a question about the state of the apostle John by translating a parchment written by John that apparently Joseph saw in vision. After that Oliver "became exceedingly anxious to have the power to translate bestowed upon him."[11] A revelation told him he would "receive a knowledge concerning the engravings of old records, which are ancient," and if he asked he would "translate and receive knowledge from all those ancient records which have been hid up, that are sacred." The revelation sparked visions of piles of records awaiting translation. After Oliver's failure to translate, a revelation comforted him with the news that "other records have I, that I will give unto you power that you may assist to translate."[12]

The prospect of more records to translate would not have discouraged Joseph who apparently enjoyed his unusual gift. The harsh revelation received after 116 pages of Book of Mormon translation were lost in 1828 spoke of translation as a treasure he was in danger of losing unless he heeded God more than man. For "except thou do this, thou shalt be delivered up and become as other men, and have no more gift." The words suggest that in God's eyes, and probably Joseph's own, the "sight and power to translate" distinguished him from other men. To lose the gift would devastate his developing prophetic identity, like losing a vital organ of the self.[13] One can imagine that translating day after day for three months in 1829, dictating hundreds of thousands of words, gave Joseph pleasure. While translating, he was in his "zone," functioning at the peak of his abilities.

Three months after the publication of the Book of Mormon, Joseph went back to translating, this time working on the Bible itself, beginning with Genesis. He started in June 1830 with a revelation to Moses that prefaced the creation story in the first chapter of Genesis. Joseph called his revision and expansion of the scriptures a translation, although he had no ancient text before him other than the King James Bible. In some passages he altered a few words; in others he interwove a few verses; in the case of Moses' preface and the stories of Enoch, he added many pages of new text. But he summed up the different forms of emendations under the heading of translation, and until 1833 this was his day-to-day work. While administering church affairs and coping with catastrophes and petty personal problems, his main job was to translate the Bible, believing that he was complying with the promise given in the February 1831 revelation "my scriptures shall be given as I have appointed."[15] When they were completed, they would be printed as the Book of Mormon was. To make sure the translation reached the world, a second temple in Kirtland, to match the first in size, was designated for the lot just south of the main temple. Though never built, this second temple was meant for "the work of the printing of the translation of my scriptures."[16]

Joseph completed his work on the Bible in 1833, but in 1835, when Egyptian scrolls fell into his hands, he went back to translating. Until 1842 he worked on these ancient records which he said contained writings of Abraham and Joseph and which seemed to arrive in fulfillment of the earlier promise to Oliver Cowdery about additional sacred writings to translate. Thus from age eighteen, when he learned about the golden plates, until two years before his death, Joseph Smith translated ancient records in fulfillment of the title given him at the organization of the church, and in defiance of all expectations associated with the translation process in nineteenth-century America.

In the world at large, translation was work for the learned, almost exclusively college-educated men whose educations were distinguished by instruction in classical languages. Boys from ordinary households and girls who attended school learned to write, read, do simple arithmetic, and understand rudimentary geography and history, but not translate classical texts. Elegant young women learned French, drawing, fancy sewing, and other genteel arts suitable for polishing young women of their class, but only college-bound young men were taught Latin and learned to translate as part of their ordinary recitations. That learning set them apart as gentlemen and was considered useless for anyone else. Ministerial candidates learned Greek and Hebrew to enable them to interpret the scriptures. Those were the realms where translation went on.

Only the most learned of this college-educated class would undertake a translation of scripture. In Joseph Smith's lifetime a number of scholars retranslated the Bible from Greek or Hebrew to simplify the language and make the scriptures more accessible. In 1826, for example, Alexander Campbell, the onetime friend of Sidney Rigdon and critic of the Book of Mormon, published a new version of the New Testament that combined portions of three new translations, selected by Campbell for their intelligibility and their recognition of immersion as the proper mode of baptism.[17] In 1836 Noah Webster, the student of the American language and author of the dictionary, published a translation designed for American audiences.[18] Theirs were only two among a number meant to encourage popular study of the scriptures.[19] But the multitude of new translations only made Joseph's translation more anomalous, for he encroached on work reserved solely for the most learned men of the age. A book about American translations of the Bible said his work contained "the most astonishing claims ever made in connection with the Bible, and the most peculiar alterations of any Bible in English ever published."[20]

At a still more stratospheric level, French scholar Jean Francois Champollion first deciphered Egyptian hieroglyphics in 1822 through close study of parallel documents inscribed in three scripts on the Rosetta Stone. Discussion of the hieroglyphs entered into elite American periodicals like *The North American Review* as early as 1823, and a follow-up article in 1829 discussed Champollion's translation in the very year when Joseph Smith was translating the "reformed Egyptian" on the plates. Conceivably news of Champollion's triumph could have reached Palmyra, but only to discourage Joseph Smith not to encourage him. The translation of the Rosetta Stone was a work of the most advanced scholarship, a *tour de force* of ingenuity and learning. Champollion was a prodigy who delivered a paper on Coptic at age sixteen and was appointed professor of history at the Grenoble lyceum at age eighteen. Later a chair of Egyptology was created in the College de France especially for him.[21] Culturally Champollion dwelt in another world from the Mormon prophet. Why Joseph thought he could translate Egyptian characters as this savant did is an unanswered question for those who try to explain the prophet's life historically.

The translation problem takes a more subtle form for those who believe Joseph received the assignment to translate from heaven. Mormons believe that Joseph did not have to think up the idea of translating gold plates; Moroni told him about "two stones in silver bows," called the Urim and Thummim, and said he would find them with the buried plates. By observing that "God [had] prepared them for the purpose of translating the book," Moroni made Joseph's task obvious.[22] The question for believers is not where the notion of translation originated, but how Joseph Smith understood the strange work that had been thrust upon him. He surely knew translation was not work for the uneducated, and that in attempting to translate an unknown language he invited skepticism. Why did he find the role of translator so congenial when it was so foreign to his education and background?

Joseph's only contact with the learned world of translation came through the visit of Martin Harris to Charles Anthon, the Columbia University classics professor in 1828. One of the first outside the family to believe Joseph, Harris understandably wanted verification of Joseph's work, and, like everyone else, he associated translation with learning. The most natural course in his state of half-doubt, half-belief was to ask a learned person what he thought of Joseph Smith's translation. Anthon's and Harris's accounts of the interview differ drastically. Harris said Anthon confirmed the accuracy of the translation at first and then withdrew written certification when told the plates could not be seen because a part was sealed. Anthon said the characters were a confused medley of awkwardly scrawled figures and that he advised Harris to steer clear of Joseph Smith. Either way Harris left Anthon convinced that he could not translate the characters and that Joseph Smith could.

In the aftermath the incident came to mean more to Joseph than to Martin Harris, for it was told as the fulfillment of a biblical prophecy in which Joseph figured. Someone, possibly Joseph himself, seized upon a passage in Isaiah 29 about a learned man who was unable to read a sealed book and an unlearned man who received it despite a lack of learning: "And the vision of all is become unto you as the words of a book that is sealed, which men deliver to one that is learned, saying, Read this, I pray thee: and he saith, I cannot; for it is sealed: And the book is delivered to him that is not learned saying, Read this, I pray thee: and he saith, I am not learned."[23] Joseph saw at once that he and Anthon were the two men in the passage, the unlearned and the learned. The idea of fulfilling a biblical prophecy was gratifying, but still more important, the passage defined a role for Joseph. He was to be another kind of translator, one quite different from Anthon and his ilk, a special kind of translator foreseen in the Bible. In the retelling of the Anthon story, the Isaiah language saturated the account. In his 1832 history, Joseph took the pen from the hand of Frederick G. Williams and personally wrote the account of Anthon and Harris, who Joseph said, "came to Su[s]quehanna and said the Lord had shown him that he must go to new York City with some of the c[h]aracters so we proceeeded to coppy some of them and he took his Journy to the Eastern Cittys and to the Learned (saying) read this I pray thee and the learned said I cannot but if he would bring the plates they would read it but the Lord had fo(r)bid it and he returned to me and gave them to (me to) translate and I said [I] cannot for I am not learned but the Lord had prepared spectacles for to read the Book."[24] That passage can be read as marking Joseph's liberation from the learned's claims to a monopoly on translation. Joseph, then just twenty-two and scantily educated, could be Isaiah's unlearned man to whom the Lord gave spectacles and a gift to translate a book the learned could not understand.[25]

In the year following's Harris's New York visit, Joseph received confirmation of his somewhat precarious identity in the pages of the Book of Mormon. The book had its own translation stones and inspired translators, the most notable being King Mosiah who was called upon to translate the twenty-four gold plates of the Jaredites.

In the Book of Mormon narrative, the records were discovered after the Jaredites' extinction, and the finders of the plates were intensely curious about what happened. Ammon, an adventurer who knew about Mosiah's powers, told the possessors of the plates that the king "has wherewith that he can look, and translate all records that are of ancient date; and it is a gift from God."[26]

Joseph, of course, could see himself in that description, for no mention was made of Mosiah's learning or his mastery of other languages. Mosiah had "interpreters" just as Joseph did, and he translated with this gift.[27] Moreover, according to the Book of Mormon passage, with the command to look in the interpreters went a title; he who looked, "the same is called seer."[28] "A seer is a revelator and a prophet also," Ammon explained, "and a gift which is greater can no man have." Besides translating, "a seer can know of things which are past, and also of things which are to come, and by them shall all things be revealed." The description opened vistas beyond the work of translating. Through a seer "shall secret things be made manifest, and hidden things shall come to light, and things which are not known shall be made known by them." And all of this was not to exalt the seer himself but to advance the work of God. "Thus God has provided a means that man, through faith, might work mighty miracles; therefore he becometh a great benefit to his fellow beings."[29]

Joseph could see himself in those words, just as he found himself in Isaiah's unlearned man. He translated as Mosiah did, as a seer with interpreters rather than a scholar trained in languages. Together the Book of Mormon and Bible passage formed a tradition for Joseph's incongruous position as a translator. Rather than an ignorant man attempting an impossible task, he was a latter-day edition of Mosiah's seer with a magnificent gift that would bless the earth.

The culture of Vermont and upstate New York may have partially prepared Joseph for this peculiar role. Joseph probably knew the meaning of the word "seer" before he came across it in the Book of Mormon. Seer appears in scripture as an older name for prophet: "A prophet was beforetime called a seer."[30] In the Bible, Samuel was a seer, and the blinding of seers in Isaiah's prophecy went with the closing of the heavens and the blighting of the earth.[31] In non-biblical literature the word had a religious ring too. In Alexander Pope's translation of the *Iliad*, for example, there was "a sacred seer whose comprehensive view the past, the present, and the future knew."[32]

The word had another life in the culture of seventeenth-century magic. John Dee, the seventeenth-century practitioner of hermetic philosophy, worked with a "Prophet or Seer" who looked into stones.[33] But this older meaning was probably not available to Joseph. By the time the culture of magic made its way down through the centuries and into the neighborhood of the Smiths in New York, the word "seer" was not connected with looking into stones for lost treasures. In the affidavits on the Smith family treasure-seeking collected by Philastus Hurlbut in 1833, the neighbors never used the word "seer" to describe Joseph or the supposed treasure expeditions with his father. The neighbors frequently mentioned the use of a stone, or a glass, or a peepstone, but never a seerstone. None of the critical neighbors called Joseph a seer, though they did speak of his "seeing" with a stone.[34] If the word was in use in Palmyra, it likely had too many biblical associations for it to apply to Joseph Smith. The neighbors were trying to denigrate him with their stories of stones, and avoided intimations of a holy calling.

Mormons first applied the word seer to Joseph and combined the two words "seer" and "stone." Martin Harris, David Whitmer, Oliver Cowdery, Brigham Young, and Orson Pratt described Joseph using a seerstone to translate and receive revelations.[35] In making the connection, they joined two traditions–the holy calling of seer and the magical practice of divining with a stone. The marriage of the two words in Mormon usage summarized the changes that Joseph had to go through as he moved into his offices of seer, translator, and prophet. The word seer elevated the stones, symbolizing the redirection of the Smith family's interest in magic toward a more serious religious end. Joseph put the pursuit of treasure aside in favor of a greater calling, just as Oliver Cowdery gave up working with the rod to write for Joseph.

Although treasure-seeking was left behind, the magical culture of the stones played an important part in the development of Joseph's identity as seer and translator. The Christianity of Methodism or Presbyterianism could not have readied him for translation. In conventional Protestant Christianity, learned men translated the Bible, and pious young people became preachers like Finney or Lorenzo

Dow, not translators. The treasure-seeking stones from the magic culture, by contrast, helped Joseph move step by step into his calling. The scryer of stones looked for the unseen, whether lost objects or buried treasure. Joseph's first reaction when he brought home the Urim and Thummim was delight with the powers of the instrument. It was "ten times Better than I expected," he told Joseph Knight. "I can see any thing: they are Marvelus."[36] Though amazed at the Urim and Thummim's power, he knew from working with his own stone what to expect; he would "see." Although he had obtained his own stone from a hole dug for a well and not by a gift from heaven, practice with the stone, looking for lost objects and probably for treasure, was an initiation into "seeing" that could be transferred to translation of the gold plates in the stones of the Urim and Thummim. In fact, as work on the Book of Mormon went on, a seerstone took the place of the Urim and Thummim, blending the culture of magic with the divine culture of translation.[37]

As time went by, Joseph played down the place of magic and seerstones in his early life. After publication of the damning affidavits about money-digging in Eber Howe's *Mormonism Unvailed* (1834), he knew that involvement with magic would discredit the church. Even before that time, in 1830 he gave up using the seerstones and spoke no more about them. Conventional Christianity was fighting to protect itself from the Enlightenment critics' charges of superstition, and, to prove their rationality, Christian apologists vented their anger on the remnants of magic carried down from an earlier time when magic and religion mingled. Joseph did not want to make himself a target for attacks that would cripple the work. But neither did he repudiate the stones or deny their powers. In 1843 he wrote that a white stone would be given to all entrants into the celestial kingdom, and with that stone "all things pertaining to an higher order of kingdoms even all kingdoms will be made known."[38] The magic culture of his early life, like his inherited Christianity, though transformed was not obliterated. He must have understood that the stones had prepared him to step into the improbable roles of seer and unlearned translator.

Joseph's development as a translator did not end when he completed the Book of Mormon and relinquished the seerstones. As he went on to the Bible and the Book of Abraham, his methods changed, and interestingly he moved closer to the learned men whose powers seemed so far beyond him at the start. As he worked on the Bible, he at first made drastic changes in the revelations on Moses and Enoch received in 1830. Later as he went through the book, he appears to have been reading and rereading in search of flawed passages. The changes did not come to him in a flash of insight or a burst of revelation. As Robert Matthews notes in his study of the Joseph Smith Translation, "a passage that had been revised and recorded once was later further revised and recorded. Some passages were revised even a third time."[39] The manuscript shows signs of him searching his mind for the right words, as a more conventional translator might do. He gave up the Urim and Thummim, Orson Pratt later said, because he had become acquainted with "the Spirit of Prophecy and Revelation" and no longer needed its aid.[40] The inspiration worked in his own mind rather than through an external instrument.

The revisions themselves were more like an improved translation too. Unlike the many additional pages on Moses and Enoch now published as the Book of Moses, the subsequent revisions added a few verses or altered a word or two, clarifying meaning in small ways in the manner of the translations that sought to make the Bible more accessible to readers. Joseph obviously relied on inspiration to make the changes, since he did not work from an ancient text, but many of the changes read like a conventional translator's work.

As he rounded out his revision of the New Testament in 1833, Joseph paradoxically took up the study of Hebrew. After six years of translating the Book of Mormon and the Bible as an unlearned man, Joseph hired a Jewish scholar, Joshua Seixias, to teach Hebrew in Kirtland, Ohio. Joseph the prophet and seer sat down to learn a language from a professor. Moreover, though he never mastered Hebrew, Joseph became an avid pupil.[41] He loved the classes, advanced rapidly considering the little time he had, and began to introduce translations of Hebrew words into his sermons.[42] His excitement about translating as a seer carried over into his conventional study of languages. A revelation as he began the study instructed him to "become acquainted with all good books, and with languages, tongues, and people"—despite all of his experience of translation by divine gift.[43]

When he began work on the Book of Abraham after the church had purchased the Egyptian scrolls from Michael Chandler in 1835,

Joseph, having no knowledge of Egyptian, had to rely on inspiration to effect a translation. Although the Book of Abraham in part resembles chapters from Genesis, the text went far beyond the Bible in many respects–again an heroic alteration. But even in this reversion to the Book of Mormon methods, Joseph reached out to conventional scholarship. Instead of plunging into translation as he had with the Book of Mormon, he first worked on "translating an alphabet to the Book of Abraham, and arranging a grammar of the Egyptian language as practiced by the ancients."[44] The next year, 1836, Champollion's *Grammaire* of Egyptian, considered to be his greatest scholarly achievement, was published posthumously, and here a year earlier Joseph Smith was writing his "Grammar & Alphabet of the Egyptian Language." The manuscript shows an Egyptian character in a ruled column on the left, and opposite on the right a translation. The translations contain whole paragraphs of material for a single character, and, as the grammar went on, blend into the translation that eventually became the Book of Abraham. But on the first page the grammar lays down rules for understanding Egyptian, using phrases like "parts of speech," and words like "verbs, participles-prepositions, conjunctions, and adverbs," the words of a grammarian and linguist.[45]

The Egyptian Grammar perplexes Mormons, who have never known whether to consider it an inspired work or exploratory experiments with an alien language.[46] As far as can be told now, Joseph's translations of the Egyptian characters do not conform to modern understanding of their meaning. They came by inspiration, not from a precocious deciphering of hieroglyphics. On the other hand, they have the appearance and in places the language of a grammar and dictionary. The work seems suspended between the world of learning and the world of divine gift. Joseph could never change himself from seer into scholar, but in this document he reached for more conventional mastery, as if he wanted to blend learning with his own special powers.[47]

Near the end of his life, in a rare moment of self-reflection, Joseph told the Saints that he knew his story strained credulity.[48] Like all religious visionaries, he understood his experience as coming from without, not from within; God, angels, the Holy Spirit directed him, not his own genius. But even so, his ego had to organize the visions and divine commands into a coherent human identity. The translation of the Book of Mormon alone required him to forge an unprecedented self-understanding for an unlearned citizen of the nineteenth century.

He took on the work with great enthusiasm, developing a momentum that propelled him from the Book of Mormon to the Bible and the Book of Abraham. He told Joseph Knight when the plates were first removed from the hill that they were "writen in Caracters, and I want them translated," and his resolve never wavered.[49] He loved translating and, rather than faltering under the strain of performing the impossible, valiantly labored on. Near the end of his life he described himself to James Arlington Bennett, his future running mate on the 1844 U.S. presidential ticket: "By the power of God I translated the Book of Mormon from hieroglyphics; the knowledge of which was lost to the world: in which wonderful event I stood alone, an unlearned youth, to combat the worldly wisdom, and multiplied ignorance of eighteen centuries."[50] In that statement, made when pressures on him were mounting, we sense the burden of living an incredible life. But those glimpses were rare. For the most part, faith in his calling and his buoyant spirit carried him through the formidable task of translating undecipherable hieroglyphics.

*NOTES*

1. Eber D. Howe, *Mormonism Unvailed; or, A Faithful Account of that Singular Imposition and Delusion, from Its Rise to the Present Time* (Painesville, OH: Printed and published by the author, 1834).

2. The classic critique of the Spaulding theory is Fawn M. Brodie, *No Man Knows My History* (New York: Alfred A. Knopf, 1945), 419-33. A more thorough study is Lester Bush, Jr., "The Spaulding Theory Then and Now," *Dialogue: A Journal of Mormon Thought* 10 (Aug. 1977): 40-69. A highly attenuated effort to revive the Spaulding theory is found in David Persuitte, *Joseph Smith and the Origins of the Book of Mormon* (Jefferson, NC: McFarland & Co., 1985), 247-55.

3. D&C 21:1.

4. Charles G. Finney, *Memoirs of Rev. Charles G. Finney, Written by Himself* (New York: A.S. Barnes Company, 1876), 19-20.

5. Joseph Smith, *History of the Church of Jesus Christ of Latter-day Saints,* 6 vols. (Salt Lake City: Deseret Book Co., 1956), 1:146.

6. D&C 20:5; James B. Allen, "Emergence of a Fundamental: The Expand-

ing Role of Joseph Smith's First Vision in Mormon Religious Thought," *Journal of Mormon History* 7 (1980): 43-61.

7. Dean C. Jessee, ed., *The Papers of Joseph Smith, Volume 1: Autobiographical and Historical Writings* (Salt Lake City: Deseret Book Co., 1989), 95.

8. *Wayne Sentinel*, 26 June 1829, reprinted in Francis W. Kirkham, *A New Witness for Christ in America: The Book of Mormon*, 2nd ed. (Independence, MO: Press of Zion's Printing and Publishing Co., 1947), 148.

9. *Advertiser and Telegraph* (Rochester), 31 Aug. 1829, in Kirkham, *New Witness for Christ*, 151. Compare the *Gem* (Rochester), 5 Sept. 1829, ibid., 151-52.

10. *Painesville Telegraph* (Ohio), 16 Nov. 1830; Dec. 1830, in Kirkham, *New Witness for Christ*, 433, 439.

11. *History of the Church*, 1:35-36; D&C 7.

12. D&C 8:1, 11; 9:2.

13. D&C 3:11, 12.

14. For the whole story of the revision, see Robert J. Matthews, *"A Plainer Translation": Joseph Smith's Translation of the Bible: A History and Commentary* (Provo, UT: Brigham Young University Press, 1975).

15. D&C 42:56.

16. D&C 94:10.

17. Alexander Campbell, *The Sacred Writings of the Apostles and Evangelists of Jesus Christ, Commonly Styled the New Testament*, trans. from the original Greek by George Campbell, James McKnight, and Philip Doddridge (Buffaloe, Brook County, Virginia, 1826; revised and republished, 1832).

18. Noah Webster, *The Holy Bible, in the Common Version with Amendments of the Language* (New Haven, 1833).

19. Margaret T. Hills, *The English Bible in America* (New York: American Bible Society, 1961); E. B. O'Callaghan, *A List of Editions of the Holy Scriptures and Parts Thereof, Printed in America Previous to 1860* (Albany: Musen and Rowland, 1861).

20. P. Marion Simms, *The Bible in America: Versions that Have Played Their Part in the Making of the Republic* (New York: Wilson-Erickson, 1936), 235, 248.

21. John T. Irwin, *American Hieroglyphics: The Symbol of the Egyptian Hieroglyphics in the American Renaissance* (New Haven, CT: Yale University Press, 1980), 4-6, 8; John A. Wilson, *Signs and Wonders Upon Pharaoh: A History of American Egyptology* (Chicago: University of Chicago Press, 1964), 17-19.

22. Jessee, *Papers of Joseph Smith*, 1:278.

23. Isa. 29:11-12.

24. Jessee, *Papers of Joseph Smith*, 1:9.

25. Joseph Knight's telling of Joseph's translation incorporated the same language: "He bing an unlearned man did not know what to Do. Then the Lord gav him Power to Translate himself. Then ware the Larned men Confounded, for he, By the means he found with the plates, he Could translate

those Caricters Better than the Larned." Dean Jessee, ed., "Joseph Knight's Recollection of Early Mormon History," *BYU Studies* 17 (Autumn 1976): 35.

26. Mosiah 8:13.

27. Mosiah 8:13

28. Mosiah 8:13.

29. Mosiah 8:16-18.

30. 1 Sam. 9:9.

31. 1 Chr. 9:22; Isa. 29:10.

32. *Oxford English Dictionary,* 9:395, citing Pope's 1718 translation.

33. O.E.D. 9:395; D. Michael Quinn, *Early Mormonism and the Magic World View* (Salt Lake City: Signature Books, 1987), 37-38.

34. The affidavits on the Smith family which Philastus Hurlbut collected used the words "stone," or "peek-stone," or "peepstone," rather than seer-stone, though sometimes referring to "seeing" in a stone. Rodger I. Anderson, *Joseph Smith's New York Reputation Reexamined* (Salt Lake City: Signature Books, 1990), 70, 118, 120, 122, 125, 126, 131, 137, 142, 144, 148, 149, 153, 154, 155. The traditional usage of "seer," going back to the seventeenth century and preserved in dictionaries, may have been revived by the Mormons rather than coming out of neighborhood folk magic. Quinn, *Early Mormonism and the Magic World View,* 37-38.

35. Richard Van Wagoner and Steve Walker, "Joseph Smith: 'The Gift of Seeing,'" *Dialogue: A Journal of Mormon Thought* 15 (Summer 1982): 48-68; reprinted in this compilation.

36. Jessee, "Joseph Knight's Recollection," 33.

37. There is evidence that the translation stone was given him after he lost the Urim and Thummim when the 116 pages disappeared. Van Wagoner and Walker, "Joseph Smith," 54.

38. Van Wagoner and Walker, "Joseph Smith," 63; D&C 130:9-11.

39. Matthews, *"A Plainer Translation," 61.*

40. Ibid., 40.

41. Brodie, *No Man Knows My History,* 169.

42. Smith, *History of the Church,* 6:307-308. For an extreme example of using foreign languages, see Brodie, *No Man Knows My History,* 292. Joseph demonstrated his proficiency in Hebrew to Josiah Quincy in April 1844. Josiah Quincy, *Figures of the Past,* new ed. (Boston: Little Brown, and Co., 1926), 325.

43. D&C 90:15 (8 Mar. 1833).

44. Smith, *History of the Church,* 2:238.

45. *Joseph Smith's Egyptian Alphabet & Grammar* (Salt Lake City: Modern Microfilm Co., n.d.).

46. Jay M. Todd, *The Saga of the Book of Abraham* (Salt Lake City: Deseret Book Co., 1969), 252-55.

47. For comparisons of Joseph Smith's translation of the papyri to conventional Egyptology, see the special journal issues devoted to the topic:

*Dialogue: A Journal of Mormon Thought* 3 (Summer 1968); *Sunstone* 4 (Dec. 1979); and *BYU Studies* 11 (Summer 1971).

48. Smith, *History of the Church*, 6:317.

49. Jessee, "Joseph Knight's Recollection of Early Mormon History," 33.

50. Cited in Van Wagoner and Walker, "Joseph Smith," 50.

# 5.

# Joseph Smith: "The Gift of Seeing"

*Richard S. Van Wagoner*
*and Steven C. Walker*

Analysis of eyewitness accounts of the Book of Mormon translation is long overdue. Studies of the statements of early witnesses[1] have not attempted to clarify the method of translation, even though testimony is occasionally contradictory, often tainted with bias, always sketchy. We retrace history's footsteps to the scene of the translation in pursuit of better understanding of how the Book of Mormon was translated.

The primary witness to the translation of the Book of Mormon record is the translator himself. But Joseph Smith's procedural descriptions are too brief and general to be of much help. In an 1831 church conference in Orange, Ohio, Joseph's older brother Hyrum requested a firsthand account of the coming forth of the Book of Mormon. The prophet vetoed the idea: "It was not intended to tell the world all the particulars of the coming forth of the Book of Mormon; it was not expedient for him to relate these things."[2] Joseph maintained this closed-mouth attitude on the subject of the translation throughout his life. His first recorded account of the process, in an 1833 letter to N. E. Seaton, is typically terse: "The Book of Mormon is a record of the forefathers of our western tribes of Indians, having been found through the ministrations of an holy angel, and translated into our own language by the gift and power of God."[3]

In 1835 he gave an even more abbreviated version to "Joshua the Jewish Minister": "I obtained them [the plates] and translated them into the English language by the gift and power of God and have been preaching it ever since."[4] Joseph's 1838 account in the *Elder's Journal* adds the additional detail of Urim and Thummim assistance: "Moroni, the person who deposited the plates ... told me where they were; and gave me directions how to obtain them. I obtained them, and the Urim and Thummim with them, by the means of which I translated the plates and thus came the Book of Mormon."[5]

The prophet's 1842 description of the translating procedure, in the Wentworth Letter, is no more specific: "Through the medium of the Urim and Thummim I translated the record, by the gift and power of God."[6] Public interest in church history, stirred by this letter, impelled the *Times and Seasons* to initiate an 1842 serial publication of the prophet's history of the church, which provides an amplified statement on Book of Mormon translation: "Immediately after my arrival there [Harmony, Pennsylvania] I commenced copying the characters off the plates. I copied a considerable number of them, and by means of the Urim and Thummim I translated some of them, which I did between the time I arrived at the house of my wife's father in the month of December [1827], and the February following."[7]

The prophet's final statement about the translation procedure, in a 13 November 1843 letter to James Arlington Bennett, adds little more to our understanding of the process: "By the power of God I translated the Book of Mormon from hieroglyphics; the knowledge of which was lost to the world: in which wonderful event I stood alone, an unlearned youth, to combat the worldly wisdom, and multiplied ignorance of eighteen centuries."[8]

To find exactly what the prophet meant in his repeated insistences that the plates were translated through the medium of Urim and Thummim by the gift and power of God, we must turn to other eyewitness accounts. Martin Harris[9] served Joseph as the first of several scribes in the work of translation.[10] His description of the method of translation is specific, though we have it only at second hand. Edward Stevenson, later of the First Council of Seventy, recorded the testimony of his friend Harris: "The Prophet possessed a seer stone, by which he was enabled to translate as well as from the Urim and Thummim, and for convenience he used the seer stone. ... By aid of the seer stone, sentences would appear and were read by the Prophet and written by Martin, and when finished he would say, 'written,' and if correctly written that sentence would disappear and another appear in its place, but if not written correctly it remained until corrected, so that the translation was just as it was engraven on the plates, precisely in the language then used."[11] Martin served as scribe only between 12 April 1828 and 14 June 1828, when his part in the loss of the first 116 pages of completed manuscript cost him the privilege of further transcription.

The second scribe to serve Joseph was his wife, Emma. In 1879 Emma, interviewed by her son Joseph Smith III, concerning important events in early church history, explained, "In writing for your father I frequently wrote day after day, often sitting at the table close by him, he sitting with his face buried in his hat, with the stone in it, and dictating hour after hour with nothing between us. ... The plates often lay on the table without any attempt at concealment, wrapped in a small linen table-cloth, which I had given him to fold them in."[12] Emma's service as scribe, interrupted as it must have been by the necessity of household chores, was at best brief. Her handwriting has not been found on any original manuscript material now available.[13]

Full-time transcription did not become possible again until a young schoolteacher, Oliver Cowdery, arrived 5 April 1829. Cowdery wrote in 1834: "These were days never to be forgotten–to sit under the sound of a voice dictated by the inspiration of heaven. ... Day after day I continued uninterrupted to write from his mouth, as he translated with the Urim and Thummim, or, as the Nephites would have said, 'Interpreters,' the history or record, called 'The Book of Mormon.'"[14] When Cowdery returned to the church in 1848, Reuben Miller recorded in his diary that Oliver confirmed his testimony to the Council Bluffs, Iowa, Saints: "I wrote with my own pen, the entire Book of Mormon [save a few pages], as it fell from the lips of the Prophet Joseph Smith, as he translated it by the gift and power of God, by means of the Urim and Thummim, or as it is called by that book, 'holy interpreters.'"[15] (The bracketed material is Cowdery's.)

After approximately two months of translating at the Isaac Hale home in Harmony, Pennsylvania, Joseph was invited by a friend of

Cowdery, David Whitmer, to continue the translation work at his father's farm on the north end of Seneca Lake near Fayette, New York. Thus the Whitmer family witnessed the Book of Mormon translation process as the manuscript grew day by day throughout June 1829. Elizabeth Ann Whitmer, who married Oliver Cowdery in 1832, recorded in 1870, when she was fifty-five: "I cheerfully certify that I was familiar with the manner of Joseph Smith's translating the Book of Mormon. He translated the most of it at my Father's house. And I often sat by and saw and heard them translate and write for hours together. Joseph never had a curtain drawn between him and his scribe while he was translating. He would place the director[16] in his hat, and then place his face in his hat, so as to exclude the light."[17]

David Whitmer, one of the Three Witnesses to the Book of Mormon, served as scribe during this brief period. He provides us with more specific information about the translation procedure than any other person. In 1887 he published a booklet in Richmond, Missouri, entitled *An Address to All Believers in Christ,* which includes this detailed description: "I will now give you a description of the manner in which the Book of Mormon was translated. Joseph Smith would put the seer stone into a hat, and put his face in the hat, drawing it closely around his face to exclude the light; and in the darkness the spiritual light would shine. A piece of something resembling parchment would appear, and on that appeared the writing. One character at a time would appear, and under it was the interpretation in English. Brother Joseph would read off the English to Oliver Cowdery, who was his principal scribe, and when it was written down and repeated by Brother Joseph to see if it was correct, then it would disappear, and another character with the interpretation would appear. Thus the Book of Mormon was translated by the gift and power of God, and not by any power of man."[18]

Whitmer reiterated that account on many occasions, explaining the translation process in a consistent fashion: "Joseph did not see the plates in translation, but would hold the interpreters to his eyes and cover his face with a hat, excluding all light, and before him would appear what seemed to be parchment on which would appear the characters of the plates on a line at the top, and immediately below would appear the translation in English."[19] In an 1881 interview with the *Kansas City Journal,* David Whitmer even details characteristics of the seer stone (multiplied by an enthusiastic reporter into two stones): "I, as well as all of my father's family, Smith's wife, Oliver Cowdery, and Martin Harris were present during the translation. The translation was by Smith, and the manner as follows: He had two small stones of a chocolate color, nearly egg shaped and perfectly smooth, but not transparent, called interpreters, which were given him with the plates. He did not use the plates in the translation, but would hold the interpreters to his eyes and cover his face with a hat, excluding all light."[20]

Whitmer explicitly confronted the general confusion between the seer stone and the Nephite "interpreters," or Urim and Thummim, when he tried to set the record straight through a friend, Edward Traughber: "With the sanction of David Whitmer, and by his authority, I now state that he does not say that Joseph Smith ever translated in his presence by aid of Urim and Thummim; but by means of one dark colored, opaque stone, called a 'Seer Stone,' which was placed in the crown of a hat, into which Joseph put his face, so as to exclude the external light. Then, a spiritual light would shine forth, and parchment would appear before Joseph, upon which was a line of characters from the plates, and under it, the translation in English; at least, so Joseph said."[21]

Other early witnesses tend to corroborate Whitmer's account. Joseph Knight, Sr., a close friend of Joseph Smith, recorded an account of the translation process, possibly as early as 1833: "Now the way he translated was he put the urim and thummim into his hat and Darkened his Eyes then he would take a sentence and it would appear in Brite Roman Letters then he would tell the writer and he would write it then that would go away the next Sentence would Come and so on."[22]

Emma Smith's father, Isaac Hale, provides a valuably frank perspective of the translation process because of the hostility he came to harbor toward son-in-law Joseph Smith during the few months the translation proceeded in the Hale home: "The manner in which he [Joseph Smith] pretended to read and interpret, was the same as when he looked for money-diggers, with a stone in his hat, and his hat over his face, while the Book of Plates were at the same time hid in the woods."[23]

Michael Morse, husband of Emma Smith's sister, Trial Hale,

described the procedure as he witnessed it, a description remarkably consistent with previous accounts. He is quoted in 1879 by W. W. Blair, of the First Presidency of the Reorganized Church of Jesus Christ of Latter Day Saints: "When Joseph was translating the Book of Mormon, [Morse] had occasion more than once to go into his immediate presence, and saw him engaged at his work of translation. The mode of procedure consisted in Joseph's placing the Seer Stone in the crown of a hat, then putting his face into the hat, so as to entirely cover his face, resting his elbows upon his knees, and then dictating word after word, while the scribes–Emma, John Whitmer, O. Cowdery, or some other wrote it down."[24]

These eyewitness accounts to the translation process must be viewed in proper perspective. Most were given in retrospect and may be clouded by the haze of intervening years. Many were reported secondhand, subject to skewing by nonwitnesses. Yet there are persistent parallels among these scattered testimonies. Consensus holds that the "translation" process was accomplished through a single seer stone from the time of the loss of the 116 pages until the completion of the book. Martin Harris's description of interchangeable use of a seer stone with the interpreters, or Urim and Thummim, refers only to the portion of translation he was witness to–the initial 116 pages. The second point of agreement is even more consistent: The plates could not have been used directly in the translation process. The prophet, his face in a hat to exclude exterior light, would have been unable to view the plates directly even if they had been present during transcription.

A mental picture of the young Joseph, face buried in a hat, gazing into a seer stone, plates out of sight, has not been a generally held view since the early days of the church. The view raises some difficult questions. Why, for example, was such great care taken to preserve the plates for thousands of years if they were not to be used directly in the translation process? Is it possible that they were to serve primarily as evidence to the eleven witnesses of the Book of Mormon that the record did in fact exist?

The concept of a single seer stone is another problem area, for we have been taught since the prophet's day that the Urim and Thummim were used. The term itself is problematic. The Book of Mormon does not contain the words "Urim and Thummim." Ammon describes the instrument as "the things ... called interpreters"–"two stones which were fastened into the two rims of a bow" which were "prepared from the beginning" and "handed down from generation to generation, for the purpose of interpreting languages" (Mosiah 8:13, 28:13-14). Joseph Smith adds in the Pearl of Great Price that "God had prepared them for the purpose of translating the book" (JS-H 1:35). Furthermore, the Nephite interpreters were not referred to as Urim and Thummim until 1833, when W. W. Phelps first equated the two in the first edition of the *Evening and Morning Star*: "It was translated by the gift and power of God, by an unlearned man, through the aid of a pair of Interpreters, or spectacles–(known, perhaps in ancient days as Teraphim, or Urim and Thummim)."[25]

That the prophet should have used a seer stone rather than the Nephite interpreters is puzzling in itself. Martin Harris's 1875 mention of convenience in using a seer stone may refer to the fact that by all accounts the Nephite interpreters were large.[26] An additional reason for using the seer stone Harris conveniently omits, since it directly involved him. David Whitmer explains that after Martin Harris lost the first 116 pages of Book of Mormon manuscript, "'the Lord' took from the prophet the Urim and Thummim and other wise expressed his condemnation. By fervent prayer and by other wise humbling himself, the prophet, however, again found favor, and was presented with a strange, oval-shaped, chocolate-colored stone, about the size of an egg only more flat, which, it was promised, should serve the same purpose as the missing Urim and Thummim. ... With this stone all of the present Book of Mormon was translated."[27]

When Zenas H. Gurley, editor of the RLDS *Saints' Herald*, interviewed Whitmer in 1855 and specifically asked if Joseph used his "'Peep stone' to finish up the translation," David replied that "he used a stone called a 'Seers stone,' the 'Interpreters' having been taken away from him because of transgression. The 'Interpreters' were taken from Joseph after he allowed Martin Harris to carry away the 116 pages of Ms of the Book of Mormon as a punishment, but he was allowed to go on and translate by the use of a 'Seers stone' which he had, and which he placed in a hat into which he buried his face, stating to me and others that the original character appeared upon parchment and under it the translation in English."[28]

Whitmer's accounts also find support in the *Historical Record* of the church: "As a chastisement for this carelessness, the Urim and Thummim was taken from Smith. But by humbling himself, he again found favor with the Lord and was presented a strange oval-shaped, chocolate colored stone, about the size of an egg, but more flat which it was promised should answer the same purpose. With this stone all the present book was translated."[29]

Joseph had apparently possessed this seer stone for several years before using it in the translation process, despite the accounts of a divine "presentation." Willard Chase, a neighbor of the Smiths in Palmyra, New York, relates how the stone was discovered on his property: "In the year 1822, I was engaged in digging a well. I employed Alvin and Joseph Smith to assist me. ... After digging about twenty feet below the surface of the earth, we discovered a singularly appearing stone, which excited my curiosity. I brought it to the top of the well, and as we were examining it, Joseph put it into his hat, and then his face into the top of his hat. ... The next morning he came to me, and wished to obtain the stone, alleging that he could see in it; but I told him I did not wish to part with it on account of its being a curiosity, but I would lend it."[30]

Confirmation of Chase's account is made by Martin Harris in 1859: "Joseph had a stone which was dug from the well of Mason Chase twenty-four feet from the surface. In this stone he could see many things to my certain knowledge."[31] Wilford Woodruff, writing in 1888, recalled that Joseph Smith found the "sears stone ... by revelation some 30 feet under the earth."[32]

Several accounts document that Joseph often carried the Chase seer stone on his person between 1822 and 1830. In an 1826 trial, "on the request of the court he exhibited the stone. It was about the size of a small hen's egg, in the shape of a high-instepped shoe. It was composed of layers of different colors passing diagonally through it. It was very hard and smooth, perhaps by being carried in the pocket."[33] Martin Harris in 1859 recalled an incident that occurred in the early 1820s: "I was at the house of his father in Manchester, two miles south of Palmyra village, and was picking my teeth with a pin while sitting on the bars. The pin caught in my teeth and dropped from my fingers into shavings and straw. I jumped from the bars and looked for it. Joseph and Northrop Sweet also did the same. We could not find it. I then took Joseph on surprise, and said to him–I said, 'Take your stone.' I had never seen it, and did not know that he had it with him. He had it in his pocket. He took it and placed it in his hat–the old white hat–and placed his face in his hat. I watched him closely to see that he did not look to one side; he reached out his hand beyond me on the right, and moved a little stick and there I saw the pin, which he picked up and gave to me. I know he did not look out of the hat until after he had picked up the pin."[34]

A third attestation of the prophet's possession of a seer stone is the difficulty between Joseph and the family of his 1825 employer, Josiah Stoal, a difficulty which apparently arose from Joseph's reputation with such a stone. According to the prophet's mother, Stoal "came for Joseph on account of having heard that he possessed certain keys by which he could discern things invisible to the natural eye,"[35] and engaged him to seek Spanish treasure near the Susquehanna River. Stoal, who later became a member of the church, related that the young Joseph, who was in his employ for some five months, "pretended to have skill of telling where hidden treasures in the earth were by means of looking through a certain stone."[36] Joseph explains the incident in some detail in the Pearl of Great Price: "In the month of October, 1825, I hired with an old gentleman by the name of Josiah Stoal, who lived in Chenango county, State of New York. He had heard something of a silver mine having been opened by the Spaniards in Harmony, Susquehanna county, State of Pennsylvania; and had, previous to my hiring to him, been digging, in order, if possible, to discover the mine. After I went to live with him, he took me, with the rest of his hands,[37] to dig for the silver mine at which I continued to work for nearly a month, without success in our undertaking, and finally I prevailed with the old gentleman to cease digging after it" (JS-H 1:56).

Though Stoal professed "implicit faith" in Joseph's psychic abilities, the Stoal family remained unconvinced. In 1826 Peter Bridgeman, a nephew of Stoal's wife, preferred charges against Joseph Smith as a "disorderly person and an imposter"–charges evidently referring to Joseph's "glass looking" psychic abilities. Though the full court record has not yet been discovered and recorded accounts of the trial fail to agree on all points, there is consensus that the Stoal family became convinced that Josiah Stoal was squandering his resources and urged him to stop.[38]

Another account corroborating Joseph's habit of carrying a stone on his person comes from Lucy Smith, the prophet's mother: "That of which I spoke, which Joseph termed a key, was indeed, nothing more nor less than the Urim and Thummim, and it was by this that the angel showed him many things which he saw in vision; by which also he could ascertain, at any time, the approach of danger, either to himself or the Record, and on account of which he always kept the Urim and Thummim about his person."[39] Since the Urim and Thummim was too large, by all accounts, to be concealed on Joseph's person, Mother Smith must have been referring here not to the Nephite interpreters but to the Chase seer stone.

That a seer stone was divinely prepared for Joseph's use is suggested in the Book of Mormon. Alma 37:23 reads: "I will prepare unto my servant Gazelem, a stone, which shall shine forth in darkness unto light, that I may discover unto my people who serve me, that I may discover unto them the works of their brethren, yea, their secret works, their works of darkness, and their wickedness and abominations." "Gazelam," with a slight difference in spelling, is identified, in three sections of the Doctrine and Covenants (78:9, 82:11, 104:26, 43), as Joseph Smith. W. W. Phelps, scribe and personal friend to the prophet, declared in Joseph Smith's funeral sermon that the prophet was "Gazelam" in the spirit world.[40]

The prophet related in his Pearl of Great Price account that during Moroni's first conversation with him 23 September 1823, "the vision was opened to my mind that I could see the place where the plates were deposited, and that so clearly and distinctly that I knew the place again when I visited it" (JS-H 1:42). Joseph does not relate how the vision was opened to his mind, but parallel accounts indicate that it may have been through the Chase seer stone.[41] Martin Harris recalled in 1859: "Joseph had before this described the manner of his finding the plates. He found them by looking in the stone found in the well of Mason Chase. The family had likewise told me the same thing."[42]

Willard Chase, on whose property the stone was discovered, points out that in 1827 Joseph Smith, Sr., explained to him "that some years ago, a spirit had appeared to Joseph his son, in a vision, and informed him that in a certain place there was a record on plates of gold; and that he was the person that must obtain them. He [Joseph

Smith] then observed that if it had not been for that stone, he would not have obtained the book."[43]

Henry Harris, an acquaintance of the Smith family, confirms these accounts: "He [Joseph Smith] said he had a revelation from God that told him they were hid in a certain hill and he looked in his stone and saw them in the place of deposit."[44] Further corroboration is provided by W. D. Purple, who had taken notes for Judge Albert Neely during Joseph Smith's 1826 trial: "Smith, by the aid of his luminous stone, found the Golden Bible, or the book of Mormon."[45] And in 1856, after attending a meeting of the Board of Regents of the University of Deseret, Judge Hosea Stout recorded in his journal that "President Young exhibited the 'seer's stone' with which the Prophet Joseph discovered the plates of the Book of Mormon."[46]

The prophet's 1838 account of the manner in which he discovered the plates, though it makes no mention of the Chase seer stone, does not preclude its use: "Moroni, the person who deposited the plates, from whence the Book of Mormon was translated, in a hill in Manchester, Ontario County, New York, being dead, and raised again therefrom, appeared unto me, and told me where they were; and gave me directions how to obtain them."[47] The seer stone could have been the medium through which Moroni's instructions were given. The fact that the Smith brothers who shared Joseph's bedroom were not disturbed by Moroni's visitation adds support to the possibility of a seer stone vision.

Lest the prophet's omission of mention of such matters be taken as proof they did not occur, it should be noted that his hesitation to divulge details of the coming forth of the Book of Mormon might be expected in light of the vitriolic public reception of his accounts of sacred matters. If the early response of a nonbelieving Methodist minister as recorded in the Pearl of Great Price is typical, it is obvious why Joseph would hesitate to provide detailed disclosure: "I took occasion to give him an account of the vision which I had had. I was greatly surprised at his behavior; he treated my communication not only lightly, but with great contempt, saying it was all of the devil, that there were no such things as visions or revelations in these days; that all such things had ceased with the apostles, and that there would never be any more of them" (JS-H 1:21). Given that sort of reaction, it is not surprising that Joseph seldom discussed the Chase seer stone, and showed it only to trusted associates.

Historical evidence indicates that he retained possession of this stone for a brief period after the completion of the Book of Mormon translation. In early 1830 Martin Harris, who had consented to finance publication of the book, was unable to come up with the necessary funds quickly. Hyrum Smith and others became impatient and suggested that Joseph send some of the brethren to Toronto, Ontario, to attempt to sell the copyright. David Whitmer records the prophet's use of the seer stone in seeking inspiration on the matter: "Joseph looked into the hat in which he placed the stone, and received a revelation that some of the brethren should go to Toronto, Canada, and that they would sell the copy-right of the Book of Mormon. Hiram Page and Oliver Cowdery went to Toronto on this mission, but they failed entirely to sell the copy-right, returning without any money. Joseph was at my father's house when they returned. I was there also, and am an eye witness to these facts. Jacob Whitmer and John Whitmer were also present when Hiram Page and Oliver Cowdery returned from Canada. Well, we were all in great trouble; and we asked Joseph how it was that he had received a revelation from the Lord and the brethren had utterly failed in their undertaking. Joseph did not know how it was, so he enquired of the Lord about it, and behold the following revelation came through the stone: *'Some revelations are of God: some revelations are of man; and some revelations are of the devil.'*"[48]

David Whitmer indicated that the seer stone was later given to Oliver Cowdery: "After the translation of the Book of Mormon was finished early in the spring of 1830 before April 6th, Joseph gave the Stone to Oliver Cowdery and told me as well as the rest that he was through with it, and he did not use the Stone anymore."[49] Whitmer, who was Cowdery's brother-in-law, stated that on Oliver's death in 1848, another brother-in-law, "Phineas Young, a brother of Brigham Young, and an old-time and once intimate friend of the Cowdery family came out from Salt Lake City, and during his visit he contrived to get the stone from its hiding place, through a little deceptive sophistry, extended upon the grief-stricken widow. When he returned to Utah he carried it in triumph to the apostles of Brigham Young's 'lion house.'"[50]

Whatever the exact circumstances of its acquisition, the Chase seer stone remained in Brigham Young's possession until his death in 1877.[51] Hosea Stout described in detail the stone President Young displayed to the University of Deseret Board of Regents on 25 February 1856, "a silecious granite dark color almost black with light colored stripes some what resembling petrified poplar or cotton wood bark. It was about the size but not the shape of a hen's egg."[52]

This same seer stone was carried by President Wilford Woodruff to the dedication of the Manti temple in 1888: "Before leaving I consecrated upon the Altar the sears stone that Joseph Smith found by Revelation some 30 feet under the earth carried by him through life."[53] Another description of the stone was given by Richard M. Robinson when he returned from a Southern States mission in 1899 and presented a strange coin he felt might be of Nephite origin to President Lorenzo Snow. Robinson relates that President Snow "went and got the money purse or leather bag that President Young had brought to the Rocky Mountains with him, also the Seer Stone and said, 'This is the Seer Stone that the Prophet Joseph used. There are very few worthy to view this, but you are.' He handed the Seer Stone to me and I couldn't express the joy that came to me and took that stone in my hands. Words are not equal to the task of expressing such a sublime joy! He then told me to hand the Seer Stone to my wife and I handed it to her. He then blessed us with the greatest blessing I have ever heard fall from the mouth of man! The Seer Stone was the shape of an egg though not quite so large, of a gray cast something like granite but with white stripes running around it. It was transparent but had no holes, neither in the end or in the sides. I looked into the stone, but could see nothing, as I had not the gift and power of God that must accompany such a manifestation."[54]

Though we seldom hear the Chase seer stone mentioned in the church today, it remains in the possession of the First Presidency. Joseph Fielding Smith, as an apostle, made clear that "the Seer Stone which was in the possession of the Prophet Joseph Smith in early days ... is now in the possession of the Church."[55] Elder Joseph Anderson, Assistant to the Council of the Twelve and longtime secretary to the First Presidency, clarified in 1971 that the "Seer Stone that Joseph Smith used in the early days of the Church is in possession of the Church and is kept in a safe in Joseph Fielding Smith's office. ... [The stone is] slightly smaller than a chicken egg, oval, chocolate in color."[56]

The final word as to what happened to the Nephite interpreters or Urim and Thummim is usually thought to be the Pearl of Great Price account in Joseph Smith-History 1:59-60: "At length the time arrived for obtaining the plates, the Urim and Thummim, and the breastplate. ... By the wisdom of God, they remained safe in my hands, until I had accomplished by them what was required at my hand. When, according to arrangements, the messenger called for them I delivered them up to him: and *he has them in his charge unto this day, being the second day of May, one thousand eight hundred and thirty-eight*" (italics added).

Though "them" in this account could refer solely to the plates, Patriarch Zebedee Coltrin, an early acquaintance of Joseph Smith, related in an 1880 high priests' meeting in Spanish Fork, Utah, that he had once asked Joseph what he had done with the Urim and Thummim and that "Joseph said he had no further need of it and he had given it to the angel Moroni. He had the Melchizedek Priesthood, and with that Priesthood he had the key to all knowledge and intelligence."[57] Joseph Smith apparently did not have the Nephite interpreters after the completion of the Book of Mormon translation; Moroni had them in his possession when they were shown to the Three Witnesses in June 1830. David Whitmer explained to Orson Pratt and Joseph F. Smith in 1878 that he, Martin Harris, and Oliver Cowdery, in fulfillment of a promise made in Doctrine and Covenants 17:1, were shown "a table with many records or plates upon it, besides the plates of the Book of Mormon, also the Sword of Laban, the Directors–i.e., the ball which Lehi had–and the Interpreters."[58]

If the Nephite interpreters were in fact returned to Moroni before June 1830, as the evidence strongly suggests, then why are so many references made to "Urim and Thummim" in church history after this date? Wilford Woodruff's journal entry describing a Quorum of the Twelve meeting held 27 December 1841 in Nauvoo, Illinois, shows the problem: "The Twelve, or part of them, spent the day with Joseph the Seer, and he confided unto them many glorious things of the Kingdom of God. The privileges and blessings of the priesthood, etc. I had the privilege of seeing for the first time in my day, the *Urim and Thummim*" (italics added).[59]

Yet Brigham Young, attending the same meeting, recorded: "I met with the Twelve at brother Joseph's. He conversed with us in a familiar manner on a variety of subjects, and explained to us the Urim and Thummim which he found with the plates, called in the Book of Mormon the Interpreters. He said that every man who lived on the earth was entitled to a seer stone, and should have one, but they are kept from them in consequence of their wickedness, and most of those who do find one make an evil use of it; he showed us his *seer stone*" (italics added).[60]

Which apostle was mistaken? Was there actual confusion of objects or simply confusion of terminology? We suggest that the discrepancy results from the popularity of Urim and Thummim terminology. Jane Manning James, a black convert living in Joseph's Nauvoo home, uses the "Urim and Thummim" terminology in her autobiographical reminiscence: "One morning I met Brother Joseph coming out of his mothers room he said good morning and shook hands with me. I went in to his mothers room she said good morning bring me that bundle from my bureau and sit down here. I did as she told me, she placed the bundle in my hands and said, handle this and after I had done it she said sit down. Do you remember that I told you about the Urim and Thummim when I told you about the book of Mormon, I answered yes mam. She then told me I had just handled it, you are not permitted to see it, but you have been permitted to handle it. You will live long after I am dead and gone and you can tell the Latter-day Saints, that you was permitted to handle the Urim and Thummim."[61] Lucy Clayton Bullock, wife to Brigham Young's clerk, Thomas Bullock, also tells of "seeing the urim and thummim" during the Nauvoo period.[62]

The brother apostles Orson and Parley P. Pratt relate separate accounts of the Urim and Thummim being used to "translate" the book of Abraham from the Egyptian papyri. Parley was quoted in 1842 as having said: "The Pearl of Great Price is now in course of translation by means of the Urim and Thummim and proves to be a record written partly by the father of the faithful, Abraham, and finished by Joseph when in Egypt."[63] Orson added in 1878: "The Prophet translated the part of these writings which, as I have said, is contained in the Pearl of Great Price, and known as the Book of Abraham. Thus you see one of the first gifts bestowed by the Lord for the benefit of His people, was that of revelation, the gift to translate by the aid of the Urim and Thummim."[64] Wilford Woodruff similarly associates the Urim and

Thummim with the translation of the Egyptian papyri: "The Lord is blessing with power to reveal the mysteries of the kingdom of God; to translate by the Urim and Thummim ancient records and hieroglyphics old as Abraham or Adam."[65]

In short, the term "Urim and Thummim" appears repeatedly. Joseph Smith's personal secretary, William Clayton, records that in 1843 Hyrum Smith "requested Joseph to write the revelation [on celestial marriage] *by means of the Urim and Thummim* [italics added], but Joseph in reply said he did not need to, for he knew the revelation perfectly from beginning to end."[66] President Heber C. Kimball testified in 1853, after the Chase seer stone had been brought to Salt Lake City by Phineas Young: "Has Brother Brigham got the Urim and Thummim? Yes, he has everything that is necessary for him to receive the will and mind of God to this people."[67]

In addition to Joseph's use of a seer stone in "translation" work with the Book of Mormon and the book of Abraham, evidence suggests that several of the early revelations recorded in the Doctrine and Covenants may have come through this medium. Orson Pratt, who lived for a time in the prophet's home, related in 1878 "the circumstances under which revelations were received by Joseph ... he [Elder Pratt] being present on several occasions of the kind. ... At such times Joseph used the 'seer stone' when inquiring of the Lord, and receiving revelations, but that he was so thoroughly endowed with the inspiration of the Almighty and the spirit of revelation that he often received them without any instrument or other means than the operation of the spirit upon his mind."[68] Headings to eight sections in the present LDS Doctrine and Covenants–3, 6, 7, 11, 14-17–describe revelations received from July 1828 through June 1829 by "Urim and Thummim." David Whitmer, who stated he was "present when Brother Joseph gave nearly every revelation that is in the Book of Commandments,"[69] records "Brother Joseph giving the revelations of 1829 through the same stone through which the Book was translated. ... He then gave up the stone forever."[70]

Revelations given through the seer stone at the Whitmer home in Fayette, New York, during 1829 include not only sections 14 through 17, but also section 18. Headnote references, which were not added until the 1921 edition of the Doctrine and Covenants, list sections 14-17 as having been given through "Urim and Thummim," but David

Whitmer also mentions the 18th section (which directs him and Oliver to select the first Quorum of the Twelve) as having come through the Chase seer stone.

Section 10:1 describes the "power given unto you to translate by the means of the Urim and Thummim." But the reference to Urim and Thummim is a retrospective addition which does not appear in the original revelation in the Book of Commandments (Chapter IX).[71] This change first appeared in the 1835 edition of the Doctrine and Covenants (sec. 36:1). The prophet's handwritten 1832 account of his early history says "the Lord had prepared spectacles for to read the Book,"[72] and he did not begin to use the phrase "Urim and Thummim" to describe his translation vehicle until after W. W. Phelps equated the interpreters with the "Urim and Thummim" in an 1833 *Evening and Morning Star* article.

President Joseph Fielding Smith thought all "statements of translations by the Urim and Thummim" after 1830 "evidently *errors*."[73] If by "Urim and Thummim" we mean exclusively the Nephite interpreters, President Smith is correct. A more feasible explanation, however, is advanced by Apostle Orson Pratt: "The Urim and Thummim is a stone or other substance sanctified and illuminated by the Spirit of the living God, and presented to those who are blessed with the gift of seeing."[74] Evidence suggests that the prophet Joseph Smith used the term "Urim and Thummim" in a much broader fashion than we have become used to. After Martin Harris had lost the 116 pages of the completed Book of Mormon manuscript, Lucy Smith said that Moroni appeared to Joseph and demanded the return of the Nephite interpreters. The prophet responded: "I did as I was directed, and as I handed them to him, he remarked, 'If you are very humble and penitent, it may be you will receive them again; if so it will be on the twenty-second of next September [1828].' After the angel left me I continued my supplications to God, without cessation, and on the twenty-second of September, I had the joy and satisfaction of again receiving the Urim and Thummim, with which I have again commenced translating, and Emma writes for me."[75]

Though Joseph's account appears at first glance to refer to the return of the Nephite interpreters, an 1870 statement by Emma Smith indicates that Joseph in all likelihood meant the Chase seer stone: "Now the first that my husband translated was translated by the use of the Urim and Thummim, and that was the part that Martin Harris lost, after that he used a small stone, not exactly black, but was rather a dark color."[76]

Another Joseph Smith application of the term "Urim and Thummim" to mean "seer stone" is recorded in the journal of Wandle Mace, a Nauvoo acquaintance of the prophet. Mace explains that a group of church members in England had been using two seer stones in exploring "magic or astrology." These two stones, often referred to as the "Sameazer Stones," were given to Joseph Smith's cousin, George A. Smith, who brought them to the prophet in Nauvoo. Mace records that "Apostle Smith gave them to Joseph the prophet who pronounced them to be a Urim and Thummim–as good as ever was upon the earth–but he said, 'They have been consecrated to devils.'"[77]

These stones could not have been the Nephite interpreters, yet Joseph specifically calls them "Urim and Thummim." The most obvious explanation for such wording is that he used the term generically to include any device with the potential for "communicating light perfectly, and intelligence perfectly, through a principle that God has ordained for that purpose," as John Taylor would later put it.[78]

Though a seer stone is referred to many times in the early days of the church as "Urim and Thummim," the reference is not always to the Chase seer stone. The prophet used several seer stones during his lifetime. One of the accounts of his 1826 trial in New York records testimony that "Prisoner [Joseph Smith] laid a book up on a white cloth, and looking through another stone which was white and transparent. ... Prisoner pretended to him that he could discover objects at a distance by holding this white stone to the sun or candle; that prisoner rather declined looking into a hat at his dark colored stone, as he said that it hurt his eyes."[79]

Philo Dibble, a friend of Joseph Smith who made early replicas of the Smith brothers' death masks, preserved a third stone used by the prophet in Nauvoo: "At the time of the martyrdom, [Dibble] rescued a small seer stone, at the Nauvoo Mansion House, from falling into the hands of the apostates. He brought this seer stone across the plains. Later, as curator of church history, he showed the death masks, the seer stone, and other items of historical value on his lecture tours throughout the territory of Utah."[80] Though a description of this stone is not given, it is definitely not the Chase seer stone, which was still in the possession of Oliver Cowdery. It may well be the same stone that the prophet showed to the Quorum of Twelve in 1841, which Wilford Woodruff referred to as the "Urim and Thummim" and which Brigham Young called a seer stone.

Brigham Young documents that Joseph had more than one seer stone: "I met with President W. Richards and the Twelve on the 6th. We spent the time in interesting conversation upon old times, Joseph, the plates, Mount Cumorah, treasures and records known to be hid in the earth, the gift of seeing, and how Joseph obtained his *first* seer stone" (italics added).[81]

Joseph Smith further expanded the meaning of "Urim and Thummim" on 2 April 1843, in response to a William Clayton question: "God and the planet where he dwells is like crystal, and like a sea of glass before the throne. This is the great Urim & Thummim whereon all things are manifest both things past, present & future and are continually before the Lord. The Urim & Thummim is a small representation of this globe. The earth when it is purified will be made like unto crystal and will be a Urim & Thummim whereby all things pertaining to an inferior kingdom or all kingdoms of a lower order will be manifest to those who dwell on it. and this earth will be with Christ Then the white stone mentioned in Rev. c2 v17 is the Urim & Thummim whereby all things pertaining to an higher order of kingdoms even all kingdoms will be made known and a white stone is given to each of those who come into this celestial kingdom, whereon is a new name written which no man knoweth save he that receiveth it. The new name is the key word."[82]

Though all events surrounding the coming forth of the Book of Mormon are not yet fully known, some things seem clear: Joseph Smith discovered a "singular-looking seer stone" in 1822 which not only served as a medium through which, according to numerous descriptions, all of the present Book of Mormon was translated but which also played a vital role in the discovery of the Nephite record. "Urim and Thummim," the traditional nomenclature for the Nephite interpreters which were used as the medium for translating the 116 Book of Mormon manuscript pages Martin Harris lost, has a broader meaning; any mechanism capable of eliciting the mind and will of God can correctly be referred to as "Urim and Thummim." Apparent historical discrepancies between references to the Nephite interpreters and the prophet Joseph Smith's seer stones evaporate once this generic use of "Urim and Thummim" is understood. Whatever the actual device used, the prophet in 1842 provided the most important insight about his Book of Mormon translation: "Through the medium of the Urim and Thummim I translated the record by the gift and power of God."[83]

*NOTES*

1. Two excellent discussions of primary sources are James E. Lancaster, "By the Gift and Power of God–The Method of Translation of the Book of Mormon," *Saints' Herald* 109 (15 Nov. 1962): 798-817, and Robert F. Smith, "Translation of Languages," a 1980 unpublished account of primary sources respecting the Book of Mormon translation, privately circulated.

2. Minutes of general conference, 25 Oct. 1831, cited in Far West Record, 13, archives, Historical Department, Church of Jesus Christ of Latter-day Saints, Salt Lake City, Utah; hereafter LDS archives.

3. Joseph Smith et al., *History of the Church of Jesus Christ of Latter-day Saints*, B. H. Roberts, ed., 7 vols. (Salt Lake City: Deseret Book Co., 1974), 1:315; hereafter *History of the Church*.

4. Warren Cowdery, Manuscript History of the Church, Book A-1:121-22, LDS archives.

5. *Elder's Journal* 1 (July 1838): 43.

6. Joseph Smith, "Church History," *Times and Seasons* 3 (Mar. 1842): 707.

7. Joseph Smith, "History of Joseph Smith," *Times and Seasons* 3 (May 1842): 772.

8. *Times and Seasons* 4 (Nov. 1843): 373.

9. Harris, a family friend of the Smiths, was one of the few persons outside the family to know of the "plates of gold" prior to their retrieval from the Hill Cumorah in 1827.

Joseph Knight, Sr., close friend and neighbor of the Smiths, also knew of the plates: "I went to Rochester on business and resumed by Palmyra to be there about the 22nt of September I was there several days I will say there was a man near By By the name of Samuel Lawrence he was a Sear and he had Bin to the hill and knew about the things in the hill and he was trying to obtain them he had talked with me and told me the Conversation he had with the personage which told him if he would Do right according to the will of god he mite obtain the 27nt Day of September next and if not he never would have them. Now Joseph was some affraid of him that he mite be a trouble to him he therefore sint his father up to Sams as he called him near night to see if there was any signs of his going away that night he told his father to stay till near Dark and if he saw any signs of his gang you till him if I find him there I will thrash the stumps with him" (Joseph Knight, Sr., untitled and undated manuscript in LDS archives written between the last date of entry mentioned in the manuscript, 1833, and Knight's death in 1847).

Brigham Young in 1855 mentioned an additional person, "a fortune-teller ... who knew where those plates were hid. He went three times in one summer to get them . . . the same summer in which Joseph did get them ... He had not returned to his home from the last trip he made for them more than a week or ten days before Joseph got them" (*Journal of Discourses*, 26 vols. [Liverpool, Eng.: F. O. and S. W. Richards, 1853-86), 19 July 1857, 5:55; hereafter *Journal of Discourses*).

10. Dean C. Jessee, "The Original Book of Mormon Manuscript," *BYU Studies,* Spring 1970, 259-78, lists the scribes as Martin Harris, Emma Smith, Oliver Cowdery, Reuben Hale, John Whitmer, and David Whitmer. The prophet's brother, Samuel H. Smith, is also mentioned as a scribe in the Kirtland Letterbook, 1829-35, 1-6, LDS archives.

11. Edward Stevenson, "One of the Three Witnesses," *Deseret News,* 30 Nov. 1881; reprinted in *Millennial Star* 44 (6 Feb. 1882): 86-87.

12. *Saints' Herald* 26 (1 Oct. 1879): 289-90.

13. Jessee, "Original Manuscript," 276-77.

14. *Messenger and Advocate* 1 (Oct. 1834): 14.

15. Reuben Miller Diary, 21 Oct. 1848, LDS archives; also *Deseret News,* 13 Apr. 1859.

16. In Book of Mormon editions from 1830-1920, Alma 37:24 read "directors" instead of the present "interpreters." RLDS Book of Mormon editions have retained the original and printer's copies reading of "directors."

17. Original not available; cited in William McLellin letter to "My Dear Friends," from Independence, Missouri, Feb. 1870, in library/archives, Reorganized Church of Jesus Christ of Latter Day Saints, Independence, Missouri; hereafter RLDS archives.

18. David Whitmer, *An Address to All Believers in Christ* (Richmond, MO: n.p., 1887), 13.

19. *Kansas City Journal,* 5 June 1881.

20. Ibid.

21. *Saints' Herald* 26 (15 Nov. 1879): 341.

22. Joseph Knight, Sr., account, LDS archives.

23. *The Susquehanna Register,* 1 May 1834, cited in Eber D. Howe, *Mormonism Unvailed* (Painsville, OH: Eber D. Howe, 1834), 77.

24. *Saints' Herald* 26 (15 June 1879): 190-91.

25. Phelps was church printer in Independence, Missouri, and editor of the *Evening and Morning Star.* He was also publisher of the Book of Command-

ments, and while living in Joseph Smith's Kirtland home assisted the 1835 First Presidency in compiling the first edition of the Doctrine and Covenants.

26. William Smith, the prophet's brother, described the interpreters as "too large for Joseph's eyes; they must have been used by larger men" (William Smith interview by J. W. Peterson and W. S. Pender, 4 July 1891, reported in *The Rod of Iron* 3 [Feb. 1924]: 6-7; *Saints' Herald* 79 [9 Mar. 1932]: 238). Professor Charles Anthon, retrospectively recalling Martin Harris's description, agreed: "These spectacles were so large that if a person attempted to look through them, his two eyes would have to be turned towards one of the glasses merely, the spectacles in question being altogether too large for the breadth of the human face" (Anthon to E. D. Howe, 17 Feb. 1834, in *Mormonism Unvailed,* 17). Though Anthon's account seems exaggerated, Martin Harris refutes that the lenses were "about two inches in diameter, perfectly round, and about five-eighths of an inch thick at the centre. ... They were joined by a round bar of diver, about three-eights of an inch in diameter, and about four inches long, which with the two stones, would make eight inches." Harris read proofs of this article before publication and verified the accuracy of the reporting (see *Tiffany's Monthly,* June 1859, 165-66).

27. *Chicago Inter-Ocean,* 17 Oct. 1886; also *Saints' Herald* 33 (13 Nov. 1886): 706.

28. "Questions asked of David Whitmer at his home in Richmond Ray County Mo. Jan. 14 1885 relating to book of Mormon, and the history of the Church of Jesus Christ of LDS by Elder Z. H. Gurley," holograph in LDS archives. Another supportive account is a Whitmer interview recorded in the *Chicago Tribune,* 17 Dec. 1885: "The plates were never restored to Joseph—nor the spectacles, but a different Urim & Thummim—one oval or kidney-shaped—a seer's stone, which he pieced in his hat, and, face in hat, he would see character and translation on the stone." Whitmer's account is also corroborated by William E. McLellin, an early member of the Quorum of the Twelve: "After the 116 pages were lost Joseph translated the rest of the Book of Mormon with a stone" (*Saints' Herald* 19 [1 Aug. 1872]: 473).

29. The *Historical Record. Devoted Exclusively to Historical, Biographical, Chronological and Statistical Matters,* 632, LDS archives.

30. Howe, *Mormonism,* 241-42. The use of seer stones in upstate New York was not unusual. *Wayne Sentinel,* 27 Dec. 1825, refutes: "A few days since was discovered in this town, by the help of a mineral stone (which becomes transparent when pieced in a hat and the light excluded by the face of him who looks into it provided he is fortunes favorite) a monstrous potash kettle in the bowels of old Mother Earth, filled with purest bullion."

31. *Tiffany's Monthly,* June 1859, 163.

32. Wilford Woodruff Journal, 18 May 1888, holograph in LDS archives.

33. W. D. Purple's account in *The Chenango Union,* 3 May 1877, cited in

Francis W. Kirkham, *A New Witness For Christ in America*, 2 vols. (Independence, MO: Zion's Printing and Publishing Co., 1951), 2:365.

34. *Tiffany's Monthly*, June 1859, 164.

35. Lucy Mack Smith, *Biographical Sketches of Joseph Smith The Prophet, And His Progenitors for Many Generations* (Liverpool, Eng.: Published for Orson Pratt by S. W. Richards, 1853), 91-92.

36. *Fraser's Magazine*, Feb. 1873, 229-30.

37. Martin Harris adds that Stoal's "hands" included "Mr. Beman (Alva), also Samuel Lawrence, George Proper, Joseph Smith, jr., and his father, and his brother Hiram Smith" (*Tiffany's Monthly*, June 1859, 164).

38. The trial, reported in *Fraser's Magazine*, Feb. 1873, and *Chenango Union*, 3 May 1877, has long been disputed: But in 1971 Judge Neely's bill of costs for the trial ($2.68) was discovered. This document designates Joseph Smith as "the glass-looker" and charges him with a "misdemeanor" (Marvin S. Hill, "Joseph Smith and the 1826 Trial: New Evidence and New Difficulties," *BYU Studies*, Winter 1972, 222-33). Joseph Smith's cousin, Church Historian George A. Smith, was apparently referring to this case when he related in 1855 that Joseph Smith "was never found guilty but once ... the magistrate, after hearing the witnesses, decided that he was guilty, but as the statutes of New York did not provide a punishment for casting out devils, he was acquitted" (*Journal of Discourses*, 2:213).

39. L. Smith, *Sketches*, 106.

40. Joseph Smith Funeral Sermon in W. W. Phelps Papers, LDS archives. In a 10 April 1854 letter to Brigham Young, Phelps, who served as Joseph Smith's scribe in Kirtland, Ohio, states that Gazelam refers to "The Light of the Lord" (Brigham Young Letter Collection, LDS archives).

41. An interesting account related by Joseph Knight, Sr., suggests that Emma Smith's involvement in the recovery of the plates on 22 September 1827 was shown in vision through the Chase Seer Stone: "Joseph says when can I have it [the Nephite Record] the answer was the 22nt Day of September next if you bring the right person with you Joseph says who is the right person the answer is your oldest Brother But before September Came his oldest Brother Died [Alvin died 19 November 1823] then he was disappointed and did not [k]now what to do but when the 22nt day of September came he went to the place and the personage appeared and told him he could not have it now But the 22nt day of September next he might have the Book if he brot with him the right person Joseph says who is the right person the answer was you will know then he looked in his glass and found it was Emma Hale daughter of old Mr. Hale of Pennsylvany" (Knight manuscript, LDS archives).

42. *Tiffany's Monthly*, June 1859, 169.

43. Cited in Howe, *Mormonism Unvailed*, 246-47.

44. Henry Harris Affidavit cited in Kirkham, *New Witness*, 1:133.

45. *Chenango Union*, 3 May 1877.

46. Juanita Brooks, ed., *On the Mormon Frontier: The Diary of Hosea Stout*, 2 vols. (Salt Lake City: University of Utah Press/Utah Historical Society, 1964), 2:593.

47. *Elder's Journal*, 1 July 1838, 43.

48. Whitmer, *Believers in Christ*, 31-32.

49. Ibid.

50. David Whitmer interview in *Des Moines Daily News*, 16 Oct. 1886.

51. President Brigham Young's estate included two seer stones. His daughter, Zina Young Card, in a letter to her cousin, Apostle F. D. Richards, related: "There is a matter that I wish to lay before you, that weighs upon my mind, and seems very important to me. I refer to some very sacred articles I bought at the sale of my father's personal effects,–articles that never should have been given up to the idle gaze; but being brought out, my mother and myself felt it a wish of our hearts to get them, that their sacredness might not be sullied.

"They are: two sear-stones and an arrow point. They are in the possession of President Woodruff now, and very properly too, but I feel dear cousin, that they should ever be the property of the President of the Church, and not of individuals; that at his demise, they are not retained as they were before among 'personal effects,' but considered ever the legitimate property of God's mouth-piece" (Card to Richards, 31 July 1896, F. D. Richards Letter Collection, LDS archives).

In addition to the seer stones, President Young also possessed a "bloodstone" which he wore about his neck on a chain "when going into unknown or dangerous places." (See display #1076, Brigham Young Collection, Daughters of Utah Pioneers Museum, Salt Lake City, Utah).

52. Brooks, *Hosea Stout*, 2:593.

53. Wilford Woodruff Journal, 18 May 1888. Though the reason for the consecration is not given, Orson Pratt refuted in 1873 that through the medium of Urim and Thummim, "which the Lord God has ordained to be used in the midst of his holy house, in his Temple ... books of genealogy, tracing individuals and nations among all people back to ancient times will be revealed" (*Journal of Discourses* 16:260).

54. "The History of a Nephite Coin," a personal experience of Elder Richard M. Robinson of Grantsville, Utah, recorded 30 Dec. 1934, LDS archives.

55. Joseph Fielding Smith, *Doctrines of Salvation*, 3 vols. (Salt Lake City: Deseret Book, 1956), 2:225.

56. David C. Martin, *Restoration Reporter* 1 (June 1971): 8.

57. High Priests Record, Spanish Fork, Utah, Sept. 1880, 128, LDS archives.

58. Orson Pratt and Joseph F. Smith to President John Taylor and Council of the Twelve, 17 Sept. 1878, cited in *Millennial Star* 40 (9 Dec. 1879): 772.

59. Wilford Woodruff Journal, 27 Dec. 1841.

60. Eldon J. Watson, ed., *Manuscript History of Brigham Young*, 27 Dec. 1841; also in "History of Brigham Young," *Millennial Star* 26 (20 Feb. 1864): 118.

61. Jane Manning James Autobiography, 19, holograph in LDS archives; reference courtesy of Linda King Newell.

62. Lucy Clayton Bullock, Biographical sketch, LDS archives.

63. *Millennial Star* 3 (July 1842): 47.

64. *Journal of Discourses*, 25 Aug. 1878, 20:65.

65. Wilford Woodruff Journal, 19 Feb. 1842.

66. Statement of 16 Feb. 1874, cited in B. H . Roberts, *A Comprehensive History of The Church of Jesus Christ of Latter-day Saints, Century 1*, 6 vols. (Provo, UT: Brigham Young University Press, 1965), 2:106.

67. *Journal of Discourses*, 13 Aug. 1853, 2:111.

68. "Report of Elders Orson Pratt and Joseph F. Smith," *Millennial Star* 40 (16 Dec. 1878): 787.

69. David Whitmer, *An Address to All Believers in the Book of Mormon* (Richmond, MO: n.p., 1887), 3; also *All Believers in Christ*, 30.

70. Whitmer, *Believers in the Book of Mormon*, 3.

71. Robert Woodford, "Historical Development of the Doctrine and Covenants," Ph.D. diss., Brigham Young University, 1974, presents strong evidence that section 10 was given in May 1829 as originally recorded in the Book of Commandments and not in the summer of 1828 as stated in the heading of current editions of the Doctrine and Covenants.

72. Kirtland Letterbook, 1829-35, 106, LDS archives.

73. Smith, *Doctrines of Salvation*, 2:225.

74. N. B. Lundwall, *Masterful Discourses of Orson Pratt* (Salt Lake City: Bookcraft, 1962), 452.

75. L. Smith, *Sketches*, 126.

76. Emma Smith Bidamon to Emma Pilgrim, 27 Mar. 1870, RLDS archives. Joseph described the interpreters in his 1842 Wentworth Letter as "two transparent stones set in the rim of a bow." But Martin Harris described them in an 1859 *Tiffany's Monthly* interview as "white, like polished marble, with a few grey streaks." An interview with David Whitmer ("The Golden Fables," *Chicago Times*, 7 Aug. 1875) clarifies this confusion by explaining the interpreters as "shaped like a pair of ordinary spectacles, though much larger, and at least half an inch in thickness, and perfectly opaque save to the prophetic vision of Joseph Smith."

77. Wandle Mace Journal, 66, microfilm in LDS archives. Priddy Meeks, a Nauvoo acquaintance of Joseph Smith, recorded in his journal, *Utah Historical Quarterly* 10 (Oct. 1842): 80: "It is not safe to depend on peepstones in any case where evil spirits have the power to put false appearance before them while looking in a peepstone. ... That is my experience in the matter; also the

Patriarch Hyrum Smith ... stated that our faith was not strong enough to overcome the evil influences."

Imitative use of a seer stone in the early days of the church was demonstrated by Book of Mormon witness Hiram Page who, in September 1830, "had in his possession a certain stone, by which he had obtained certain 'revelations' concerning the upbuilding of Zion, the order of the Church, etc., ... many—especially the Whitmer family and Oliver Cowdery—were believing much in the things set forth by this stone" (*History of the Church*, 1:110). Doctrine and Covenants 28:11 responded for Oliver Cowdery: "Thou shalt take thy brother, Hiram Page between him and thee alone, and tell him—that those things which he hath written from that stone are not of me, and that Satan deceiveth him."

78. *Journal of Discourses*, 24 June 1833, 24:262-63.

79. *Frazier's Magazine*, Feb. 1873, 229-30.

80. *Millennial Star* 11 (Jan. 1849): 11-12.

81. Manuscript History of the Church, 6 May 1849, LDS archives. The Quorum of the Twelve Minutes of this date record that the Brethren spent the "evening in conversation upon many little incidents connected with finding the Plates, preserving them from the hand of the wicked, & returning them again to Cumorah, who did it &c, also about the gift of seeing & how Joseph obtained his first seer stone. Treasures known to exist in the earth of money & records."

82. William Clayton Diary, 2 Apr. 1843, cited in Andrew F. Ehat and Lyndon W, Cook, *The Words of Joseph Smith* (Provo, UT: BYU Press, 1980), 169.

83. Joseph Smith, "History of the Church," *Times and Seasons* 3 (Mar. 1842): 707.

# 6.

# Joseph Smith, the Mormons, and Antebellum Reform—A Closer Look

*Newell G. Bringhurst*

HAROLD BLOOM IN HIS WIDELY READ *THE AMERICAN RELIGION: THE Emergence of the Post-Christian Nation* devotes a significant portion of his discussion to Mormonism, wherein he characterizes Joseph Smith as "an authentic religious genius, unique in [American] history." Smith's "genius," according to Bloom, was manifested in bringing together within Mormonism several "fundamental principles" that comprised what Bloom termed "the American religion."[1] Bloom, in characterizing Mormonism "the American religion," gave substance to a statement made by the great nineteenth-century Russian writer Leo Tolstoy who had become acquainted with the LDS church and its beliefs as the result of correspondence between his daughter, Tatyana, and Susa Young Gates—the talented, articulate daughter of Brigham Young.[2]

Despite his extensive discussion of Mormonism, however, Bloom overlooks one important topic: the relationship between early Mormonism and antebellum reform within American society in the period before the American Civil War. Bloom's oversight is not surprising given the author's observation that the Mormon church today, in combination with their supposed arch-rivals, fundamentalist Baptists and other American evangelicals, have become "socially, politically, and economically reactionary bastions of the American establishment." Bloom attributes Mormonism's current anti-reformist position to what he labels "a reaction-formation against both Joseph Smith and Brigham Young."[3]

In a similar vein Lawrence Foster in his seminal 1981 study, *Religion and Sexuality: The Shakers, the Mormons, and the Oneida Community,* while not characterizing Joseph Smith an antebellum reformer, suggests that Mormonism's founder fits the archetype of those "displaced New Englanders" living in the "burned-over" district of New York State "attracted to an extraordinary range of crusades aimed at the perfection of mankind, the achievement of millennial happiness."[4] More recently, Kenneth Winn, in *Exiles in a Land of Liberty: Mormons in America, 1830-1846,* noted that Joseph Smith and his followers represented "religious protest against the pervasive disorder plaguing antebellum America." Mormons, according to Winn, saw themselves as active proponents of what he labels traditional "republican values." Winn, while not characterizing Joseph Smith or his followers as antebellum reformers, or even using the term "reform" to describe their activities, does label Latter-day Saint efforts to restore "republican values" as a crusade "to redeem the nation."[5]

More to the point, Geoffrey F. Spencer, in an engaging essay entitled "Anxious Saints: The Early Mormons, Social Reform, and Status Anxiety," asserts a direct relationship between early Latter-day Saint concerns for certain social issues, including temperance, slavery, the changing status of women, and the desire of Americans, generally, to deal with these same issues. Spencer, moreover, suggests that early "Mormon efforts to reshape society could be understood as an attempt to restore a status that was seen to be diminished and to resolve anxieties created by the emergence of a pluralistic, changing social environment." Specifically, Spencer sees Mormon reform activities within the context of what he terms "status anxiety."[6] But Spencer also stated that such "status anxiety" was not unique to the Latter-day Saints, noting that "the issues of moral reform were one way through which" any cultural group, be they Latter-day Saints or otherwise, "acts to preserve, defend or enhance the dominance of its own style of living within the total society."[7]

Looking to the ideas presented by Spencer and others as a point of departure, it would appear that Joseph Smith and the Latter-day Saint movement that he founded can be better understood within the context of the broader movement to bring about significant social, political, and economic reform within American society during the first half of the nineteenth century. Like other nineteenth-century reformers, Joseph Smith was influenced by his background, especially the economic and social situation of his family. The future Mormon leader, during the years prior to 1830 and the formation of the Latter-day Saint movement, had good reason for deep anxieties about the social-economic status of himself and his family. Born on 23 December 1805 in Sharon, Vermont, Joseph Smith, Jr., fourth child in a family of nine, was exposed to unsettled, uprooted conditions in a frontier environment. By the time young Joseph was eleven, his parents, Joseph Sr. and Lucy Mack Smith, had moved their family in and out of nine different New England communities.

In addition, young Joseph was forced to deal with the uncertainties of life within a lower middle-class family. His father, Joseph Sr., due to continuing economic misfortune, had difficulty providing for his family. After repeatedly failing as a farmer in various parts of New England and unable to establish himself as a merchant, the elder Smith in 1816 moved his family west to Palmyra, New York.[8] Looking for a new beginning in this frontier environment, he hoped to benefit from the boom generated by the recent completion of the Erie Canal. But by the time he arrived with his family, the best farming land had been taken and the boom had subsided into hard times culminating in the Panic of 1819.[9] These difficulties, combined with successive crop failures, ruined the elder Smith's hope for future wealth. This adversity, moreover, "may have driven [Joseph Sr.] to excessive drinking, a habit he apparently retained until his conversion to Mormonism many years later."[10]

As for young Joseph, he, along with his brothers and sisters, "received scant schooling" because of the compelling need to secure employment to supplement the family's meager income.[11] Young Joseph worked as a day laborer on various neighboring farms. He also hired himself out to certain individuals as a "money-digger" for buried treasure. Money-digging through the use of various devices including "seer stones" was "a common form of folk magic practiced primarily by the poor and itinerant in New England and western New York."

But it was generally "opposed" or looked down upon "by middle and upper-class Americans."[12] Young Joseph, in fact, was brought to trial in Bainbridge, New York, in 1826 as a "glasslooker," at which time various friends and associates were interrogated as to his personal character.[13]

Joseph Jr.'s money-digging activity combined with the family's general poverty caused the Smiths to be socially snubbed by their more affluent, middle-class neighbors. The Smiths were forced to endure such humiliation even though, in the words of one commentator, they "were, on the whole, good, decent, hard-working people who should have fared better."[14] Such ostracism apparently "took its greatest toll" on Joseph Jr.'s mother, Lucy Mack, a "fiercely proud and socially ambitious" woman. Lucy, moreover, found the Smith family's chronic economic difficulties particularly galling, given that the Smiths and Macks were both of prominent New England stock. Ancestors on both sides of the family had "accumulated a substantial amount of property," and "achieved political distinction in state and local offices" in Massachusetts. However, the family's economic decline began with the migration to Vermont of Asael Smith, Joseph Jr.'s grandfather. This decline accelerated following the marriage of Lucy to Joseph Sr. in 1796.[15]

Within the Smith family, moreover, Joseph Sr. apparently failed to fulfill the traditional role of male patriarchal dominance. Joseph Sr.'s problems with alcohol might have been a contributing factor. Whatever the case, his wife Lucy assumed a "strong role" in overseeing family affairs, at least equal to that of Joseph Sr. "Assertive, proud, inclined to self-importance," Lucy, according to one writer, presented "an interesting contrast" to Joseph Sr., who was characterized as a "reticent" personality. Thus Lucy and *not* Joseph Sr. was apparently "the greatest influence" on Joseph Jr. during the future Mormon leader's early years.[16] Further overshadowing Joseph Sr. was Alvin, the oldest son. According to at least one observer, "It was he who worked the farm and was the mainstay of the family."[17] Thus when Alvin suddenly died in November 1823 of complications resulting from bilious colic, the loss was profoundly felt. Joseph Jr. lamented the loss of his brother, characterizing him "as the noblest of my father's family."[18]

Exacerbating all these difficulties was the Smith family's unsettled religious situation. Long before Joseph Jr.'s birth, both of his grandfathers had broken away from the traditional churches of New England, despite their Puritan roots. Both grandfathers, however, retained fervent religious beliefs, variously millennialistic and mystical, but could find no home within various organized churches.[19] In turn, Joseph Sr. and Lucy also manifested "religious heterodoxy." Accordingly they both rejected the negative view of humanity evident in the Calvinistic tenets of New England Congregationalism. They believed, instead, that free will and one's own ability could influence his or her own salvation. Eschewing various established churches, they embraced "Christian primitivism" or a return to "true" Christianity as taught at the time of Jesus, believing that various innovations within the established churches down through the ages had corrupted the true faith.[20]

There were further complications when conflict developed within the Smith family over religious practice and belief when Lucy joined the Presbyterian church following the family move to Palmyra. She was joined by two sons and one daughter.[21] Other family members, however, held back, including her husband and young Joseph. The elder Smith, despite his own deeply held mystical, universalistic beliefs, steadfastly refused to join the Presbyterians or any other church, even in the face of his wife's persistent admonitions.[22] It appears that Joseph Jr. "was distressed by [this] religious conflict between his parents."[23] Young Joseph responded by agreeing to attend church with his mother but "did not find the experience edifying."[24]

Further aggravating his situation, young Joseph himself was caught up in the religious fervor of the Second Great Awakening affecting Palmyra and other parts of the "burned-over" district of western New York.[25] As a result, a number of denominations vied for his allegiance causing further inner turmoil. Joseph Jr. later confessed that "my mind became somewhat partial to the Methodist sect and I felt some desire to be united with them." But he held back, adding, "So great were the confusion and strife among the different denominations, that it was impossible for a person as young as I was and so unacquainted with man and things to come to any certain conclusion who was right and who was wrong. My mind ... was greatly excited, the cry and tumult were ... great and incessant."[26]

Deeply troubled, Joseph Jr. sought divine guidance and in the wake of a "vision" was allegedly instructed to join none of the existing denominations. Over the next several years young Joseph allegedly experienced a number of other "visions" or divine visitations culminating in his writing of the Book of Mormon, completed in 1830.[27]

The Book of Mormon served as the basis for a new church founded by Smith and a small group of followers, including members of his own family, on 6 April 1830. Smith himself assumed the title of "first elder" indicating "his preeminence over the whole church."[28] Thus for Joseph Smith, this new denomination, ultimately known as the Church of Jesus Christ of Latter-day Saints (or Mormon church), resolved the sharp religious divisions within his own family while at the same time allaying his own deeply felt anxiety concerning the "true" source of religious authority.[29] Joseph Smith, moreover, apparently hoped that revenue generated from sales of copies of the Book of Mormon would help ease his own family's chronic financial problems.[30]

The Book of Mormon, besides serving as the basis for this new and, in many ways, unique American religious denomination,[31] can be viewed as a clarion call for radical reform, that is, the need to resolve the multitude of problems, political, economic, as well as social, plaguing American society during the antebellum period. Alexander Campbell, in commenting on the Book of Mormon, noted that Joseph Smith's work "decides all of the great controversies–infant baptism, ordination, the Trinity, regeneration, the fall of man, the atonement, transubstantiation, fasting, penance, church government, religious experience, the call of the ministry, the general resurrection, eternal punishment, who may be baptized, and even the questions of free masonry, republican government, and the rights of man."[32]

While Campbell was a less-than-sympathetic critic by virtue of his leadership within the rival Disciples of Christ (from which the Mormon church drew many of its early converts), he was perceptive in noting the deep concerns expressed in the Book of Mormon relative not just to specific religious-sectarian issues, but also social, political, and economic problems which Campbell alluded to under the category of "republican government, and the rights of man." Thus the Book of Mormon can be viewed as a document of strong social-economic protest. According to one noted scholar of American religious history, "The single most striking theme in the Book of Mormon is that it is the rich, the proud, and the learned who find themselves in the hands of an angry God. Throughout the book, evil is most often depicted as the result of pride and worldliness that comes from economic success and results in oppression of the poor."[33] Indeed within the Book of Mormon, one of its protagonists, Jacob, proclaimed, "But wo unto the rich, who are rich as to the things of the world. For because they are rich they despise the poor, and they persecute the meek, and their hearts are upon their treasures, wherefore, their treasure is their God. And behold, their treasure shall perish with them also."[34] In other places the rich found themselves under attack. Alma, a well-known Book of Mormon prophet, condemned those who "persist in the wearing of costly apparel" and who set their "hearts upon the vain things of the world." He warned that if they "persist in turning [their] backs upon the poor and the needy they shall be hewn down and cast into the fire except they speedily repent."[35]

Lawyers along with merchants came under the sharpest attack as economic oppressors. Also denounced were vain, learned clergymen more concerned about their own ornate clothing and general appearance than conditions of the poor and needy in their midst.[36] In general, the main focus of divine displeasure were "the interlocking themes of pride, wealth, learning, fine clothing, and oppression of the poor."[37] By contrast, the Book of Mormon clearly identified with the plight of the poor and downtrodden.

As for specific remedies, the Book of Mormon called for radical reform, a new religious-political order based on economic equality and communal cooperation. Smith's work lamented the current division of American society "into classes."[38] The "ideal" society was one in which "there should be equality among all men." There would be no idle people. All would labor "with their own hands for their support, in all cases save it were in sickness, or in much want."[39] The Book of Mormon described in glowing terms a "golden age" in which "every man did deal justly one with another" and during which "they had all things common among them; therefore there were not rich and poor, bond and free, but they were all made free, and partakers of the heavenly gift."[40]

In general, the Book of Mormon was a critique of the "rampant exploitative individualism" that characterized the larger American society during the Jacksonian period. Thus it rejected the accepted norm or "ideal" of the "self-made man" who could achieve success through individual initiative. "The good of the community took precedence over individual self-interest."[41] It has also been suggested that Smith's work had an "anti-capitalistic quality" to it.[42] Whatever the case, the Book of Mormon "projected a utopian vision that challenged the political, economic, and social values of antebellum America."[43] It anticipated the ultimate destruction of "an old way of life" and the subsequent building of "a new social order from the ground up."[44]

The Book of Mormon found a ready audience, despite the radical tone of its basic message, or more precisely because of it, and the fledgling Mormon church grew rapidly. From some 290 converts at the end of 1830, the movement more than doubled to over 680 within a year after Smith's own migration from New York to the Midwest in 1831. At that time two new Mormon settlements were formed: the first at Kirtland, Ohio, where Smith maintained his principal residence with his wife, Emma Hale, whom he had courted and married in January 1827, and the second established in the then frontier community of Independence, Missouri. By 1835 total church membership stood at 8,835, a thirteen-fold increase in just four years! And three years later, in 1838, this number had doubled to 17,881, with over 10,000 (a majority) living in Mormonism's principal gathering place of northwestern Missouri.[45]

The "earliest [Mormon] disciples" were "men and women of modest means and little education."[46] "Most converts," noted one writer, "had a history of [geographic] mobility, economic insecurity, dissatisfaction with contending sects and hope[d] for a millennium in which discord and hardship would be eliminated and status in the Lord's kingdom would depend upon spiritual rather than material values."[47] In general, they were "characteristically poor, uprooted, unschooled, and unsophisticated" like Joseph Smith himself.[48] Thus they not only responded to the basic message contained in the Book of Mormon, but also identified with the Mormon leader in terms of their own social-economic backgrounds. For example, Brigham Young, who joined the church in 1832 and would emerge as a principal Mormon leader, had been raised in such desperate poverty that his family was broken up when he was just fourteen in the wake of his mother's death in 1815. Leading a nomadic existence while living in various communities throughout upstate New York, Young tried with limited success to make a living variously as a carpenter, painter, and glazer prior to joining the Mormon movement.[49] Young, like Smith, was "denied the opportunity of formal schooling and occasions to cultivate ... social graces." As a result, Young "retained deep resentment against the social distinctions of the churches of his youth."[50] Other notable Mormon leaders, including John Taylor, Wilford Woodruff, Lorenzo Snow, Heber C. Kimball, Parley and Orson Pratt, came from similar backgrounds in that they were "poor farmers or artisans barely finding funds to meet their needs" prior to joining the church.[51]

Joseph Smith, moreover, possessed a number of striking personal qualities which aided him in commanding the allegiance of his followers. In his physical appearance, he was imposing, "muscular," standing six feet tall, and considered "very handsome, except for his nose, which was aquiline and prominent."[52] According to one writer, "he had remarkably blue and compelling eyes under heavy eyelashes, thick blond eyebrows, a high, slanting forehead and light auburn hair." His face "was sensitive" and "he looked at others directly, with an open and sympathetic interest" while possessing a smile that was "easy and warm."[53] Although another account characterized his "gaze" as "veiled and slightly mysterious."[54] Whatever the case, Smith's wife, Emma, was reported to have remarked that "no painting could catch his expression, which was always changing in reflection of his thoughts and feelings."[55] In addition, Smith possessed a certain "charisma" particularly evident while speaking. He projected "intense feeling" according to one writer, in delivering sermons whereby "the blood drained from his face, leaving a frightening, almost luminous pallor."[56] These varied qualities enabled Joseph Smith to command and hold the allegiance of his followers.

As Mormon leader, Joseph Smith implemented certain practices in the spirit of reform manifested in the Book of Mormon while at the same time consolidating his own power or control over his followers. Smith promoted active, widespread participation by members of his church. "Exceedingly egalitarian," in the words of one writer, the Mormons had "no professional clergy." Virtually all adult male members (but no females) were ordained to offices within the Mormon priesthood.[57] Such egalitarianism was also evident in Mormon doctrine, in particular, Joseph Smith's assertion, through revelation, that virtually *all* humankind would be saved, even non-believers along with the wicked and unrighteous. Despite such a universal view, however, the "degrees of glory" in the hereafter would vary with the "highest degrees" reserved to practitioners of the true faith, that is, Mormonism.[58] Also providing greater opportunity for his followers, Smith established special positions of leadership for his most capable and loyal followers. These included an "assistant president" plus two counselors to aid him in running the church, a Quorum of Twelve Apostles along with a Quorum of Seventies to direct the church's expanding missionary work, and two high councils to directly supervise affairs in the rapidly growing Mormon settlements in Kirtland and Independence.[59]

But at the same time Smith increased his own power over the whole church. In March 1835 Smith, through revelation, established himself as church president, or premier officer "over the whole church." The powers of this office were enhanced by Smith's designation as "seer, revelator, translator and prophet."[60] Accordingly Smith made frequent use of personal revelations to instruct and direct his followers, which gave further divine sanction to his authority. Smith's published revelations appeared, first, in a Book of Commandments, brought forth in 1833, and two years later in an expanded volume known as the Doctrine and Covenants. The latter work, ultimately canonized as holy scripture in 1835, was upheld by the Mormons on a par with the Book of Mormon and the Old and New Testaments.

In the meantime Smith asserted his role as a reformer in another important way. In February 1831 he called for a new economic order. The Law of Consecration and Stewardship established in February 1831 through revelation was "a prescription for transforming the highly individualistic economic order of Jacksonian America into a system characterized by economic equality, socialization of surplus incomes, freedom of enterprise, and group economic self-sufficiency."[61] Members of the church were expected to "consecrate" or "deed" to the church all of their property. In turn, the church would then grant an "inheritance" or "stewardship" to every family out of the properties so received. It was hoped and expected that the consecrations would exceed the stewardships. Out of this surplus the church would then grant stewardships to poorer and younger members of the church.[62]

The Law of Consecration and Stewardship was designed as a

"leveler" to bring about a condition of relative temporal equality among church members. It was in the spirit of the "ideal" egalitarian society suggested in the Book of Mormon and further described in a later revelation given by Joseph Smith. The Mormon leader proclaimed: "It is not given that one man should possess that which is above another, wherefore the world lieth in sin."[63] Smith's effort paralleled attempts by other groups of antebellum Americans to implement their own forms of economic communitarianism, in particular the Shakers under Ann Lee and the followers of Robert Dale Owen at New Harmony. The Mormon system, however, was less all-inclusive or in the words of one writer, "more aliken to farm tenancy than to the true communal agriculture practiced by the Shakers and New Harmomists."[64] The Mormon system "aimed at equality in consumption" rather than equality "in the capital controlled or managed by individuals." Individuals "were to be given responsibilities proportionate to their need, circumstances, and capacities."[65] As one writer has suggested, "The spirit of true Marxian communism–'from each according to his ability, to each according to his need'–was implicit in the whole system."[66]

Despite the relative moderation of the Mormon Law of Consecration and Stewardship, this experiment was less than successful and abandoned by Joseph Smith in August 1834–less than four years after its implementation. Smith and other leaders could persuade "only about half" of those church members living in Independence, Missouri, to participate in the program "and those [doing so] almost invariably [were] the poorer."[67] Further upsetting Mormon efforts was the forced expulsion from Independence of those Latter-day Saints living in that community during the summer of 1833 by hostile non-Mormons leery of not just Mormon communitarianism but of Mormons, generally.[68]

A significant amount of Missouri/anti-Mormon hostility stemmed from anxiety concerning Latter-day Saint views on the issue of black slavery–rapidly emerging as the *most critical* issue among antebellum reformers. Joseph Smith and his followers assumed a basic anti-slavery position.[69] The expression of Mormon anti-slavery attitudes is not surprising given that Smith along with the vast majority of his Latter-day Saint followers were from nonslave-holding regions of the northeast. Reflecting this attitude, the Book of Mormon condemned human bondage in general, despite its concurrent and seemingly contradictory racist concepts, that is, a belief that the Indians' dark skin was related to their degraded condition and the product of unrighteous behavior.[70]

Joseph Smith, moreover, expressed his own deep anxieties relative to the disruptive potential of black slavery in American society in response to the 1832-33 South Carolina secession crisis. Through a 25 December 1832 revelation destined to become one of the most famous in Mormon canon, Smith predicted that numerous wars would "shortly come to pass, beginning at the rebellion of South Carolina." In time "the Southern States shall be divided against the Northern States" and war ultimately spread to "all nations." Even more ominous, black slaves would be involved in these apocalyptic events: "And it shall come to pass, after many days, slaves shall rise up against their masters, who shall be marshaled and disciplined for war."[71] Such cataclysmic expectations clearly fit in with basic Mormon millennialistic beliefs.

Reflective of Mormon anti-slavery views was a July 1833 newspaper article entitled "Free People of Color" published in the Mormons' official *Evening and Morning Star* outlining the procedures necessary for free blacks to migrate to the slaveholding state of Missouri. It stated: "So long as we [the Latter-day Saints] have no special rule in the church as to people of color, let prudence guide." It concluded, "[I]n connection with the wonderful events of this age much is doing towards abolishing slavery and colonizing the blacks in Africa."[72] Non-Mormon Missouri reaction to this article was swift and violent. Combined with their perceived suspicions of the Mormons generally, this newspaper article triggered the Latter-day Saints' forced removal from Jackson County, Missouri, in 1833.[73] Mormon anti-slavery views were, moreover, a significant factor in the complete expulsion of all Latter-day Saints from Missouri some five years later in the wake of organized mob violence sanctioned by the state's governor and other officials. The so-called Mormon Missouri War of 1838-39 culminated in Joseph Smith's own near execution and six-month confinement in the Liberty County jail.[74] Despite their violent expulsion from Missouri, Smith and his followers continued to express general anti-slavery views over the course of the next five years, although they remained aloof from, and indeed, condemned the actions of militant abolitionists such as William Lloyd Garrison, Theodore Weld, Frederick Douglass, and others. Smith and his followers, moreover, carefully distinguished their own views from those of various anti-slavery organizations including the American Colonization Society and the American Anti-slavery Society.[75]

Joseph Smith showed himself to be an antebellum reformer in other ways, particularly following the Mormon migration to and settlement of Nauvoo, Illinois, the Mormons' primary gathering place after 1839. Smith personally directed the Mormon migration to Nauvoo, which by the mid-1840s boasted some 12,000 residents, making it the second largest city in the entire state.[76] In addition to his role as religious leader, Smith took charge of both economic and political affairs within the burgeoning city. In promoting the city's economy, Smith did not formally reinstitute the recently abandoned Law of Consecration and Stewardship.[77] But he did encourage close, economic cooperation among his followers in developing local farming, the mainstay of the Mormons' economy, along with various mercantile and commercial enterprises. To further this end, he directed establishment of the Nauvoo Agricultural and Mechanical Association in 1841.[78]

Politically, Nauvoo secured what one writer has labeled "a quasi-sovereign government," thanks to a liberal city charter secured by Smith from the state government of Illinois. This charter gave the city council power to "make, ordain, establish and execute all such ordinances not repugnant to the Constitution of the United States or of this state." It made the city's mayor a particularly powerful figure, granting him legislative, executive, as well as judicial authority–the latter, by virtue of the mayor's concurrent position as chief justice of the municipal court.[79] The charter, moreover, allowed Smith and his followers to organize and maintain their own armed force. Nominally a part of the Illinois state militia, the Nauvoo Legion, consisting of every able-bodied male resident between eighteen and thirty-five, came to number "some five thousand men" by 1844.[80] This military organization was the result of Smith's deep concern for the safety of his followers in the wake of the Mormons' brutal, bloody expulsion from Missouri–an act sanctioned, indeed, carried out by local and state officials.[81]

Joseph Smith himself exercised significant political and military power due to his membership on the Nauvoo City Council, and ultimately his role as the city's mayor, plus his office as commander or lieutenant general of the Nauvoo Legion. He used his authority to promote certain reforms. The city allowed no saloons or public drinking establishments, a situation in sharp contrast to other frontier communities. If citizens of Nauvoo wanted to drink, they were required to buy their alcohol from a shop specifically licensed for this purpose and to consume it in the privacy of their own homes.[82] This enforcement of public temperance was in the spirit of the Mormon Word of Wisdom. Based on a revelation given by Joseph Smith in February 1833 during the Mormon sojourn in Kirtland, Ohio, the Word of Wisdom called for abstinence from "wine or strong drink" proclaiming them "not good ... for the belly."[83] Joseph Smith's call for Mormon abstinence took place during a time when a rising tide of temperance agitation culminated in the rise of the so-called "Cold Water Army," and was most evident in the formation of some 5,000 temperance societies by 1834.[84] Similarly, the Nauvoo City Council enacted a strong anti-vagrancy ordinance directed against idle persons and others who could not "give a good account of themselves." Such individuals were subject to a $500 fine and a six-month jail sentence. The council even sought to limit public utterances of "profane and indecent language."[85] In another move to enforce public morality, Joseph Smith, along with other members of the Nauvoo City Council, acted against the proprietors of a local brothel when news of its operation came to their attention in October 1842. The city council pronounced the brothel a "public nuisance" and ordered a detachment of the Nauvoo Legion to demolish the building in which this enterprise was located.[86]

On a more elevated level, Joseph Smith, acting as Mormon church leader, concerned himself with various other issues affecting women. A fundamental issue involved the proper role and place of women in the church. The church manifested a definite male, patriarchal orientation evident from its earliest days and reflected in the Book of Mormon and the Doctrine and Covenants. In the words of one scholar who has carefully examined these two works, both conveyed the stark assumption that "women are insignificant–or at least less significant than men."[87] Accordingly, the Book of Mormon referred to only six women by name, in sharp contrast to the hundreds of men so mentioned–a logical situation given this work's primary focus on relationships within male-dominated societies.[88] Similarly, the Doctrine and Covenants was "generally addressed to 'men' or assumed an all-male audience."[89] It gave minimal attention to women, referring to them a mere five times in contrast to the mention of men, by name, over 400 times![90]

The limited role allowed women in the church is nowhere more evident than in the fact that women were not allowed ordination to church priesthood offices.[91] This restriction held even though women, from the earliest days of the Mormon movement, manifested what has been characterized as two special spiritual gifts, the ability to heal the sick through blessings or prayer, and the gift of speaking in tongues.[92] Also, during the Mormon sojourn in Kirtland, a female member of the church named Hubble "professed to be a prophetess of the Lord ... and had many revelations" in affirming the truthfulness of the Book of Mormon.[93]

In upholding a strong male, patriarchal role within his movement, Smith was apparently influenced by two basic factors: first, it is possible that Smith was reacting against his childhood environment within his own family, where his mother, Lucy, a strong, dominant individual, had exerted an influence at least equaling and perhaps exceeding that of his father. Joseph Sr., by contrast, seemed a weaker or more benign figure. Second, Smith might have been responding to what one author has termed "the feminization of American culture," the increasingly strong role played by women in various religious denominations within the larger American society during the early nineteenth century.[94]

Despite Mormonism's strong patriarchal male orientation, Joseph Smith found himself under increased pressure from women in his movement following the Mormon migration to Nauvoo. Mormon females, in particular married women, became more assertive apparently as the result of increased responsibilities within their families–a consequence of the absence of their husbands. A large number of Mormon males left their families in response to calls by church authorities to serve as missionaries, leaving their wives primarily responsible for their families.[95] Pressure from such increasingly independent and assertive Mormon women culminated in the formation of the Relief Society in March 1842. Some 1,341 women involved themselves in this new organization, a number representing 10-15 percent of Nauvoo's Mormon population. These women chose as their first president none other than Emma Smith, the strong-willed wife of Joseph Smith![96] The major announced objectives of the Relief Society were "to seek out and relieve the distressed" and "to watch over the morals–and be very careful of the character and reputation of [its] members." In seeking "to house the homeless and provide work for widows" and help other dependent people, the Relief Society's role was similar to that of numerous other contemporary women's auxiliaries and benevolent and reform societies throughout the United States. Such organizations by the 1840s numbered in the thousands.[97]

Relief Society activities, moreover, soon expanded into the spiritual realm. In fact, Joseph Smith's own assertive mother, Lucy, suggested that "the organization could provide the opportunity for women to refresh each other spiritually." Thus members of the organization engaged in testimony bearing, gospel instruction, and occasionally spoke in tongues. More important, Joseph Smith himself apparently granted the Relief Society additional powers. Smith characterized this organization as "a select Society ... a kingdom of priests as in Enoch's day" to whom "the keys of the kingdom are about to be given." He further stated that the officers in the organization, Emma Smith and her two counselors, were "not only set apart, but ordained" to "administer to the sick and comfort the sorrowful." According to another account, "several other sisters were also ordained and set apart to administer in these holy ordinances."[98] These allusions to "priests," "keys" to be given, and "ordinations" have caused some writers to suggest that Joseph Smith was on the verge of granting Mormon women the powers, if not the actual offices, of the Mormon priesthood. The suggestion that Joseph Smith was about to move in such a radical direction has emerged as a sharp point of debate among certain writers as well as spokespersons within the Mormon church.[99] Ultimately, however, the whole issue of the Mormon priesthood *vis à vis* the Relief Society became moot with the formal disbanding of the women's organization in 1844 just two years after its formation. This move came in reaction to attacks by certain Relief Society members to the still secret but highly controversial practice of Mormon polygamy.[100]

Indeed, Joseph Smith's introduction of polygamy to a small, select group of followers in 1841, followed by its divine sanctioning through revelation on 12 July 1843, represents the Mormon leader's most radical effort to "reform" or alter the role of women within the basic structure of the family.[101] Smith's sanctioning of plural marriage appears to be a bold departure, running counter to his earlier teachings in the Book of Mormon, which contained five separate denunciations of polygamy, linking this practice with "fornication," "whoredoms," and various problems of family disorganization.[102]

But, in fact, Joseph Smith began to move away from his initial monogamous position shortly after publication of the Book of Mormon. In July 1831 Smith apparently suggested that plural marriage would be introduced at some future date.[103] It also appears that Joseph Smith himself may have taken at least one plural wife as early as the mid-1830s while still living in Kirtland.[104] But it was not until 1841 that Joseph Smith unveiled the practice of plural marriage to a small group of his most trusted followers, including Brigham Young and Heber C. Kimball.[105] The precise number of women taken as plural wives by each of Smith's close associates was "very restricted," usually numbering just "two or three."[106] By contrast, Joseph Smith took unto himself a considerably larger number of women, despite strong protests and opposition from his first wife, Emma. The precise number of women who became Smith's plural wives is difficult to determine, with varied estimates ranging from twenty-seven all the way up to eighty-four![107]

Joseph Smith's precise motives for implementing plural marriage are difficult to determine. On a doctrinal level, Smith's introduction of this extremely controversial practice represents a critical stage in the evolution of Mormon theology. Through a series of important revelations and various statements given between 1841 and 1844, Smith introduced a number of significant doctrinal concepts, including the introduction of sacred, secret temple ceremonies, as essential for complete Mormon salvation, along with several revolutionary concepts concerning the nature of God and humankind's own relationship to the supernatural. Accordingly, Mormons viewed God as not only anthropomorphic (humanlike in basic form and substance), but also as plural. In promoting the latter concept, Smith asserted the existence of numerous divine beings throughout the total expanse of the universe. Smith, moreover, preached an even more radical concept that humans currently living upon the earth had the potential to become "gods" ultimately assuming dominion over worlds of their own through a process known as "eternal progression." Ultimate godhood, however, could be secured only though the strict adherence to various Mormon ordinances and practices, including plural marriage. Indeed, the practice of plural marriage would serve as an effective means for faithful Mormon males to produce the largest possible number of offspring to be subject to his exalted godlike authority in the hereafter.[108]

Joseph Smith in introducing plural marriage was apparently also influenced by an antebellum American society experiencing profound social change. One scholar has suggested that Mormon polygamy represented "an attempt to restore earlier patriarchal patterns in marriage" currently under attack. "At the deepest level [Mormon polygamy] was a fundamental protest against the careless individualism of romantic love, which seemed to threaten the very roots of family life and social solidarity."[109] Smith, perhaps, was also influenced by one additional factor: the prevalence of various forms of marital experimentation, particularly evident among various groups in the upstate New York environment where he had grown up. These ranged from the Shaker religion directed by Ann Lee which preached complete sexual abstinence, with male and female members living completely separate from each other, to the Oneida Community under John Humphrey Noyes which preached "complex marriage," a practice that involved sexual relations with multiple partners.[110]

In sharp contrast to the secrecy surrounding the introduction of plural marriage, Joseph Smith was very open in promoting himself as a reform candidate for president of the United States in 1844. Rejecting the two major parties, Smith ran as an Independent. But at the same time he adopted a broad-based reform platform clearly influenced by the two major parties, the Whigs and the Democrats, and the small but highly visible Liberty party. Echoing the Whigs, the Mormon leader called for the reestablishment of the national bank. Smith also expressed ardent expansionist views not unlike those of the Democratic party under the leadership of James K. Polk. Thus Smith opposed British claims to Oregon, advocated the annexation of Texas, and, if it could be arranged peacefully, annexation of both Canada and Mexico as well. Like the reformist, anti-slavery Liberty party,

Smith called for the abolition of black slavery. This would be accomplished through gradual, compensated emancipation with revenues gained from the sale of public lands. Three additional reforms not on the agendas of the existing political parties included prison reform whereby virtually all imprisoned convicts would be freed, a call for a reduction in the size of the U.S. Congress by half and reduction in its pay, and a proposal that the president of the United States be given authority to suppress mobs and protect the constitutional rights of all citizens, irrespective of the wishes of any state governor.[111]

To direct his campaign, Joseph Smith utilized a newly created political organization, the Council of Fifty. While separate and distinct from the Mormon church, the council was made up almost entirely of Latter-day Saints. This organization dispatched more than 300 spokesmen throughout the United States who organized dozens of political rallies in major cities in the East and the Midwest.[112] Expressing confidence of ultimate victory, Smith and his backers talked about building "a coalition of the oppressed" including, interestingly enough, American Catholics who like the Mormons were a despised religious minority and victims of persistent antebellum mob violence.[113]

What success Smith would have achieved in the political arena will never be known. The Mormon leader was killed by an armed mob on 27 June 1844 while imprisoned at Carthage, Illinois. Smith's arrest and subsequent death came at the end of a chain of events stemming from Smith's introduction of plural marriage. This practice had generated increasing controversy in the church as more and more Latter-day Saints became aware of its existence. By June 1844 a group of Mormon dissidents had completely broken away from Joseph Smith, denouncing him as a "fallen prophet." They formed their own organization and commenced publication of their own newspaper, *The Nauvoo Expositor,* which openly attacked Joseph Smith and plural marriage. In response, Smith, acting in his capacity as Nauvoo's mayor, had the newspaper declared a "public nuisance" and ordered destruction of the press along with all available copies of the newspaper. Smith, however, quickly realized the explosive situation caused by this clear violation of basic First Amendment rights. Thus he agreed to be taken into custody and stand trial on the charges brought against him. Smith did this to stem the rising tide of anti-Mormon violence generated by local non-Mormons which threatened to escalate into full-scale civil war. But Smith's arrest was not enough to prevent his own death at the hands of a well-organized mob composed of local citizens unwilling to let the legal process take its course.[114]

In conclusion, Joseph Smith and the early Mormon movement reflected many aspects of the reform impulse which characterized American society during the antebellum period. This was evident in Smith's advocacy of such reforms as temperance, prison reform, and the abolition of slavery. But such proposals were minor parts of a much larger reform program whereby Smith and his followers envisioned the creation of an entirely new social and economic order to be built on the ruins of what they felt to be a fundamentally corrupt and decadent American society tottering on the edge of imminent collapse.[115] Mormon communitarianism and the practice of plural marriage would be important, essential components in hastening the creation of this "new heaven and new earth." Indeed, the Latter-day Saints, as reflected in their name, believed the Millennium and Second Coming to be imminent. While the radical new society envisioned by Joseph Smith and his early followers did not come to pass, the Mormon movement or Church of Jesus Christ of Latter-day Saints, which numbered some 26,000 members at the time of Smith's death in 1844, has grown to over 10 million members in the 1990s. An ironic consequence of this growth is that the present-day Mormon church, as a major American denomination, exerts significant influence not in advocating radical reform as envisioned by Joseph Smith more than 150 years ago, but rather as a fundamentally conservative organization supporting the status quo of American society, taking care not to upset existing political, economic, and social institutions.

*NOTES*

1. Harold Bloom, *The American Religion: The Emergence of the Post-Christian Nation* (New York: Simon and Schuster, 1992), 77-128. According to Bloom (103): "What I call the American Religion is a far larger and more diffuse phenomenon than is the Church of Jesus Christ of Latter-day Saints, and as

such seems to me to have three fundamental principles. The first is that what is best and oldest in us goes back well before Creation, and so is no part of the Creation. The second is rather than a belief founded upon mere assent. The third is that loneliness of belated American time, and the American experience of the abyss of space."

2. For a discussion of Tolstoy and his relationship to Mormonism, see Leland A. Fetzer, "Tolstoy and Mormonism," *Dialogue: A Journal of Mormon Thought* 6 (Spring 1971): 13-29.

3. Bloom, *The American Religion*, 118.

4. Lawrence Foster, *Religion and Sexuality: The Shakers, the Mormons, and the Oneida Community* (New York: Oxford University Press, 1981), 129.

5. Kenneth Winn, *Exiles in a Land of Liberty: Mormons in America, 1830-1846* (Chapel Hill: University of North Carolina Press, 1989), 2-3. The so-called "republican ideology" that the Mormons sought to preserve, according to Winn, "rested on the foundation of a virtuous citizenry composed of independent property-owning men whose self-reliance, civic spirit, and hardy disdain for enfeebling luxury separated them from the very wealthy and the very poor ... The republican citizen scorned luxury ... Republican government balanced precariously between anarchy and tyranny. Good citizens were expected to arm themselves, form militias, and exercise constant vigilance in putting down challenges that threatened to upset this fragile equilibrium."

6. Geoffrey F. Spencer, "Anxious Saints: The Early Mormons, Social Reform, and Status Anxiety," *John Whitmer Historical Association Journal* 1 (1981): 43-53.

7. Ibid., 45. Spencer in making this statement paraphrases the observations made by Joseph Gusfield in *Symbolic Crusade: Status Politics and the American Temperance Movement* (Urbana: University of Illinois Press, 1963), 3.

8. For three different views of Joseph Smith, relative to his early life and activities, see Fawn M. Brodie, *No Man Knows My History*, 2d ed. (New York: Alfred A. Knopf, 1971), 1-82; Donna Hill, *Joseph Smith: The First Mormon* (New York: Doubleday, 1977), 32-97; Richard L. Bushman, *Joseph Smith and the Beginnings of Mormonism* (Urbana: University of Illinois Press, 1984).

9. Winn, *Exiles in a Land of Liberty*, 7.

10. This according to Marvin Hill, *Quest for Refuge: The Mormon Flight from American Pluralism* (Salt Lake City: Signature Books, 1989), 1. In n8, 190, the author lists a number of contemporary accounts discussing the elder Smith's drinking problems.

11. Winn, *Exiles in a Land of Liberty*, 7.

12. Hill, *Quest for Refuge*, 3. For the most detailed discussion of Joseph Smith's involvement with money digging and magic, generally, see D. Michael Quinn, *Early Mormonism and the Magic World View* (Salt Lake City: Signature Books, 1987).

13. Hill, *Quest for Refuge*, 11.

14. Winn, *Exiles in a Land of Liberty,* 11.

15. Ibid., 6-8.

16. Hill, *Joseph Smith,* 38. Another writer "expressed the opinion that Joseph's mother provided his motivation" in that she "'had the intellect' and spurred her son on with visions of his greatness." As quoted in Hill, *Joseph Smith,* 456, n7. Evidence of Lucy's strong role in directing family affairs is suggested in her own autobiography: Lucy Mack Smith, *Biographical Sketches of Joseph Smith the Prophet and His Progenitors for Many Generations* (Liverpool, Eng.: S.W. Richards, 1853). See in particular, 38-115.

17. Hill, *Joseph Smith,* 59-60.

18. Ibid., 59. By contrast, Joseph Jr. "was very saucy and insolent to his father" on at least one occasion, according to the statement of Issac Hale, his father-in-law, 20 Mar. 1834, as contained in Brodie, *No Man Knows My History,* 439.

19. Winn, *Exiles in a Land of Liberty,* 9-10.

20. Hill, *Quest for Refuge,* 4; Winn, *Exiles in a Land of Liberty,* 9.

21. Hill, *Joseph Smith*; Winn, *Exiles in a Land of Liberty,* 11. Lucy's motives for taking the lead in trying to get her family to associate with a congregation at this particular time, given the Smiths' "religious tradition of family heterodoxy," is not completely clear. Winn has suggested that Lucy was caught up in "the religious fervor" of the Second Great Awakening and, like other women of the time, "played the role of God's fifth column in this movement, subverting irreligion in the household." Perhaps, also, joining an established congregation would help in the Smith family's quest for social reliability.

22. Ibid. Joseph Sr.'s mystical beliefs were bolstered by several "visions" or divinely inspired "dreams" which anticipated and in some respects paralleled those that would be experienced by Joseph Jr. See Lucy Mack Smith, *Biographical Sketches,* 54-57, 72-75,76.

23. Hill, *Joseph Smith,* 48.

24. Winn, *Exiles in a Land of Liberty,* 11.

25. Whitney R. Cross's classic study, *The Burned-over District: The Social and Intellectual History of Enthusiastic Religion in Western New York* (New York: Cornell University Press, 1950), remains the essential starting point for examining the religious enthusiasm affecting this region.

26. Joseph Smith, Jr., *History of the Church of Jesus Christ of Latter-day Saints,* 2d ed. (Salt Lake City: Deseret Book, 1978), 2:34.

27. What actually occurred relative to Joseph Jr.'s various "visions" and his subsequent writing or "transcription" of the Book of Mormon have been and continue to be topics of intense debate. For a good starting point for three different views, see the early chapters of Brodie, *No Man Knows My History;* Hill, *Joseph Smith;* and Bushman, *Joseph Smith and the Beginnings of Mormonism.*

28. Hill, *Quest for Refuge,* 27.

29. As suggested by Winn, *Exiles in a Land of Liberty,* 17. Mario S. De Pillis

in "The Quest for Religious Authority and the Rise of Mormonism," *Dialogue: A Journal of Mormon Thought* 1 (Spring 1966): 68-88, presents the classic argument in this regard.

30. Hill, in *Quest for Refuge,* 19-20, and (particularly) 195-96, nn1-11, presents documentary evidence showing how this was the case.

31. Jan Shipps, *Mormonism: The Story of a New Religious Tradition* (Urbana: University of Illinois Press, 1985), is the most significant and articulate work in discussing Mormonism in terms of its distinctiveness.

32. Alexander Campbell, "The Book of Mormon Reviewed and Its Divine Pretensions Exposed," *Painesville Telegraph,* 15 Mar. 1831; reprinted in *Campbell's Delusions: An Analysis of the Book of Mormon, With An Examination of Its Internal Evidences, and a Refutation of Its Pretenses to Divine Authority* (Boston, 1832), 13.

33. Nathan O. Hatch, *The Democratization of American Christianity* (New Haven, CT: Yale University Press, 1989), 117.

34. Book of Mormon, 2 Ne. 6:62-64 (2 Ne. 9:30, LDS).

35. Ibid., Alma 3:93 (5:53-56, LDS); Alma 3:97 (10:14-17, LDS).

36. Ibid., 3 Ne. 3:11-16 (3 Ne. 6:11-14, LDS); Mormon 4:50-51, 54 (8:37, 394 1, LDS).

37. Hatch, *The Democratization of American Christianity,* 119.

38. Book of Mormon, 4 Ne. 1:28 (4 Ne. 26-27, LDS).

39. Ibid., Mosiah 11:152-54 (27:3-5, LDS).

40. Ibid., 4 Ne. 1:3-4 (4 Ne. 2-3, LDS).

41. Foster, *Religion and Sexuality,* 139.

42. Mark Leone, in his *Roots of Modern Mormonism* (Cambridge, MA: Harvard University Press, 1979) 16, was the first writer to use this term. This assertion has been echoed more recently by Marvin S. Hill, *Quest for Refuge,* 17, who qualified his use of the term by stating that such "anti-capitalism ... had more to do with the divisive, pluralistic character of capitalism than to permanent ideological objections to it." R. Laurence Moore, in *Religious Outsiders and the Making of Americans* (New York: Oxford University Press, 1986), 42, suggests that Mormon "anti-capitalism" rested on opposition to "the atomistic individualism of a society that thrived on competition and conflict."

43. Moore, in *Religious Outsiders and the Making of Americans,* 42.

44. Foster, *Religion and Sexuality,* 143. In making this observation, Foster stands in opposition to the interpretation presented by Kenneth Winn in his *Exiles in a Land of Liberty* who argues that the primary objective of Joseph Smith, the Book of Mormon, and the Mormon movement was the restoration and perpetuation of American "republicanism" and the values within that ideology. I tend to find Foster's basic assertions more convincing than those of Winn.

45. This according to "official" church statistics given in the *Deseret News*

*1991-92 Church Almanac* (Salt Lake City: Deseret News, 1990), 333. The 10,000 living in Missouri are cited by Winn in *Exiles in a Land of Liberty,* 102.

46. As noted by Hill in *Quest for Refuge,* 16. A recent effort to examine the social-geographic origins of the earliest Mormon converts is Marvin S. Hill, "The Rise of Mormonism in the Burned-Over District: Another View," *New York History* 61 (1980): 411-30. Also see Mario S. De Pillis, "The Social Sources of Mormonism," *Church History* 38 (1968): 50-79; and "A Brief Essay on Mormon Socioeconomic Origins and Their Possible Relationship to Latter-day Saint Racial Attitudes" as contained in Newell G. Bringhurst, *Saints, Slaves, and Blacks* (Westport, CT: Greenwood Press, 1981), 213-17.

47. Hill, *Joseph Smith,* 102.

38. Hatch, *The Democratization of American Christianity,* 121.

49. For two discussions of Young's early life and subsequent conversion to Mormonism, see Leonard J. Arrington, *Brigham Young: American Moses* (New York: Alfred A. Knopf, 1985), 7-30; and Newell G. Bringhurst, *Brigham Young and the Expanding American Frontier* (Boston: Little, Brown & Co., 1986), 1-24.

50. As noted by Hatch, *The Democratization of American Christianity,* 121.

51. As described by Hill in *Quest for Refuge,* 16.

52. According to Brodie, *No Man Knows My History,* 32.

53. According to the description of Hill, in *Joseph Smith,* 62.

54. According to Brodie, *No Man Knows My History,* 32.

55. As noted by Hill, in *Joseph Smith,* 62.

56. According to Brodie, *No Man Knows My History,* 32.

57. Moore, *Religious Outsiders and the Making of Americans,* 42. Smith had earlier suggested the principle of a "lay clergy" in the Book of Mormon, Mosiah 11:55 (27:4 LDS), "priests and teachers should labor with their own hands for their support."

58. Doctrine and Covenants 85:4-12 (88:14-50, LDS).

59. Ibid., 104:11b-18 (107:22-40, LDS).

60. Ibid., 104:42 (107:91-92, LDS).

61. Leonard J. Arrington, Feramorz Y Fox, and Dean L. May, *Building the City of God: Community & Cooperation Among the Mormons* (Salt Lake City: Deseret Book, 1976), 13.

62. Instructions relative to this plan contained in Doctrine and Covenants 42:8b-10c (42:30-35, LDS).

63. Ibid., 49:3e (49:20, LDS).

64. Brodie, *No Man Knows My History,* 106.

65. Arrington, Fox, and May, *Building the City of God,* 16.

66. Brodie, *No Man Knows My History,* 106.

67. Hill, *Joseph Smith,* 149.

68. Brodie, *No Man Knows My History,* 140, has suggested that "Missouri had particularly resented the communistic nature of the Mormon settlement"

in Nauvoo. In a manifesto drawn up by local Missouri settlers in Independence, the Mormons were described as "deluded fanatics or weak and designing knaves ... in claiming revelations direct from heaven, especially that God had given them this country for an inheritance." Other causes for the Mormons' expulsion from Jackson County included non-Mormon suspicions concerning Mormon attitudes toward the Indians as well as toward black slavery. For an account of the circumstances surrounding the expulsion of the Mormons from Missouri, see Warren A. Jennings, "Factors in the Destruction of the Mormon Press in Missouri, 1833," *Utah Historical Quarterly* 35 (Winter 1967): 56-76.

69. Bringhurst, *Saints, Slaves, and Blacks,* contains an extensive discussion of such attitudes. See esp. 3-83.

70. Book of Mormon, Alma 15:10 (27:9, LDS). Other relevant verses include: Mosiah 1:44, 5:20 (2:13-7:15, LDS); Alma 15:10, 19:112, 20:50, 20:64, 12:131, 22:23, 24:22 (27:9; 43:29; 43:45-49; 44:2- 48:10-11 50:22; 53:17, LDS). Discussion of Book of Mormon racist concepts are particularly evident in 1 Ne. 3:134 (1 Ne. 12:23, LDS) and 2 Ne. 4:33-3 5 (2 Ne. 5:21-24, LDS) where certain individuals are cursed with a "skin of blackness" and the Lamanites become "a dark and loathsome, and a filthy people full of idleness and all manner of abomination." Although this same work holds out the possibility of ultimate redemption whereby the descendants of the Lamanites, the present-day Indians, would lose "their scales of darkness" and become "a white and delightsome people" provided they become "civilized" and adopt the true faith of Mormonism. See 2 Ne. 12:83-84 (2 Ne. 30:6, LDS).

71. Doctrine and Covenants 87, LDS (not in RLDS Doctrine and Covenants).

72. *Evening and Morning Star,* July 1833.

73. Jennings, "Factors in the Destruction of the Mormon Press in Missouri, 1833," 56-76.

74. Stephen C. LeSueur, *The 1838 Mormon War in Missouri* (Columbia: University of Missouri Press, 1987), is the most thorough analysis of the Mormon conflict in Missouri and the Mormons' ultimate expulsion.

75. Bringhurst, *Saints, Slaves, and Blacks,* esp. 15-33, and 54-83, discuss the characteristics and evolution of Mormon anti-slavery attitudes and efforts to distinguish their own attitudes from those of other American anti-slavery advocates.

76. Robert B. Flanders, *Nauvoo: Kingdom on the Mississippi* (Urbana: University of Illinois Press, 1965), is a good starting point in seeking an understanding of this important period.

77. Although Joseph Smith had through revelation attempted a revival of the Law of Consecration and Stewardship in modified form in 1838 during the Mormon sojourn, it was soon abandoned. One aspect of this effort was retained, the so-called "law of tithing" whereby church members were re-

quired to pay a tithe or a tenth "of all their interest annually." Doctrine and Covenants 106 (119, LDS), 120, LDS (not in RLDS Doctrine and Covenants).

78. Flanders, *Nauvoo,* 144-78, discuss such activities. See 48-55 for a description of the formation of the Nauvoo Agricultural and Mechanical Association, various laborers' cooperative industries, along with the organization of producers' and consumers' cooperatives over the next five years.

79. Ibid., 98-99.

80. This figure is given by Hill, *Joseph Smith,* 97.

81. Formation of the Nauvoo Legion followed naturally from earlier Mormon-armed efforts at self-protection in the wake of non-Mormon attacks, specifically Zion's Camp of 1834 and the later formation of the much more controversial Danites in Missouri in 1838.

82. Brodie, *No Man Knows My History,* 268.

83. Doctrine and Covenants, 86:1 b-c (89:5, 7, LDS).

84. As noted in Brodie, *No Man Knows My History,* 166. For a discussion of temperance reform within the context of American society at large, see Joseph Gusfield, *In Symbolic Crusade: Status Politics and the American Temperance Movement.* It should be noted that the Word of Wisdom also called for a prohibition on the consumption of tobacco noting that "tobacco is not for the body, neither for the belly, and is not good for man;" as well as "sparing use" of the "flesh ... of beasts and of the fowls of the air." By contrast, "All grain is ordained for the use of man and of beasts, to be the staff of life." Doctrine and Covenants 86:2b-c (89:12-14, LDS). Smith's admonitions, calling for the limited consumption of animal flesh and fowl, were not unlike the recommendations concurrently being promoted by such American dietary reformers as Sylvester Graham.

85. Brodie, *No Man Knows My History,* 269.

86. Ibid., 268-69.

87. As noted by Melodie Moench Charles, "Precedents for Mormon Women from Scriptures," 45, 49, in *Sisters in Spirit: Mormon Women in Historical and Cultural Perspective,* eds., Maureen Ursenbach Beecher and Lavina Fielding Anderson (Urbana: University of Illinois Press, 1987).

88. Ibid., 48.

89. Ibid., 45.

90. Ibid., 48.

91. For one discussion of this issue within the context of contemporary controversy, see Grethe Baliff Peterson, "Priesthood and Latter-day Saint Women: Eight Contemporary Definitions," 249-68, in Beecher and Anderson, *Sisters in Spirit.*

92. This is discussed by Linda King Newell in "Gifts of the Spirit: Women's Share," 113-14, in Beecher and Anderson, *Sisters in Spirit.*

93. Ibid., 114. Newell also notes "a remarkable prophecy" given by Elizabeth Ann Whitney "concerning the Indians" on 10 October 1833. Smith,

however, reacted against the actions of women such as Hubble. His concern was evident in a February 1831 revelation in which "none other" than Joseph Smith was "appointed unto you to receive commandments and revelations." Doctrine and Covenants, 43:1 (43:2-3, LDS).

94. Ann Douglas, in *The Feminization of American Culture* (New York, 1977), discusses this important development. According to Douglas, 97, "[T]he nineteenth century minister moved in a world of women. He preached constantly to women; he administered what sacraments he performed largely for women; he worked not only for them but with them, in mission and charity work of all kinds."

95. As suggested by Jill Mulvay Derr, in "Making of Mormon Sisterhood," in Beecher and Anderson, *Sisters in Spirit,* 156-58.

96. Ibid., 158. The standard work dealing with Joseph Smith's first wife, Emma, is Linda King Newell and Valeen Tippetts Avery, *Mormon Enigma: Emma Hale Smith* (New York: Doubleday, 1984).

97. As noted by Derr, "Making of Mormon Sisterhood," 158. Keith E. Melder, *Beginnings of Sisterhood: The American Woman's Rights Movement, 1800-1850,* examines this development within the larger American society.

98. Newell, in "Gifts of the Spirit: Women's Share," in Beecher and Anderson, *Sisters in Spirit,* 115.

99. For two somewhat different views on the issue of the Relief Society *vis à vis* ordination of women to the priesthood, see Derr, "Making of Mormon Sisterhood," 116, and Newell, "Gifts of the Spirit: Women's Share," 114-15, Beecher and Anderson, *Sisters in Spirit.*

100. Derr, "Making of Mormon Sisterhood," 161-63.

101. Doctrine and Covenants, 132, LDS (not in RLDS Doctrine and Covenants).

102. As noted by Foster, *Religion and Sexuality,* 132. Foster's work is the most reliable standard treatment tracing the early development and evolution of Mormon polygamy. Specific Book of Mormon anti-polygamous passages include Jacob 1:15, RLDS and LDS; Jacob 2:31-34, 33, 35-37, 41, 45-47 (2:23, 24, 26, 27, 28, 32, 35, LDS); 2:54-55 (3:5, LDS); Mosiah 7:2, 7, 20 (11:2, 4, 14, LDS); and Ether 4:48 (10:5, LDS).

103. Foster, *Religion and Sexuality,* 136.

104. Ibid., 138.

105. For three discussions of the responses of Young and Kimball to plural marriage, see Arrington, *Brigham Young,* 100-102; Bringhurst, *Brigham Young and the Expanding American Frontier,* 54-56; Stanley B. Kimball, *Heber C. Kimball: Mormon Patriarch and Pioneer* (Urbana: University of Illinois Press, 1981), 86-102.

106. Foster, *Religion and Sexuality,* 154.

107. Ibid., 151.

108. Ibid., 143-44,179.

109. Ibid., 139.

110. As with his discussion of the Mormons, Lawrence Foster's *Religion and Sexuality,* 21-122, represents the most scholarly discussion of the marital practices of these two groups.

111. Joseph Smith's platform, with an introduction by Richard D. Poll, has been reprinted under the title "Joseph Smith's Presidential Platform," *Dialogue: A Journal of Mormon Thought* 3 (Autumn 1968): 17-36.

112. Klaus J. Hansen, *Quest for Empire: The Political Kingdom of God and the Council of Fifty in Mormon History* (East Lansing: University of Michigan Press, 1967), is the standard work on the role and activities of the Council of Fifty.

113. Winn, *Exiles in a Land of Liberty,* 205-206.

114. Dallin H. Oakes and Marvin S. Hill, *Carthage Conspiracy: The Trial of the Accused Assassins of Joseph Smith* (Urbana: University of Illinois Press, 1975), is the standard work discussing this tragic event and the trial of those implicated in Smith's assassination.

115. Foster, *Religion and Sexuality,* and Winn, *Exiles in a Land of Liberty,* both assert that Mormon perceptions of a decadent American society on the verge of collapse motivated Mormon actions during this period.

# 7.
# Rediscovering the Context of Joseph Smith's Treasure Seeking

*Alan Taylor*

ONE NIGHT IN 1811 IN ROYALTON, VERMONT, JOSEPH SMITH, SR., dreamed he was in a barren, silent, lifeless field. A spirit advised the elder Smith to eat the contents of a box that promised "wisdom and understanding." Immediately, "all manner of beasts, horned cattle, and roaring animals, rose up on every side in the most threatening manner possible, tearing the earth, tossing their horns, and bellowing most terrifically all around me, and they finally came so close upon me that I was compelled to drop the box, and fly for my life."[1] The elder Smith's mystical encounter introduces us to the realm of folk magic experienced, and later transcended, by his celebrated son, the Mormon prophet, Joseph Smith, Jr. An examination of the prophet's early years reveals a world apparently alive with the inexplicable: guardian spirits, divining rods, seer stones, and treasures that move in the ground.

To comprehend these beliefs, we need to reconstruct the cultural context of rural America in the early nineteenth century, a context where treasure-seekers were neither fools nor deceivers, where treasure-seeking was part of an attempt to recapture the simplicity and magical power associated with apostolic Christianity. To recapture that context we need to exorcise the persistent spirit of Philastus

Hurlbut, whom I am using here to represent the entire nineteenth-century cult of rationality that so complicates our attempt to understand people in the past who mixed magic with their Christianity. For we today have inherited that cult's rigid insistence that magic and Christianity are polar opposites when in fact they have usually been inseparable and natural allies.

Magic is a particular way of looking at the universe. Magic perceives the supernatural as inseparably interwoven with the material world while the pure "religion" of definition divorces the two, separating them into distinct dimensions. Magic detects supernatural entities throughout our natural environment, intermediaries between man and God, spirits both good and evil that can hurt or help men and women both materially and spiritually. To minimize harm and secure benefit, people who believe they dwell in a magical cosmos practice rituals intended to influence the spiritual beings, the supernatural entities. In contrast, abstract "religion" strips the natural environment of its spirits and relocates God's divine power to a distant sphere. The sharp distinction between "magic" and "religion" seems clear and straightforward, but anthropologists and religious historians have repeatedly discovered that magic and religion have at most times and in most places been interwoven. Few people anywhere have ever possessed a religious faith shorn of hope that through its pursuit they could manipulate the supernatural for protection and benefit in this life as well as the next. Moreover, our century's neat distinction between magic and religion is laden with the value judgment that magic is superstitious, deluded, and irrational, if not downright evil, while religion is the lofty, abstract expression of our highest ideals.[2]

Hurlbut was a Mormon apostate who, in 1833, zealously collected affidavits in Palmyra and Manchester, New York, from people who described the Smith family's treasure-seeking. Hurlbut's affidavits (and subsequent anti-Mormon writers) implied that treasure-seeking was an ignorant superstition whose devotees were either credulous dupes or cunning con-men equally driven by materialistic greed.[3] Convinced that the Smiths were neither credulous nor devious, Mormon historians long denied that the family sought material treasure with occult methods. In the process, they implicitly accepted Hurlbut's premise that actual treasure-seekers were indeed deluded by superstition or driven by greed.[4] This acceptance is readily understandable given that over the course of the nineteenth century, most Americans came to live in a disenchanted world that discredited magic; by the late nineteenth century, treasure beliefs seemed too incredible, too fantastic for anyone but fools or con-men to pursue. Consequently, evidence that the Smiths were deeply involved in treasure-seeking is disconcerting for those Mormons who accepted the equation of treasure-seeking with ignorant superstition and cunning greed.

Indeed, although most recent Mormon historians recognize the Smiths' treasure-seeking, they remain sufficiently haunted by Hurlbut's premise to minimize folk magic's long-term influence on Joseph Smith, Jr., and its significance to the early Mormon faith.[5] The root of the problem is that, in assessing treasure seeking's meaning, historians are tempted to posit too stark a dichotomy between tradition and modernity, between magic and religion. They stress the ancient roots, continuity, and unity of occult beliefs across time and space. They refer to a wide array of very different belief complexes—Rosicrucianism, freemasonry, divining, alchemy, phrenology, astrology, visions, dreams, faith-healing—from different times and places as if their differences were unimportant—as if the essential point was that they were all occult, that they were all magical, that they were, in effect, all parts of a traditional world that had not yet discovered truly abstract religion and rational inquiry.

By treating occult beliefs as a whole they miss the fact that specific beliefs are extremely revealing about the particular culture in place and time that develops them. Consequently they imply that the early Republic's treasure-seekers subscribed to a set of beliefs unchanged from the ancient Egyptians. Surely they are correct that venerable folk beliefs provided the intellectual raw materials exploited by the treasure-seekers, but they slight a second critical element: the degree to which those seekers actively, energetically, and innovatively reworked those beliefs to meet the challenges of their own place and time. To recognize the treasure-seekers' creativity we need to shed our assumption that what we call tradition was an immutable monolith. We cannot fully understand the treasure seekers if we continue to think of them as simple anachronisms, as practitioners of the timeless occult who were oblivious to, or rebellious against, the larger, cosmopolitan culture's trend toward empirical rationalism.[6]

Indeed, I would argue that Joseph Smith Jr.'s transition from treasure-seeker to Mormon prophet was natural, easy, and incremental and that it resulted from the dynamic interaction of two simultaneous struggles: first, of seekers grappling with supernatural beings after midnight in the hillsides, and, second, of seekers grappling with hostile rationalists in the village streets during the day. Confronted with uncooperative spirits and with rationalism's challenge, over time the treasure-seekers adopted more complex and explicitly empirical techniques. Aware that the respectable considered them credulous fools, the seekers were determined to prove to themselves, if not to others, that they were in fact careful and canny investigators of the supernatural. In their quasi-scientific religiosity, these treasure-seekers were much more akin to their contemporaries, the spiritualists, than to ancient and medieval magicians. This is especially evident in the life of Joseph Smith's first and most important convert, Martin Harris: fellow treasure-seeker, and witness and financier of the Book of Mormon.

Three interrelated characteristics loom large in every account of Martin Harris: substantial agricultural prosperity, limited formal education, and a restless religious curiosity. He was an honest, hard-working, astute man honored by his townsmen with substantial posts as fence-viewer and overseer of highways but never with the most prestigious offices: selectman, moderator, or assemblyman.[7] In the previous generation in rural towns like Palmyra substantial farmers like Harris would have reaped the highest status and most prestigious offices. But Harris lived in the midst of explosive cultural change as the capitalist market and its social relationships rode improved internal transportation into the most remote corners of the American countryside. The agents of that change were the newly arrived lawyers, printers, merchants, and respectable ministers who clustered in villages and formed a new elite committed to "improving" their towns and their humbler neighbors. The village elites belonged to a new self-conscious "middle class," simultaneously committed to commercial expansion and moral reform. Because of their superior contacts with and knowledge of the wider world, the new village elites reaped higher standing and prestigious posts from their awed neighbors.[8]

Utterly self-confident in their superior rationality and access to urban ideas, the village elites disdained rural folk notions as ignorant, if not vicious, superstitions that obstructed commercial and moral "improvement." Through ridicule and denunciation, the village middle class aggressively practiced a sort of cultural imperialism that challenged the folk beliefs held by farmers like Martin Harris.[9] Harris's material prosperity was comparable to the village elite's but, because of his hard physical labor and limited education, culturally he shared more with hardscrabble families like the Smiths. A village lawyer needed only scan Harris's gray homespun attire and large stiff hat to conclude that a farmer had come to town. A village minister could tell from Harris's "disputatious" arguments for "visionary" religion that this was a country man who preferred reading his Bible to attending learned sermons.

A proud and sensitive man, Harris disliked the village elites for belittling his culture and for preempting the status that in the previous generation in rural towns like Palmyra would have gone to substantial farmers. Because western New York's village elites cooperated through membership in Masonic lodges, Harris's involvement in the anti-Masonic movement attests to the resentful suspicion he felt toward men with extensive external contacts and greater worldly knowledge. But this does not mean that he withdrew into a timeless, unchanging folk culture in utter rejection of the wider world and its new ideas. Instead he tried to defend his beliefs by proving to himself and others that the village elites' ridicule was misplaced, that the supernatural world of angels, spirits, and demons was every bit as "real" and subject to scientific understanding as the natural world, that indeed the supernatural was just that extension of the natural that men did not yet fully comprehend but could and would if they were willing to "experimentally" explore the spiritual dimension. In effect he meant to refute the respectable people's condescension by demonstrating that he was more wise than they, that his investigations opened the secrets of existence in a manner that the narrow-minded elite foreclosed. Small wonder then that his favorite biblical quotation, paraphrased from 1 Corinthians 1:27, was "God has chosen the weak things of this world to confound the wise."

Like the Smiths and thousands of other rural folk in the arc of hill towns stretching from Ohio east to Maine, Harris was a "Christian primitivist," a religious seeker who thoroughly scoured his Bible and his dreams in a determined effort to directly know his God. Dissatisfied with abstract religion, primitivists sought tangible contact with the divine. Terrified of living alienated and isolated from God's voice, seekers longed for the reassurance of regular spiritual encounters in dreams, visions, inner voices, and uncanny coincidences. They aptly called their search "experimental religion." The early Republic's seekers insisted that the established denominations had lost the original simplicity and spiritual power of the apostolic Christian church when the faithful experienced miracles and spoke in tongues. They believed that their day's respectable denominations had lapsed into empty forms and rituals that deadened their members' ability to reestablish direct mystical contact. By insisting on direct, individual encounters with divinity, seekers disdained any temporal authority that presumed to govern individual conscience. They hoped to reestablish the apostolic Christian churches where members helped one another to directly experience the divine. Confident that this reestablishment would usher in the Millennium, every seeker played a crucial role in a critical struggle with cosmic consequences. Every moment and every action raised the stakes as the climactic conflict between Christ and Antichrist drew nearer. This was the sort of role that Martin Harris longed to play. Most "Christian primitivists" found their way into the Methodists, Freewill Baptists, or Christians, as did Harris temporarily, but neither he nor the Smiths felt satisfied with any existing church for long.[10]

Harris's restless search for sustained encounters with God and his angels led him to associate with the nearby Smith family, who shared his concerns. By the 1820s the Smiths had achieved local notoriety with the village respectables and local influence among the rural folk for their expertise with visions, dreams, and treasure-seeking. Contrary to Hurlbut's assumptions, there was no contradiction between the Smith's religious seeking and their treasure-seeking. Indeed, for the Smiths and many other hill-country Christian primitivists, treasure-seeking was an extension of their "experimental religion." It represented a cross-fertilization of material desire and spiritual aspiration. Sure that they dwelled in a magical landscape alive with both evil (demons) and good spirits (angels), treasure-seekers believed that Christ would reward those who battled evil, certainly in the next life, and perhaps with a treasure in this one. They proceeded with a sort of empirical spirituality, testing their faith against guardian spirits and using prayers, Bibles, and religious pamphlets in their digging rituals.

They insisted that the presence of anyone of dubious morality or incomplete faith doomed the attempt to recover a treasure. It was no accident that the Smiths' leading collaborator in their Palmyra treasure-seeking was Willard Chase, a Methodist preacher.[11] Because of this intersection with religious seeking I prefer to call them treasure-seekers rather than the more sordid-sounding money-diggers. And if we recognize this intersection, then they do not appear such a bad lot for the Smiths to have associated with.[12]

One interpretation current among Mormon historians sees Joseph Smith, Jr., as a reluctant treasure-seeker egged on by his father and neighbors who ill-understood the spiritual purpose of his gifts and twisted them to material ends.[13] This sets up a false distinction between what was inseparable in treasure-seeking (at least, in treasure-seeking as practiced by the Smith family): spirituality and materialism. Moreover, never in his life did Joseph Smith do anything by halves, always plunging forward with apparently boundless enthusiasm, conviction, and energy. It rings false to read his treasure-seeking differently. Recognizing this, Mormon historian Michael Quinn recently observed, "It really seems pointless for Mormon apologists to continue to deny the extent and enthusiasm of Joseph Smith, Jr.'s, participation in treasure-digging throughout the 1820s."[14]

Instead of seeing young Joseph's treasure-seeking as an early and reluctant false step we ought, as Jan Shipps argued years ago, to regard it as an essential early stage of a life-long process by which he grappled with the supernatural in search of the spiritual power that came by accumulating divine wisdom. She wrote, "If the prophet's preference for leaving the money-digging part of his career out of the picture is ignored ... a pattern emerges which leaves little room for doubting that Smith's use of the seerstone was an important indication of his early and continued interest in extra-rational phenomena, and that it played an important role in his spiritual development."[15] Joseph Smith eagerly pursued treasure-seeking as a peculiarly tangible way to practice "experimental religion," as an opportunity to develop his spiritual gifts through regular exercise in repeated contests with guardian spirits. Because it was the contest itself that interested him, the repeated failure to recover gold did not discourage his efforts. Joseph was after something more than mere material wealth: by accumulating spiritual understanding he hoped to attain divine power. He earnestly wanted to become godlike. So he wore a silver Jupiter talisman inscribed, "Make me, O God, all powerful," and testified that when he looked at his seerstone he "discovered that time, place and distance were annihilated; that all the intervening obstacles were removed, and that he possessed one of the attributes of Deity, an All-Seeing Eye."[16]

He began small by grappling with the guardian spirits of treasure troves in nocturnal, ritualistic digging expeditions but, through such experiences, matured his concerns toward his ultimate role as the Mormon prophet. By the time he recovered the treasure he sought, it was no longer the mammon of a few years earlier but instead a book of divine knowledge. Translating and publishing that book accelerated his pursuit of divine knowledge's power as he became a prophet guiding a growing number of devoted seekers. If we see Smith's spiritual engagement as a continuum beginning at age fourteen in 1820 and continuing through treasure-seeking and the transitional recovery of the gold plates to his role as the Mormon prophet, then we should not be surprised that he and his followers described what he saw in 1827 differently in 1840 than they did in 1830, that their understanding evolved from talking of guardian spirits to describing angels representing Christ. If we see Smith engaged in a lifelong struggle to master spiritual knowledge, then it is natural that he and his followers continuously reinterpreted earlier episodes.[17]

Characteristically, Harris felt torn between his fervent desire to experience what the Smiths described and his wary determination to test carefully their abilities, to convince himself that the village scoffers were wrong. Because he was determined to answer rational skepticism, rather than reject its validity, Harris continuously sought empirical evidence to buttress the Smiths' claims. He tested young Joseph's ability to divine with his seerstone the location of a pin hidden in shavings and straw. Like a scientist trying to replicate a colleague's experiments, Harris went treasure-seeking and sought to direct his dreams to encounters with the guardian treasure spirits that the Smiths described. After Smith secured the plates, Harris took two assistants (treasure lore held that at least three men were necessary for a successful dig) to Cumorah to look for the stone box and claimed to see it vanish into the bowels of the earth. In search of contradictions, Harris separately interrogated various members of the Smith family about Joseph's discovery. Although initially denied permission to see the plates, Harris hefted the covered plates and carefully reasoned from their weight that they must be gold or lead, metals the impoverished Smiths could not have purchased. Then he resorted to experimental religion's ultimate test–private prayer–and believed he obtained divine confirmation in an inner voice that urged him to believe the Smiths and assist their translation. Finally, his eager visit to Professor Charles Anthon and other cosmopolitan experts with the transcribed hieroglyphics attests that he respected worldly learning and felt confident it could promote young Joseph's discovery if the learned would only recognize the evidence Harris laid before them.[18]

To conclude, if we recognize the late treasure-seekers' sincere spirituality and quasi-scientific rationality, then we can detect important continuities with early Mormonism.[19] Just as religious aspiration informed treasure-seeking, magic persisted within early Mormonism, as Michael Quinn has so thoroughly documented.[20] Joseph used his seerstone to find and translate the gold plates and cherished that stone for the rest of his life. Other Mormons–including David Whitmer, Hiram Page, and Brigham Young–used their own seerstones to seek divine messages, and Oliver Cowdery employed his gift with witch-hazel rods to divine answers to spiritual questions. As president of the LDS church, the pragmatic, rational Brigham Young testified that he believed in astrology and insisted that treasures were real instruments of divine power: "These treasures that are in the earth are carefully watched, they can be removed from place to place according to the good pleasure of Him who made them and owns them."[21]

Early Mormons persisted in practicing magic because they nurtured a magical world view where the material and the spiritual were interwoven in the same universe. But their cosmology was much more than the timeless occult; indeed, it was imbued with the same spirit of rational inquiry that characterized late treasure-seekers and the spiritualists, for in addition to spiritualizing matter, as did traditional magic, Mormon cosmology also materialized the spiritual. This rendered the supernatural ultimately comprehensible by purposeful human inquiry. As Joseph Smith wrote, "There is no such thing as immaterial matter. All spirit is matter, but it is more fine or pure, and can only be discerned by purer eyes; we cannot see it; but when our bodies are purified we shall see that all is matter."[22] He explained, "A *spirit* is as much matter as oxygen or hydrogen."[23] He added, "God the father is material, Jesus Christ is material. Angels are material. Space is full of materiality. Nothing exists which is not material."[24] In this view, miracles are not incomprehensible interventions from a distinct supernatural dimension but instead natural phenomena that humans cannot yet understand but eventually will *if through "experimental religion" they pursue spiritual understanding*. For, like the late treasure-seekers, early Mormons conceived of their faith as a progressive, scientific perfection of man's ability to comprehend the cosmos.[25]

Through Joseph Smith's agency, treasure-seeking evolved into the Mormon faith. Indeed, Mormon theology represented a continuation of the concerns he had previously pursued through treasure-seeking. An empirical search for divine knowledge and power recurs in his plan of salvation which explains that God's plan for humankind is that they advance in knowledge and power by dealing with matter on the earth. Smith insisted, "A man is saved no faster than he gets knowledge, for if he does not get knowledge, he will be brought into captivity by some evil power in the other world, as evil spirits will have more knowledge, and consequently more power than many men who are on the earth."[26] As with Smith's early treasure-seeking contests, obtaining divine exaltation was a matter of learning to understand and control the supernatural laws already known by the most advanced supramaterial being, God. Human beings pursued God in this progressive, unending struggle to comprehend and, so, master the universe; in 1844 Joseph Smith explained, "As man is God once was: as God is man may become."[27]

Smith adapted treasure-seeking's promise that the deserving would ultimately reap tangible rewards that were simultaneously and inseparably spiritual and material. A revelation of his describes how the exalted would "inherit thrones, kingdoms, principalities, and powers, dominion over all heights and depths.... then shall they be above all, because all things are subject unto them. Then shall they be gods, because they have all power, and the angels are subject unto them" (D&C 132).[28] But, unlike the treasure-seekers who hoped to unite search and recovery in this world, Smith divided the two into different stages in the soul's eternal continuum: seekers were to use this world to perfect themselves but look for their proper reward *only* in the future state, and *not* after midnight in this probationary world's glacial till. This division of search and reward enabled Mormonism to survive, while the earlier and similar New Israelites, a religious sect in Middletown, Vermont, collapsed when its promise of material reward through treasure-seeking in this world failed.[29]

In this transformation of treasure-seeking into early Mormonism we see the fruit of the two interactive struggles: of seekers with the supernatural, of magic with reason. Smith had dual reasons for redirecting treasure-seeking's spirituality. First, his personal progressive struggle with spiritual beings for divine knowledge gradually led him to see that the search for literal treasure in this world was a dead end. Second, he recognized that a reputation for treasure-seeking was a handicap in communicating his message to an audience increasingly committed to rationality and a more abstract understanding of religion. To further his proselytizing mission, he and his followers deemphasized his early supernatural explorations as a treasure seer, a deemphasis that has ever since led some Mormons to doubt that he was ever so involved and anti-Mormons to charge that he was insincere. Perhaps it is now possible to recognize that Mormonism's founders were deeply and enthusiastically involved in folk magic but that this does not undermine the sincerity of the Mormon faith.[30]

*NOTES*

1. Lucy Mack Smith, *Biographical Sketches of Joseph Smith, the Prophet, and His Progenitors for Many Generations* (1853; reprint ed. New York: Arno Press, 1969), 57.

2. I. C. Jarvie and Joseph Agassi, "The Problem of the Rationality of Magic," in Bryan R. Wilson, ed., *Rationality* (Oxford: Blackwell, 1970); S. F. Nadel, "Malinowski on Magic and Religion," in Raymond Firth, ed., *Man and Culture; An Evaluation of the Work of Bronislaw Malinowski* (New York: Humanities Press, 1957); and Keith V. Thomas, *Religion and the Decline of Magic* (New York: Scribner 1971), 25-77, 636-68.

3. E. D. Howe, *History of Mormonism: or a Faithful Account of That Singular Imposition and Delusion* (Painesville, OH: E. D. Howe, 1840), 231-64; Pomeroy

Tucker, *Origin, Rise and Progress of Mormonism* (New York: D. Appleton, 1867), 20-22.

4. See, for example, Hugh Nibley, *The Myth Makers* (Salt Lake City: Bookcraft, 1961).

5. See, for example, Richard L. Bushman, *Joseph Smith and the Beginnings of Mormonism* (Urbana: University of Illinois Press, 1985); Donna Hill, *Joseph Smith: The First Mormon* (Garden City, NY: Doubleday, 1977); Marvin S. Hill, "Joseph Smith and the 1826 Trial: New Evidence and New Difficulties," *BYU Studies* 12 (Winter 1972): 223-33; and Linda King Newell and Valeen Tippetts Avery, *Mormon Enigma: Emma Hale Smith* (Garden City, NY: Doubleday, 1984).

6. Here I differ with D. Michael Quinn, "Early Mormonism and the World View of Folk Magic" (paper presented at the Mormon History Association Annual Meeting, 48-49, May 1986, copy in my possession), and with Ronald W. Walker, "Martin Harris: The First Convert" (paper presented at the Mormon History Association Meeting, May 1986, published as "Martin Harris: Mormonism's Early Convert," in *Dialogue: A Journal of Mormon Thought* 19 [Winter 1986]: 29-43). For a fuller statement of my views on the unique nature of the treasure-seeking practiced in America during the early Republic, see Alan Taylor, "The Early Republic's Supernatural Economy: Treasure-Seeking in the American Northeast, 1780-1830," *The American Quarterly* 38 (Spring 1986). My views on the volatility of cultures labeled "traditional" have been influenced by E. J. Hobsbawm and Terence Ranger, eds., *The Invention of Tradition* (New York: Cambridge University Press, 1983), and Alfred Young, "English Plebeian Culture and Eighteenth-Century American Radicalism," in Margaret Jacob and James Jacob, eds., *The Origins of Anglo-American Radicalism* (London: Allen and Unwin, 1983).

7. See Walker, "Martin Harris," my source for information about Harris.

8. See Paul E. Johnson, *A Shopkeeper's Millennium: Society and Revivals in Rochester, New York, 1815-1837* (New York: Hill and Wang, 1978).

9. Bushman, 6-7, 71-72.

10. Marvin S. Hill, "The Shaping of the Mormon Mind in New England and New York," *BYU Studies* 9 (Spring 1969): 355-56; Nathan O. Hatch, "The Christian Movement and the Demand for a Theology of the People," *Journal of American History* 67 (Dec. 1980): 545-67.

11. Bushman, 72.

12. Taylor.

13. Bushman, 69-76.

14. Quinn, 48.

15. Jan Shipps, "The Prophet Puzzle: Suggestions Leading Toward a More Comprehensive Interpretation of Joseph Smith," *Journal of Mormon History* 1 (1974): 14, reprinted in this compilation.

16. Quinn, 61; Francis W. Kirkham, ed., *A New Witness of Christ in America, the Book of Mormon*, 2 vols. (Salt Lake City: Utah Printing Co., 1951), 2:365-66.

17. Shipps, 12-14.

18. I have imposed my interpretation on evidence from Ronald W. Walker, "The Persisting Idea of American Treasure Hunting," *BYU Studies* 24 (Fall 1984 [mailed Spring 1986]): 429-60; Quinn, 47; and Bushman, 104-105).

19. Hill, "The Shaping of the Mormon Mind," 351.

20. Quinn, 35-38.

21. Ibid., 51.

22. Klaus J. Hansen, *Mormonism and the American Experience* (Chicago: University of Chicago Press, 1981), 28.

23. Thomas F. O'Dea, *The Mormons* (Chicago: University of Chicago Press, 1957), 120.

24. Hansen, 71.

25. Sterling M. McMurrin, *The Theological Foundations of the Mormon Religion* (Salt Lake City: University of Utah Press, 1965), 2, 6, 13.

26. O'Dea, 130.

27. Hansen, 72.

28. Also in ibid., 79.

29. Barnes Frisbie, *The History of Middletown, Vermont in Three Discourses* (Rutland, VT: Tuttle and Co., 1867), 43-59.

30. Shipps, 13-14.

# 8.

# Joseph Smith: America's Hermetic Prophet

*Lance S. Owens*

*You don't know me–you never will. You never knew my heart. No man knows my history. I cannot tell it; I shall never undertake it. I don't blame anyone for not believing my history. If I had not experienced what I have, I could not have believed it myself.*

–Joseph Smith, 7 April 1844

If there is a religion uniquely and intrinsically American–a religion worked from America's soil and cast in the ardent furnace of its primal dreams–that religion must be Mormonism. Founded in 1830 by twenty-four-year-old Joseph Smith, the Church of Jesus Christ of Latter-day Saints (as it is formally named) has emerged from relative insularity during the mid-twentieth century to become a worldwide movement now numbering 10 million members. Patriotic, conservative, influential, and vastly wealthy, modern Mormonism is a mainstay of American society.

Despite its success and respectability, however, a fundamental crisis looms before Joseph Smith's church–and the crux of the predicament is Smith himself. Today's Mormonism is being forced into an uncomfortable confrontation with its early nineteenth-century origins–an inevitable encounter given the importance of the founding prophet to his religion. From the start, Joseph Smith has been cast by his church as a man more enlightened than any mortal to walk the earth since the passing of the last biblical apostles. No historical life could be granted a more mythological tenor than his. To Mormons, Joseph Smith is simply "The Prophet." He bears the *imago Christi.* He alone stands as doorkeeper to the last dispensation of time; to him angels came and restored God's necessary priestly "keys" and powers; he built the temple and taught the ancient rituals which make gods of men and women.

But now, more than 150 years after his death, Smith's place in Western religious history is undergoing an important and creative reevaluation. Historians and religious critics alike are examining him anew. And in history's newest reading of Smith's life, themes unrecognized by its orthodox interpreters are quickly moving to stage center. Quite simply, modern Mormonism, guardian of the prophet's story, has no idea what to do with the rediscovered, historical, and rather occult Joseph Smith.

Several years ago, Harold Bloom's boldly original work, *The American Religion,* offered an introduction to this unknown prophet. The true American religion, pronounces Bloom, is a kind of Gnosticism, which is in itself a surprising enough declaration. But as evidence of this American gnosis, and as first hero of his story, Bloom gives us Joseph Smith. Of the man himself, Bloom judges: "Other Americans have been religion makers. ... But none of them has the imaginative vitality of Joseph Smith's revelation, a judgment one makes on the authority of a lifetime spent in apprehending the visions of great poets and original speculators. ... So self-created was he that he transcends Emerson and Whitman in my imaginative response, and takes his place with the great figures of our fiction."[1] And of Smith's religious creation: "The God of Joseph Smith is a daring revival of the God of some of the Kabbalists and Gnostics, prophetic sages who, like Smith himself, asserted that they had returned to the true religion. ... Mormonism is a purely American Gnosis, for which Joseph Smith was and is a far more crucial figure than Jesus could be." Smith is not just "a prophet, another prophet, but he is the essential prophet of these latter days, leading into the end time, whenever it comes."[2]

Bloom's coupling of Smith to the Gnostic tradition has aroused animated disagreement among students of Mormonism and Gnosticism alike. Several questions crucial to modern Gnostic studies are raised by this dialogue: What is the relationship of later "Gnostic" movements to classical Gnosticism? Were rudiments of the tradition conveyed to postclassical groups by historical links such as oral transmissions, myths, and texts? Was it instead the independent product of a recurrent type of creative vision? Or are dual forces of historical transmission and primary Gnostic experience generally interdependent, even occultly linked? While Smith had some historical connection with late remnants of Gnosticism conveyed by Renaissance Hermeticism and Kabbalah, his religious creation nonetheless is clearly derived in largest part from a personal experience. Was that primal creativity "Gnostic"? If so, how did it relate to the matrix of tradition?

These questions defy simple declarations. Nonetheless Smith did apparently espouse Gnostic themes, including the necessity of continuing, individual revelation as the source of salvific knowledge. Smith and his religion thus eschewed theology in favor of the dynamic process of revelation. The result was best summarized in what Bloom calls "one of the truly remarkable sermons ever preached in America," a discourse delivered by the prophet on 7 April 1844. Known as the King Follett Discourse, it was Smith's last major address to his church, presented just ten weeks before his death at age thirty-eight.

"There are but very few beings in the world who understand rightly the character of God," he said. "If men do not comprehend the character of God, they do not comprehend their own character." Within humankind there is an immortal spark of intelligence, taught the prophet, a seed of divine intellect or light that is "as immortal as, and coequal with, God Himself." God is not, however, to be understood as one and singular. Turning to an oddly kabbalistic exegesis of the first three words of the Hebrew text of Genesis, Smith pronounced that there are a multitude of Gods which have emanated from the First God, existing one above the other without end. He whom humankind calls God was himself once a man; and man, by advancing in intelligence, knowledge, and consciousness, may be exalted with God, may *become as God.*

Near the beginning of his ministry in 1833, Smith declared that "the glory of God is intelligence," eternal and uncreated. Those who wish to find a Gnostic in Smith have pointed out that he used the word "intelligence" interchangeably with "knowledge" in his prophetic writings during this period. Indeed, they suggest, his words might be read poetically to proclaim that God's glory *is* gnosis—a gnosis that saves woman and man by leading them together to a single, uncreated, and intrinsically divine Self.

II

Joseph Smith a modern Gnostic prophet? Certainly nowhere within the vast domains of American religion did this proclamation cause more amazement than within Mormonism itself. But Bloom (a self-proclaimed "Jewish Gnostic") is no casual observer; his knowledge of gnosis and Kabbalah is tempered by vast experience critiquing their creative matrices. His thesis deserves—and is receiving—attention. Joseph Smith is taking on a new visage, and words like "gnostic," "kabbalistic, " and "Hermetic" have suddenly gained a place in the vocabulary employed by those trying to understand him.

In this form, Joseph Smith's story is, of course, almost entirely unknown to his church. The oft-repeated orthodox version of the story—and the mythic function of that story—remain so central to the Mormon past and present that it must be heard before exploring the evolving (and heretical) rereading.

This story begins around 1820, when the adolescent Smith retired to a grove near his family's farm in Palmyra, New York, and knelt in prayer. Troubled over his own deep religious yearnings and uncertain where to turn for sustenance, he felt compelled to petition God's mercy. "The Lord heard my cry in the wilderness," he wrote in his diary several years later, "and while in the attitude of calling upon the Lord a pillar of light above the brightness of the sun at noonday came down from above and rested upon me and I was filled with the spirit of God and the Lord opened the heavens upon me and I saw the Lord."[3] When he came to himself again, he was lying on his back, totally drained of strength, looking up at heaven. This was the new prophet's first vision.

The young man apparently told several people about his experience, but, outside his own closely knit family, the account was met with general derision. Then in 1823 there came a second manifestation. On the night of 21 September, while Smith was again engaged in prayer, a light suddenly began to fill his room. Within the light there appeared an angelic being. "His whole person was glorious beyond description, and his countenance truly like lightning," recounted Smith.

The angel, named Moroni, explained that a book was deposited in a nearby hill, a record written upon gold plates by the ancient inhabitants of the American continent. Smith was instructed that in due time he would be allowed to obtain the record and translate it. No sooner had the messenger departed and the vision ceased than it began again. Three times the messenger came, each time repeating exactly the same message. As the cock crowed dawn, the final apparition ended. Smith's experience had occupied the entire night.

That day Smith visited the hill. Straightway he found the location shown him in the vision and there unearthed a stone box containing the plates. The angel Moroni again appeared, however, warning Smith that he could not yet remove the plates from their resting place. Instead he would need to return to the spot on this same day each year for four years. Only on the fourth visit would he be allowed to remove the treasure and begin the work of translation. Smith did as instructed, and four years later, on 22 September 1827, the angel delivered the record to his charge.

Soon after obtaining the records, Smith began his translation. The record was engraved upon the plates in "reformed Egyptian," a language he read by gazing into the "Urim and Thummim," the sacred implements of biblical seers, delivered to him with the plates. Called the Book of Mormon after its last ancient redactor and scribe, the record purportedly contained an abridged history of America's ancient inhabitants, descendants of a Jewish clan who fled Jerusalem shortly before destruction of the first temple in 586 B.C.E. Led by their patriarch, the wandering Israelites had built a boat and launched themselves into the ocean, and were eventually washed ashore somewhere in the Americas. Their descendants multiplied greatly in the new land, but were plagued by fratricidal divisions. A few of the people remained loyal to God, the prophets, and their heritage as descendants of Israel, while many more became unbelieving pagans.

According to the book, Christ appeared after his resurrection to teach this American remnant of Israel. For a century thereafter the converted Christians lived in peace, but inevitably dissension returned. About 400 years after Christ's visitation there came a final series of great wars in which the barbarous unbelievers vanquished the last of Christ's people. Prior to this final catastrophe, the golden records constituting the Book of Mormon were hidden to await the time when God would call them forth again.

The call came in 1830. In March of that year 5,000 copies of the Book of Mormon were printed. A few weeks later the Church of Christ (as it was first named) was established with Joseph Smith as its "prophet, seer, and revelator." Though central to the events, the Book of Mormon was only one element in the complete "restoration." Smith soon produced several other less noted pseudepigraphic works, prophetic texts attributed to ancient figures such as Enoch, Abraham, and Moses.

After the angel Moroni (who returned to retrieve the golden plates from Smith), several other angelic messengers also came bearing "keys" pertaining to the true church of God–priestly powers and consecrations lost in the great apostasy overtaking Christianity after its first centuries. John the Baptist appeared and ordained Smith and a disciple to the lesser, or "Aaronic," priesthood, granting the authority to baptize. Next came a visitation of the apostles Peter, James, and John, who ordained Smith to the higher priesthood after the ancient order of Melchizedek. By 1836 Elijah, Moses, and Christ had all appeared to the new prophet, restoring the fullness of God's power and truth.

Duly ordained to the restored priesthood, and with Book of Mormon in hand, Smith's disciples fanned out across the northeastern states. Their message was simple: the ancient church of God had been restored with its powers and priesthood and with a reopened canon—a restoration accomplished by God through a modern prophet.

The flock grew quickly. By 1836 a Mormon communal society flourished at Kirtland, Ohio (near Cleveland), and a second gathering of Latter-day Saints (as Smith's disciples called themselves) was taking form on the Missouri frontier. But between 1837 and 1839 a series of disasters struck. First, amidst a general financial collapse, the Kirtland community was abandoned. Then the new Zion in Missouri came under violent persecution, culminating in the "Mormon War," a conflict that finally forced all Mormons out of the state under threat of extermination in 1839. After this debacle, the beleaguered Mormon refugees retreated to Illinois and to the new city named by the prophet "Nauvoo."

Over the next four years the Mormon settlement at Nauvoo emerged from a swampy backwater to become, in 1844, one of the largest cities in the state of Illinois. Nearly 20,000 converts answered the call to Smith's new Zion, 4,000 of them arriving from England alone. Handsome brick houses and shops lined the city's well-planned streets; river boats unloaded at its Mississippi docks. And on the bluff above, overlooking the city and river, masons raised a new temple after the ancient order of Solomon.

But behind a facade of success, danger encompassed the prophet. By the spring of 1844 rumors of his multiple marriages and sexual liaisons, of strange rituals and unorthodox teachings, heralded growing turmoil within the Mormon community. Plots abounded. Events were quickly escalating towards scandal and open schism. In early June prominent Mormon dissidents assembled a press in Nauvoo with the intent of publishing a paper exposing Smith's secret teachings, including the practice called polygamy. The first (and only) issue of the paper did just that, creating an intolerable situation for Smith. He responded by declaring the press a public nuisance and ordering it destroyed.

This act of obstructing a free press played directly into his enemies' hands: the prophet had proved himself a theocratic tyrant. He was charged with treason and commanded by the governor of Illinois to surrender himself. Hoping to prevent the mob violence sure to be directed at Nauvoo if he resisted or fled, Smith surrendered to jail in the nearby but hostile village of Carthage, well aware that he would probably never be allowed to escape alive. As expected, his most rabid enemies quickly gathered to Carthage, and on 27 June 1844 a mob with painted faces–composed in part of the militia assigned by the governor to protect him–battered down the jail doors and shot to death both Joseph and his older brother Hyrum.

## III

This summary of Smith's history is widely canonized in published accounts of his life. But another side to the story is now emerging. More than ten years ago a bizarre series of events focused attention on several other even more curious facts that had never before been integrated into accounts of Joseph Smith's story. When added, they change its tenor entirely.

In the early 1980s an obscure book dealer in Salt Lake City named Mark Hofmann began unearthing a series of previously unknown documents relating to the early history of Mormonism. Most troublesome of these was a letter purportedly written in 1830 by one of Smith's first disciples. Brimming with references to treasures and enchantments, the letter related how Smith actually obtained the Book of Mormon not from an angel, but from a magical white salamander which transfigured itself into a spirit. When disclosed publicly in 1985, the "salamander letter," as it became known, received prominent discussion in the national media and stimulated intense new activity in circles studying early Mormonism.

Unsettled by the damaging publicity brought by the letter, Mormon church authorities began negotiating with Hofmann to purchase other "newly discovered" materials, particularly any that might impugn orthodox versions of their history. These secret dealings tragically unraveled after a Mormon historian involved with the documents was the victim of a brutal bomb murder. Complex forensic investigations revolving around the murder eventually revealed the "salamander letter" and several companion documents to be bogus, the pathologically intuitive creations of Hofmann, a master forger turned bomb maker and killer.[4]

By then, however, several historians had already undertaken detailed reevaluations of Smith, focusing careful attention on any overlooked associations he might have had with things magical. Ironically, investigators soon brought to the surface a wealth of unquestionably genuine historical evidence–much of it long available but either misunderstood, suppressed, or ignored–substantiating that Smith and his early followers had multiple involvements with magic, irregular Freemasonry, and traditions generally termed "occult."

## IV

Though it is a work still very much in progress, Joseph Smith's story is now being pieced together in a new and entirely unorthodox fashion.[5]

Beginning in his late adolescent years, Smith was first recognized by others to have paranormal abilities, and between 1822 and 1827 he was enlisted to act as "seer" for several groups engaged in treasure digging. Not only did he possess a "seer stone" into which he could gaze and locate things lost or hidden in the earth, but it has recently become evident that this same stone was probably the "Urim and Thummim" later used to "translate" portions of the Book of Mormon. According to contemporary accounts, Smith would place his "seer stone" in the crown of his hat and then bend forward with his arms upon his knees and his face buried in the hat. Gazing into the stone while in this posture, he would visualize and then dictate the words to a scribe seated nearby.

The treasure digging had also involved magical rituals, and it is likely that Smith knew at least the rudiments of ceremonial magic during his adolescent years. A possible occult mentor to the young Smith has also been identified, a physician named Luman Walter(s), who was a distant cousin of Smith's future wife and a member of the circle associated with the early treasure quests. According to contemporary accounts, Walter(s) was not only a physician but a magician and mesmerist who had traveled in Europe to obtain "profound learning," probably including knowledge of alchemy, Paracelsian medicine, and Hermetic lore.

Other pieces of evidence add to the picture. Three very curious parchments and a dagger owned by Smith's brother Hyrum have been carefully preserved by Hyrum's descendants as sacred relics, handed down from eldest son to eldest son after his death. Family tradition maintained that they were religious objects somehow used by Hyrum and Joseph. When finally scrutinized by individuals outside the family, they were recognized as the implements of a ceremonial magician. The dagger bears the sigil of Mars. The three parchments, each apparently intended for a different magical operation, are inscribed with a variety of magic symbols and sigils.

Another heirloom also fell into perspective: a silver medallion, owned by Joseph Smith and reputedly carried on his person at the time of his murder in Carthage jail, was identified as a talisman. It is inscribed front and back with the magic square and sigil of Jupiter, the astrological force associated with the year of Smith's birth. All these items could have been constructed using the standard texts of ceremonial magic available in the late eighteenth and early nineteenth centuries: Cornelius Agrippa's *Occult Philosophy,* Ebenezer Sibly's *Occult Sciences,* and Francis Barrett's *The Magus.*

In this light the visit of the angel Moroni takes on another aspect. The angel appeared on the night of the autumnal equinox, between midnight and dawn—hours auspicious for a magical invocation. Smith made his subsequent visits to the hill on the same day for the next four years. When he finally retrieved the plates, it was the eve of the equinox, in the first hour after midnight. A contemporary account suggests that he was required to take a consort (his wife) with him, to ride a black horse, and to dress in black—all lending a further magical tenor to the operation.

Historians puzzled over how this information fit into the more familiar story. Were the magical parchments used to invoke the angel Moroni or the other angelic visitors? And above all, how does this relate to the doctrinal substance and evolution of Mormonism, which seems outwardly devoid of a magical tenor?

## V

While ceremonial magic was a virtually unknown, or at least little documented, element in Mormonism as encountered by Smith's followers, other occult aspects of his religion were evident. The most obvious was its irregular Masonic connections. In 1842, two years before his death, Smith had embraced Masonry. But long before his own initiation as a Mason in Nauvoo, he had traveled in company with Masons, who included, among other prominent disciples, Brigham Young. Smith's earliest connection with the Craft probably came with the initiation of his brother (and close companion) Hyrum as a Mason around 1826, just shortly before Joseph began work on the Book of Mormon.[6]

Sometime before 1826, Joseph may even have had contact with a historically important Masonic figure named Captain William Morgan. Morgan published the first American-authored exposé of Masonic rites at Batavia, New York, in 1826; his disappearance (and presumed murder) just before the book's printing was widely judged to be an act of Masonic vengeance and sparked a national wave of fierce anti-Masonic activity. Given their close geographic proximity (they lived about twelve miles apart), it is quite possible that Morgan and Smith met; one nineteenth-century Masonic historian even suggested that Smith influenced Morgan.

Interestingly, in 1834 Morgan's widow, Lucinda, converted to Mormonism along with her second husband, George Washington Harris. Harris was also a Mason and had been an associate of William Morgan. Joseph Smith became closely acquainted with George and Lucinda around 1836, and sometime thereafter he entered into an intimate relationship with Lucinda. Eventually Lucinda became one of Smith's ritually wed "spiritual wives," although she remained married to Harris.

The prophet's connection with Masonry after 1841 became extremely complex. In June 1841 efforts to establish a Masonic lodge at Nauvoo began, and a few months later a dispensation for it was granted by the Grand Lodge of Illinois. On 15 March 1842 the Nauvoo lodge was installed and Joseph Smith initiated. The next day he was passed and raised to the sublime degree of Master Mason. Two days later Smith organized a Female Relief Society, perhaps intending it to be a Masonic auxiliary, or the beginning of an "adoptive," androgynous new Mormon Masonry. Eventually every officer of the Female Relief Society also became a spiritual wife and consort of Smith's, with his first wife, Emma, acting as its president (a situation complicated by the fact that Emma did not completely understand her husband's relationships with the other women).[7]

The last three years before Smith's murder in 1844 were unquestionably the most creative period in a uniquely creative life. Shortly after his Masonic initiations, he began formulating the rituals that would be instituted in his own Mormon temple, then still under early phases of construction in Nauvoo. Six weeks later Smith gave a first version of this "endowment" (as the ritual was subsequently called) to a "Holy Order" of nine disciples, all of whom were Master Masons. Many elements of the "endowment" ritual directly paralleled Masonic ceremony, a fact plainly evident to participants. Smith explained to his followers that Masonry was a somewhat corrupted remnant of the ancient priesthood God had commissioned him to restore in its fullness. In turn, essentially every prominent male figure in the Mormon church who was present as an adult in Nauvoo became a Master Mason.

Another unusual element entered the matrix of Smith's creativity around this time. From his associations with ceremonial magic and Masonry, Smith had almost certainly heard of Kabbalah. But in 1841 a Jew named Alexander Neibaur, raised in the Polish borderlands of Prussia, educated at the University of Berlin, and familiar with Kabbalah, joined the Mormon church. He migrated to Nauvoo, and there became Smith's frequent companion and tutor in Hebrew. Documentation has recently come to light suggesting that Neibaur not only knew of Kabbalah, but may have possessed in Nauvoo a copy of its classic text, the Zohar. Smith probably gained some familiarity with the Zohar while under Neibaur's tutelage. Indeed it appears that Smith's 7 April 1844 declaration of a plurality of Gods was supported by an exegesis of the first Hebrew words of Genesis *(Bereshith bara Elohim)* drawn from the opening section of the Zohar.[8]

During the period after 1841, Smith introduced the practice of plural "celestial marriage" (which later evolved into Mormon polygamy) to a small group of his most trusted followers. In this era not only men, but a few women, including Lucinda Harris, secretly took a "plural" spouse. The sacred wedding ritualized by Smith was a transformative union that anointed men and women to become "priests and priestesses," "kings and queens," and then ultimately gods and goddesses, the dual creative substance of divinity in eternal, Tantric intercourse. The ceremony was intended to be performed in the holiest precincts of the new temple. By late 1843 Smith revealed several ritual extensions to the "endowment," all of which were ultimately incorporated into Mormon temple ceremony. This legacy of mysterious initiatory rituals revealed between 1842 and 1844 remains more or less unaltered as the sacred core of Mormonism.

Fifty years later, at the end of the nineteenth century, leaders of the Utah church would still occasionally state in private that the Mormon temple ritual embodied "true Masonry"—a fact unknown to most modern Mormons. But then, of course, almost all of this history is unknown to the average modern Mormon. Even well-educated Latter-day Saints today seldom understand the origins of the compass and square embroidered upon the breasts of the ritual garment worn by temple initiates. Nonetheless the relationship of these rituals with Joseph Smith's occult vision and the concurrent introduction of Masonry in Nauvoo is becoming the subject of intense interest.[9]

## VI

In the autumn of 1994 pieces of the prophet puzzle began falling into place, revealing a unifying pattern behind the unusual array of historical information outlined above. Joseph Smith's quest for a sacred golden treasure buried in dark earth, his involvement with ceremonial magic, his angelic visitations, the pseudepigraphic texts he "translated," his declaration of Masonry as a remnant of the priesthood, and his restoration of a temple with its central mystery of a sacred wedding—all could be fitted into one very recently recognized context: Hermeticism.

Not only did Smith have many documented associations with historical legacies of Hermeticism such as magic and Masonry, but his religious creation also evidences several parallels with Hermetic ideas. John L. Brooke, professor of history at Tufts University, has recently explored this subject in a seminal 1994 study of Mormonism and Hermeticism, *The Refiner's Fire: The Making of Mormon Cosmology, 1644-1844.*[10] Brooke notes the "striking parallels between the Mormon concepts of coequality of matter and spirit, of the covenant of celestial marriage, and of an ultimate goal of human godhood and the philosophical traditions of alchemy and Hermeticism, drawn from the ancient world and fused with Christianity in the Italian Renaissance." In this light Harold Bloom's poetic reading of Joseph Smith as a "Gnostic" takes on broader nuances: though Bloom does not mention it, Smith's religion-making imagination was allied in several ways with remnants of a Hermetic tradition frequently linked to gnosticism.

The investigations of Smith's connection with Hermeticism are focusing new attention on an oft-ignored claim of esoteric lore: the importance of Hermeticism in the evolution of early American religious consciousness and political culture. This has broad implications for our understanding of the new nation's religious history. During the seventeenth and eighteenth centuries, a complex alloy of Hermeticism and alchemical mysticism developed within Europe's religious crucible, displaying radical aspirations for Christian reformation. Brooke documents how this intersection between dispensational restorationism and the Hermetic occult flowed into early American culture and religion: among

Quakers, Pietists, and perfectionists coming to Pennsylvania and New Jersey between about 1650 and 1730; through the "culture of print" conveyed by alchemical and Hermetic texts brought from Europe; and in the development of late eighteenth-century esoteric Masonry with its rich foundations in Kabbalistic, Hermetic, and alchemical mythology.

As a young man in the company of occult treasure seekers, drawing magic circles and battling enchantments in the New York and Pennsylvania countryside, Joseph Smith probably first learned about this alternative and very unpuritanical religious vision. He may even have heard the old Rosicrucian legend of a seventeen-year-old prophet named Christian Rosenkreutz and the mysterious "Book M" that he translated.[11] Certainly he would have learned about the Philosopher's Stone and alchemy's transmutational mystery. Soon after, the eighteen-year-old Smith found his own sacred treasure buried in the earth, a treasure golden and yet–as alchemical lore promised–of substance more subtle than vulgar gold. Gazing into his seer stone, he saw in the Book of Mormon's golden plates a record of ancient fratricidal oppositions and of a Christ who brought union.

For a decade, Brooke suggests, Smith's emergent Hermetic theology was disguised under the coloring of traditional Christian restorationism. But in the last years of his life, the veil was parted: "At Nauvoo he publicly and unequivocally announced his new theology of preexistent spirits, the unity of matter and spirit, and the divinization of the faithful, and he privately pursued the consummation of alchemical-celestial marriage as the ultimate vehicle to this divinity. The alchemical-hermetic term of *coniunctio* powerfully summarizes the resolution that Smith had achieved at Nauvoo by the summer of 1844. He had established a theology of the conjunction–the unification–of the living and the dead, of men and women, of material and spiritual, of secular and sacred, all united in a 'new and everlasting covenant' over which he would preside as king and god. In these circumstances the conventional boundary between purity and danger, right and wrong, law and revolution, simply melted away. ... In effect the greater Mormon emergence can be visualized as metaalchemical experience running from opposition to union, an experience shaped and driven by the personality of Joseph Smith."[12]

VII

How this strange Hermetic religion evolved into today's Mormon church is a question awaiting detailed study, particularly as the contours of Joseph Smith's vision become more sharply defined. I can here give only a rough summary of what followed Smith's death.

Smith established no clear order of prophetic succession, and in the chaotic period after his martyrdom several followers claimed his office and prophetic mantle. Brigham Young, long a loyal apostle to Smith, emerged as the natural organizational leader and was eventually proclaimed the new "prophet, seer, and revelator," a position he held until his death three decades later. Forced to abandon Nauvoo in the winter of 1846, Young led his people through their difficult flight to the valley of the Great Salt Lake and there organized the new Mormon society.

Young staunchly defended the teachings and rituals presented by Smith in Nauvoo, including the temple ceremonies and the doctrines relating to polygamy. Isolated in the Rocky Mountain wilderness, he hoped to realize Smith's millennial dreams and establish Zion unhampered by a hostile world. But it was not to be. With the full force of the U.S. government and a Victorian public morality marshaled against the Mormon church, the practice of polygamy had to be publicly abandoned in 1890. After its defeat in that epochal battle, Mormonism slowly found accommodation with the world it had fled. In the process, many elements of Smith's mystery religion were necessarily veiled or attenuated, and, by the late twentieth century, perhaps largely forgotten.

For students of religion, the prophet Joseph Smith today remains a grand American enigma: too potent a force to be dismissed without comment, and yet too complex for facile categorization. In the final analysis, I must agree with Bloom that "we do not know Joseph Smith, as he prophesied that even his own could never hope to know him. He requires strong poets, major novelists, accomplished dramatists to tell his history, and they have not yet come to him."[13] But the tides may be shifting. While the prophet still awaits his poets, historians are examining with new wonder this most extraordinary chapter in American religious history.

*NOTES*

1. Harold Bloom, *The American Religion* (New York: Simon and Schuster, 1992), 98, 127,

2. Ibid., 99, 123.

3. Dean C. Jessee, ed., *The Papers of Joseph Smith,* vol. 1 (Salt Lake City: Deseret Book Co., 1989), 6. For a detailed examination of Smith's early years, see Richard L. Bushman, *Joseph Smith and the Beginnings of Mormonism* (Urbana: University of Illinois Press, 1984). Despite many interpretive limitations, Smith's best overall biography remains Fawn M. Brodie, *No Man Knows My History* (New York: Alfred A. Knopf, 1945; 2d ed., 1971).

4. See Linda Sillitoe and Allen Roberts, *Salamander: The Story of the Mormon Forgery Murders* (Salt Lake City: Signature Books, 1988); and Steven Naifeh and Gregory White Smith, *The Mormon Murders* (New York: Weidenfield & Nicolson, 1988).

5. Smith's associations with occult traditions in early America are comprehensively detailed in D. Michael Quinn, *Early Mormonism and the Magic World View* (Salt Lake City: Signature Books, 1987; 2d ed., 1998). For an interpretive reading of this history, see Lance S. Owens, "Joseph Smith and Kabbalah: The Occult Connection," *Dialogue: A Journal of Mormon Thought* 27 (Fall 1994): 117-94.

6. The interactions of Smith and his religion with the Masonic tradition are fully documented in Michael W. Homer, "'Similarity of Priesthood in Masonry': The Relationship between Freemasonry and Mormonism," *Dialogue: A Journal of Mormon Thought* 27 (Fall 1994): 1-113.

7. Emma's role in these events is comprehensively reviewed in an excellent biography by Linda King Newell and Valeen Tippetts Avery, *Mormon Enigma: Emma Hale Smith* (New York: Doubleday, 1984).

8. Owens, 178-84.

9. It has occasionally been suggested that Masonic revenge was somehow involved in Smith's murder. While clear evidence for this is lacking, the assertion deserves comment. Smith's secret–and, by some interpretations, loosely "Masonic"–religious practices clearly impelled the many groups seeking his death, and Masons undoubtedly were present among his assailants at Carthage. Indeed, as musket balls ripped his body, Smith stood in the window of Carthage jail, raised his arms to the square, and with his last breath began to address his brothers with the old Masonic distress call: "Oh Lord my God, is there no help for the widow's son?" In the midst of these words, he tumbled from the window, dead.

10. John L. Brooke, *The Refiner's Fire: The Making of Mormon Cosmology, 1644-1844* (New York: Cambridge University Press, 1994).

11. See the "Fama Fraternitatis" and "Confessio Fraternitatis," along with

the accompanying discussion, in Frances A. Yates, *The Rosicrucian Enlightenment* (London: Routledge & Kegan Paul, 1972), 238-51.

12. Brooke, 281.

13. Bloom, 127.

# 9.
# How Joseph Smith Resolved the Dilemmas of American Romanticism

*Eugene England*

WHEN I WAS FIFTEEN, I FIRST READ JOSEPH SMITH'S "KING FOLLETT Discourse." I was captivated, swept up in new emotions and vistas. Reading this sermon, the most complete we have from the prophet, opened to me for the first time a clear sense of myself as an eternal being, uncreated and indestructible, the same kind of being as God, destined to be like him, at home in an infinite universe pregnant with incredible possibilities. I wandered under the stars in a kind of ecstasy or lay in my sleeping bag on our back lawn and considered the unnumbered worlds out there, rolling on in great orders of evolutionary development, with beings beyond my imaginings in their thoughts and activities, yet like myself or what I might be. I trembled in my delight with life and the future.

Fifteen years later, as a graduate student at Stanford University, I reread those same, and other, writings of Joseph Smith. And because I was a different person, now trained in classic rationalist thought as well as susceptible to emotional Romantic perspectives, I saw some other things, such as this: "The things of God are of deep import; and time and experience and careful and ponderous and solemn thoughts can only find them out. Thy mind, O man, if thou wilt lead a soul unto salvation, must stretch as high as the utmost heavens and search into and contemplate the darkest abyss and the broad expanse of eternity."[1]

I was chilled at the prophet's vision of a universe ultimately tragic: one dependent for its continued existence on the opposition of good and evil and even opposition between good things; one in which only a genuine, costly struggle against evil and between good alternatives makes possible the progress of intelligences; one where there is no relief from the pains of growth and of continual effort within a context of inexorable laws that govern not only physical but moral and spiritual reality—no relief except to learn to live in harmony with those laws; one in which God is limited, unable to strike through the mask of the world or dissolve it as merely a symbol of deeper reality or save me from myself with his irresistible grace—a universe in which I can never be a purely autonomous individual, completely free to pursue my creative will, but must come to terms with immutable conditions of reality and of development within that reality, especially the condition that I can never fully know or be myself except in relationship, in community, in the painful, intimidating struggle to love, to respond to, and give myself to, other individuals and God. I learned that I must work out my salvation in "fear and trembling."

I also learned, not long after my adolescent response to Joseph Smith, that my response could be called an epiphany of Romantic optimism, that it was very much like what Ralph Waldo Emerson inspired in a whole generation of American writers and thinkers of the 1830s and 1840s. And I found, at Stanford, that much of my later response could very well be called Classical realism. Romantic optimism and Classical realism are nothing new, and a switch from one to the other not at all unusual. What is unusual is that the same person, Joseph Smith, in the same body of writing, intensely evoked both in me, and that he did not just move me from one to the other, but helped me to resolve the great dilemmas that that age-old polarity has posed: law versus freedom, reason versus emotion (or head versus heart), community versus the individual, the necessity but limitations of language. And I have become convinced that a crucial test of a genuine and great religious figure, one that Joseph Smith meets extremely well (better than his critics and even many of his friends have recognized) is that his work embodies both Romantic and

Classical tendencies in creative tension. He reveals theoretical and practical resolutions to the dilemmas I have mentioned that come not as mere didactic answers but as more exciting and inclusive questions, new visions of possibility, moving symbols, and energizing patterns of ritual and literal action–genuine synthesis rather than simplistic choice or polar destructiveness.

Of course, as I also learned in my studies at Stanford, certain great secular writers, in their best poetry and fiction, have also tried to work out, with varying success, resolutions to these dilemmas. Some of the very greatest resolutions came out of or directly followed the Romantic rebellion of the early nineteenth century, that crucial watershed in human history when major issues that had divided and energized human beings from earliest times were brought to explosive focus and produced detonations that changed human thought and history. Henry David Thoreau, Herman Melville, Emily Dickinson, Frederick Goddard Tuckerman, and others were able at certain points in their work to take the best of the Romantic spirit from the European pioneers William Wordsworth and Samuel Coleridge and John Keats and to integrate Romantic forces with Classical ones; thus they were not mere rebels or reactionaries, like so many of their contemporaries, but creative forgers of solutions to some of the most profound epistemological and ontological questions.

I am convinced that Joseph Smith, like these great writers (but independent of their influence), developed through what can be called Romantic and Classical stages, creatively resolved Romantic and Classical conflicts, and integrated Romantic and Classical tendencies in himself, but he did not do so only in the symbolic structures of art or behind fictional masks but in explicit doctrines which he claimed were revealed and also appeared in church practice and in the hard realities of his own daily life. The prophet developed these resolutions in revelations that came pragmatically, in response to developing problems and various specific questions and in a way that is progressive, that reaches its height in the "King Follett Discourse" near the end of his life and tantalizes us with the promise of further development. Many of the writers of his age, on the other hand, declined after the high point of their balanced achievement–I think of Wordsworth, Tennyson, Thoreau, Emerson, Hawthorne–or were only able to maintain it briefly, in a few of their best works, such as Keats, Melville,

Dickinson. And the writers, though some belatedly, have been quite universally admired despite (and even *because of*) the complexities and contradictions and difficulties of interpretation that their struggles toward resolution produced. Yet similar complexities in Joseph Smith have led him to be, outside his own church, quite universally misunderstood and villified.

But that may be changing now, and my purpose here is to add a reasonable impetus to that change. Jan Shipps, the most eminent non-Mormon historian of Mormonism today, in what she calls "the prophet puzzle," was one of the first to recognize that the apparently antithetical elements in Joseph Smith, which have been ignored by most Mormon writers and used by others, particularly Fawn Brodie, in *No Man Knows My History,* to discredit him, can be combined into a coherent picture of a genuine religious figure, like other complex religious figures and creative geniuses. She writes: "The approach I am suggesting here ... might allow us to reconcile enough of the inconsistency to reveal, not a split personality, but a splendid, gifted–pressured, sometimes opportunistic, often troubled–yet for all of that, a larger-than-life *whole* man."[2]

Shipps has some excellent ideas about avenues that might be followed in such an attempt. But for me her major contribution was in making the suggestion that Joseph's complexity be seen positively and examined carefully–and that a deeper look at the intellectual and cultural currents of his time, and at comparable figures, would help us.

Another non-Mormon, prominent American literary critic Harold Bloom, in his book on American religion, calls Joseph Smith *the* American prophet, whose "religion-making imagination" is unique in our history.[3] Bloom sees Joseph Smith's central contribution as restoring "the Bible's sense of the theomorphic," that is, the understanding that humans are genuinely made in the image of God and thus their highest capacities are divine, and also bringing back the ancient Hebrew concept of theurgy, that God's purposes and progress depend on ours. Bloom frankly admits he cannot explain how Joseph Smith recovered these unique ancient concepts except through revelation. His main point, however, is that whatever the source of these ideas, they are the ones that have been most crucial to the quintessentially American sense of the god-like potential of humans and they continue to "mark the limits" of modern spirituality in America. This is, of course, a remarkable confirmation of Jan Shipps's claim that Mormonism is a genuinely "new religious tradition,"[4] as different from traditional Christianity as primitive Christianity was from Judaism, and it is also a confirmation of my central thesis, that Joseph Smith, through his own genius and the revelations he received, created doctrine and an organization that are unique in successfully resolving the dilemmas that came to a head in early-nineteenth-century American thought.

It is only a bit disconcerting that such important new perspectives, which I think are a central key to understanding Joseph Smith, and therefore to understanding the Restored Gospel, should have come from non-Mormons. But it is seriously troubling that Mormon scholars have not yet been as effective as Shipps and Bloom in countering the influence of Brodie and laying groundwork for breaking its hold on non-Mormon thinking with new paradigms for thinking about Joseph Smith. And I am most troubled that we students of rhetoric and literary critics, especially experts in the thought and the writers of the Romantic Age, should have been leading the way and have not, so let me lay out some suggestions for future work.

The great Romantics, those who found real solutions to their dilemmas, would not have agreed with Emerson that not only words but things are directly symbolic, that nature is merely "the symbol of the spirit," "a metaphor of the human mind."[5] Their experience and conviction was that nature has its own independent reality, diverse, even contradictory to human feeling and purpose. And that was Joseph Smith's experience and belief. He had what could be called Romantic inclinations toward optimism, toward a more organic, individualistic world view, toward ancient and nonrational patterns for salvation. But Joseph Smith, unlike Emerson, did not succumb to some form of Transcendentalism, which despite its rhetorical opposition to Calvinism continued the central assumptions of Calvinist theology, such as that the universe, including humans, is a creation out of nothing and merely symbolic and that God's *will*, his omnipotent decisions, and *our* wills, which are essentially expressions of his, determine what is true and good.

Emerson's "Self-Reliance" was really a dangerous kind of God-reliance, ultimately a surrender to personal impulse as if it were divine authority, and it clearly pointed his later disciples, less protected by inherited good habits, toward sheer automatism, complete loss of freedom and moral chaos. Unlike any religious movement around him, except the Episcopalian and perhaps the Unitarian, Joseph Smith's revealed theology was *rationalistic* rather than voluntaristic; it gave ultimate authority to what he called "irrevocable" law rather than to God's will: "Element had an existence from the time God had. The pure principles are principles that can never be destroyed. They may be organized and reorganized, but not destroyed. Nothing can be destroyed. They never can have a beginning or an ending; they exist eternally."[6] In other words, given eternal natural laws, that is, those "pure principles of element ... that never can be destroyed," God's laws are *descriptive* of how things are, not *prescriptive* of how he wills them to be.

Joseph Smith thus struck straight to the heart of the major epistemological and ontological dilemma the great Romantics struggled with. And his resolution was no mere compromise but can be understood as an integration of the great Romantic impulses and Classical realities. By the end of his life he had articulated, not systematically but in developing responses to dynamic practical problems and questions in the total life of the community he led, a full-fledged theology of salvation that transcended the Classical rationalist extremes of both traditional high church Christianity and Enlightenment secularism and that also avoided the Romantic, emotionalistic, and voluntaristic extremes of Calvinism, Revivalism, and Transcendentalist pantheism. Like the great Romantics, he somewhat naturalized deity and deified nature,[7] but he did not in doing so make God into a mere intellectual or mystical natural force or all nature into God. Instead he encountered and eventually described a God who is literally an exalted man, a genuine person living in a real environment of time and space, of what he termed "element" and "spirit" (or matter and energy) and of co-existent beings and of laws which govern the relationships and development of all. Alone among Christian religious leaders, he struck down the notion of creation out of nothing by an omnipotent God, with its encouragement to Romantic excesses in the belief that "Anything is possible!" He taught that "The Elements are eternal"; that "Intelligence was not created, neither indeed can be." It is a rational universe, consistent and amenable to empirical scientific exploration.

But it is also an organic universe, shot through with refined spirit matter and light, by which it is constantly in communication with the Gods who sustain it and pregnant with purposes toward which God moves it that are beyond the ken of mere empirical science. And those purposes center in a way of salvation much like the "circuitous journey," the central Romantic myth of salvation through the soul's profitable breaking out from primal unity and stasis into experience and struggle and then returning to higher unity with itself and God. Like the great Romantics, Joseph accepted a myth of the Fall that made it a "fortunate" fall, but he learned through revelation that the story is a literal reality that God himself has passed through to become God. And he received scriptures that taught the story as a literal original archetype in the fall of the first fully human parents, Adam and Eve, one which had to be literally completed in the sacrificial love and atoning suffering of the "second Adam," Christ, and lived through by each individual human: That fall and atonement, both of which were fully intended and approved by God, moved humankind out from mere innocence into a moral universe of choice and struggle, of failure and growth, which was indeed the best of all *possible* worlds; it was the only kind where, given the limitations placed on God's power by universal laws and selfexistent free intelligences, individuals could genuinely face new environments, experience good and evil, learn to develop real virtue rather than merely preserve innocence, and through faith in Christ's unconditional love, have faith in themselves and the courage to repent and thus grow and develop literally toward Godhood. The result is not unity of human activity through secularization but through making all things sacred.

These two basic *ontological* principles, specific resolutions to the Romantic question about the ultimate nature of the universe and divinity and about the purpose and nature of human experience in a dangerous world, also have *epistemological* implications that speak directly to the Romantic anxieties. Through revelations, Joseph found an attractive balance between nominalism and realism, one that can be compared to that of the great Romantic poets. He did not believe literally in Platonic universals: orders of reality are all equally real for him, not mere shadows of others, and he was poignantly aware of the tragic limitations of language, especially when written, aware that even God must communicate with his children "in their weakness, after the manner of their language" (D&C 1:24). But neither could he be a nominalist; events and objects, though independently real, are for him related to each other by basic eternal laws, especially by the unifying powers of creative intelligence—of which language is one power, one of the many that we all share, in embryonic form, with God, the original "Word." In the "King Follett Discourse," Joseph refers to "chaotic matter—which is element, and in which dwells all the glory."[8] It seems that order, in God's creative act, is wrought from a pluralistic chaos of discrete, equally real particulars, but a chaos that is unified in the sense that because of those "pure principles of element" or laws of the nature of things the chaos is *potent,* genuinely responsive to the creative powers of God in rational, lawful ways and responsive in similar ways to the lesser powers of humans. And these powers are embodied in mind and language, characteristics God and his children share as literally related beings. The 88th section of the Doctrine and Covenants ties the divine mind and the cosmic creative power of Christ together with human perception through the media of physical and spiritual light, which are pronounced to be the same. All this provides a metaphysics of form that counters both the extreme philosophical realism the Romantics reacted against and the debased philosophical idealism (or nominalism) which too many succumbed to and which has contributed to the excessive breakdown in structure of some modern literature and rhetoric.

There is much here that needs further exploration, especially in comparison to the other great Romantic synthesizers. For instance, Hawthorne's struggle with the story of the fortunate Fall behind a fictional mask gives much of the power to his finest works, *The Scarlet Letter* and "My Kinsman, Major Molineux," but he was clearly afraid, as Joseph Smith was not, to come out explicitly against the religious orthodoxy of his time. Melville, who let his skepticism push him to the heights of fictional struggle and then for a while into the ultimate escape from that Romantic dilemma, complete fictional silence, afterwards gave us, in *Billy Budd,* perhaps our most powerful study of the great dilemma of freedom and order. Joseph Smith struggled throughout his life with that dilemma; he not only produced one great resolution for it in the apparently Romantic concept of consecration and stewardship in a Zion society patterned after the ancient order of Enoch, but rationally implemented that concept in literal united orders and the political kingdom of God. The Romantic utopians, with an optimistic view of humanity, believed that ideal *structures* would correct all ills; the Classical realists, for instance those (with a negative view of humankind) who designed the American constitution, believed the best they could do was minimize political exploitation through pitting power against power. Different from both extremes, Joseph Smith taught that human nature was essentially neutral or, better, a potential; that only a development in humanity's basic nature through religious means could bring political and economic salvation; but that certain forms, both as experiments and as continuing symbols, could help bring that about.

Perhaps most intriguing is the working out in Joseph Smith of that *central* Romantic dilemma, reason versus emotion. If we are better to know him, better know his history, which he said we would never know until the judgement day, we must know both his heart and his mind, much better than we have. This requires that we look honestly at all the data, the scriptures, the personal writings, *especially* the sermons and letters, which more than any single thing reveal the mind of a man of Joseph Smith's complexity and spiritual genius–but also at the reports of friends and enemies, the difficulties, the conflicts. Jan Shipps is right that "the entire project must be approached with an open mind, a genial spirit, and a determination to follow the evidence that appeals to reason from whatever source it comes, wherever it leads. Only then will the outcome be a picture of the prophet and an account of the foundations of the Mormon faith which will be convincing to both tough minds, which demand empirical facts, and *tender* minds, comfortable in the presence of leaps of faith."[9] But we must, I think, in order to know his heart and mind and see their unique Romantic and Classical integration, be able to understand as quintessential the wholesome combination of what seem to many to be conflicting activities–such as on the day the prophet spent in the temple at Nauvoo, Illinois, working up a sweat cleaning and painting in the morning, followed by a study class, washing, and dressing in sacred robes for ritual temple worship, followed by a prayer and testimony meeting in which gifts of the spirit were manifest, followed by a feast of raisins and cakes and then music and dancing.[10] Or to see as essentially revealing this report from the young apostle George A. Smith: "Joseph asked my opinion of W. W. Phelps as an editor. I told him I thought Phelps the sixth part of an editor, that was the satirist. When it came to the cool discretion entrusted to an editor in the control of public opinion, the soothing of enmity, he was deficient and would always make more enemies than friends. But for my part I would be willing, if I were able, to pay Phelps for editing a paper, provided nobody else should have the privilege of reading it but myself.

"Joseph laughed heartily and said I had the thing just right. At the close of our conversation, Joseph wrapped his arms around me and pressed me to his bosom and said, "George A., I love you as I do my own life." I felt so affected I could hardly speak."[11]

*NOTES*

1. Joseph Smith, "Letter to the Church from Liberty Jail," Mar. 1839, in Joseph Smith et al., *History of the Church of Jesus Christ of Latter-day Saints,* ed. B. H. Roberts (Salt Lake City, 1905), 3:295.

2. Jan Shipps, "The Prophet Puzzle: Suggestions Leading Toward a More Comprehensive Interpretation of Joseph Smith," *Journal of Mormon History* 1 (1975): 3-20; reprinted in this compilation.

3. He gave the chapter on Joseph Smith as a lecture at the University of Utah, 15 Nov. 1990; transcript in my possession.

4. See her *Mormonism: The Story of a New Religious Tradition* (Urbana: University of Illinois Press, 1988).

5. "Nature," in Ralph Waldo Emerson, *Emerson: Selected Prose and Poetry,* ed. Reginald Cook (New York: Holt, Rinehart, and Winston, 1950), 19.

6. "The King Follett Discourse: A Newly Amalgamated Text," ed. Stan Larson, *BYU Studies,* Winter 1978, 203.

7. See M. H. Abrams, *Natural Supernaturalism* (New York: Norton, 1971).

8. Larson, "King Follett Discourse," 203.

9. Shipps, "Prophet Puzzle," 7.

10. Diary of Samuel Whitney Richards, 1824-1909, 17-18, typescript, Special Collections, Harold B. Lee Library, Brigham Young University, Provo, Utah; cited in Truman Madsen, "Joseph and the Sources of Love," *Dialogue: A Journal of Mormon Thought* 1 (Spring 1966): 131.

11. Diary of George A. Smith, 15 May 1843, typescript, archives, Historical Department, Church of Jesus Christ of Latter-day Saints, Salt Lake City, Utah.

# 10.
# The Psychology of Religious Genius: Joseph Smith and the Origins of New Religious Movements

*Lawrence Foster*

THE NATURE OF GENIUS–ESPECIALLY RELIGIOUS GENIUS–IS AN ELUSIVE and controversial topic. Great and recognized creativity in fields such as art, science, or politics has been the subject of extensive investigation without leading to clear and generally agreed upon criteria for assessing and accounting for such achievement. Religious genius, especially the prophetic leadership of founders of new religious movements, has proven even more difficult to evaluate with any degree of openness and objectivity. Adherents to new faiths often accept at face value prophetic claims to having had direct communication with the divine, while naive critics and apostates in equally one-dimensional fashion tend to see nothing but fraud and delusion in such claims. Neither approach begins to do justice to complexities that characterize the classic foundational phenomena that noted American psychologist William James explored so convincingly in his still unsurpassed analysis of the psychology of religious genius, *The Varieties of Religious Experience*.[1]

This essay focuses on one particularly well-documented case of religious genius–that of Mormon prophet Joseph Smith, founder of a rapidly-growing religious movement that now numbers more than 10 million members worldwide. Joseph Smith's motivation and the psychological dynamics that made possible both his successes and failures have proven highly controversial, both in his own time and today. Critics of Smith such as Fawn Brodie have often found him opaque and disingenuous. They have speculated that his was a highly conflicted personality with enormous powers to rationalize his own impulses as being the will of God. Devout Latter-day Saints, on the other hand, have often ignored whole areas of Smith's personality and actions, creating an almost unbelievable paragon who could do nothing wrong as he consistently attempted to do God's will. Despite the apparent polarization of opinion, recent scholarship increasingly has seen Smith as a complex figure who nevertheless creatively attempted to come to terms with and fuse seemingly conflicting elements within his personality and his world into a new synthesis.[2]

The analysis that follows is an admittedly speculative personal reflection on elements that need to be kept in mind in understanding the psychological dynamics of Joseph Smith's creativity. I begin with some general observations on the nature of great religious creativity and prophetic leadership, drawing on the work of scholars such as William James, Anthony F. C. Wallace, Kenelm Burridge, and others. The core of the article then presents a new hypothesis about one possible element in Joseph Smith's psychology that might help explain some of his most puzzling and disturbing actions associated with his concerted effort to introduce plural marriage among his followers during the last three years of his life. Finally, I ask whether the hypothesis about Joseph Smith's psychological characteristics may help us in understanding the psychological dynamics of other great prophets and foundational religious figures throughout history.

## I

Great religious creativity, as many scholars have argued, always begins with a problem or complex series of problems that the future prophet finds deeply disturbing. To use psychological jargon, "cognitive dissonance" is always present. Individuals who eventually become prophets find this dissonance more disturbing than do many of their contemporaries, and they seek with unusual intensity to try to make sense of both their personal lives and their world. The dissonance for religious geniuses—as opposed to geniuses in art, science, or politics—focuses with unusual intensity on *value* conflicts and inconsistencies. Ultimately, as anthropologist Kenelm Burridge suggests, the prophetic figure attempts "to initiate, both in himself as well as in others, a process of moral regeneration."[3]

How does this process take place in the prophetic figure? Anthropologist Anthony F. C. Wallace has presented a classic description of the way in which new religions—or as he calls them "revitalization movements"—originate in a context of high social disorder and perceived stress.[4] Based on a consideration of hundreds of different groups on five continents, Wallace concludes: "With a few exceptions, every religious revitalization movement with which I am acquainted has been originally conceived in one or several hallucinatory visions by a single individual. A supernatural being appears to the prophet-to-be, explains his own and his society's troubles as being entirely or partly a result of the violation of certain rules, and promises individual and social revitalization if the injunctions are followed and the rituals practiced, but personal and social catastrophe if they are not."

Wallace observes that thereafter the "prophet feels a need to tell others of his experience, and may have definite feelings of missionary or messianic obligation. Generally he shows evidence of a radical inner change in personality soon after the vision experience: a remission of old and chronic physical complaints, a more active and purposeful way of life, greater confidence in interpersonal relations, the dropping of deep-seated habits like alcoholism. ... Where there is no vision (as with John Wesley), there occurs a similarly brief and dramatic moment of insight, revelation, or inspiration, which functions in most respects like the vision in being the occasion of a new synthesis of values and meanings."[5]

One need not accept the value judgment Wallace makes when he refers to such visionary experiences as "hallucinatory" (that is, not literally true) to accept his general description of what happens in such instances as strikingly similar to the case of Joseph Smith. Young Joseph, though highly talented, was at loose ends initially—viewed by some as a pleasant and outgoing ne'er-do-well who spent much of his time hunting for hidden treasure. The series of visions he had in his teens ultimately led to the transformation of his life and the founding of the Church of Jesus Christ of Latter-day Saints. Although surviving accounts of Joseph Smith's first vision are far from consistent on points of detail, such as whether one or several figures appeared to him, they do indicate that young Joseph was deeply disturbed by the competing claims to religious truth that were being put forward in his area. Joseph was bright enough to understand that such mutually exclusive claims simply could not all be true. Eventually he would conclude that he had been specially called by God to introduce a new religious synthesis that would integrate and supersede all previous ones.[6]

All this is well-known among scholars of Mormon history. But what were the *psychological* dynamics that led young Joseph to see visions and be open to the notion that he was specially called by God to lead the way in developing a new synthesis of truth, and later a new social system, including polygamy? To place this issue into a larger context, let us return to the perspectives of William James in *The Varieties of Religious Experience* and realize that religious prophets, including Joseph Smith, are in some sense, at least initially, "sick," "disturbed," or "abnormal." Successful, as opposed to unsuccessful, religious prophets eventually work through their psychological disturbance by creating a new synthesis, but the intensity of their drive always continues to owe something to the magnitude of the problems they feel they have escaped by developing their new understanding of reality.

James is particularly eloquent in discussing the psychology of religious genius in individuals for whom "religion exists not as a dull habit, but as an acute fever." Genius in such individuals, according to James, is frequently associated with "symptoms of nervous instability": "Even more perhaps than other kinds of genius, religious leaders have been subject to abnormal psychic visitations. ... Often they have led a discordant inner life, and had melancholy during part of their career. They have known no measure, been liable to obsessions and fixed ideas; and frequently they have fallen into trances, heard voices, seen visions, and presented all sorts of peculiarities which are ordinarily classed as pathological. Often, moreover, these pathological features in their career have helped to give them their religious authority and influence."[7]

James explains how psychological disorder may contribute to

greatness in a person who also has a "superior intellect": "The cranky person has extraordinary emotional susceptibility. He is liable to fixed ideas and obsessions. His conceptions tend to pass immediately into belief and action; and when he gets a new idea, he has no rest till he proclaims it, or in some way 'works it off' ... Thus, when a superior intellect and a psychopathic temperament coalesce ... in the same individual, we have the best possible condition for the kind of effective genius that gets into the biographical dictionaries. Such men do not remain mere critics and understanders with their intellect. Their ideas possess them, they inflict them, for better or worse, upon their companions or their age."[8]

James also emphasizes that even if religious inspiration may often occur in psychologically unstable or disordered individuals, that fact does not necessarily discredit the *fruits* of such inspiration. He quotes Dr. Henry Maudsely's statement: "What right have we to believe Nature under any obligation to work by means of complete minds only? She may find an incomplete mind a more suitable instrument for a particular purpose. It is the work that is done, and the quality of the worker by which it is done, that is alone of moment; and it may be no great matter from a cosmical standpoint, if in other qualities of character he was singularly defective–if indeed he were a hypocrite, adulterer, eccentric or lunatic."[9] James concludes that the only ultimate test of the validity of religious inspiration is practical–in Jesus' words, "By their fruits ye shall know them." He concludes: "If there were such a thing as inspiration from a higher realm, it might well be that the neurotic temperament would furnish the chief condition of the requisite receptivity."[10]

One final observation needs to be added before we can briefly explore one possible approach to understanding Joseph Smith's psychological states and how they may have influenced some of his most controversial beliefs and actions. The line between health and illness, between normal mood swings and those that might be called extreme, is a fine one indeed. It is often difficult for a contemporary psychiatrist who has worked closely with a patient to make an accurate diagnosis. To diagnose with confidence someone long dead, even when extensive records exist on his or her life, is far more difficult and speculative. The observations that follow are therefore intended to be suggestive, not definitive. These observations will have served their purpose if they open up new possibilities for better understanding aspects of Joseph Smith's beliefs and behavior that might otherwise appear opaque or incomprehensible.

II

My ongoing interest in the psychology of Joseph Smith's religious experience and its impact on his actions has been greatly stimulated by nearly two decades of intensive research as a non-Mormon scholar into the origin and early development of plural marriage among the Latter-day Saints.[11] Initially, I tried to separate my concerns about Joseph Smith's religious and sexual drives, avoiding reductionistic approaches while attempting to make sense of the extraordinarily complex religious and social phenomena associated with the early development of the Mormon movement. Clearly Joseph Smith, like any dynamic personality *can* be analyzed using a variety of different psychological and other perspectives. How convincing any one such approach can be as an *explanation* of what actually made him tick remains highly questionable since reality is always far more complex than any single way of conceptualizing reality can be.[12]

Ultimately, however, the psychological question continued to recur. Why did Joseph Smith feel so preoccupied with introducing plural marriage among his followers during the last three years of his life between 1841 and 1844 that he eventually put many other vital aspects of his prophetic leadership at risk? Was there some hidden psychological key that could help make sense of this seemingly obsessive drive? As difficult as understanding the introduction of polygamy may have been, it ultimately proved not to be the most challenging task. A variety of factors including biblical precedent, concerns for expanding kinship ties in a socially chaotic environment, and Joseph Smith's own strong sex drive all made plural marriage an idea with considerable power for the Mormon prophet in Nauvoo, Illinois, during the early 1840s.[13]

The most intractable problem associated with the early development of polygamy, instead, was something else. One curious bit of evidence simply did not make sense. William Marks, president of the Nauvoo Stake high council and a man of unquestionable honesty and integrity, emphatically insisted that Joseph Smith had approached him in the spring of 1844, shortly before his martyrdom, and had said: "This doctrine of polygamy or Spiritual-wife System, that has been taught and practiced among us will prove our destruction and overthrow." According to Marks, Smith went on to say that he had been "deceived, in reference to its practice," that it was "wrong," and that Marks should go to the high council and prefer charges against all who practiced the doctrine, while Joseph would "preach against it, with all my might, and in this way we may rid the church of this damnable heresy."[14]

Apart from this remarkable statement from a man of unimpeachable honesty, there is evidence from both LDS and RLDS sources that Joseph Smith may indeed have talked about abandoning polygamy near the end of his life. In *Mormon Enigma*, a superb biography of the Mormon prophet's wife Emma Hale Smith, Linda King Newell and Valeen Tippetts Avery refer to the minutes of an 1867 meeting within the RLDS church in which a man named Hugh Herringshaw stated that he had "heard Joseph tell the 12 that they must abandon polygamy and turned to Brigham Young and asked if he was willing to do so. Young said he had been asleep. Then Joseph spoke upon the matter as only he could talk denouncing the doctrine of polygamy. Brigham replied that he and Taylor had determined what course they would pursue."[15] A year earlier, in 1866, Brigham Young had conceded in a carefully qualified statement, "Joseph was worn out with it, but as to his denying any such thing I never knew that he denied the doctrine of polygamy. Some have said that he did, but I do not believe he ever did."[16]

I believe that these and other reports that could be cited accurately reflect the tenor of statements made by Joseph Smith during the last months of his life. If Smith did indeed talk to Marks and to his closest associates among the Twelve about possibly stopping polygamy, such statements are extraordinary in the context of 1844 Nauvoo. For three years, Joseph Smith had engaged in a major, carefully orchestrated effort to introduce plural marriage among his closest followers in the Quorum of the Twelve and other high church councils. He himself had led the way by taking at least sixteen wives besides Emma in a full physical sense during that time. He had put enormous pressure on unwilling associates such as Heber C. Kimball and Orson Pratt to accept the belief and practice, and as many as thirty of his closest associates had taken plural wives under his influence, committing themselves in very tangible form to the new beliefs and practices.[17]

How under such circumstances would it even have been conceivable for Joseph Smith to talk about rejecting plural marriage without forfeiting all credibility with his closest associates? One could understand why he might have feigned such an intent with an associate such as William Marks, who opposed polygamy, but if he actually spoke in such terms to members of the Twelve who were already living in polygamy, how could such statements possibly be explained? Was Smith, as some of his previously most loyal followers at the time asserted, losing touch with reality during his final months in Nauvoo?[18]

A compelling psychological approach to explaining this and other puzzling features of the Mormon prophet's behavior during this period was suggested to me by a Mormon psychiatrist, Dr. Jess Groesbeck.[19] For nearly two years, I dismissed his suggestion as reductionistic, but gradually the explanatory power of the interpretation came to seem more and more compelling to me. Groesbeck argued that many aspects of Joseph Smith's behavior, especially during the last years of his life, appeared strikingly similar to behavior that psychiatrists associate with manic-depressive syndromes. Although one could understand that any individual under the pressures Joseph Smith faced might have experienced substantial mood swings, in the Mormon prophet's case those mood swings appear so severe that they may be clinically significant. Groesbeck also pointed out that there is substantial evidence that tendencies toward manic-depression tend to be inherited. Although many people are aware that one of Joseph Smith's brightest and most appealing sons, David Hyrum, tragically lapsed into insanity and spent the last years of his life in a mental institution, few realize at least six other male descendants of the Mormon prophet also have suffered from psychological disorders, including manic-depression.[20] The possibility that Joseph Smith himself may also have been subject to similar tendencies cannot be discounted.

What are some of the characteristics of psychological mania, and how do such states reflect themselves in behavior? According to Harold I. Kaplan and Benjamin J. Sadock's *Comprehensive Textbook of Psychiatry/IV*:

> The critical clinical feature for a manic episode is a mood that is elevated, expansive, or irritable. The associated symptoms include hyperactivity, pressure of speech, flight of ideas, diminished need for sleep, increased self-esteem to the point of grandiosity, extreme distractibility, short attention span, and extraordinarily poor judgment in the interpersonal and social areas. ...
>
> The person speaks more rapidly, thinks more rapidly, or moves more rapidly. The person frequently requires much less sleep and has apparently limitless energy. Many people with a manic illness feel that they are highly creative during these attacks. The reason, in part, is because there is a flooding of consciousness with ideas and associations that at times are imaginative and creative but that at other times are idiosyncratic and of little artistic merit. ...
>
> Although the elevated mood is often described as euphoric and cheerful and having an infectious quality, it is characterized by an absence of selectivity and an unceasing driven quality. Mania is also characterized by an extremely poor frustration tolerance, with resulting heightened irritability. A manic patient may be quite humorous, good natured, and friendly until frustrated in some trivial way. The good humor then promptly disappears and is replaced by anger and even rage. ...
>
> The increased activity often takes the form of sexual promiscuity, political involvement, and religious concern. ...
>
> The manic episode may or may not include psychotic symptoms. The impairment of judgment may not be sufficiently severe to justify a psychotic diagnosis. Delusions and hallucinations are not unusual. The context is usually consistent with the dominant mood. It is quite common for the person to communicate with God and to have it revealed that he or she has a special purpose or mission. Patients frequently describe themselves as an "organ" of God through whom God speaks to the world.[21]

In the various forms of manic-depressive illness, the manic highs alternate in bipolar fashion with periods of depression.[22] Current diagnostic opinion, described by psychiatrists Frederick K. Goodwin and Kay Redfield Jamison in their pathbreaking study *Manic-Depressive Illness* (New York: Oxford University Press, 1990),[23] emphasizes that manic-depressive illness expresses itself in an extraordinarily complex variety of forms, on a spectrum of intensity ranging from relatively mild, cyclothymic ups and downs that would be hard to distinguish from normal mood swings to extreme highs and lows that clearly display full-blown psychosis. At the extreme end of the manic-depressive spectrum, the bipolar I form of the syndrome, individuals feel the full force of manic excitement or depressive despair. During their manic phases, they feel invincible and often do outrageous things. In full psychotic manias, individuals lose touch with reality, experience delusions and hallucinations, and lack any sense of judgment in interpersonal relations. At the other extreme, depression can become so severe that individuals can come to feel utterly hopeless and eventually may commit suicide if not treated.

A milder form of manic-depressive illness, bipolar II, typically involves recurrent depressions alternating with brief "hypomanic" (less than manic) periods of several days to a week or more when they feel mildly euphoric and full of self-confidence and energy.

It is often very hard to determine whether an individual is experiencing the bipolar II form of manic-depression needing treatment or just a normal period of enthusiasm or low spirits, but the recurrent nature of the experience is diagnostically important. In the mildest, cyclothymic forms of the manic-depressive spectrum, the distinction between normal expressions of enthusiasm or low spirits and those suggesting illness is particularly difficult to determine.[24]

III

How do descriptions of psychological mania square with Joseph Smith's actions during the last three years of his life in Nauvoo between 1841 and 1844? To anyone who has worked closely with the records of the Mormon prophet's life during those final years, the parallels are striking. Only a few key elements can be highlighted here, especially as they relate to his involvement with introducing the belief and practice of plural marriage among his closest followers.

Most obvious is the Mormon prophet's extraordinary expansiveness and grandiosity throughout this period. During the last year of his life, to mention only the most well-known examples, Smith served as mayor of Nauvoo and head of his own private army, became "king" of his secret Kingdom of God that he anticipated would eventually encompass all of North and South America, ran for president of the

United States (that effort was cut short by his martyrdom), and was the "husband" in some sense of dozens of wives.[25] About a year before his martyrdom, he declared: "Excitement has almost become the essence of my life. When that dies away, I feel almost lost."[26] Those who supported Joseph Smith during his last years were impressed by his sense of divine mission and his feeling that he was discovering the very secrets of the universe. Those who opposed him, including some of his previously most loyal lieutenants such as William Marks and William Law, thought instead that he had slipped his moorings and become a "fallen prophet," unfit to lead the church he had founded.

In no area were Joseph Smith's manic qualities more evident than in his efforts to introduce and practice polygamy during the last three years of his life. The point at which Joseph Smith began systematically to introduce polygamy to his closest associates has strong suggestions of mania. As Danel Bachman, summarizing the account by Helen Mar Kimball, wrote: "Brigham Young, Heber C. Kimball, and John Taylor [key members of the Quorum of the Twelve Apostles who were returning from England] arrived in Nauvoo on July 1, 1841. ... Joseph Smith was waiting at the landing with a company of horsemen. As soon as the missionaries disembarked from the boat, he rushed them to dinner at his home, not even giving them time to visit their own families. Vilate Kimball thought that this discourtesy continued after dinner when Smith brought the entire party to the Kimball home. The Prophet, wrote Helen Kimball, 'seemed unwilling to part with my father and from that time kept the Twelve in Council early and late.' Helen said her mother 'never dreamed that he was during those times revealing to them the principles of Celestial Marriage' or that her trials were about to begin."[27]

If the initial systematic attempt to introduce the concept of plural marriage among his closest associates bespeaks possible manic enthusiasm on Joseph Smith's part, his subsequent surge of activity with the sixteen or more women with whom he appears to have sustained sexual relations as plural wives (the full number may have been much greater) is even more suggestive of the hypersexuality that often accompanies manic periods. Some earlier writers such as Fawn Brodie, who have closely investigated the evidence on Joseph Smith's plural relationships, have suggested that he was in effect essentially a lusty, good-natured libertine giving vent to impulses that more cautious individuals keep under better control. I have increasingly come to the conclusion, however, as did Brodie upon later reflection, that this argument cannot adequately explain the extent of Smith's sexual relationships and activities. Something more surely was involved.[28]

Clinically significant manic episodes often alternate with correspondingly deep states of depression. Once again it must be noted that many individuals experience mild depression and that such states of mind are not uncommon during periods of severe stress. Whether such periods of depression were clinically significant in Joseph Smith's case remains debatable. That he *did* have periods of severe depression and discouragement during the last years of his life is, however, indisputable.

One such period was described by one of his plural wives, Mary Rollins Lightner. She recalled Smith saying: "I am tired, I have been mobbed, I have suffered so much from outsiders and from my own family. Some of the brethren think they can carry this work on better than I can, far better. I have asked the Lord to take me away. I have to seal my testimony to this generation with my blood. I have to do it for this work will never progress until I am gone for the testimony is of no force until the testator is dead. People little know who I am when they talk about me, and they will never know until they see me weighed in the balance in the Kingdom of God. Then they will know who I am, and see me as I am. I dare not tell them, and they do not know me."[29]

Although this was recounted many years later, it seems to reflect accurately the spirit of many of Joseph Smith's private statements during his last days, including those in which he allegedly expressed doubts about polygamy. His sermon of 7 April 1844 at the funeral of King Follett may appropriately serve as his own epitaph. In this sermon, he described his glorious vision of men progressing to the achievement of full godlike powers. He declared in his conclusion, which George A. Smith said referred to plural marriage, "You never knew my heart; no man knows my history; I cannot tell it. I shall never undertake it. If I had not experienced what I have, I should not have known it myself. ... When I am called at the trump of the archangel, and weighed in the balance, you will all know me then."[30]

Here, it seems to me, was a profoundly lonely man, poignantly aware of the inability of the world (or even himself) to understand the underlying significance of his ideas and mission and seeing with stark clarity that he was about to be overwhelmed by forces he had helped set loose but which were beyond his control. Throughout his life, Joseph Smith was painfully aware of his singularity and never able to escape it.

Where does all this leave us with regard to understanding the dynamics of Joseph Smith's psychology and its impact on his beliefs and practices? It must be emphasized again that the analysis presented here about Joseph Smith's possible tendencies toward manic-depressive mental states is not intended as anything but an hypothesis. It is in no way intended to reduce the mystery–and the greatness–of Joseph Smith's accomplishments. Even if this hypothesis be true, the ultimate question remains not the *origin* of Smith's genius but the *fruits* of that genius.

To restate one of William James's observations, "If there were such a thing as inspiration from a higher realm, it might well be that the neurotic temperament would furnish the chief condition of the requisite receptivity."[31] It may be that only individuals whose inhibitions are bypassed by various forms of mania may be able to convince themselves and others that their insights emanate directly from God or other higher spiritual powers.

It must further be emphasized that individuals with manic-depressive tendencies can be extremely effective leaders, especially during times of crisis. One striking example is Oliver Cromwell, the great Puritan general and leader of England during the 1640s and 1650s, who never lost a battle and who dealt with a host of issues that would have destroyed any lesser person.[32] A related example, Abraham Lincoln, who was subject to recurrent depressive states (though probably not manic-depression), nevertheless showed extraordinary creativity in handling the most intractable crisis the United States has ever faced and has been recognized by both scholars and the general public as the greatest president this country has ever had.[33] And in the twentieth century, Winston Churchill, himself with the cyclothymic tendencies that ran throughout his distinguished lineage, led England to victory over the Nazis in World War II at a time when an individual with less manic drive might well have assumed that defeat was inevitable.[34]

Thus William James's insistence that the *fruits* of religious inspiration must be considered apart from the *sources* of such inspiration must be seriously considered. Even if cyclothymic or manic-depressive psychological states may arguably have provided much of the *occasion* for Joseph Smith's remarkable creativity, the validity of the *product* of that inspiration must be judged on its own merits. Nonbelievers no doubt will still continue to see Joseph Smith's creativity as a product of his own fertile mind, but devout Saints may equally well see that creativity as an emanation from the divine.[35]

IV

If this hypothesis about the impact of possible manic-depressive tendencies on Joseph Smith's complex religious creativity holds up under scrutiny, does it also suggest any new insights for understanding the creativity of other great foundational religious figures and the origins of new religious movements as well? Although a fuller investigation, both cross-culturally and cross-temporally, would be necessary to establish how frequently manic-depressive states may have influenced foundational religious figures, a convincing argument can be made that such figures have sometimes exhibited behavior that could be described as manic-depressive and that such a hypothesis may help explain otherwise puzzling aspects of their prophetic careers.

Among the individuals I have studied most intensively who exhibited behavior suggesting manic-depression are Ann Lee, founder of the Shaker movement, and John Humphrey Noyes, founder of the perfectionist community at Oneida, New York. The candid reminiscences of Ann Lee in the rare 1816 *Testimonies of the Life, Character, Revelations and Doctrines of Our Ever Blessed Mother Ann Lee, and the Elders with Her*, vividly describe how she was subject both to periods of extraordinary euphoria when she had visions of walking with Jesus Christ as her Lord and Lover and seeing glory after glory, as well as other visions in which she felt herself living literally in the uttermost depths of hell with those in unbearable suffering and torment.[36] As historian Clarke Garrett has suggested in a sophisticated reconstruction using contemporary evidence, Lee's untimely death at age forty-eight in 1784 may not only have been due to the physical and mental abuse she had suffered, but also to heavy drinking associated with severe depression during the last year of her life.[37]

The thoroughly documented case of John Humphrey Noyes is

even more suggestive of manic-depression. Indeed, historian Michael Barkun, who has worked extensively with manuscript materials relating to Noyes's early life, has argued that Noyes may provide almost a classic illustration of the manic-depressive syndrome.[38] Noyes's emotionally devastating three weeks in New York City in May 1834, for example, saw him swing from extraordinary euphoria and direct self-identification with Christ to the depths of depression in which he was unable to sleep, wandered the streets among down-and-outers and prostitutes at night, and consumed copious amounts of cayenne pepper and other stimulants to try to convince himself that he really existed.[39] Throughout Noyes's subsequent career, though he never faced such near-total collapse, he continued to experience wide mood swings. Whenever serious crises would develop in his Oneida Community, for example, he would go away, sometimes for months or years at a time, leaving responsibility for straightening out problems to trusted subordinates.[40]

In their insightful analysis in *Manic-Depressive Illness*, psychiatrists Frederick K. Goodwin and Kay Redfield Jamison discuss as illustrations four other important religious leaders who appear to have exhibited manic-depressive tendencies.[41] Most notable and well-documented of their cases is that of Martin Luther, the initiator of the Protestant Reformation and founder of the Lutheran movement. As Luther himself and his biographers such as Roland Bainton, Heiko A. Oberman, Erik Erikson, and H. G. Heile have shown,[42] he was subject at times to periods of the most profound depression, with even psychotic and suicidal components, going back to childhood. At other times, he experienced periods of exaltation and extraordinary energy, during which he showed an astonishing verbal and literary productivity.

In many ways similarly complex was George Fox, founder of the Religious Society of Friends, better-known as Quakers. Fox, like some other key Quaker leaders such as James Nayler, was subject to extreme mood swings with apparently psychopathological elements. William James, for instance, cites the entry in Fox's *Journal* when he describes feeling called to go to Litchfield in the middle of winter, take off his shoes, and walk through the town during market-day crying out, "Woe to the bloody city of Litchfield! Woe to the bloody city of Litchfield!" Yet Fox was an enormously capable and level-headed person at other times, and his organizational efforts were largely responsible for the Quakers being the only significant religious group originating during the period of the Puritan Revolution to survive to the present.[43]

Sabbatai Sevi, whose messianic claims convulsed much of the Jewish community of Europe, the Middle East, and North Africa during the seventeenth century, is another figure who illustrated classic manic-depressive behavior, with sharp alternation between days of anguish and ecstasy. Gerschom Scholem's magisterial study of Sevi's life and impact leaves no doubt about his wide mood swings and the tremendous emotional impact of the "frenzied ecstasy" that his associate Nathan of Gaza helped channel into a powerful millenarian movement.[44]

Emmanuel Swedenborg, the eighteenth-century Swedish scientist, philosopher, and mystic whose ideas profoundly influenced a variety of movements from nineteenth-century spiritualism to more recent new age and occult groups, also exhibited manic behavior and wide mood swings after his mid-fifties. He began having a series of dreams, ecstatic visions, and trances that led him to spend the last third of his life producing a prolific series of writings, including *Heaven and Hell, from Things Heard and Seen.*[45]

Beyond such cases, one cannot help speculating that the most influential of all religious founding figures, Jesus of Nazareth, called the Christ by his followers, may have been subject to manic-depressive tendencies. Of course, the primary records are so limited and the accretions of interpretation so great that almost nothing can be stated with historical certainty about Jesus except that he lived and had a profound impact on those who knew him best. Nevertheless, if one could look freshly at the reported events of Passion Week, for example, one might at least wonder whether such activities may not suggest manic-depressive behavior. Jesus' actions riding into Jerusalem on a donkey while ecstatic followers spread their garments and leafy branches in front of him on the road and shouted Hosanna, or scourging the money changers from the temple, when juxtaposed with Jesus' profound depression shortly before his final arrest when he felt that his soul was "very sorrowful, even unto death" (Mark 14:34), "and being in agony ... his sweat became like great drops of blood falling on the ground" (Luke 22:44), could raise the question of whether something more than normal mood swings may have been present in Jesus' experience as well.[46]

Irrespective of whether any particular foundational religious figure may or may not have experienced cyclothymic or manic-depressive states, the question nevertheless remains how and why such states may contribute to great creativity, especially religious creativity. Let us touch briefly on the question of the relationship between manic-depression and artistic creativity, before returning to the question of its role in religious prophetic leadership. In a recent investigation of the links between artistic creation and mood disorders, for example, psychiatrist Kay Redfield Jamison found that in forty-two award-winning playwrights, poets, and novelists, rates of treatment for emotional illness (mainly depression or manic-depression) were vastly more common than one would expect in the general population. For example, whereas only 5 percent of the general population had ever been treated for a major depression, Jamison found that 13 percent of the novelists, 28 percent of the poets, 38 percent of the artists, and 50 percent of the playwrights she interviewed in depth had undergone such treatment.[47] Why should this be the case?

At a session on the creative mind at the annual meeting of the American Psychiatric Association in San Francisco in 1989, "panelists argued that at the heart of artistic expression lies the process of change: changes in mood, in perception, in energy levels. 'The creative process involves a cycle of disruption and re-integration in response to stress,' said Frederick J. Flach. ... If it is true that the cycle occurs in all of us ... it is also true that some people–artists–undergo it more frequently. In some of them, the process of re-integration after disruption fails. 'Mental illness,' suggested Dr. Flach, 'is a failure in the regulation of this process.'"[48]

Even more than in other types of artistic creativity, religious creativity shows what a fine line separates insanity and social disorganization from ecstasy and the highest visionary reorganization of the individual and society. The prophet, as Kenelm Burridge suggests, is both a dangerous and a necessary person, an adventurer who puts himself at risk in order to try more fundamentally than the average person to make sense of his confusing world. As Burridge notes: "It is not appropriate to think of a prophet as reduced in size to a schizophrene or a paranoid, someone mentally sick. In relation to those to whom he speaks a prophet is necessarily corrupted by his wider experience. He is an 'outsider,' an odd one, extraordinary. Nevertheless, he specifically attempts to initiate, both in himself as well as in others, a process of moral regeneration."[49]

The result in many cases is only partially successful. Perhaps one reason that prophets so often face martyrdom or early death is that they have attempted to take on too much. Like Moses, they may be able to lead their followers to the edge of the promised land yet be unable to enter it themselves. Just as for every positive genetic mutation there are hundreds that are destructive, so too, I would argue, for every successful prophet there are hundreds of other would-be prophets who fail to realize their promise.[50] And even "successful" prophets often fall short of their ideals. Although prophets' experiences are deeper and richer than those of their followers, prophets, even the greatest of prophets, are not omniscient. Inevitably they are striving toward goals that to some extent can never be fully achieved.[51]

*NOTES*

1. The edition cited here is William James, *The Varieties of Religious Experience: A Study in Human Nature* (New York: New American Library, 1958). I am grateful to Syracuse University Press for permission to use some material in this article that first appeared in my book *Women, Family, and Utopia: Communal Experiments of the Shakers, the Oneida Community, and the Mormons* (copyright 1991 by Syracuse University Press).

2. For an early call to consider Joseph Smith in all his complexity, see Jan Shipps, "The Prophet Puzzle: Suggestions Leading Toward a More Comprehensive Interpretation of Joseph Smith," *Journal of Mormon History* 1 (1974): 3-20. Especially revealing recent treatments are Gary James Bergera's articles "Joseph Smith and the Hazards of Charismatic Leadership," *John Whitmer Historical Association Journal* 6 (1986): 33-42, and "Toward 'Psychologically Informed' Mormon History and Biography," *Sunstone* 16 (Dec. 1991): 27-31. For some of the classic psychological reductionist accounts, see Isaac Woodbridge Riley, *The Founder of Mormonism: A Psychological Study of Joseph Smith, Jr.* (New York: Dodd, Mead, 1902); Bernard De Voto, "The Centennial of Mormonism," *American Mercury* 19 (Jan. 1930): 1-13; Fawn M. Brodie, *No Man Knows My History: The Life of Joseph Smith, the Mormon Prophet*, 2d. ed. rev. and enl. (New York: Alfred A. Knopf, 1972), 418-21; and Louis J. Kern, *An Ordered Love: Sex Roles and Sexuality in Victorian Utopias–the Shakers, the Mormons, and the Oneida Community* (Chapel Hill: University of North Carolina Press, 1981),

137-43. Marvin Hill, "Secular or Sectarian History? A Critique of *No Man Knows My History*," *Church History* 33 (Mar. 1974): 78-96, analyzes the tendency toward psychological reductionism that is present in her revised edition. For treatments of Smith as a paragon who could do no wrong, see almost any of the works published by official Mormon publishers such as Deseret Book Company.

3. Kenelm Burridge, *New Heaven, New Earth: A Study of Millenarian Activities* (New York: Schocken, 1969), 162. For a compelling example of Burridge's analysis of a single cult leader, see his *Mambu: A Study of Melanesian Cargo Movements and Their Social and Ideological Backgrounds* (New York: Harper & Row, 1970).

4. Anthony F. C. Wallace, "Revitalization Movements," *American Anthropologist* 38 (Apr. 1956): 264-81. For the work that most directly influenced Wallace's formulation of his "revitalization movement" theory, see his *The Death and Rebirth of the Seneca* (New York: Vintage, 1972). A revealing attempt to use Wallace's theory to deal with the dynamics of American religious history is William G. McLoughlin, *Revivals, Awakenings, and Reform* (Chicago: University of Chicago Press, 1978).

5. Wallace, "Revitalization Movements," 270-71.

6. For a summary of some of the major issues involved with Joseph Smith's "first vision" experience and a bibliographic essay on major studies, see my "First Visions: Personal Observations on Joseph Smith's Religious Experience," *Sunstone* 8 (Sept.-Oct. 1983): 39-43. More recent studies such as Richard L. Bushman, *Joseph Smith and the Beginnings of Mormonism* (Urbana: University of Illinois Press, 1984), have expanded our understanding of the social context of Smith's religious concerns but have added little to our understanding of the psychological dynamics of his religious experiences. For a preliminary listing of studies that could be used to reconstruct the visionary components of later products of Smith's religious creativity such as the Book of Mormon, see my *Religion and Sexuality: The Shakers, the Mormons, and the Oneida Community* (Urbana: University of Illinois Press, 1984), 294-97; and Scott C. Dunn, "Spirit Writing: Another Look at the Book of Mormon," *Sunstone* 10 (June 1985): 16-26.

7. James, *Varieties of Religious Experience*, 24.

8. Ibid., 36.

9. Ibid., 33. Brigham Young made a similar point in a sermon on 9 November 1856, when he reported how, shortly after he became attracted to Mormonism, he responded to a man who attacked Joseph Smith's character at every conceivable point. Young told the man that he had never seen Smith and did not know his personal character, but that the doctrine was what mattered. "He may get drunk every day of his life, sleep with his neighbor's wife every night, run horses and gamble, I do not care anything about that, for I never embrace any man in my faith. But the doctrine he has produced

will save you and me, and the whole world; and if you can find fault with that, find it" (*Journal of Discourses*, 26 vols. [Liverpool, Eng.: LDS Bookseller's Depot, 1855-86], 9: 77-78).

10. James, *Varieties of Religious Experience*, 37. James's acute sensitivity to the implications of abnormal psychology for profound religious experience may have been due, in part, to the fact that he had also experienced many of the extraordinary states about which he wrote. See Harvey Mindess, *Makers of Psychology: The Personal Factor* (New York: Human Sciences Press, 1988), 35-44.

11. For an account of how my interests in this area developed, see "A Personal Odyssey: My Encounter with Mormon History," *Dialogue: A Journal of Mormon Thought* 16 (Autumn 1983): 87-98. My major findings are reported in *Religion and Sexuality* and *Women, Family, and Utopia*.

12. On this point, see Foster, "Personal Odyssey," esp. 96-97. A rather apologetic example of how Joseph Smith's experiences could be analyzed using the perspectives of Freud, Jung, Adler, Ego Psychology, Erik Erikson, and so forth, is T. L. Brink, "Joseph Smith: The Verdict of Depth Psychology," *Journal of Mormon History* 3 (1976): 73-83. More revealing of the substantial contribution that different analytical approaches can offer in understanding one complex personality is Mindess, *Makers of Psychology*, 147-68.

13. See Foster, *Religion and Sexuality*, 125-46, and *Women, Family, and Utopia*, 124-33.

14. Letter of 15 June 1853, printed in *Zion's Harbinger and Baneemy's Organ* 3 (7 July 1853): 52-54. Marks reaffirmed this statement in a letter dated 23 October 1859 that appeared in the first issue of the *True Latter-Day-Saint's Herald* 1 (Jan. 1860): 22-23, and in a letter to Hyrum Faulk and Josiah Butterfield on 1 October 1865, in the archives of the Reorganized Church of Jesus Christ of Latter Day Saints, Independence, Missouri (hereafter RLDS archives).

15. Council of the Twelve Minutes, Book A, 6 Apr. 1865-12 Apr. 1889, RLDS archives, as quoted in Linda King Newell and Valeen Tippetts Avery, *Mormon Enigma: Emma Hale Smith–Prophet's Wife, "Elect Lady," Polygamy's Foe* (Garden City, NY: Doubleday, 1984), 179.

16. Brigham Young address, 8 Oct. 1866, Brigham Young papers, LDS archives, as quoted in Newell and Avery, *Mormon Enigma*, 179. In support of the idea that Joseph Smith may have seriously considered ending polygamy in Nauvoo, it may be significant that he apparently did not take additional plural wives himself after November 1843. Newell and Avery, *Mormon Enigma*, 179.

17. For the most important accounts of this process, see Charles E. Shook, *The True Origin of Mormon Polygamy* (Cincinnati: Standard, 1914); Newell and Avery, *Mormon Enigma*; Foster, *Religion and Sexuality* and *Women, Family, and Utopia*; Danel Bachman, "A Study of the Mormon Practice of Plural Marriage before the Death of Joseph Smith," M.A. thesis, Purdue University, 1975;

Richard S. Van Wagoner, *Mormon Polygamy: A History* (Salt Lake City: Signature, 1976); and Brodie, *No Man Knows My History*. Impressively thorough documentation of the polygamous households in Nauvoo between 1841 and Joseph Smith's death is presented in George D. Smith, "Nauvoo Roots of Mormon Polygamy, 1841-46: A Preliminary Demographic Report," *Dialogue: A Journal of Mormon Thought* 27 (Spring 1994): 1-72.

18. In a profound reflection based on his extensive study of Joseph Smith and his role in Mormon Nauvoo, Robert Bruce Flanders explores this possibility in his "Dream and Nightmare: Nauvoo Revisited," in F. Mark McKiernan, Alma R. Blair, and Paul M. Edwards, eds., *The Restoration Movement: Essays in Mormon History* (Lawrence, KS: Coronado, 1973), 141-66. On page 152, for example, Flanders speculates that "in 1844, Smith was losing control of many of his affairs, and perhaps of himself."

19. Personal conversation with R. Jess Groesbeck in May 1988 immediately following Valeen Tippetts Avery's Mormon History Association Presidential Address, which was subsequently published as "Irreconcilable Differences: David H. Smith's Relationship with the Muse of Mormon History," *Journal of Mormon History* 15 (1989): 3-13. For Groesbeck's published speculations, see his "The Smiths and Their Dreams and Visions: A Psycho-Historical Study of the First Mormon Family," *Sunstone* 12 (Mar. 1988): 22-29. I am grateful to Dr. Groesbeck for sharing with me other unpublished materials he has written about Joseph Smith's psychology.

20. For discussions of David Hyrum Smith's case, see Valeen Tippetts Avery, *From Mission to Madness: Last Son of the Mormon Prophet* (Urbana: University of Illinois Press, 1998); Avery, "Irreconcilable Differences"; and Newell and Avery, *Mormon Enigma*, 288-95. Of the six other male descendants diagnosed as having mental disorders, one committed suicide at about age forty-five after showing signs of manic-depression, and another, who had been diagnosed as schizophrenic (dementia paradoxia), also committed suicide. Documents in my possession from a living associate of the Smith family. Name withheld by request. On 22 May 1993 in Lamoni, Iowa, I corroborated examples of manic-depression in the family with a Joseph Smith, Jr., descendant.

21. Harold I. Kaplan and Benjamin J. Sadock, *Comprehensive Textbook of Psychiatry/IV*, 4th ed. (Baltimore: Williams & Wilkins, 1985), 761.

22. It is also important to note that some individuals apparently are subject only to depressive states. Treatment of such individuals is handled differently from treatment of those who experience manic-depressive states.

23. For a recent popular treatment of the subject that is also utilized here, see Patty Duke and Gloria Hochman, *A Brilliant Madness: Living with Manic-Depressive Illness* (New York: Bantam, 1992). The presentation in the following paragraphs is highly compressed. Anyone interested in understanding the full dimensions of manic-depressive experience should closely consult Goodwin

and Jamison's fascinating 938-page analysis. To an extent rare in medical texts, it conveys the personal dimension of the manic-depressive spectrum, with both its positive and negative elements.

24. Even with living individuals, diagnosis of manic-depression is difficult because the symptoms can mimic other types of mental disorder. Reliable diagnosis of someone no longer living is even more difficult, particularly if the symptoms are mild. If Joseph Smith suffered relatively mild forms of manic-depression, knowing whether his behavior represented normal volatility of mood or possible illness would be difficult to determine with any degree of conclusiveness. I have, nevertheless, been encouraged to pursue the manic-depressive hypothesis by positive reactions from both Mormon and non-Mormon scholars. For example, Kay Redfield Jamison, in a letter to me on 7 May 1992, responded to the preliminary version of my argument in *Women, Family, and Utopia*, 161-66, by saying: "[Y]ou make a very convincing case. It has always seemed that Joseph Smith would be a likely candidate."

25. For discussions of this period of Joseph Smith's life, see Joseph Smith, Jr., *History of the Church of Jesus Christ of Latter-day Saints: Period I*, ed. Brigham H. Roberts, 6 vols., 2d ed. rev. (Salt Lake City: Deseret Book Co., 1948), vols. 4 and 5; Brigham H. Roberts, *A Comprehensive History of the Church of Jesus Christ of Latter-day Saints: Century I*, 6 vols., (Salt Lake City: Deseret News Press, 1930), vol. 2; Brodie, *No Man Knows My History*; Donna Hill, *Joseph Smith: The First Mormon* (Garden City, NY: Doubleday, 1977); Robert Bruce Flanders, *Nauvoo: Kingdom on the Mississippi* (Urbana: University of Illinois Press, 1965); Klaus J. Hansen, *Quest for Empire: The Political Kingdom of God and the Council of Fifty in Mormon History* (East Lansing: Michigan State University Press, 1967); Newell and Avery, *Mormon Enigma*; Foster, *Religion and Sexuality*; and Bachman, "Plural Marriage."

26. Sermon on 14 May 1843, as reported in Joseph Smith, Jr., *History of the Church* 5:389.

27. Bachman, "Plural Marriage," 179, based on Helen Mar Whitney, "Scenes in Nauvoo," *Woman's Exponent* 10 (15 Aug. 1881): 42.

28. Although this was the emphasis in the original edition of *No Man Knows My History*, Brodie's "Supplement" to the second, revised and enlarged edition in 1971, pages 405-25, increasingly emphasizes theories of psychological disorder in trying to explain the Mormon prophet's behavior.

29. Mary Rollins Lightner, Remarks at Brigham Young University, 5, 14 Apr. 1905.

30. *Latter-day Saints' Millennial Star* 5 (Nov. 1844): 93. See the letter of George A. Smith to Joseph Smith III, 9 Oct. 1869, as reproduced in Raymond T. Bailey, "Emma Hale: Wife of the Prophet Joseph Smith," M.A. thesis, Brigham Young University, 1952, 84.

31. James, *Varieties of Religious Experience*, 37.

32. Both Robert S. Paul, *The Lord Protector: Religion and Politics in the Life*

*of Oliver Cromwell* (Grand Rapids, MI: Eerdmans, 1964), and Christopher Hill, *God's Englishman: Oliver Cromwell and the English Revolution* (New York: Harper, 1972), convincingly document Cromwell's manic-depressive tendencies. Cromwell's manic-depressive behavior is also discussed in H. Belloc, *Cromwell* (London: Cassell, 1934); Antonia Fraser, *Cromwell: The Lord Protector* (New York: Knopf, 1973); and W. D. Henry, "The Personality of Oliver Cromwell," *Practitioner* 215 (1975): 102-10.

33. All the standard biographies of Lincoln discuss his depressive tendencies and the problems they caused for those who had to deal with him. See especially James G. Randall, *Lincoln the President: Springfield to Gettysburg* (New York: Dodd, Mead, 1945); R. W. Hudgins, "Mental Health of Political Candidates: Notes on Abraham Lincoln," *American Journal of Psychiatry* 130 (1973): 110; and Stephen B. Oates, *With Malice Toward None: The Life of Abraham Lincoln* (New York: New American Library, 1977). Goodwin and Jamison, *Manic-Depressive Illness*, 358, note that although Ronald R. Fieve, *Moodswing: The Third Revolution in Psychiatry* (New York: William Morrow, 1975), describes Lincoln as a "mild bipolar manic-depressive," "the evidence for hypomania is far less clear-cut than for his serious depressions."

34. For discussions of Churchill's sharp alternation between periods of depression and high energy, tremendous drive, and sometimes questionable judgment, see Martin Gilbert, *Churchill: A Life* (New York: Henry Holt, 1991); John Pearson, *The Private Lives of Winston Churchill* (New York: Touchstone, 1991); A. Storr, *Churchill's Black Dog, Kafka's Mice, and Other Phenomena of the Human Mind* (New York: Grove Press, 1988); and Lord C. M. W. Moran, *Winston Churchill: The Struggle for Survival, 1940-1965: Taken from the Diaries of Lord Moran* (Boston: Houghton, Mifflin, 1966).

35. Of course, any effort to use psychological theories to understand major religious figures inevitably will be dismissed as "reductionistic" by devout believers. But the manic-depressive hypothesis appears to me to be less reductionistic than many other psychological approaches because it does not imply any necessary judgment about the quality of the product of the experience. Furthermore, as Anthony F. C. Wallace noted to me in a letter of 4 August 1992 after reading an earlier draft of this article, "One advantage of the [manic-depressive] hypothesis is that it answers, to some degree at least, the tricky question of timing. Why did the prophet have his revelation just when he did rather than months before or later? In a sense the choice of date becomes random, a function of the cyclical mental evolution of the prophet's mood."

36. *Testimonies of the Life, Character, Revelations, and Doctrines of Our Ever Blessed Mother Ann Lee, and the Elders with Her* (Hancock, MA: J. Talcott & J. Teming, Junrs., 1816). Other primary sources also make this point clearly. For secondary starting points, that suggest these issues, see Ann White and Leila S. Taylor, *Shakerism: Its Meaning and Message* (Columbus, OH: Fred. J. Heer,

1904), and Edward Deming Andrews, *The People Called Shakers: A Search for the Perfect Society*, new enl. ed. (New York: Dover, 1963).

37. Clarke Garrett, *Spirit Possession and Popular Religion: From the Camisards to the Shakers* (Baltimore: Johns Hopkins University Press, 1987), 195-213.

38. Barkun indicated to me that after reading one of his papers on Noyes, a psychiatrist commented to him that Noyes's experiences provided almost a classic example of the manic-depressive syndrome. See Michael Barkun, "'The Wind Sweeping Over the Country': John Humphrey Noyes and the Rise of Millerism," in Ronald L. Numbers and Jonathan M. Butler, eds., *The Disappointed: Millerism and Millenarianism in the Nineteenth Century* (Bloomington: University of Indiana Press, 1987), 153-72; and "The Visionary Experiences of John Humphrey Noyes," *Psychohistory Review* 16 (Spring 1988): 313-34.

39. John Humphrey Noyes's graphic description of the episode was published in his *Confessions of John H. Noyes. Part I: Confession of Religious Experience, Including a History of Modern Perfectionism* (Oneida Reserve, NY: Leonard, 1849). For other primary evidence relating to his extremes of emotion, see the edited collections by George Wallingford Noyes, *Religious Experience of John Humphrey Noyes, Founder of the Oneida Community* (New York: Macmillan, 1923), and *John Humphrey Noyes: The Putney Community* (Oneida, NY: By the Author, 1931). The most relevant secondary studies of Noyes are Robert Allerton Parker, *A Yankee Saint: John Humphrey Noyes and the Oneida Community* (New York: G. P. Putnam's Sons, 1935), and Robert David Thomas, *The Man Who Would Be Perfect: John Humphrey Noyes and the Utopian Impulse* (Philadelphia: University of Pennsylvania Press, 1977).

40. One of the reasons for Noyes's success in staying in control of the Oneida Community throughout virtually its entire existence was his willingness to step aside during periods of crisis until his loyal associates were able to resolve major problems by appealing to his authority and principles in his absence. If such flexibility were more common among charismatic figures, perhaps fewer of them would be killed or deposed.

41. Goodwin and Jamison, *Manic-Depressive Illness*, 360-63.

42. Roland H. Bainton, *Here I Stand: A Life of Martin Luther* (New York: New American Library, orig. ed. 1950); Heiko A. Oberman, *Luther: Between God and the Devil*, trans. Eileen Walliser-Schwarzbart (New York: Image, 1992); Erik Erikson, *Young Man Luther: A Study in Psychoanalysis and History* (New York: Norton, 1962); and H. G. Haile, *Luther: An Experiment in Biography* (Princeton: Princeton University Press, 1980).

43. James, *Varieties of Religious Experience*, 25-26. For similar examples, see *The Journal of George Fox*, rev. ed. by John L. Nickalls (London: Religious Society of Friends, 1975). Tendencies toward emotional excess among early Quakers are thoroughly documented in standard scholarly treatments of the movement, including William C. Braithwaite, *The Beginnings of Quakerism*, 2d ed. rev. by Henry J. Cadbury (York, England: William Sessions Limited, 1970),

and John Punchon, *Portrait in Grey: A Short History of the Quakers* (London: Quaker Home Service, 1984).

44. Gerschom Scholem, *Sabbatai Sevi: The Mystical Messiah*, trans. R. J. Zwi Wesblowsky (Princeton: Princeton University Press, 1973). On page 126 Scholem describes Sevi's symptoms, "with almost absolute certainty," as "manic-depressive."

45. Goodwin and Jamison, *Manic-Depressive Illness*, 362-63, present evidence that Swedenborg's major visionary experience at age fifty-six was associated with an attack of acute mania. For vivid descriptions of Swedenborg's role as a seer and his subsequent impact, see Slater Brown, *The Heyday of Spiritualism* (New York: Pocket Books, 1972); J. Stillson Judah, *The History and Philosophy of the Metaphysical Movements in America* (Philadelphia: Westminster Press, 1967); and Colin Wilson, *The Occult* (New York: Vintage Books, 1973).

46. Many scholars have been unwilling to deal frankly with early Christianity using the same criteria they apply to the analysis of other religious movements. Jesus, in particular, is always treated as *sui generis*. If Jesus and some other figure are reported to have done something descriptively similar, the framework used for analysis often is quite different.

A case in point relates to the Quaker James Nayler. Scholars readily agree that psychological excess characterized his behavior on 24 October 1656 when he rode into Bristol while followers sang and chanted, "Holy, holy, holy, Lord God of Israel," and spread their garments before him. Nayler, one of the most eloquent of the early Quaker leaders, was punished for his "blasphemy" by brutal whipping, imprisonment, and having his tongue bored through with a red-hot iron before saying, shortly prior to his death: "There is a spirit which I feel, which delights to do no evil nor to revenge any wrong, but delights to endure all things in hope to enjoy its own in the end." For a detailed analysis of this episode, see the chapter on "Nayler's Fall" in Braithwaite, *Beginnings of Quakerism*, 241-78.

If orthodox Christianity asserts that Jesus must be viewed as both "wholly man" and "wholly God," then perhaps scholars should at least consider whether the full complexity of human psychological dynamics, with both its heights and depths, may not have characterized his life as well.

47. *Chronicle of Higher Education*, 21 June 1989, A2, A6, based on Kay Redfield Jamison, "Mood Disorders and Patterns of Creativity in British Writers and Artists," *Psychiatry* 52 (May 1989): 125-34. Also see Goodwin and Jamison, *Manic-Depressive Illness*, 332-56, and Kay Redfield Jamison, *Touched with Fire: Manic Depressive Illness and the Artistic Temperament* (New York: Free Press, 1993). Ibid., 240-60, raises the question whether treatment of manic-depressive disorders may inhibit some forms of great creativity. As with almost every aspect of manic-depressive illness, there are no simple answers. Also see Kay R. Jamison, et al., "Clouds and Silver Linings: Positive Experiences

Associated with Primary Affective Disorders," *American Journal of Psychiatry* 137 (Feb. 1980): 198-202.

48. *Chronicle of Higher Education*, 21 June 1989, A6.

49. Burridge, *New Heaven, New Earth*, 162.

50. A recent analysis, for example, argues that many of the post-World War II problems of the Bruderhof religious movement were due to the depressive tendencies of Heine Arnold, who led the group from 1957 to 1982. See Julius Rubin's *The Other Side of Joy: Religious Melancholy Among the Bruderhof* (New York: Oxford University Press, 1998), and his larger study, *Religious Melancholy and Protestant Experience in America* (New York: Oxford University Press, 1994).

51. This point, which is central to my analysis of religious leadership, is also developed in my article "James J. Strang: The Prophet Who Failed," *Church History* 50 (June 1981): 182-192, and in *Religion and Sexuality*, 245-47.

# 11. Toward an Introduction to a Psychobiography of Joseph Smith

*Robert D. Anderson*

## BASIC ASSUMPTIONS

WERE A MORMON PSYCHOTHERAPIST TO ATTEMPT A PSYCHOBIOGRAPHY of Joseph Smith, I believe the first decision should be identifying his or her theological assumptions. These assumptions not only determine audience, but in turn are determined by whether the author takes a professional position or writes as a believing member of the LDS church. The writer's stance necessarily leads to certain conclusions and eliminates others.

Nowhere is this more true than in the area of spiritual claims. An extreme example of this demonstrates the changing assumptions of our own culture. During the witch-craze of Western Europe from about 1350 to 1650 C.E. thousands of people, mostly women, were condemned to death for confessing under torture to actions now considered impossible. These included flying through the air on forked sticks or animals, meeting in "covens" during "Sabbats" where they sacrificed infants, brewed storms, created plagues, illnesses, impotency, or infertility, and engaged in sexual relations with demons, called incubus (male) and succubus (female).

Some 350 years after these events, historian Joseph Hansen

wrote a naturalistic approach to the witch-craze. He believed confessions were the result of coercion, usually torture, and witch/demonic interactions did not occur. Two years later Catholic Jesuit scholar Robert Schwickerath responded to Hansen's work, commenting that the "one-sided *a priori* treatment of the [sixteenth-century Catholic] scholastics was fatal; and it would be well if the book were studied by Professors of Philosophy and Theology." He added quotes by other Catholic leaders: "[W]e now know how much is purely natural which even the most enlightened men of their age formerly account supernatural." Schwickerath acknowledged that "belief in incubus and succubus which played a most important part in the witch trials, are now rejected ... by the best Catholic theologians." Nevertheless, he stated that Hansen's book was "based on a false suppostion in denying the existence of evil spirits, and consequently leads to wrong conclusions."[1]

What credence, in a psychobiographical study of a Mormon–in this case, the first Mormon–concerning the supernatural should be allowed? Let us move along a sliding scale, from totally supernatural to totally natural explanations. In the process, my own position will become clear.

To many believing Mormons, virtually all that Joseph Smith did was a result of commandments from God. This was the position of the LDS church during its first 100 years, and continues to surface in many church manuals and sermons. As recently as 1976 Mormon apostle Ezra Taft Benson criticized two Mormon historians for suggesting that envirornmental factors–such as the temperance movement of the 1830s–may partly explain the background of Joseph Smith's 1833 health-related revelation on the Word of Wisdom.[2] According to this view, external secular influences should be largely discarded. Smith thus is not so much a man of his time, nor a result of his own psychology, but a product of the influence of the Holy Ghost. Outside the Mormon church, Jesuit scholar H. Becher takes basically the same position in his biography of the sixteenth-century founder of his priesthood order, *Ignatius of Loyola*[3]: "Even a lack of psychological analysis may be admissible as long as one sees and correctly portrays the workings of God in the Saint."

In this position, there is virtually nothing important about Joseph Smith to understand psychologically, and no significant psychobiography can be attempted. Such histories of Smith simply reiterate his story, along with experiences from his mother, other acquaintances, friends, and enemies, without close scrutiny or analysis. They continue to be found in church books and manuals. Most non-Mormon historians consider them of limited value at best.[4]

The next step along this continuum is acknowledging Joseph Smith's statement that "a prophet is a prophet only when he is acting as such."[5] Here Smith's supernatural acts of translation and revelation are still largely exempt from psychological and environmental inquiry, but in his daily life he can be understood as a man of the nineteenth-century American frontier as well as of some limited psychological forces. This is the position of most present-day academic Mormon historians, who expect that psychological forces result in a view of Smith as mostly healthy and his underlying motivations as fundamentally charitable.

Yet comments here by most Mormon historians seem timid. In the words of one writer: "there has been little effort to uncover the background modes of thought, the controlling categories and assumptions, of Joseph Smith himself."[6] Even if one suspects that some aspects of Smith's daily life contained psychological conflict, there is immediate challenge. Mormon Jungian psychoanalyst C. Jess Groesbeck has proposed Smith may have had an unresolved "split" in his personality, an internal conflict between two contending systems of morality: "[Joseph Smith] basically could not unite these two aspects of himself[:] ... that side which believed in a single relationship to his wife ... versus that side that believed in multiple plural relationships to other women. ... In my opinion Joseph sensed he was not going to be able to heal the split in his life ... [H]ad Joseph lived his life longer, he might have united the opposites ... and the split ... within him." Groesbeck was soon countered by another Mormon psychiatrist: "There is great danger in interpreting manifest dream content without access to the latent dream material. There is even greater danger in interpreting the dreams of a prophet. ... Prophets dream dreams of things past, present, and future." Thus even day-to-day mundane mental functions of a prophet escape psychological evaluation.[7]

If Smith's motives have been little examined, his revelations remain completely exempt from psychological interpretation. This approach contains two essential elements: (1) the acts of a prophet–

when "acting as such"–contain no psychological influence, (2) and God does not work through the psyche of a prophet but is external to it. Such a man is little more than a tool or machine worked by God. In fact, this is how Smith's translation of the Book of Mormon has been described.[8]

The next move toward a secular approach is controversial and calls for closer examination. At this level God might work through the psyche of a saint or prophet, whose conflicts appear not only in his ordinary living but constitute an important element in his visions and spiritual calling. Here the essential ingredient is not only acknowledging psychological forces–healthy or pathological–but their fusion with spiritual forces that use these psychological struggles to express the will of God.

I know of no published work in orthodox Mormonism that represents such a view, but at least two authors imply such in their writings about the Book of Mormon. One believes that the core of the book is authentic history but that Smith added elements from his own life and time to it.[9] The other believes there is no historical basis for the book but nonetheless subscribes to its spiritual value,[10] a position also held by some members of the Reorganized Church of Jesus Christ of Latter Day Saints.[11] Aside from this, Smith's revelations remain exempt from psychological or environmental influence. Outside the Mormon church, this fused approach is best represented by the work of Jesuit psychoanalyst William W. Meissner on the life of Ignatius of Loyola.[12] This, I propose, is the next step for Mormon psychohistorians.

All of the above approaches assume that God, supernatural forces, and spiritual experiences exist, but in the last approach they are not of interest to the psychobiographer. In the words of Meissner: "If the theologian allows that Ignatius was the recipient of great mystical graces and that the miraculous course of his inspired saintly career was the work of God's grace guiding and inspiring him at every step of the way, on this subject the psychoanalyst can say neither yea or nay. The interpretation lies beyond the scope of his methodology and theory. The psychoanalyst is concerned with only those aspects of his subject that reflect basically human motivation and the connections of psychic meaning–whether or not the patterns of behavior have religious or spiritual meaning. ... His method and his perspective do not include the theological nor the spiritual. If he is wise he will leave those considerations to theologians and spiritual writers. The psychoanalyst is in no position to deny or exclude any actions, effects, or purposes of God. His is simply not interested in them since his approach has nothing to say about them."[13]

There is considerable difference between assuming God and the supernatural while ignoring them and refusing either to assume or deny such sources for visionary, prophetic, inspired translations, statements, and acts. The existence of God lies not only beyond the psychoanalyst's interest but, as a scientist, beyond his or her knowledge. This does not deny the possibility; it simply insists that from a position of science and history, miracles have not been established as fact and cannot be assumed. I am among the first to acknowledge Meissner's contributions which, while scientific, are not science, as well as those of historians writing as believing Mormons or Christians who, while enlightening, do not write academic history.

One can acknowledge that the scientist or historian—or anyone, for that matter—may miss vital elements by refusing to acknowledge the spiritual. Perhaps such subjective experiences will forever be outside scientific replication, and science and history may forever miss ultimate causality. Nevertheless, as a psychiatrist within the field of medicine, I have only one possible response when such supernatural claims are admitted for consideration: I must respond by saying that I have no psychiatric experience mixed with collective knowledge in the professional literature to evaluate such happenings, including the effect of such phenomena on personality. I do not deny the possibility, nor do I deny my interest. I simply insist that supernatural experiences lie beyond scientific knowledge, and from a position of science they cannot be assumed. At the same time, if I as a person of science wished to write as a religious believer, I would have an obligation to inform my audience that I am stepping outside my professional role and to provide for them the suppositions with which I begin—or am attempting to support—that color my work.

If I maintain my position as scientist, my approach has two other consequences probably even less appealing to believers. First, it allows that all religious belief and experience may be naturalistic and therefore subject to unrestrained psychological examination. In the case of St. Ignatius, instead of excluding religious and theological considerations from scrutiny, the psychobiographer asks, "Can his visions and religious life be explained by natural means?" If we attempted a psychobiography of Joseph Smith, we would be expected to do the same. Second, such a consideration may ask if claims of obedience to God are being used not only to excuse but justify behavior no matter how flagrant. Belief in supernatural influences can become an escape from possibilities that are otherwise difficult. This same consideration applies to others, such as Ignatius. But even if one believes that the visions, spiritual and mystical experiences–as well as leadership qualities–of Ignatius resulted only from natural abilities, childhood trauma, and psychopathological responses to adult stress, in the eyes of Catholics he is still admirable. His simple life was characterized by vows of chastity and poverty. Many Mormons, on the other hand, would probably believe that the supernatural claims of Joseph Smith must be preserved at all costs. Otherwise, what are we to do, for example, with Smith's polygamy, including his attempts to marry pubsecent girls, as well as his sexual activities with these girls and with already-married women?[14] Eliminate the supernatural and we are left with what appears to be emotional rape. Perhaps this is why, despite the twenty-year-old challenge by non-Mormon historian Jan Shipps to find a solution to "The Prophet Puzzle,"[15] relatively nothing has been done.

We are now at the center of a growing conflict, and the literature here is massive. Some Mormons insist that all historical accounts are subjective in the sense of being interpretations only; so a believer's interpretation is as valid as a non-believer's, both representing interpretations based on mutually incompatible but non-verifiable premises. But some historical issues are testable facts not subject to interpretation. To believe contrary to the evidence that something in the past happened the way that tradition says it happened "is not a matter of justified subjectivity but simply of incoherent commitment to the irrational."[16]

Repeatedly non-believing historians have debated this position with devout historians.[17] Neither denying nor assuming spiritual experience, they must of necessity exclude the hand of God in events: "The reason for this aspect of academic history is both clear and persuasive. What sense data exist to reveal God's hand? If such data existed, whose God would it reveal? Because God is not sensible, data dealing with him is nonsense and speculative. Were historians to admit such nonsense data, they would lose much of their shared universe of discourse which allows them to evaluate theories. Personal, inspired speculation with no data would become as valid as hard documents, and chaos would replace orderly criticism. ... [A]cademic history, like science, has limited its universe of discourse to sense data. God and his action, in history, being non-sensible, therefore, do not fall within the bounds of that universe of discourse. ... [B]ehind this limitation of subject matter was an attempt to facilitate communication among historians. ... Were historians to accept revelations and other metaphysical data, communication would be greatly hindered because individuals from different religious traditions could not agree on which revelations were to be accepted or rejected. ... Should [the believer] seek evidence of God's action in history, let him turn to his faith, for academic history can never provide proof for something which its methodology excludes."[18] And again some refuse to hear this required position. They continue to insist that subjective non-reproducible, non-observable spiritual experiences must be accepted as fact or possible fact, not just as an unknown that has not been proven and cannot be assumed.

The historian or scientist may personally believe in miracles but must exclude them from his or her professional products. Historian Michael Grant, in his biography of Jesus, understands this position: "It is true that words ascribed to the risen Christ are beyond the purview of the historian since the resurrection belongs to a different order of thinking. ... Accordingly, therefore, to the cold standard of humdrum fact, the standard to which the student of history is obliged to limit himself, these nature-reversing miracles did *not* happen."[19]

In fact, this position is stronger than "clear and persuasive"; I believe it is necessary if we are to talk with anyone outside our own circles. The usual arguments against this are that all history requires interpretation and that the secular historian's position is, like everyone else's, personal opinion colored by predetermined and unconscious prejudice. This denies two countering considerations: (1) some history is simple documentation and does not require interpretation; and (2) some historians are capable of rising above themselves, altering previously-accepted beliefs and accepting unpleasant truths. This is one of the distinguishing contrasts between science or academic history and religious fundamentalism. In addition, the belief that "faith and revelation" (which are above rational evaluation) lead to the "one true perspective" fails "to acknowledge ... that nearly 21,000 other sectarian perspectives would thus be above rational evaluation too, and all other denominations would be as true as theirs, which of course they cannot accept. In other words, historians of Mormonism must accept Mormon Truth claims. In like manner, historians of Catholicism must accept Catholic Truth claims and the Catholic Holy Spirit as a reliable indicator of those claims, which of course would automatically nullify Mormon Truth claims. The same must obtain of historians of eastern Orthodoxy, Lutheranism, and the remainder of the almost 21,000 Christian denominations. Since it would not be possible for historians of religion to write about other religions or denominations without accepting *their* Truth claims, no historian of one perspective could critically analyze another perspective with any validity because he or she would have to accept the latter's Truth perspective. Historiographers would be turned back into pre-Enlightenment 'story-tellers' or 'defenders of the faith' called by the church 'to summon events from the past' and write 'faith-promoting history.'"[20] Thus such a position leads to the conclusion that one must accept not only God and the supernatural, but Mormon truth claims about God and the supernatural. The argument is circular, and concludes where it begins, with accepting the claims of Joseph Smith.

This then is the predicament: take a position from science and you exclude the supernatural; take a position from religion and your conclusions support your assumptions. The way we solve such problems in our ordinary lives is to follow the instructions Galileo attempted to teach the Catholic church 350 years ago: coordinate your assumptions with external objective reality; emotional certainty by itself is not enough. We cannot and will not find objective evidence for the visions of Joseph Smith, but his ability to translate ancient records is another matter. A scientist or academic historian will take a close look at the Book of Mormon when archaeology says he or she should.

To summarize: I believe we can attempt no truly satisfactory psychobiography of Joseph Smith if we consider his motivations and behavior the result of supernatural experiences only. Nor can we fully understand his life if we consider both naturalistic and supernatural events because difficulties in his psychological makeup which result in questionable behavior will be attributed to obedience to God, not to underlying psychological reasons. Such a psychobiograpy when it appears will be by believers for believers and be understood as "faith-promoting." Few outside historians will take it seriously because the author will have abandoned the common ground of naturalistic assumption–daily "humdrum fact"–required of his or her position in the world of science.

A true psychobiography of Joseph Smith can be done only if naturalistic assumptions are made and if all of Smith's writings–inluding canonized scripture–and interactions are considered psychologically. (Again, this position does not deny the possibility of the supernatural, but acknowledges that supernatural experiences are not established as scientific fact and must be ignored for heuristic reasons.) This would be difficult if we relied solely on Smith's reputed autobiography–*The History of the Church*–for two reasons: (1) as Fawn Brodie has stated, Smith wrote it with the public in mind, not as an uncensored confession; and (2) it has been so compromised by past Mormon historians that it is of little value as autobiography. Source material does exist in his mother's preliminary biography, in acquaintances' accounts of Joseph and the Smith family during Joseph's teenage years, in early courtroom testimonies, in affidavits from New York, and in testimonies from his wife's neighborhood. These, together with the Book of Mormon, which as his first artistic creation would likely be the most revealing of his personality, give us some evidence of underlying motives and unconscious thought processes.

## METHODOLOGY

Psychiatry is that branch of medicine dealing with the diagnosis and treatment of mental dysfunction, and the term "psychiatrist" is reserved for physicians–graduates of medical schools–who have taken added specialty training in psychiatry. That area of psychiatry focusing on the mental forces and maneuvers of a person to modify these forces into successful social adaptation is referred to generally as "(psycho)dynamic psychiatry." Its most intense form is psychoanalysis, a subspecialty of psychiatry that is a collection of knowledge and a body of theory, as well as a specific form of treatment for certain patients.

Psychoanalysis began with Sigmund Freud around 1900 and for sixty years dominated psychiatry. In the absence of other theories, it over-extended itself into the treatment of severe psychotic mental illnesses, now known to be partly, or largely, genetically determined. In the last thirty years the leadership role of psychoanalysis has been replaced with technical laboratory methods and their results in the burgeoning fields of neurophysiology and psychopharmacology. This has allowed psychiatrists to modify, but not cure, severe forms of mental illness by medication. The next fifty years hold promise that the study of mental forces will unite with technical studies of brain chemistry, and we will be able to explain in neurophysiologic terms why the loss of a mother when a child is two years old will probably result in certain types of adult mental disturbance. Freud anticipated this,[21] and today some "psychoanalysts" are active in laboratory research in those areas.

The term "psychoanalyst" is not legally regulated throughout most of the United States, and the title frequently may be claimed by anyone, including the uneducated and charlatan. Within the profession, it is usually reserved for the 10 percent of psychiatrists (and more recently psychologists and social workers) who have completed four to six or more years of advanced training in the thirty-five or so psychoanalytic institutes accredited by the American Psychoanalytic Association. Others who use the term "psychoanalyst" are expected (but not required) to explain that their use of the term is not the usual or standard definition.

The American Psychoanalytic Association and its psychoanalysts continue to exercise major influence on all areas of treatment of the mentally ill. Their training courses welcome psychiatrists, psychologists, registered nurses, and social workers; and the body of knowledge they have accumulated over the last ninety years has filtered not only into the practices of mental health professionals but into our whole lives. For example, every modern government has "think tanks" of professionals using psychoanalytic knowledge in trying to understand the actions of other governments and in evaluating their leaders. Psychoanalytic knowledge is imparted in high schools and has become universal. Both Hollywood and Madison Avenue have people knowledgeable in psychodynamic understanding and manipulation who use these techniques successfully and without moral compunction. Psychoanalytic treatment has been modified and some of its methods help in treating all mentally disturbed patients. Its most extreme form of treatment, using a couch and "free association" in frequent sessions extending over years, continues to be the treatment of choice for a smaller but carefully selected percentage of patients.

That segment of psychoanalytic thinking that does not deal with development of theory or treatment of patients, but instead focuses on culture, art, history, politics, and literature is referred to as applied psychoanalysis. Attempts to enhance our understanding of individuals by their writings or known life is termed psychobiography. It began early in the psychoanalytic movement. Freud's first attempts to apply psychoanalytic concepts outside of psychoanalysis proper were in 1897. Three years later in his *Interpretation of Dreams* (1900) he again referred to Sophocles' *Oedipus Rex* and *Hamlet.*[22] In 1907 he wrote on Jensen's *Gravida,*[23] then on *Leonardo da Vinci* (1910),[24] and on the paranoid process of Schreber (1911).[25] Since then the psychobiographical literature has greatly expanded. Classic works include Ernst Kris's *Explorations in Art* (1952), Phyllis Greenacre's *Swift and Carroll* (1955), Richard and Editha Sterba's *Beethoven and His Nephew* (1954), and of course Erik Erikson's *Young Man Luther* (1958) and *Gandhi's Truth* (1970).

One division of applied psychoanalysis attempts to study personalities and interactions of fictional people in literature without necessarily using this material to understand the author. This approach has aided our appreciation of some of the greatest works such as the writings of Shakespeare. A collection of thirty-three such papers was made by M. D. Faber in 1970.[26] These studies, which open the door to understanding the *unconscious* processes and interplay among *fictional* people, fit into the object-relations theory of development which presently dominates psychoanalytic discussions. Bruno Bettelheim's writings on the meaning behind fairy tales is related.[27] The cultural phenomena of belief in witches, vampires, devils, and nightmares were studied by Ernst Jones[28] in a work which reflected early psychoanalytic preoccupation with sexual frustration.

However, the greatest contributions of psychobiography have been to expand our ideas about the personality of authors.[29] Difficulties in such endeavors are carefully reviewed in important papers by Heinz Kohut[30] and John Mack. Mack adds the provocative thought that applied analysis will provide in coming generations the greatest legacy of psychoanalysis.[31] Harry Trosman[32] identifies various cultural and humanistic sources of Freud's pursuits and then discusses art and literature. This work, along with the small book by Fritz Schmidl,[33] provides extensive bibliographies. These lists demonstrate progress from fumblings and errors to more precise, careful work. Other studies are speculative in the extreme, and two works by Freud are now considered unfortunate setbacks.[34]

Alliances between psychoanalysis and history have been encouraged in the past. In 1958 William Langer, president of the American Historical Association, challenged colleagues to seek deeper psychological meaning in their studies.[35] The response has varied from mixed to hostile. Historians emphasize that there is no such thing as objective history, but they do live in a world where there are historical facts and documentations. This, happily, allows them to keep their feet on the ground. In contrast, the world of psychodynamic psychiatry is far more a world of feelings, thoughts, misrememberings, forgettings, fantasy, analogy, allegory, and metaphor. No wonder some historians give little credence to attempts to make sense of ephemeral mental material which does not seem to be connected. Freud knew this: "[In the use of applied psychoanalysis] we should have to be very cautious and not forget that, after all, we are only dealing with analogies and that it is dangerous, not only with men but also with concepts, to tear them from the sphere in which they have originated and been evolved."[36] Analogy is not a good way to establish historical fact, and history cannot be reduced to psychological explanation. Western historian Bernard DeVoto understood this: "Psycho-analysis has no value whatever as a method of arriving at facts in biography. ... [The first condition of biography must be] absolute, unvarying, unremitted accuracy."[37] But psychoanalytic application and attention to factual detail are compatible, and psychoanalytic interpretation and understanding may add texture to the historical picture, fill in aspects of personal meaning and motive, and provide continuity to a history that has gaps. DeVoto found little value in applied psychoanalysis except as a plaything. Consequently, his conclusions concerning the Book of

Mormon lacked comprehension: "a yeasty fermentation, formless, aimless and inconceivably absurd ... a disintegration."[38]

When psychiatrists enter the world of history, they are strangers in a strange land. They are trained to interact with a live and reactive patient, not someone distant or dead for 150 years. Interaction between therapist and patient is the central focus and the means for, if not a cure, then improvement. Clarification, confrontation, interpretation, and repeatedly working through an issue describes the observable process. It is speculative work, which only gains assurance over time and in the interaction. Every dynamic psychiatrist has had the experience of making a painful interpretation he or she felt was accurate, only to have the patient exclaim, "No!" then break into sobs and correct the therapist with an even more painful truth, newly discovered by the therapist's near-miss. It is this dynamic interplay that we do not have in an applied psychoanalytic approach to a dead man or woman.

Add to this the fact that a person not only reflects his or her own personal, familial development but his or her time and place. It is difficult to shift spheres of influence, much less gain insight by guesswork in the inner wellsprings of a person's emotions and thinkings. Time veils many things and there will be aspects of anyone's life that will never be understood, even with the full cooperation of a live patient. These difficulties tempt a psychohistorian to become reductionistic instead of reductive in finding certain conclusions where only incomplete information and partial solutions are available: "Reductionism, the 'nothing but' fallacy, which attempts to reduce complex psychological and creative processes to roots in the unconscious, is the most dangerous tendency. ... Closely related to this is 'the originological fallacy,' the invoking of antecedent experiences or early drives to explain the subject's later behavior. I would add to these 'the critical period fallacy,' which attempts to build a study of a man's life around a certain 'key' period of development, and 'eventism,' the discovery in some important episode in a man's life of not only the prototype of his behavior but *the* turning point in his life from which all subsequent events and work are derived. Both these oversimplifications lend artistic grace to a biographical study, but also impose unnatural order, shape, and direction to the often rather amorphous nature and fitful course of a human life, even that of a great man."[39]

The above emphasizes the necessary tension and balance between the historical and the psychological. If this latter view becomes too strong, then "psychopathology becomes a substitute for the psycho-historical interface. ... the psychopathological idiom for individual development ... [replaces] the idiom for history, or psychohistory. When this happens there is, once more, no history."[40]

If a balance is maintained, then looking at symptomatic or general behaviors can be productive. From our psychodynamic perspective and experience, there is reason to believe that all of us derive part of our motives and uniqueness from psychologically meaningful events in our past, most strongly and enduringly in our childhood. Might this be true also for a prophet? At the least, such considerations add depth to understanding. The concern is that the subject might be reduced to a stilted figurine to fit a psychodynamic model, while the full richness of his or her life is left unexplained. No live patient fits any mold and sooner or later will emotionally bristle when he or she senses the therapist's attempt to do so. Some of this will happen with psychobiography because live interaction, corrections, modifications, and elaborations by the patient are not available to us. The patient is not there to challenge, correct, and change our tendency to simplify. It will also happen because no one has direct first-hand experience with a culture from the past.

Some now believe that the greatest impediment to good psycho-biography is the author's own emotional relationship to his or her subject. These "countertransferences" may "distort the [biographers'] material so that their discussion may actually reveal more about themselves than about their subjects."[41] Psychobiographers are not limited to writing about people they admire or love, but also those considered profoundly destructive, and this can bend their studies into attempts at debunking. No one can write completely free of bias, but it is important to know where one's prejudices lie. This may be especially true of religious figures. For this reason, clarifying the underlying theological assumptions, as discussed earlier, is necessary. Some readers will find the scientific position untenable. The goal of psychobiography is explanation and understanding, but sometimes such explanation and understanding may be unattractive. Describing a personality that rationalizes, changes his or her story, deceives, and abuses others is unavoidable in any honest study, while mislabeling or avoiding these qualities results in incomplete or even censored history. The best psychobiographers, like the best psychotherapists, use their emotional reactions to their subjects and patients as stepping stones to further understanding of the unconscious.[42]

What psychobiography does have, despite the absence of a live patient, are two areas of collective knowledge and known experience. Techniques used in applied psychoanalytic investigation are adapted from techniques of psychoanalytic treatment. If Joseph Smith were in dynamic psychotherapy, he would have the right to begin the sessions anywhere, under the guide of free association—to say anything and everything that comes to mind with preferably no editing at all—and our job would be to follow, understand, decipher, confront, and clarify. Where will he take us?

Patients tell their life story and emphasize problem areas repeatedly in treatment. But some areas of conflict are too painful to discuss and feel directly, so patients use a number of methods, both conscious and unconscious, to modify their pain. They may talk about a friend with similar problems or discuss a movie or book that contains problems similar to their own. They may divide their history into two or more parts, discussing some segments one day and filling in the remaining segments on other days. The more painful the incident, the more repetitious the patient will be in "working through" the problem. If the pain of sadness is too much on one day, they may reverse it into an inappropriate euphoria which will break down in the next days or weeks. Their dreams will repeat their life stories and conflicts, disguised by exaggeration, displacement, reversal, projection onto others, condensing and combining stories, and so forth. Their mental fantasies will repeat their problem and frequently show dramatic wished-for solutions and compensations, some reasonable and some impossible.

Over time the psychotherapist begins to know the life story well and becomes acquainted with the psychological "defenses" the patient uses to repeat yet half-avoid facing pain. The patient will speak in metaphor, simile, allegory, fantasy. We can expect that the mental maneuvers, styles, and defenses of the author will be represented in his or her work. This is most true if the work was his or her first or early work and if the work was "spontaneous" and close to the therapeutic process of "free association," as perhaps was his dictation of the Book of Mormon.

The therapist may learn the patient's methods so well that he or she can anticipate the next session's content—only to find him- or herself surprised on occasion when the patient demonstrates a new technique. What becomes increasingly important is not the life story but its modifications which the patient brings to treatment. These modifications–exaggerations, similarities, aversions, combinings, reversals, eliminations, projections, forgettings, denials, imagined compensations, division of the story into two or more parts, etc.–are what help us understand the patient and assist him or her to face pain and more successfully adapt to life. What we wait to see are patterns. Meissner states: "The data of analytic investigation are subtle, hidden, and masked behind the veil of manifest content. ... The causal links are nowhere immediate or evident. The proof rests on a welter of facts, opinions, reactions, behaviors in various contexts, comments in letters and other writings. No single fact or connection will validate the hypothesis, but it begins to take on meaning and consistency in the light of the total complex of facts, data, and their integrating interpretations."[43]

The second principle is overdetermination. "The problem of determinism in psycho-analysis is a point that bothers unsympathetic critics of psycho-analysis. Freud insisted that strict determinism prevailed in respect of psychic acts; there are no 'accidents.' For example, 'free associations,' the basis of dream analysis and of therapy, is 'free' only in the sense that it is not hampered by the censorship of 'logical,' 'rational' thought and *mores.* It is not, however, undetermined."[44] This also depends on the amount of material extant, and if no pertinent material exists there can be no psychobiography. But we do have material with Joseph Smith–from himself, his mother, outsiders–and we can theorize his mental productions in the Book of Mormon. Overdetermination comes in two forms: the fact that the same word or symbol refers to many elements in the unconscious thought process, and that a single unconscious drive or pattern of behavior will manifest itself in numerous different conscious manifestations. This makes the evidence abundant and self-confirming. If one adds this to outside observations–by family, friends, enemies–it seems possible to complete the historian's task of reconciling, interpreting, and confirming evidence, as well as the psychohistorian's task of explaining.

Let us take an example from Joseph Smith's life: his first known run-in with the law. Shortly after he turned twenty years old—four years before the Book of Mormon was published—he was arrested as a "disorderly person and imposter." He spent one night in jail, was found "guilty" in a "trial" (probably a type of preliminary hearing or examination) that received some local attention, and was encouraged to leave the area to avoid further punishment.[45] Mormon historian Marvin Hill says that Smith "experienced shame ... in 1826 when he was brought to trial. ... It is significant that Joseph Smith never mentioned this trial in any of his writings."[46] Hill's statement is half correct, for seven years later Smith assisted his close friend, Oliver Cowdery, in writing about this trial: "some very officious person complained of him [Joseph Smith] as a disorderly person, and brought him before the authorities of the country; but there being no cause of action he was honorably acquitted."[47]

Joseph's subsequent avoidance in discussing this trial suggests that he did experience shame and humiliation. If the principle of overdetermination applies, then this trial might appear in the Book of Mormon in unconscious representation. Smith's emotional upheaval might appear in a dream of a volcanic explosion or perhaps transformed into physical assault and injury. Or the trial might be represented as just that: a literal court trial. Or perhaps it will show as a judgment from God, or persecution by evil men. If this trial appears, we will want to place it into continuity: other aspects of Smith's life before and after it should be represented in metaphor and allegory but in proper sequence in the Book of Mormon. If the trial was a profound emotional experience, we could expect that it would appear more than once, again expecting it to be in proper sequence with the rest of his life. As we do with live patients, we listen until it becomes clear we are hearing allegorically, metaphorically, and in fantasy a repetition of major incidents. However, once again of even greater interest to us is to see how Smith changes his real-life trial into Book of Mormon incidents, for when we begin to see such patterns we begin to understand him and his motives. We wait to see an internally consistent chronological pattern and repetitive psychological style.

This then is one challenge: to what extent, if any, can the Book of

Mormon be understood as an autobiography of Joseph Smith? Such a psychobiography would be both interpretive essay and psychological detective story. But if this inquiry is successful, can repeated psychological patterns in Smith's alteration of his dramatic life into Book of Mormon stories be discerned? If so, then this level of writing can be advanced to another and allow an expanded question: Can such observations contribute to a psychological understanding of Smith, and with this information, alongside his mother's biography and other outside information, can we develop a reasonably complete psychoanalytic profile of Joseph Smith?

From the beginning with Joseph Smith there has been not only an alternate story to the official version, but a contradictory one. Depending on one's outlook, this has been curse, burden, challenge, opportunity, or blessing. Some alternate stories were plausible but with inadequate documentation; others failed as contradictory evidence was discovered. With each failure, some Mormons felt reassured that Smith's original stories were confirmed. However, this is no longer true. Recent historical discoveries not only add to the alternate version but are incompatible with the canonized story. This has created something of a "crisis in Mormon historiography" and divided many Mormons into "traditionalists" and "New Mormon Historians."[48] The problem has become intense because church leaders have reacted with a degree of defensiveness that suggests the threat they feel. They have typically sided with "traditionalists" and their response to those grappling with historical documentation has oscillated between uncharitable and cruel.[49] A naturalistic psychobiography of Joseph Smith, if successful in demonstrating repeated styles of psychological defense and patterns of thinking–even within the Book of Mormon–that parallel his life, would provide explanations and motivations for Smith's behavior as well as possibly fill in gaps in recent discoveries. It would add more challenges to the traditional story of the founding of Mormonism and enlarge the present controversy.

## ADDENDUM

Attempts to use a clinical diagnosis of manic-depressive illness to help explain Joseph Smith's personality is, in my opinion, so filled with problems that it deserves special scrutiny. The necessary symptom for a diagnosis of manic-depressive illness, now called Bipolar Affective Disorder, is a discrete episode of mania with or without episodes of depression. Usually beginning in the late teens or early twenties, the first episode(s) is likely precipitated by stress such as birth, death, loss of employment, or divorce. As the illness unfolds, it takes on a life of its own with episodes occurring independently of the stresses of life. But the illness may create havoc in the patient's life. It is a periodic illness with recurrence throughout one's life. As is the case with all psychiatric diagnoses, the illness is determined by clumpings of symptoms ("syndromes") seen in a patient in a clinical setting.

In the early and mid-1970s lesser manic episodes not severe enough to warrant hospitalizations were split off from full mania and termed "Bipolar Affective Disorder, type II." This questionable distinction was supported by statistical studies of patients who were younger than more severe "Bipolar I" patients at onset, tended to be female with greater chronicity to the illness, had families which had relatives with a similar degree of mania, etc. Some were "rapid cyclers" or the episodes seemed connected to seasonal affective disorder or premenstrual syndrome. Some patients experienced the onset of the illness when prescibed standard antidepressant medication.

Researchers continued to divide Bipolar II patients into lifelong forms of even lesser intensity, termed cyclothymia and hyperthymia. Both of these "unofficial" illnesses require the occurrence of hypomania–a distinct period of at least a few days of mild elevation of mood, positive thinking, and increased activity level, but without the severe impairment of full manic episodes. It is not easy to distinguish "hypomania" from simple happiness except perhaps by its inappropriate timing, and it becomes increasingly difficult to distinguish these illnesses from other mental health problems or even normal everyday variations. Even with interviews with a live patient and family members, the symptoms are termed "subsyndromal" or "subclinical," suggesting uncertainty. Some may have intermittent mild depression ("cyclothymics"), but some, these researchers suggest, have hypomania woven habitually and consistently into their personality. One researcher proposes these characteristics for this "hyperthymic" temperament: cheerful, overoptimistic, or exuberant; warm, people-seeking, and extroverted; overtalkative and jocular; overconfident, self-assured, boastful, or grandiose; habitual short sleeper, including weekends; high energy level, full of plans and improvident activities; overly involved and meddlesome; uninhibited, stimulation-seeking, or promiscuous. But where is the necessary episodic nature of the illness required for the diagnosis?

These last descriptions put us over the line from episodic illness into general personality types, and the closest present official description to this type is "narcissistic personality disorder," as these researchers acknowledge. In addition, these researchers suggest the possibility that some patients with the turbulent "borderline personality disorder" may in fact have a disguised form of "cyclothymia." These are ideas rich for research, but such diagnoses are difficult to delineate in a live patient, and impossible to discern from a distance of more than 150 years. I agree that Bipolar Affective Disorder may appear in a myriad of subtle forms and believe these suggestions hold promise, but almost anything can be put into such categories, and we are obligated to follow the descriptions of illness that have some reasonable clarity.

Researchers in these studies focus on neurobiology and pay little attention to psychology. These illnesses are seen as a result of the body's internal clock going awry to its own independent drumbeat, but possibly affected by how much light hits the retina of the eye, or menstrual-cycle biochemistry. These lesser subdivisions of "Bipolar Affective Disorder, type II" (types III, IV, V, VI?) are speculative, and I believe we should stay at the first level of theorizing by trying to fit Joseph Smith into known and clearly distinguishable categories or combinations of distinguishable categories of illness. Trying to place him into a speculative form of Bipolar Affective Disorder that is actually a description of a personality type, or deciding that he has one of the subtle atypical forms of the illness, difficult to discern even in a real live patient, only stirs an already muddy pool. If this is allowed, then almost anything can be permitted.

These lesser forms of Bipolar Affective Disorder–type II and the unofficial so-called cyclothymic and hyperthymic individuals–assuming both are bipolar illnesses–may demonstrate artistic creativity. The introversion and self-doubt of mild depression contributes to insights and reflection on the human condition, and then hypomania provides the energy for the creative work.

It seems to me that proponents of a clinical manic-depressive diagnosis for Joseph Smith must demonstrate repeated episodes of illness in Smith that reversed his usual temperament, and were minimally or not at all precipitated by external factors. Where is such a description of periodicity from his friends or enemies? Without this periodicity of reversal, there can be no real diagnosis of any form of Bipolar Affective Disorder. I do not doubt that he had periods of depression especially toward the end of his life, but these seem to have been in response to his environment. He was steadily being entrapped by his enemies in retaliation for his own doings. He may indeed have had periods of elation following narrow escapes, imprisonment, conquests, etc. Quotes from Smith that excitement had become his essence of life suggests a chronic steady condition, not an episodic one. I find it difficult to believe that there was a period in Smith's life when he was not making grandiose claims.

How does any form of Bipolar Affective Disorder explain the Book of Mormon, Smith's revelations, or the Book of Abraham? At best, it only provides Smith with thoughtful introspection when depressed and energy when hypomanic. It contributes little to the explanation for these "miracles." Non-Mormon proponents of manic-depressive diagnosis must provide further naturalistic–psychological–explanations for these texts. Mormon proponents, on the other hand, escape this problem. But with no objective evidence for the Book of Mormon as actual history, all thoughtful outsiders (as well as some insiders) see it as a product of early nineteenth-century America. Mormon proponents of manic-depressive diagnosis must be certain that they see nothing significant in the Book of Mormon that reflects Smith's personal life, his readings, his local religious experiences, or the national scene. They must also explain how Smith's revelations and translations escaped contaminations from Bipolar Affective Disorder such as overstatement or grandiosity; or, at the other end of bipolarity, exaggerated despair and condemnation.

Here are some of the issues that a diagnosis of Bipolar Affective Disorder does not address: the results of an unstable and deprived childhood with too many moves and periods of near-starvation; the results of a traumatic childhood surgery; the effects of being raised in a family with an alcoholic father, a mother predisposed to depression, and repeated failures and minimal esteem in the community; and the effect of being raised in the subculture of magical delusion, requiring deceit of self and others. I agree that Smith demonstrated grandiosity, but I see it as a progressive development going out of control toward the end of his life. It may be that he suffered from an atypical, strange form of Bipolar Affective Disorder in addition, but I do not believe he fits into established categories of the illness. The strongest evidence for this diagnosis is probably his family history, but family members had an incomprehensible burden of conflict to carry. (This could lead to suicide. Schizophrenia is not one of the bipolar spectrum of illnesses.)

Several years ago, paying attention to the recurrent depressive episodes in Joseph's mother and the life-long mental illness of his son, I seriously considered Bipolar II but abandoned it for the reasons given. Frankly I was sorry, for I would have liked to find an explanation for Smith's later excesses that was outside of his control. Other intellectuals in the Mormon world would understand this wish.

If proponents of a manic-depressive diagnosis for Joseph Smith are trying to observe a periodic illness so minimal or atypical that it looks like a general personality type, why avoid the obvious and not investigate personality types? (This would still allow normal everyday ups and downs and episodes of euphoria and temporary hypomania in response to conquests and successes.) The main writers on personality types are psychoanalysts, not family statisticians. Here the writings are so voluminous that one hardly knows where to begin, for the study of the "narcissistic personality" has preoccupied them for thirty years, along with their intense investigation of the first three years of life and the consequent development of "Object Relations" metapsychology which continues to dominate any theoretical discussion. Even so, I do not think any single personality type will adequately explain Joseph Smith. Finally, I would encourage the idea that explaining Joseph Smith requires looking beyond just his genetic makeup, internal conflicts, or personality, but also to interactions between him and his followers, for they contributed to his creation as a prophet. Here the nidal point is easy to see, for it was described by the unsophisticated farmer and wagon master Peter Ingersoll and published in 1834.

Any explanation should encompass that description. This description, like so much else in his life, nudges the diagnosis toward psychology and away from the organic/genetic.

Let me open this discussion to further dialogue by asking if the following striking example of hypomania in the Book of Mormon is the result of Bipolar Affective Disorder in Joseph Smith or a result of psychological defensiveness. The specific example occurred during a war between the Lamanites and Nephites, and also between the Lamanites and their former brothers, the Anti-Nephi-Lehies. In the middle of these slaughters the herioic missionary-swordsman Ammon breaks forth into a cry of joy, his heart brimming over for the salvation of the victims in the Kingdom of God (Alma 26). He sets aside the carnage, mayhem, dislocations, devastation, deaths, rapes, dismemberings, torturings, burnings, and grievings that would have resulted from the continuing hand-to-hand combats with savages driven by hatred.

If the hypomania of Ammon, as an alter-ego for Joseph Smith, cannot be connected to specific incidents in the latter's life, then the diagnosis is likely Bipolar Affective Disorder. But if this hypomania can be connected to some devastating humiliation in Jospeh Smith's life, then I believe it suppports understanding this hypomanic episode as a *psychological defense of compensating reaction-formation.* The clues are probably found in the chapters before and after Ammon's curious Ode to Joy.[50]

*NOTES*

1. Joseph Hansen, *Zauberwahn, Inquisition and Hexenprozess im Mittelalter* (Munich, 1900). The response by Robert Schwickerath, S.J., is in the *American Catholic Quarterly Review* 27 (1902): 475-516, entitled "Attitude of the Jesuits in the Trials for Witchcraft." For a brief overview of the witch trials, see H. R. Trevor-Rober, *The European Witch-Craze of the Sixteenth and Seventeenth Centuries and other Essays* (New York: Harper & Row, 1967), 90-192; R. H. Robbins, *The Encyclopedia of Witchcraft and Demonology* (New York: Crown Publishers, 1965); and R. D. Anderson, "The History of Witchcraft: A Review With Some Psychiatric Comments," *American Journal of Psychiatry* 126 (June 1970): 1727-35.

2. Ezra Taft Benson, *The Gospel Teacher and His Message* (Salt Lake City: Church Educational System, 1976), 11-12, quoted by D. Michael Quinn, "On

Being a Mormon Historian (and Its Aftermath)," in George D. Smith, ed.: *Faithful History: Essays on Writing Mormon History* (Salt Lake City: Signature Books, 1992), 69-111.

3. H. Becher, S.J., "Ignatius as Seen by His Contemporaries," in *Ignatius of Loyola: His Personality and Spiritual Heritage, 1556-1956*, ed. F. Wulf, S.J. (St. Louis: Institute of Jesuit Sources, 1977), 69-96, at 70. Also in W. W. Meissner, S.J., "Psychoanalytic Hagiography: The Case of Ignatius of Loyola," *Theological Studies* 52 (1991): 3-33.

4. Lawrence Foster, "New Perspectives on the Mormon Past: Reflections of a Non-Mormon Historian," in Smith, *Faithful History*, 113.

5. Joseph Smith, Jr., et al., *History of the Church of Jesus Christ of Latter-day Saints*, 6 vols., ed. B. H. Roberts (Salt Lake City: Deseret Book Co., 1951), 5:265.

6. Gary F. Novak, "Naturalistic Assumptions and the Book of Mormon," *BYU Studies* 30 (Summer 1990): 23-40.

7. C. Jess Groesbeck, "Joseph Smith and His Path of Individuation: A Psychoanalytical Exploration in Mormonism," Aug. 1986, privately circulated; tape-recorded version with response by James Morgan available on tape through Sunstone Foundation, Salt Lake City.

8. James E. Lancaster, "The Translation of the Book of Mormon," in Dan Vogel, ed., *The Word of God: Essays on Mormon Scripture* (Salt Lake City: Signature Books, 1990), 97-112; Dean C. Jessee, "Joseph Knight's Recollection of Early Mormon History," *Brigham Young University Studies* 17 (Autumn 1976): 29-39, esp. 35-36.

9. Blake T. Ostler, "The Book of Mormon as a Modern Expansion of an Ancient Source," *Dialogue: A Journal of Mormon Thought* 20 (Spring 1987): 66-123.

10. Mark Thomas, "Lehi's Doctrine of Opposition in Its Nineteenth and Twentieth Century Contexts," *Sunstone* 13 (Jan. 1989): 52; and his "The Meaning of Revival Language in The Book of Mormon," *Sunstone* 8 (May-June 1983): 19-25. See also his "Rhetorical Approach to The Book of Mormon," 1992, privately circulated.

11. William D. Russell, "A Further Inquiry into the Historicity of the Book of Mormon," *Sunstone* 7 (Sept.-Oct. 1982): 20-24.

12. William W. Meissner, S.J., *Ignatius of Loyola: The Psychology of a Saint* (New Haven, CT: Yale University Press, 1992), 346-58.

The term "Jesuit psychoanalyst" deserves some discussion. Sigmund Freud, an atheist, referred to himself as "The Godless Jew" and believed that religion was an illusion. Toward the end of his life he wrote his "war cry against religion," entitled "The Future of an Illusion" (*Standard Edition*, vol. 21 [London: Hogarth Press, 1961]). Freud believed that the therapeutic effects of psychoanalysis resulted from the successful disintegration of the Oedipal conflict. Religion was an adult form of this conflict and would be abandoned when the conflict dissolved. However, this was not his followers' subsequent experience, who instead watched their patients' conflicts alter into more refined and adaptive behaviors. Today the therapeutic effects of psychoanalysis are understood to come not from interpretation but the internalization of the patient-doctor relationship which lays down added unconscious psychic structures through which conflict is modified. Even toward the end of successful analysis, unusual stress might bring back symptoms of insomnia, anxiety, depression, etc., albeit in brief and less intense forms. Note how this changes things: involvement in religion might be one form of a refined cultural adaptation. The question then turns, not on religious participation, but on the adaptive and flexible forms of religion and their coordination with reality. Fundamental religions, holding firm beliefs in opposition to new knowledge, do not fare well in this view.

Meissner, with 200 papers and nine books, is a leader at the interface between psychiatry and religion. In 1961 he published the *Annotated Bibliography in Religion and Psychology* (New York: Academy of Religion and Mental Health), and in 1984 his *Psychoanalysis and Religious Experience* (New Haven: Yale University Press) proposed that religion is an adult form–mature and immature–of transitional object. In his "The Pathology of Belief Systems" (*Psychoanalysis and Contemporary Thought* 15 [2]: 99-128), he distinguishes between the verifiable validity of a religion and the measurement of its pathology. In his "The Cult Phenomenon and the Paranoid Process" (*The Psychoanalytic Study of Society* 12:69-95), he finds similarity in the mental underpinnings of both processes, whether in the first or nineteenth century after Jesus Christ.

On a personal note, he is a man of wide humanity that has no flavor of fundamentalism. His critique of some of my preliminary writings has been very useful.

13. This quote is a composite from Meissner's large biography of Ignatius in n12 and his earlier work reference in n3. However, the critical second sentence of the second paragraph has been removed from the later, larger work.

14. Linda King Newell and Valeen Tippets Avery, *Mormon Enigma: Emma Hale Smith; Prophet's Wife, "Elect Lady," Polygamy's Foe* (Garden City, NY: Doubleday & Co., 1984), 65, 100-101, 146-47.

15. Jan Shipps, "The Prophet Puzzle: Suggestions Leading Toward a More Comprehensive Interpretation of Joseph Smith," *Journal of Mormon History* 1 (1974): 3-20; reprinted in this compilation.

16. Richard Sherlock, "The Gospel Beyond Time: Thoughts on the Relation of Faith and Historical Knowledge," in Smith, *Faithful History*, 53n.

17. Articles may be found in many volumes of *Dialogue: A Journal of Mormon Thought*, as well as in *Sunstone*. Many of the best of these arguments have been gathered together in Smith, *Faithful History*.

18. This quote is a composite from two letters from Michael T. Walton in *Sunstone* 8 (Nov.-Dec. 1983): 2, and 11 (Jan. 1987): 6.

19. Michael Grant, *Jesus: An Historian's View of the Gospels* (New York: Collier Books, 1977), 13, 39.

20. Edward H. Ashment, "Historiography of the Canon," in Smith, *Faithful History*, 292.

21. "We have found it necessary to hold aloof from biological considerations during our psycho-analytic work and to refrain from using them for heuristic purposes," Freud wrote, "so that we may not be misled in our impartial judgement of the analytic work we shall have to find a point of contact with biology; and we may rightly feel glad if that contact is already assured at one important point or another" ("The Claims of Psycho-Analysis to Scientific Interest. Part II (C)" [1913], in *Psychological Works of Sigmund Freud* [London: Hogarth Press, 1955], 13:181-82 [hereafter *Standard Edition*]). "Biology is truly a land of unlimited possibilities," he added. "We may expect it to give us the most surprising information and we cannot guess what answers it will return in a few dozen years to the questions we have put to it. They may be of a kind which will blow away the whole of our artificial structure of hypotheses" ("Beyond the Pleasure Principle," *Standard Edition*, 18:7-64). Finally, "We may look forward to a day when paths of knowledge and, let us hope, of influence will be opened up leading from organic biology and chemistry to the field of neurotic phenomena. That day still seems a distant one [in 1926]" ("The Question of Lay Analysis," *Standard Edition*, 20:231).

22. See Freud, Letter #71 (17 Oct. 1897), *Standard Edition*, 1:265-66; Freud, "The Interpretation of Dreams," *Standard Edition*, 4:263-66.

23. S. Freud, "Delusion and Dreams in Jensen's *Gravida*," *Standard Edition*, 9:3-95.

24. Freud, "Leonardo da Vinci and a Memory of his Childhood," *Standard Edition*, 11:59-137.

25. Freud, "Psychoanalytic Notes on an Autobiographical Account of a Case of Paranoia," *Standard Edition*, 12:9-82.

26. M. D. Faber, *The Design Within: Psychoanalytic Approaches to Shakespeare* (New York: Science House, 1970).

27. Bruno Bettelheim, *The Uses of Enchantment: The Meaning and Importance of Fairy Tales* (New York: Alfred A. Knopf, 1976).

28. Ernst Jones, *On the Nightmare* (New York: Liverright, 1951).

29. See Gary James Bergera, "Toward 'Psychologically Informed' Mormon History and Biography," *Sunstone* 15 (Dec. 1991): 27-31. I consider this excellent review an expansion on the ideas in this section.

30. Heinz Kohut, "Beyond the Bounds of the Basic Rule," *Journal of the American Psychoanalytic Associaiton* 19 (1960): 143-79.

31. John E. Mack, "Psychoanalysis and Historical Biography," *Journal of the American Psychoanalytic Association* 19 (1971), 1:143-49.

32. Harry Trosman, *Freud and the Imaginative World* (Hillsdale, NJ: The Analytic Press, 1985).

33. F. Schmidl, *Applied Psychoanalysis* (New York: Philosophical Library, 1981).

34. Freud, "Leonardo da Vinci," and W. D. Bullitt and Freud, *Thomas Woodrow Wilson: A Psychological Study* (Boston: Houghton Mifflin, 1966). See also Alan C. Elms, *Uncovering Lives: The Uneasy Alliance of Biography and Psychology* (New York: Oxford University Press, 1994).

35. W. D. Langer, "The Next Assignment," *American Historical Review* 63 (1958): 283-304.

36. Freud, "Civilization and Its Discontents," *Standard Edition*, 21:144.

37. Bernard DeVoto, "The Skeptical Biographer," *Harper's Magazine* 166 (1933): 181-92.

38. Bernard DeVoto, "The Centennial of Mormonism," *American Mercury*, Jan. 1930, 1, in Francis W. Kirkham, ed., *A New Witness for Christ in America* (Independence, MO: Zion's Printing Press, 1951), 1:352.

39. Mack, 156.

40. Robert J. Lifton, "On Psychohistory," in *Explorations in Psychohistory: The Wellfleet Papers*, eds. R. J. Lifton and E. Olson (New York: Simon and Schuster, 1974), 25.

41. Bergera, 28.

42. Mack, 155.

43. Meissner, xiv.

44. Bruce Mazlish, "Clio on the Couch," *Encounter*, Sept. 1968.

45. Fawn M. Brodie, *No Man Knows My History* (New York: Alfred A. Knopf, 1971); Jerald and Sandra Tanner, *Joseph Smith and Money Digging* (Salt Lake City: Modern Microfilm, 1970); Wesley P. Walters, "Joseph Smith's Bainbridge, N. Y. Court Trials," *Westminster Theological Journal* 36 (Winter 1974): 123-55; and Wesley P. Walters, "From Occult to Cult with Joseph Smith, Jr.," *The Journal of Pastoral Practice* 1 (Summer 1977): 121-13.

46. Marvin S. Hill, *Quest For Refuge: The Mormon Flight from American Pluralism* (Salt Lake City: Signature Books, 1989), 11, 193n62.

47. *Messenger and Advocate* 2 (Oct. 1835): 200-201.

48. These articles may be found throughout the journals of *Sunstone* and *Dialogue*. Some of the best have been collected into Smith, *Faithful History*.

49. See Lavina Fielding Anderson, "The LDS Intellectual Community and Church Leadership: Contemporary Chronology," *Dialogue: Journal of Mormon Thought* 26 (Spring 1993); and also D. Michael Quinn, "On Being a Mormon Historian (and Its Aftermath)," in Smith, *Faithful History*, 69-112.

Intellectuals in the Mormon church are becoming symbolic martyrs in a twentieth-century struggle against a sixteenth-century mentality. Mormon writer Linda King Newell summarized the conflict best when she described at the 1992 Pacific Northwest Sunstone Symposium events that followed release of *Mormon Enigma: Emma Hale Smith* (Garden City, NY: Doubleday and Co., 1984), which she co-authored with Valeen T. Avery. Within months of publication, her award-winning biography of Joseph Smith's first wife was censored by Mormon church officials and she and Avery were forbidden to speak in church meetings, teach classes, or speak about their research. With her husband and their stake president, Newell met with Elders Dallin H. Oaks and Neal A. Maxwell, authors of the ban, on 21 July 1985. Oaks, a former Utah Supreme Court Justice and past president of Brigham Young University, did not believe the ban would be lifted. He recognized that "many members consider him an intellectual given his academic background in professional history, but he doesn't want us or anyone else to be mislead." He said: "My duty as a member of the Council of the Twelve is to protect what is most unique about the LDS church, namely the authority of the priesthood, testimony regarding the restoration of the gospel, and the divine mission of the Savior. Everything else may be sacrificed in order to maintain the integrity of those essential facts. Thus, if *Mormon Enigma* reveals information that is detrimental to the reputation of Joseph Smith, then it is necessary to try to limit its influence and that of its authors."

In his statement Oaks sacrificed the search for truth to the support of dogma. The names of similarly motivated men that come to mind include Jakob Sprenger, Jean Bodin, Henri Boguet, Peter Binsfeld, Nicholas Remy, M. A. Del Rio, and Dietrich Flade. However, unlike Oaks, they were not restrained by a Constitution and Bill of Rights and are not seen in a favorable light today. The last named, the most decent of them all, attempted to resist zealous actions that overrode the search for truth, was caught, and destroyed.

50. In the above I summarized the following books and papers: F. K. Goodwin and K. R. Jamison, *Manic-Depressive Illness* (New York: Oxford University Press, 1990), 13-55, 75-151, 281-315, 332-66, 541-70; H. S. Akiskal, "New Diagnostic Concepts of Depression—The 'Soft' Bipolar Spectrum," *Masters in Psychiatry*, July 1993, 9-13; H. S. Akiskal and K. Akiskal, "Reassessing the Prevalence of Bipolar Disorders: Clinical Significance and Artistic Creativity," *Psychiatry and Psychobiology* 3 (1988): 29s-36s; H. S. Akiskal, "The Bipolar Spectrum: New Concepts in Classification and Diagnosis," in L. Grinspoon, ed., *Psychiatry Update: The American Psychiatric Association Annual Review* (Washington, D.C.: American Psychiatric Press, Inc., 1983), 271-92; G. B. Cassano et al., "Proposed Subtypes of Bipolar II and Related Disorders: With Hypomanic Episodes (or Cyclothymia) and with Hyperthymic Temperament," *Journal of Affective Disorders* 26 (1992): 127-40; R. H. Howland and M. E. Thase, "A Comprehensive Review of Cyclothymic Disorder," *Journal of Nervous and Mental Disease* 181 (1993): 485-93; G. L. Klerman, "The Classification of Bipolar Disorders," *Psychiatric Annals* 17 (Jan. 1987); D. L. Dunner, "A Review of the Diagnostic Status of 'Bipolar II.' For the DSM-IV Work Group on Mood Disorders," *Depression* 1 (1993): 2-10; and Hagop S. Akiskal, "The Prevalent

Clinical Spectrum of Bipolar Disorders: Beyond DSM-IV," *Journal of Clinical Psychopharmacology* 16 (1996): 2, Supplement 1:45-145. Peter Ingersoll's testimony is in E. D. Howe, *Mormonism Unvailed* (Painsville, OH: the Author, 1834), 323-37. For an introduction to the development of the grandiose self as part of the narcissistic personality, see Otto Kernberg, *Borderline Conditions and Pathological Narcissism* (New York: Jason Aronson, Inc., 1975), 16-18, 227-314.

# 12.
# Joseph Smith and the Hazards of Charismatic Leadership

*Gary James Bergera*

> *Would to God, brethren, I could tell you who I am! Would to God I could tell you what I know! ... But you would call it blasphemy, and there are men ... who would want to take my life.*
>
> –Joseph Smith[1]

ONE OF THE CHIEF IMPEDIMENTS TO SUCCESSFUL LEADERSHIP FACING charismatic people, whose primary claim to power is based on personal factors, is separating the self-perceptions of youth from the limitations of maturity.[2] When a charismatic person assumes a position of leadership and fails to recognize the limitations of his power, convinced he can "transform his ... fantasies into reality for his followers,"[3] he may develop what psychologists refer to as megalomaniacal fantasies, including paranoid delusions. In fact, the leader and his followers may easily experience in crisis situations "a state of childlike bliss."[4] The group may willingly surrender its ego to the leader "in order to preserve [its] love of the leader, and whatever esteem [it] experience[s] comes from the sense of devotion to the ideals and causes established in the leader's image."[5] Yet the leader may experience little resistance in influencing his followers to do things they would not do otherwise, reconfirming the breadth of his own power and the ease with which his followers are able to achieve the realization of their own dreams as defined by the leader. "Attachment and omnipotence [can] mutually reinforce one another," omnipotence turning into a "self-fulfilling prophecy" in which "everything is allowed and nothing is off limits."[6]

Joseph Smith, founder and first prophet of the Church of Jesus Christ of Latter-day Saints, more than qualifies as a charismatic religious leader. In fact, he was described by German sociologist Max Weber, who first discussed charisma in any detail, as possessing "unusual qualities ... which are attractive to others and result in special attachments, if not devotion, to his leadership."[7] The findings of subsequent researchers have echoed Weber's initial evaluation.[8] Embodying both the strengths and weaknesses of charismatic leadership, Joseph, during the final two years of his life, from 1842 to 1844, tested more than once the boundaries separating fantasy from reality, succumbing to those hazards problematic to charismatic religious leaders. In significant and, I believe, revealing ways, Joseph's leadership is a case study of the hazards confronting charismatic leadership in crisis situations.

Joseph's followers not only reinforced his claims to leadership, they accorded him even greater power by their deference to his leadership. His closest associates were unsparing in their adulation. Brigham Young insisted, for example, "if Jesus lives, and is the Savior of the world, Joseph Smith is a Prophet of God. ... His garments are as pure as the angels that surround the throne of God."[9] Another contemporary, Heber C. Kimball, emphasized: "The day will be, gentlemen and ladies, whether you belong to this Church or not when you will ... look upon [Joseph Smith] as a god."[10] "He acted not with the wisdom of Man," testified a third follower, "but with the wisdom of God."[11] And a fourth commented, "He was a great statesman, philosopher and philanthropist, logician, and last but not least the greatest prophet, seer and revelator that ever lived, save Jesus Christ only."[12]

As Joseph came to see himself, he was "one greater than Solomon,"[13] insisting that "no man ever did such a work as I."[14] "Called of my Heavenly Father to lay the foundation of this great work and kingdom in this dispensation and [to] testify of His revealed will to scattered Israel,"[15] Joseph affirmed: "If any person should ask me if I were a prophet I should not deny it, as that would give me lie."[16] Though "the world persecutes me," he told a newspaper reporter in 1843, "when I have proved that I am right and get all the world subdued under me, I think I shall deserve something."[17] "God," he proclaimed to his followers, "will make me a god to you."[18] He became, in his own words, "the voice of one crying in the wilderness,"[19] "a huge, rough stone rolling down from a high mountain,"[20] "a smooth and polished shaft in the quiver of the Almighty,"[21] and "the towering rock in the midst of the ocean, which has withstood the mighty surges of the warring waves for centuries."[22] "God Almighty is my shield," he told his followers.[23] "I am His servant."[24] To which his most loyal adherents readily acceded: Joseph, Brigham Young testified, "reigns [in heaven] as supreme a being in his sphere, capacity, and calling, as God does."[25] "I shall bow to ... brother Joseph," Young added, "under Jesus Christ."[26]

Mormon historian Danel W. Bachman has identified Joseph's use of institutionalized power (i.e., priesthood) as based on a "perception of prophetic prerogatives."[27] Simply stated, Joseph believed he had power that transcended civil law. "Such formalities," Andrew F. Ehat has written, "palled into insignificance when compared to the pervasive power of the priesthood conferred upon him by angelic messengers."[28] And it is Joseph's exercise of this conviction that offers perhaps the best evidence for the tenuousness of the grasp he may have held, at times, on reality. But the discussion of Joseph's occasional difficulty to distinguish fantasy from reality should not be construed as an attempt to address the validity of his prophetic calling. Rather, it represents an admittedly speculative attempt to better understand the mental state–the strains, pressures, conflicts, and contradictions–we all experience when expectations clash with reality. With Joseph, the effects of such struggles were perhaps more dramatic, affecting the lives of more people, than would have been the case with a lesser individual.

In many ways, near the end of his life Joseph epitomized that person who, according to psychiatrist John E. Mack, "seeks in his expectations of himself to reach beyond what ordinary men are willing or able to undertake [and who] draws upon extraordinary means of adaptation and [thus] exposes himself to great failure and disappointment. He is especially vulnerable to the development of pathological symptoms and unusual behavioral responses."[29]

Twelve examples of the extent to which Joseph may have sought to interpose his will over that normally imposed upon human behavior by external reality are: his use of military imagery, his defiance of state laws, his manipulation of the political process, his control of the financial affairs of the church and its members, the creation of the Council of Fifty, his ordination as king, his campaign for the presidency of the United States, failed prophecy, his abrogation of established church judicial procedures, his failure to specify an apparent successor, his practice of plural marriage, and the destruction of the *Nauvoo Expositor.* Each example, discussed in greater detail below, reflects what may be either maladaptive responses to Joseph's environment or possible evidence of a growing sense of self-importance and personal omnipotence.

The charter incorporating Nauvoo, Illinois, as a city—a charter designed in operation to establish an independent Mormon commonwealth in the state of Illinois[30]—authorized the creation of a municipal legion. All eligible male citizens between the ages of eighteen and forty-five were compelled to join the Nauvoo Legion, and fines were levied against men who failed to appear at parade. If nothing else, the legion became a powerful symbol of potential force and especially autonomy. By 1844 it boasted an enlistment of between 3,000-5,000 recruits, while the entire U.S. Army had only 8,453, and was theoretically not subject to the military laws of Illinois. As a result historian Robert Flanders has noted, "'Colonel,' 'Captain,' or 'General' came to replace 'Brother,' 'Elder,' or 'President' in the address of the Saints. Military trappings were for them a particular symbol of status, prestige, and reassurance."[31]

As leader of the Nauvoo Legion, Joseph Smith received from the governor of Illinois the honorific commission of lieutenant general. Josiah Quincy relates a conversation that took place between Joseph and a Protestant minister during which Joseph scolded his colleague for referring to him simply as "Joe Smith." "Considering not only the day and the place," Joseph reportedly said, "it would have been more respectful to have said Lieutenant-General Joseph Smith."[32] Eventually Joseph "came to prefer the title 'General' even to 'President' and used it in much of his correspondence," Fawn Brodie has written.

"Delighting in the pomp and splendor of parades, he called out the Legion on every possible occasion, marching at the head on his magnificent black stallion, Charlie."[33] Joseph on such occasions, one member later recalled, "looked like a god."[34]

Actually, Joseph's title of "lieutenant-general" carried no real military authority, beyond decoration, outside the municipal boundaries of Nauvoo. When the U.S. Military Academy at West Point was contacted about the legitimacy of Joseph's rank, archivist Joseph M. O'Donnell responded: "Although the Nauvoo Legion was chartered by the State of Illinois, it was not considered to be part of the state militia. ... Joseph Smith, Jr., was not a Lieutenant General in the state militia, but of a small Mormon Army established to police Nauvoo, Illinois, and to defend the state of Illinois."[35] But Joseph clearly "deemed himself born to command,"[36] regardless of the formalities of military service, at the head of an army of his own making. In the process he reinforced both for himself and his followers the extent of his and others' perceptions of the power he controlled.

Organized in mid-March 1844,[37] though revealed in principle perhaps two years earlier,[38] the Council of Fifty, intended to represent the political kingdom of God on the earth, further evidenced Joseph's growing interest in the manifestations of power during the final two years of his life. The council's stated objectives included the eventual establishment of Christ's millennial rule, the introduction of his law, the protection of his church, and the "maintenance, promulgation and protection of civil and religious liberty in this nation and throughout the world."[39] In essence, the Council of Fifty was "conceived as the nucleus of a world government for the Millennium."[40] Yet the council, either during Joseph's lifetime or after, never came to occupy the kind of executive, legislative, or judicial role Joseph had hoped for.[41] Still its formation–in theory, at least–underscores the sobriety with which Joseph took his calling as prophet and leader, as well as the preemptive legitimacy his calling afforded him as executor of God's will. Both spiritually and politically, he stood in Christ's stead–a responsibility never lost on him.[42]

This facet of Joseph's personality and approach to leadership may also be evident in his ordination as "king on earth"[43] and his subsequent bid for the presidency of the United States. Reportedly, Joseph's coronation was "a perfect secret,"[44] although rumors of its occurrence were not uncommon in Nauvoo. Illinois governor Thomas Ford later wrote, for example, that Joseph "caused himself to be crowned the anointed king and priest far above the rest [of his followers]; and he prescribed the form of an oath of allegiance to himself which he administered to his principal followers."[45]

In pushing to win the 1844 U.S. presidential election, Joseph interpreted his move as part of the Council of Fifty's plans for the establishment of Christ's kingdom on earth and the ushering in of the long-awaited parousia. "Tell the people," he announced in accepting his nomination in late January 1844, five months before his death, "we have had Whig and Democratic Presidents long enough; we want a President of the United States."[46] His closest associates agreed: "General Smith is the greatest statesman of the 19th century," wrote Willard Richards, Joseph's secretary and a member of his Quorum of Twelve Apostles.[47] By this time Joseph had also been appointed mayor of Nauvoo, a judge of the Nauvoo Municipal Court, lieutenant general of the Nauvoo Legion, and trustee-in-trust for the church; he was a steamboat owner, a real estate agent, and de facto leader of the kingdom of God. Given the heady reaffirmation of omnipotence such positions afforded him, Joseph genuinely believed that he would win the upcoming national election. And when eventually informed that no one outside of Illinois would vote for him, he countered, "The Lord will turn the hearts of the people."[48]

In his dual role as prophet-politician, Joseph willingly lent his voice to the needs of followers that he reveal their economic and political futures. In so doing, however, he sometimes taxed his prophetic abilities to the limit, issuing prophecies that went unfulfilled. In 1843, for example, he predicted that Nauvoo would become "a great city" but refused to specify "how many inhabitants will come to Nauvoo."[49] Four months later he boldly prophesied, "in the name of the Lord," that because of the failure of the U.S. government to redress the persecutions leveled at his church "in a few years this government will be utterly overthrown and wasted so that there will not be a potsherd left."[50] By the end of the year he had added, convinced of his own prophetic prerogatives, that the government "shall be broken up as a government and God shall damn them, and there shall nothing be left of them–not even a grease spot."[51] For Joseph's adherents, as well as for himself, the rhetorical impact of his prophecies may have been more immediately important than their eventual realization.

Besides authorizing the establishment of the Nauvoo Legion, the Nauvoo city charter also contained a provision that gave the municipal court "power to grant writs of *habeas corpus* in all cases arising under the ordinances of the city council."[52] Conceivably, the court had power to investigate within city limits any confinement that was in violation of city ordinances.[53] When Missouri state officers arrested Joseph on 8 August 1842 on charges that he was an accessory to an attempted murder, the court granted him a writ of *habeas corpus* to prevent his extradition to Missouri. Shortly thereafter, the city council, composed predominantly of Mormons and over which Joseph presided as mayor, passed an ordinance that specifically authorized the court to investigate the case of any person under arrest at Nauvoo. The council and court clearly acted out of deference to Joseph, amending statute and procedure to better serve his interests. Five months later the council approved an ordinance designed to protect Joseph from future Missouri persecutions. The new statute subjected any law official to a mandatory life sentence who attempted to arrest Joseph on "old Missouri charges." The ordinance stipulated that those found guilty could only be pardoned by the governor of the state with the "consent of the Mayor" of Nauvoo.[54] Joseph's confidence in the new provision is reflected in his public comments of 30 June 1843: "We have all power: and if any man from this time forth says anything to the contrary, cast it into his teeth."[55] Though the council's fears of possible harm to Joseph are understandable, the actions it took in his defense served to shield him from outside discord, perpetuating a feeling of safety and omnipotence while safeguarded at Nauvoo, at least.

When Joseph was eventually arrested in mid-1843 (outside Nauvoo), he secured the legal services of Cyrus Walker, a Whig candidate from Illinois for the U.S. House of Representatives. Evidently, Walker arranged for Joseph's release in exchange for the Mormon vote in the upcoming election. Within thirty days after having "promised Walker that he should have nine out of every ten Mormon votes,"[56] however, church leaders decided it would be more expedient to vote for his opponent, Joseph P. Hoge. Two days before the election, Hyrum Smith, Joseph's older brother, announced publicly that "he had a revelation from the Lord, that the people should vote for Mr. Hoge."[57]

Joseph's reaction is recorded in his diary: "Bro. Hyrum tells me this morning that he has had a testimony that it will be better for this people to vote for Hoge, and I never knew Hyrum say he had a revelation [and] it failed."[58] Joseph subsequently advised the assembled Saints to follow his brother's admonition, and Hoge easily carried the Nauvoo vote.[59] Joseph's apparent change of heart exhibits not only the ease with which he was able to reverse earlier commitments to serve the interests of his church; it demonstrates the control he held over his followers–the willingness of the leader and the led to reinforce the other in his needs.

Not all Saints were as receptive to their leader's actions, however. William Law, at one time Joseph's second counselor in the First Presidency,[60] came to reject openly Joseph's claim to authority. When Joseph informed Law on 8 January 1844 that he had been "dropped" from the First Presidency, Law requested that his case be aired publicly. Joseph refused because of mounting opposition from other apostates, and church leaders moved to excommunicate Law with as little outside knowledge of their proceedings as possible. Revealed procedures involving the removal or excommunication of a member of the First Presidency dictated that the case be heard by a bishop and his two counselors, assisted by twelve high priests;[61] that three separate witnesses of "long and faithful standing," whose characters were "unimpeachable" provide evidence of misconduct and that the final verdict be approved by a majority of stakes of the church;[62] and that all parties concerned be in attendance during the proceedings.[63] When charges were formally brought against Law in mid-April 1844, Apostle Brigham Young, not church bishop Newel K. Whitney, presided, and the above procedures were dispensed with. Law, his wife, and other church dissidents were excommunicated *in absentia* without having been notified of the proceedings or served with specific charges. When he learned of the court's action, Law demanded the names of his accusers and to know on what grounds he had been excommunicated. Apostle Willard Richards, who had acted as clerk during the closed trial, insisted that no record had been kept. In fact, a partial transcript in Richards's hand is currently housed in LDS church archives in Salt Lake City.[64]

Joseph's response to events surrounding the abrogation of church justice that characterized the excommunication of William Law suggests a fear of the truth and demonstrates the extent to which he was ready to manipulate organizational and judicial procedures to protect himself against attacks that might expose him to a loss of credibility and power. Tragically, he was apparently unable to appreciate the impropriety of his acts or the consequences in which they would result so convinced was he of the power he wielded.

In early 1843 brisk competition from enterprising land speculators prompted Joseph to insist that church members purchasing building lots do so only from authorized church officials. Joseph ruled that "those who come here having money and purchased without the church [and] without council must be cut off."[65] More tactful, though no less pointed, the *Nauvoo Neighbor* later requested that "all brethren ... when they move to Nauvoo, consult President Joseph Smith, the trustee in trust, and purchase their lands from him."[66] Not only were the economic principles of free enterprise discarded to benefit the stability of the church, but ecclesiastical punishment was employed as a threat to encourage compliance. The threatened loss of spiritual blessings, while no doubt an effective deterrent, represented a severe punishment to challengers of Joseph's authority.

At the time of Joseph's martyrdom in late June 1844, at least eight possible means of succession to the presidency of the church had their apparent precedents.[67] Each method had its proponents, but immediately following Joseph's death none was clearly favored, or even understood, by members generally. "Many wanted to draw off a party and be leaders," observed Brigham Young, president of the Quorum of the Twelve Apostles, whose claim was eventually accepted by a majority of members remaining with the church.[68] Apostle Wilford Woodruff recorded that the Saints "felt like sheep without a shepard, as being without a father, as their head had been taken away."[69] Organizational ambiguities surrounding the transfer of power helped foster a succession crisis during which a variety of contenders vied for control of the church. As D. Michael Quinn has written, "Joseph Smith's neglect to make explicit to the general membership an undisputed mode of succession caused thousands of his followers to falter, wander, and ultimately to reject the Church headquartered in Utah."[70]

If anyone must bear the burden of responsibility for the confusion and uncertainty that nearly overwhelmed the Saints immediately following their prophet's death, it is Joseph. Either unwilling or unable, Joseph could not foresee the necessity for such a provision, firmly believing that his power controlled even death. "I defy all the world to destroy the work of God," he pronounced, "and I prophecy they never will have power to kill me till my work is accomplished, and I am ready to die."[71]

When members of the Quorum of the Twelve Apostles returned from missions to England in 1841, many learned that Joseph had begun taking additional wives as part of his "restoration of all things." Joseph moved almost immediately to introduce his doctrine of "celestial marriage" to receptive members of the Twelve. Initially, he did so on an individual basis, devising a test of loyalty and obedience to "dramatically demonstrate the transcendence of priesthood power over civil customs ... and establish clearly in their minds that only when a couple have made a covenant for eternity by that priesthood power would they have a legitimate and eternal claim on one another."[72] The test consisted of Joseph's requesting of an apostle that he relinquish his wife to Joseph, that she might become his plural wife. This apparently continued for almost one year before one apostle, Orson Pratt, failed to pass Joseph's test in July 1842. Sensitive to the scandal that could erupt from additional failures, Joseph suspended requiring such a show of faith.

Later that same month, however, he introduced a variation of his "Abrahamic" test. Andrew Ehat reports: "The Prophet went to various parents in Nauvoo, who had marriageable daughters, tested and taught the parents these principles by requesting that they in turn teach their daughters eternal and plural marriage. With this show of faith, the parents were subsequently sealed in marriage for time and eternity."[73] Though Ehat only intimates as to the exact nature of the adapted test, it is clear that the price some paid for their own sealing for time and eternity was the marriage of their daughter to Joseph. To the parents of one such girl, Joseph confided, "The only thing to be careful of is to find out when Emma [Joseph's first wife] comes, then you cannot be safe but when she is not here, there is most perfect safety."[74]

That Joseph, fearing repercussions from his propositions to married women, would so soon thereafter employ a virtually identical test suggests a possible inability to distinguish between actions which were clearly repugnant to a majority of his followers. If Joseph's move away from asking for the wives of married men to asking for the daughters of faithful couples was intended to minimize the risk of public exposure, it shortly, and not unexpectedly, proved unsuccessful. Joseph's courtship of Nancy Rigdon, daughter of former First Presidency counselor Sidney Rigdon, became as damaging to his reputation as his attempted liaison with Apostle Orson Pratt's wife. The evidence indicates that Joseph did not appreciate adequately the probable results of his advances. Despite the far from completely unreliable play his exploits received in the press, his plural marriages continued throughout the summer of 1843.[75]

There is reason to believe that Joseph's tests may have resulted from anticipated opposition to his practices from both his brother Hyrum and his wife, Emma. Apparently never once during the first twenty-four months Joseph secretly promoted and practiced the "celestial law of marriage" did either Emma consent to her husband's taking another wife or Hyrum offer to perform or teach the secret ordinance. Joseph's tests, it may be argued, evince the possible expression of what can be termed a paranoid delusion in which not even his most faithful friends could be completely trusted without their being first required to demonstrate unconditional allegiance to his leadership. Yet the irony in Joseph's need to ascertain the reaction of his closest disciples when the two people whose love and support he craved most could not be trusted is both striking and telling. If Joseph could endure the rejection of others, he could not suffer rejection from either Hyrum or Emma, and initially refused to court their hostile responses.

When Emma did eventually accede to her husband's wishes, on condition that she select the new wives, she unknowingly chose two women, sisters, who had surreptitiously married Joseph only two months earlier. Not wanting to give Emma cause for believing she had been deceived, the two sisters allowed her to teach them the principles of plural marriage, and Joseph, rather than offend his wife by revealing the existing marriage, furthered the deception by having the sealing ordinance performed a second time.[76] Given this and other subterfuges, Emma's support was short-lived, and she soon became an active opponent of her husband's secret teachings.

If Hyrum Smith proved more difficult to convert to the principle of plural marriage than Emma, he, at least remained more faithful to its practice. In May 1843 he openly preached against "the ancient order of things as Solomon [and] David having many wives [and] concubines [which] is an abomination in the sight of God. If an angel from heaven should come down [and] preach such a doctrine [one] would be sure to see his cloven foot [and] cloud of blackness over his head, though his garments might shine as white as snow."[77] Only when Brigham Young, not Joseph, explained the doctrine to him, provided he never again speak out against his brother, did Hyrum come to accept the practice of polygamy as divine.

Not only were the theory and practice of polygamy conducted in private, but there were occasions when Joseph went to elaborate measures to conceal his own involvement. After his marriage to one young woman, the seventeen-year-old daughter of Newel K. Whitney, Joseph had her "married" to her father's brother-in-law. Her "husband" later explained: "According to President Joseph Smith['s] council & other[s] I agread to stand by Sarah Ann Whitney as to be her husband & had a pretended marriage for the purpose of bringing about the purposes of God in these last days spoken by the mouths of the prophets."[78]

Joseph, Danel Bachman notes, "must have realized that an indiscriminate advocacy of plural marriage would only intensify criticism and stiffen anti-Mormon opposition."[79] Yet this does not satisfactorily explain Joseph's misrepresentation in denying any personal involvement in polygamy whatsoever. "What a thing it is for a man to be accused of committing adultery," he quipped publicly in May 1844, after he had had at least nineteen women sealed to him, "and having seven wives when I can find only one. I am the same man, and innocent as I was fourteen years ago; and I can prove them all [i.e., his detractors] perjurers."[80] Earlier he had gone so far as to give "instructions to try those who were preaching [or] teaching on the doctrine of plurality of wives ... [because] Joseph forbids it, and the practice thereof. No man shall have but one wife."[81]

With the appearance of the *Nauvoo Expositor* in early June 1844, published by a handful of disaffected church authorities, Joseph could not help but recognize that he had been put "on trial before his whole people."[82] Had he at this point been able to trust them with the truth regarding his involvement in plural marriage, "he might have stripped the apostates of their chief weapon and freed his loyal followers from a burden of secrecy, evasion, and lying that was rapidly becoming intolerable."[83] With uncustomary foresight he reportedly confided to Nauvoo Stake president William Marks, "This doctrine of polygamy, or spiritual wife system, that has been taught and practiced among us, will prove our destruction and overthrow. I have been deceived, it is a curse to mankind, and we shall have to leave the United States soon unless it can be put down, and its practice stopped in the Church."[84]

Tragically, however, reality soon gave way to the fantasy that his opposition needed only to be suppressed to be controlled. Joseph "told the people or us that God showed him in an open vision in daylight that if he did not destroy that press, Printing Press, it would cause the Blood of the Saints to flow in the Street."[85] Calling together the Nauvoo City Council, he declared than the revelation on plural marriage referred to in the *Nauvoo Expositor* was "in answer to a question concerning things which transpired in former days, and had no reference to the present time."[86] Joseph asked the council "if they would stand by him. He also told them if they would not that he would leave them and goe to where he could rais up a people that would stand by him."[87] Again, deferring to their prophet, the council declared that the press was indeed libelous and must be destroyed. Joseph issued a proclamation to the effect that the press was a civic nuisance. Members from the Nauvoo Legion dutifully marched to the *Expositor* office, wrecked the press, pied the type, and burned every issue of the paper that could be found.

Joseph's action, the destruction of not only a newspaper but its printing press, escalated into far more than simply "a moment of bad judgement" or defiance of "the sacred precept of freedom of the press."[88] It became a "greater breach of political and legal discipline than the anti-Mormons could have hoped for. Joseph could not have done better for his enemies, since he had given them a fighting moral issue."[89] Joseph's recurrent inability to distinguish fantasy from reality is once again evident, though, unlike the preceding examples, the consequences in this final instance proved fatal.

Destruction of the *Nauvoo Expositor,* while perhaps not the most blatant expression of Joseph's mounting megalomania, was clearly its most violent manifestation. But the greatest factor contributing to his image of virtual omnipotence was not the destruction of the press or his fusion of politics and religion, but rather the acceptance of polygamy by his brother, wife, and closest associates. More than any other expression of allegiance, their willingness to obey Joseph's commands in an area so at odds with conventional Victorian morality may have contributed to what appears to be the slowly eroding of barriers separating reality from fantasy. Organizational behaviorist Manfred F. R. Kets de Vries contends, for example, that "continuous positive responses from the [leader's] direct subordinates for even his most erratic actions may be responsible for a gradual deterioration of reality testing."[90] The irony is that the leader who succeeds in pushing his movement toward the realization of their fantasies may well be on the way to his own self-destruction.[91]

The crisis that followed Joseph's death probably began at least two years preceding it. The sporadic breakdowns in the perception of reality that occurred for many in Nauvoo may have been conducive to "regressive behavior in [their] leaders as well as [themselves]."[92] Yet because the threat of change was greatest during this unstable period, many Saints may have found that their identification with their prophet was greatly facilitated, resulting in a possible "rebirth of motivation and the emergence of a cohesive group spirit within the organization."[93] Small wonder, then, that a deep sense of personal loss should have engulfed many of his adherents after Joseph's violent death as if a part of them had suddenly been taken away. What has since become evident, however, is that a move toward greater physical and mental health sometimes follows and can be related to the loss of the leader by his followers.[94] Perhaps if any benefit is to be derived from Joseph's death it is that it may have saved his followers from a similar fate.

*NOTES*

1. Recorded in Orson F. Whitney, *Life of Heber C. Kimball* (Salt Lake City: Bookcraft, 1945), 322.

2. Manfred F. R. Kets de Vries observes, for example, that charismatic individuals can hold on to "infantile wishes of all powerfulness" so that "an

excess of material, physical, or symbolic resources through which power can easily bring about pathological behavior patterns in otherwise 'normal' individuals." Kets de Vries, "Crisis Leadership and the Paranoid Potential," *Bulletin of the Menninger Clinic,* July 1977, 351-52.

3. Ibid., 352.

4. Ibid.

5. Abraham Zalesnick, "Charismatic and Consensus Leaders: A Psychological Comparison," *Bulletin of the Menninger Clinic,* May 1974, 228.

6. Kets de Vries, 353.

7. Talcott Parsons, ed., A. M. Henderson and Talcott Parsons, trans., *Max Weber: The Theory of Social and Economic Organization* (New York: Oxford University Press, 1947), 359.

8. See, for example, Zalesnick, 223; Irvine Schiffer, *Charisma: A Psychoanalytic Look at Mass Society* (Toronto: University of Toronto Press, 1973); Ann Ruth Willner, *Charismatic Political Leadership: A Theory,* Research Monograph, No. 32 (Princeton University: Center of International Studies, May 1968); Ann Ruth and Dorothy Willner, "The Rise and Role of Charismatic Leaders," *Annals of the American Academy of Political and Social Sciences,* Mar. 1965; Douglas F. Barnes, "Charisma and Religious Leadership: An Historical Analysis," *Journal of the Scientific Study of Religion,* 1978; and Michael W. Purdy, "The Unique Charismatic Influence of Joseph Smith, Founder of the Mormon Church," copy in my possession (thanks to E. Gary Smith for pointing out this study to me).

Weber's definition, implying that the charismatic leader has somehow been bestowed with powers, has been criticized as inadequate in explaining the existence of charisma in an increasingly secular world where such concepts have been largely discarded. However, within a religious frame work that emphasizes the existence of the supernatural, Weber's characterization need not necessarily be abandoned, especially when charisma is viewed by the perspective of the follower. For criticisms of Weber, see Reinhard Bendix, "Reflections on Charismatic Leadership," *State and Society* (Boston: Little, Brown, 1968); William Friedrich, "For a Sociological Concept of Charisma," *Social Forces,* 1968; Robert C. Tucker, "The Theory of Charismatic Leadership," *Daedalus,* Summer 1968; and Martin D. Spencer, "What Is Charisma?" *The British Journal of Sociology,* Sept. 1973.

9. In *Journal of Discourses,* 26 vols. (London: Latter-day Saints' Book Depot, 1854-86), 1:38; hereafter cited as JD, followed by volume and page numbers.

10. JD 5:88.

11. "Newel Knight's Journal," *Scraps of Biography* (Salt Lake City, 1883), 65.

12. Daniel Tyler, in *The Juvenile Instructor,* 1 Feb. 1892, 93.

13. In Josiah Quincy, "Figures of the Past," in William Mulder and A.

Russell Mortensen, eds., *Among the Mormons: Historic Accounts by Contemporary Observers* (Lincoln: University of Nebraska Press, 1958), 138.

14. Joseph Smith et al., *History of the Church of Jesus Christ of Latter-day Saints. Period I. History of Joseph Smith, the Prophet, by Himself,* 6 vols., B. H. Roberts, ed. and comp. (Salt Lake City: Church of Jesus Christ of Latter-day Saints, 1902-12), 6:409; cited as HC, followed by volume and page numbers.

15. Ibid., 5:516.

16. Ibid., 215.

17. In the *New York Spectator,* (23 Sept. 1843).

18. HC, 6:319-20.

19. Ibid., 273.

20. Ibid., 5:402.

21. Ibid.

22. Ibid., 6:78.

23. Ibid., 5:259.

24. Ibid., 6:305.

25. JD 7:299.

26. Ibid., 4:41.

27. Danel W Bachman, "New Light on an Old Hypothesis: The Ohio Origins of the Revelation on Eternal Marriage," *Journal of Mormon History* 5 (1978): 32.

28. Andrew F Ehat, "An Overview of the Introduction of Eternal Marriage in the Church of Jesus Christ of Latter-day Saints, 1840-1843," Nov. 1980, 2; copy in my possession.

29. John E. Mack, *A Prince of Our Disorder: The Life of T. E. Lawrence* (Boston: Little, Brown, Co., 1976), xxvi.

30. See Robert B. Flanders, *Nauvoo: Kingdom on the Mississippi* (Urbana: University of Illinois Press, 1965), 104.

31. Ibid., 112-13.

32. Quincy, in Mulder and Mortensen, 140.

33. Fawn M. Brodie, *No Man Knows My History: The Life of Joseph Smith, the Mormon Prophet,* 2nd. ed., rev. and enlarged (New York: Knopf, 1976), 270.

34. Lyman Woods, in Nels Anderson, *Desert Saints* (Chicago: University of Chicago Press, 1942), 5.

35. Joseph M. O'Donnell to Ralph L. Foster, 29 Aug. 1963, copy in my possession.

36. Peter H. Burnett, *An Old California Pioneer* (Oakland: Biobooks, 1946), 40.

37. Wilford Woodruff Journal, 10 Mar. 1844, in archives, Historical Department, Church of Jesus Christ of Latter-day Saints, Salt Lake City, Utah (hereafter LDS archives).

38. Minutes of the Council of Fifty, 10 Apr. 1880, typed copy in Special Collections, Harold B. Lee Library, Brigham Young University, Provo, Utah.

39. See revelation dated 27 June 1882, in Annie Taylor Hyde Notebook, 58-60, LDS archives.

40. Andrew F. Ehat, "'It Seems Like Heaven Began on Earth': Joseph Smith and the Constitution of the Kingdom of God," *BYU Studies*, Spring 1980, 274.

41. D. Michael Quinn, "The Council of Fifty and Its Members, 1844 to 1945," *BYU Studies*, Winter 1979, 174.

42. Cf. LDS D&C 28:2.

43. See the letter of George Miller, June 1855, in Donna Hill, *Joseph Smith: The First Mormon* (Garden City, NY: Doubleday, 1977), 485n15.

44. George T. M. Davis, *An Authentic Account of the Massacre of Joseph Smith, the Mormon Prophet, and Hyrum Smith, His Brother* (St. Louis, 1844), 7.

45. Thomas Ford, *A History of Illinois from Its Commencement as a State in 1814 to 1847* (Chicago: S.C. Griggs, 1854), 321-22.

46. HC, 6:188.

47. Willard Richards to James Arlington Bennett, 4 Mar. 1844, LDS archives.

48. "Autobiography of Dr. Ephraim Ingals," *Journal of the Illinois State Historical Society*, Jan. 1936, 295.

49. HC, 5:232.

50. Ibid., 393-94, and William Clayton Journal, 18 May 1843, LDS archives (cf. HC, 6:58).

51. *Latter-day Saints' Millennial Star* 22:455. When this last prophecy was later republished, the phrase "and God shall damn them, and there shall nothing be left of them–not even a grease spot" was omitted (see HC, 6:116).

52. The Nauvoo City Charter is reprinted in HC, 4:239-45.

53. This was Dallin H. Oaks's conclusion in "The Suppression of the *Nauvoo Expositor," Utah Law Review*, Winter 1965, 878, 880.

54. HC, 6:105-106.

55. Ibid., 5:466.

56. "The Law Interview," *Salt Lake City Daily Tribune*, 31 July 1887.

57. Ibid.

58. Joseph Smith Diary, 6 Aug. 1843, LDS archives.

59. "Law Interview."

60. Earlier Law had written: "Bro. Joseph is truly a wonderful man he is all we could wish a prophet to be" (William Law to Isaac Russell, 10 Nov. 1837, LDS archives).

61. LDS D&C 107:76, 82.

62. Revelation, 12 Jan. 1838, in "Scriptory Book of Joseph Smith," 51-52, LDS archives.

63. Nauvoo High Council Minutes, 11 July 1840, LDS archives.

64. For a sympathetic treatment of William Law, see Lyndon W. Cook, "William Law: Nauvoo Dissenter," *BYU Studies,* Winter 1982, 47-72.

65. Joseph Smith Diary, 13 Feb. 1843.

66. *Nauvoo Neighbor,* 20 Dec. 1843.

67. See D. Michael Quinn, "The Mormon Succession Crisis of 1844," *BYU Studies,* Winter 1976, 187-232, for a thorough discussion of possible means of succession.

68. Brigham Young Diary, 8 Aug. 1844, LDS archives.

69. Wilford Woodruff Journal, 8 Aug. 1844.

70. Quinn, "Succession Crisis," 232.

71. HC, 6:58.

72. Ehat, "Eternal Marriage," 8. For the best introduction to polygamy, see Richard S. Van Wagoner, *Mormon Polygamy: A History* (Salt Lake City: Signature Books, 1986).

73. Ibid., 9-10.

74. Joseph Smith to "Brother and Sister Whitney," 8 Aug. 1842, LDS archives.

75. See Danel W. Bachman, "A Study of the Mormon Practice of Plural Marriage Before the Death of Joseph Smith," M.A. thesis, Purdue University, 1975, 333-36.

76. Circuit Court Testimony, 1892, Emily D. R Young Deposition, Questions 29-33, carbon copy in LDS archives.

77. Levi Richards Journal, 14 May 1843, LDS archives.

78. Joseph C. Kingsbury, "The History of Joseph C. Kingsbury," 12-13, Special Collections, Marriott Library, University of Utah, Salt Lake City.

79. Bachman, "A Study of the Mormon Practice of Plural Marriage," 194.

80. HC, 6:411.

81. Joseph Smith Diary, 5 Oct. 1843.

82. Brodie, 375.

83. Ibid., 375-76.

84. *Zion's Harbinger and Baneemy's Organ,* July 1853.

85. George Laub Journal, in Eugene England, ed., "George Laub's Nauvoo Journal," *BYU Studies,* Winter 1978, 160.

86. *Nauvoo Neighbor,* 19 June 1844.

87. George Laub Journal, 160.

88. Hill, 2.

89. Brodie, 377.

90. Kets de Vries, 358.

91. See Manfred F. R. Kets de Vries, "The Entrepreneurial Personality: A Person at the Crossroads," *Journal of Management Studies,* 1977, 34-57.

92. Kets de Vries, "Crisis Leadership," 359.

93. Ibid.

94. See, for example, the finding of Charles K. Hofling and Joy Michael in "Favorable Responses to the Loss of a Significant Figure: A Preliminary Report," *Bulletin of the Menninger Clinic*, Nov. 1974, 528; Erich Lindeman, "Symptomology and Management of Acute Grief," *American Journal of Psychiatry*, 1944, 141-48; G. L. Engel, *Psychological Development in Health and Disease* (Philadelphia: Saunders, 1962); and C. M. Parkes, *Bereavement: Studies of Grief in Adult Life* (New York: International Universities Press, 1972).

# 13. Joseph Smith's "Inspired Translation" of Romans 7

*Ronald V. Huggins*

THIS ESSAY EXAMINES JOSEPH SMITH'S TREATMENT OF ROMANS 7 IN THE Joseph Smith Translation or "Inspired Version" of the King James Bible (JST). First, Smith's modifications of the chapter are compared to the King James Version (KJV), upon which it is primarily based, and to the Greek manuscript tradition. Second, the early nineteenth-century interpretation of the chapter is outlined as background to understanding Smith's rendition. Finally, Smith's rendition of the chapter is investigated.

## JOSEPH SMITH'S MODIFICATIONS, THE KING JAMES VERSION, AND THE GREEK TEXT

Basic sources for the study of the relation between the JST and the KJV for Romans 7 are (1) the Joseph Smith-Oliver Cowdery Bible (SCB) and (2) New Testament Manuscript 2 (NT MS 2) of the JST. The SCB (or "Marked Bible") is a stereotype edition of the KJV printed by H. & E. Phinney in Cooperstown, New York, in 1828. Joseph Smith and Oliver Cowdery bought it jointly from Palmyra printer and bookseller Egbert B. Grandin on 8 October 1829. The SCB is an 8-by-11-by-2½-inch pulpit-style Bible weighing just under five pounds.[1] Into it marks were entered (with varying consistency) indicating where and what sort of changes were to be made. These changes were then entered into separate hand-written manuscripts. The manuscript containing Romans 7 is commonly referred to as NT MS 2. NT MS 2 is made up of four folios and totals 154 pages. Romans 7 is treated on pages 123-25 of folio four.[2]

The following is the full text of Romans 7 with all the changes made in the SCB and NT MS 2 noted.

*Sigla:* 1. Additions to the SCB are in capital letters (where confusion might arise due to the close proximity of "I," this is marked by [ or ]).
2. Deletions from the SCB: {—}
3. Italicized words in the SCB which were *not* marked for removal: > <
4. Transpositions from SCB order: < > with </> or <\> in the place from which it was removed. The direction of the slash marks indicates whether the word(s) has been moved forward or backward in the text.
5. Words crossed out in NT MS 2: /—/
6. Words written between the lines in NT MS 2 are underlined.

(1) Know ye not, brethren, (for I speak to them that know the law,) how that the law hath dominion over a man ONLY as long as he liveth? (2) For the woman which hath a husband is bound by the law to >her< husband, ONLY {~~so~~} AS long as he liveth; {~~but~~} FOR if the husband be dead, she is loosed from the law of >her< husband. (3) So then, if, while >her< husband liveth, she be married to another man, she shall be called an adultress: but if her husband be dead, she is free from that law; so that she is no adultress, though she be married to another man. (4) Wherefore, my brethren, ye also are become dead to the law by the body of Christ; that ye should be married to another, {~~even~~} to him who is raised from the dead, that we should bring forth fruit unto God. (5) For when we were in the flesh, the motions of sins, which were {~~by~~} NOT ACCORDING TO the law, did work in our members, to bring forth fruit unto death. (6) But now we are delivered from the law <wherein we were held>, {~~that~~} being dead <\> TO THE LAW, that we should serve in newness of spirit, and not >in< *the* oldness of /~~the~~/ the letter. (7) What shall we say then? >Is< the law sin? God forbid. Nay, I had not known sin, but by the law: for I had not known lust, except the law had said, Thou shalt not covet. (8) But sin, taking occasion by the commandment,

wrought in me all manner of concupiscence. For without the law, sin >was< dead. (9) For <once> I was alive without TRANSGRESSION OF the law <\>, but when the commandment OF CHRIST came, sin revived, and I died. (10) and WHEN I BELIEVED NOT the commandment OF CHRIST WHICH CAME, which >was ordained< to life, I found {~~to be~~} IT CONDEMNED ME unto death. (11) For sin, taking occasion, {/~~by~~/} DENYED the commandment, AND deceived me; and by it {~~slew me~~} [I WAS SLAIN. (12) {~~Wherefore~~} NEVERTHELESS I FOUND the law {~~is~~} TO BE holy, and the commandment TO BE holy, and just, and good. (13) Was then that which is good made death unto me? God forbid; But sin, that it might appear sin </> by that which is good, <working death in me>; that sin by the commandment might become exceeding sinfulL. (14) For we know that the {~~law~~} COMMANDMENT is spiritual; but WHEN I WAS UNDER THE LAW,] I {~~am~~} [WAS YET carnal, sold under sin. (15) BUT NOW I AM SPIRITUAL For that which [I AM COMMANDED TO DO,] I do; AND THAT WHICH I AM COMMANDED NOT TO ALLOW,] I allow not. (NT MS 2 = vs 16) For what I] KNOW IS NOT RIGHT,] <I (1)> would <not (2)> {~~that~~} do <1\> <2\>; {~~but what~~} FOR THAT WHICH IS SIN,] I hate {~~that do I~~}. (vs 16 = vs 17) If then /~~I~~/ I do NOT that which I would not ALLOW, I consent unto the law, that >it is< good, AND I AM NOT CONDEMNED. (vs 17 = vs 18) Now then, it is no more I that do {~~it~~} SIN; but [I SEEK TO SUBDUE THAT sin {~~that~~} WHICH dwelleth in me. (vs 18 = vs 19) For I know that in me, that is, in my flesh, dwelleth no good thing; for to will is present with me; but {~~how~~} to perform that which is good I find not, ONLY IN CHRIST. (vs 19 = vss 20-21) For the good the I would HAVE DONE WHEN UNDER THE LAW, I FIND NOT TO BE GOOD; THEREFORE,] I do IT not. (NT MS 2: vs 21) But the evil which I would not DO UNDER THE LAW, I FIND TO BE GOOD; that, I do. (vs 20 = vs 22) Now if I do that, THROUGH THE ASSISTENCE *OF CHRIST*,] I would not DO UNDER THE LAW, /~~I no more~~/ I AM NOT UNDER THE LAW; AND it is no more /~~I~~/ <that> I [SEEK TO <\> do {~~it~~} [W]RONG, but TO SUBDUE sin that dwelleth in me. (vss 21-2 = vs 23) I find then {~~a~~} THAT UNDER THE law, that when I would do good evil {~~is~~} WAS present with me; (SCB: vs 22) for I delight in the law of God after the inward man. (vs 23 = vss 24-/~~25~~/ vs 18) {~~but~~} AND NOW] I see another law, EVEN THE COMMANDMENT OF CHRIST, AND IT IS IMPRINTED IN MY MIND (NT MS 2: vs 18; JST: /~~25~~/) {~~in~~} BUT my members ARE warring against the law of my mind, and bringing me in to captivity /~~unto sin~~/ *to* the law of sin which is in my members. (24 = JST: 26) AND IF I SUBDUE NOT THE SIN WHICH IS IN ME, <but with

the flesh /~~is subject to~~/ *SERVE* the law of sin>; O wretched man that I am! who shall deliver *me* from the body of this death? (25 = JST: 27) I thank God through Jesus Christ our Lord, <then>, THAT /[~~wit~~] (?)/ so <\> with the mind, I, myself serve the law of God <vs 23\>.

Joseph Smith's adaptation of the SCB for Romans 7 is conservative with regard to deletions. In contrast to the 168 words introduced by Smith (thirty-seven in 7:14-15 alone), only twenty-seven words were deleted from the entire chapter. Of these, ten are due to minor clarifications or stylistic changes;[3] five are due to changes in verb tense or mood;[4] and four are due to the removal of italicized words.[5] This leaves only nine deletions unaccounted for, all of which Smith probably considered unimportant: "by" twice (vv. 5 and 11); "that" three times (vv. 6, 15 = $16^2$); "do" (v. 15 = 16); "I" (v. 15 = 16); "a" (v. 21 = 23); and "in" (v. 23 = 25). Considerable pains then were taken to retain as many original SCB words as possible. Seven transpositions, however, do occur (vv. 6, 9, 13, 15 = 16, 20 = 22, 24 = 26, and 25 = 27), but these are handled in such a way as to keep as many original SCB words as possible. Indeed, the very act of transposing suggests restoration of words and phrases from incorrect secondary locations to correct original ones.

That Joseph Smith felt the KJV contained many errors and corruptions is well known.[6] The kinds of modifications he made in Romans 7 lead us further to conclude that he understood such corruptions to consist primarily of things removed or left out.[7] This observation confirms certain of Smith's own statements from around the same time. In Joseph Smith's *History of the Church*, prefacing a "revelation" dated 16 February 1832 (now D&C 76; 1835 ed., XCI), Smith reports: "Upon my return from the Amherst conference, I resumed the translation of the Scriptures. From sundry revelations which had been received, it was apparent that many important points touching the salvation of man *had been taken from* the Bible, or lost before it was compiled" (italics added).

This remark provides insight into Smith's approach to the Bible within at most only a few months of his "translation" of Romans 7.[8] A similar statement occurs in a "revelation" dated June 1830 in which God tells Moses of a time when: "[T]he children of men shall esteem my words as nought, and *take many of them from the book* which thou shall write, behold, I will raise up another like unto thee [i.e., Joseph

Smith], and they shall be had again among the children of men ..." (italics added; HC 1:245-52; Pearl of Great Price, Moses 1:41 [1851 ed., 10]).[9] The conservatism in handling the SCB for Romans 7, then, in light of these statements, suggests that Joseph Smith *did* intend to restore the ancient text of the New Testament. He apparently felt this could be best accomplished by rearranging the words of the SCB, leaving out as little as possible, and then adding whatever seemed to be lacking.[10]

However, we shall seek to demonstrate here, in agreement with several earlier studies,[11] that JST Romans 7 does not represent a restoration of the original text. If the JST is not a restoration, what is it? If what we have said is true–that Joseph Smith claimed to restore the text to its original form but did not actually do so–the issue of the validity of the JST as a revelation comes to the fore. Broadly speaking, Mormon scholars have responded to this in two ways. Some have attempted to undermine the validity of modern critical editions of the Greek New Testament by asserting that the earliest extant Greek manuscripts already represent a widely corrupted text. These writers seek to place the JST earlier still and thus for all practical purposes beyond contradiction.[12] However the abundance of early evidence makes such a position difficult to maintain. Others have sought instead to cast doubt on Smith's restorational intent.[13] Though this position is more plausible in that it deals realistically with the textual data, it still suffers from a seeming readiness to assume that if the JST is not a restoration, Smith never intended it as one. But this does not necessarily follow. Perhaps Smith honestly believed he was restoring the ancient text but failed in reality to do so. Or, worse, perhaps he was consciously involved in imposture. If Smith did not intend a restoration, why is it that "many of the early Mormon people were conditioned to think of the revision [of the Bible] as a restoration of original, lost texts," and why did Smith himself say in his journal for 15 October 1843: "I believe in the Bible, as it ought to be, as it came from the pen of the original writers"?[14] Or why a decade earlier did he allow statements like the following to appear in *The Evening and Morning Star* (July 1833): "As to the errors in the bible, any man possessed of common understanding, knows, that both the old and new testaments are filled with errors, obscurities, italics and contradictions, which must be the work of men. As the church of Christ will soon have the scriptures, in their *original purity* it may not be amiss for us to show a few of the gross errors, or, as they might be termed, contradictions" (italics added). And later: "With the old copy full of errors; with Dickinson's and Webster's polite translation, with Campbell's improved, and many more from different persuasions, how will a person of common understanding know which is right without the gift of the Holy Spirit? ... *the bible ... must be PURIFIED*! ... O what a blessing, that the Lord will bestow the gift of the Holy Spirit, upon the meek and humble, whereby they can know of a surety, *his words from the words of men!*" (italics added). Or again why did he say, as already noted, that "I resumed the translation of the Scriptures ... it was apparent that many important points touching the salvation of man had been taken from the Bible or lost before it was compiled"? And finally why does the very manner in which Smith treats the text of JST Romans 7 imply (in agreement with his statements on the matter) that he considered the language of the KJV to be essentially authentic except where (1) transpositions have occurred or (2) something has been left out? In view of these facts it seems clear that Philip Barlow's claim that "Joseph Smith himself never explained exactly how he understood his revision of the Bible" is misleading.[15] Rather the message communicated to early Mormons, whether by Smith himself or other representatives of the church, was that the JST *was* to be a restoration of the scriptures to their original purity. The actual manner in which Smith modified the text of the SCB indicates that he was attempting to carry out in practice what he had elsewhere indicated was necessary due to textual corruption. But the principles he used, starting with an English text, proceeding with a mix of common-sense corrections and harmonizations plus sporadic revelations and his own doctrinal expansions–without knowledge of the original languages and without an adequate grasp or even an interest in textual criticism–were simply not adequate to accomplish his restorational task.

Does the evidence of JST Romans 7 suggest that Smith either through "revelation" or the employment of available resources brings readers closer to the original Greek text for the chapter? From a historical point of view, a comparison between the JST and current critical editions of the Greek New Testament is out of order because Smith could not have had access to them. The appropriate procedure is to compare the JST with the Greek New Testament as it was known in his day. Still, the view of some recent writers—that the JST represents, in some sense, a supernatural restoration of the original Greek text—lifts the question to another level. Smith would not need to have access to more modern editions since he would have already moved beyond them. His modifications, in fact, should be increasingly confirmed as textual criticism brings us closer to the original New Testament text. The fact that this restorationist view exists makes at least a brief comparison of the JST with the most current edition of the Greek New Testament relevant.

As represented in the *Nestle-Aland26,* the following activity is recorded for the Greek manuscript tradition for Romans 7: At four points insertions have been made; at four more, deletions occur; and at eleven, variant readings occur. In each of these cases Smith follows the SCB whether it reflects the best and earliest manuscript evidence or not. In addition, not one of the 168 words Smith introduces, nor any of the seven transpositions of words and phrases, has any manuscript support. The situation is the same when comparing JST Romans 7 with the New Testament Greek text as understood in Smith's day.

Comment should be made in two cases having to do not with the Greek manuscript tradition but with the conjectural emendation of it. In Romans 7:6 an erroneous reading, without support from any Greek manuscript, found its way into the so-called Textus Receptus,[16] from whence it passed into the KJV: "But now we are delivered from the law, that being dead *[apothanontos]* wherein we were held ..." This, by way of a deletion, a transposition, and an insertion, Smith changed to "But now we are delivered from the law <wherein we were held>, {~~that~~} being dead <\> TO THE LAW ..." The genitive *apothanontos* is linked to *tou nomou* (the law) in the text underlying the KJV, but in the JST it now refers to the subject of the sentence (i.e., "we"): "we are delivered ... *being dead* to the law." In this Smith agrees with the Greek manuscripts, most of which have the nominative participle *apothanontes.*[17] Yet he need not have depended on revelation for this correction since it had already been made in a number of English sources familiar to his circles. Through his Methodist connection, Smith might have come into contact with it either in Wesley's *Explanatory Notes on the New Testament*(1754)[18] or with *Clarke's Commentary* (1825)[19]; or, through the Campbellite connection of Sidney Rigdon (who served as scribe for JST Romans 7) and several other early Mormons, in Alexander Campbell's edition of the Bible.[20] But Smith may have simply changed the passage independently because the idea of the law dying seemed unacceptable to him, either doctrinally or because of its conceptual peculiarity.

A second and similar instance is the relocating in the JST of the latter half of verse 25b to a position between verses 23 and 24 (after some words added by Smith):

> (v. 24 = JST v. 26) AND IF I SUBDUE NOT THE SIN WHICH IS IN ME, <but with the flesh /~~is subject to~~/ SERVE the law of sin>; O wretched man that I am! Who shall deliver me from the body of this death? (v. 25 = JST v. 27) I thank God through Jesus Christ our Lord, <then>, THAT /~~wit~~ [?]/ so <\> with the mind, I, myself serve the law of God <v. 23\>.

Here again there is no evidence for this in the Greek manuscripts themselves. A similar suggestion, however, had been made by eighteenth-century Dutch scholar Herman Venema.[21] Venema, however, favored moving the whole of verse 25b rather than only half of it, as Smith did.[22] In suggesting this modification, both men were responding to a difficulty in the text that continues to trouble interpreters: how is it that we find sandwiched between the two upbeat remarks of verses 7:25a and 8:1 the decidedly downbeat restatement of verse 7:25b? In the present century a number of scholars have dealt with this problem either by considering verse 25b a secondary gloss[23] or by rearranging the passage in which it stands (usually 7:23, 25b, 24, 25a, 8:2, 1, 3).[24]

Smith was probably unaware of Venema's position, since it does not seem to have been widely known in America at the time. That is not to say, however, that no one struggled with the apparent difficulty Venema was trying to correct. Campbell's Bible, for example, which incorporated James MacKnight's translation of the epistles, dealt with this by casting verse 25b as a question, a "diatribal false conclusion," such as occurs throughout the Romans letter (for example, 3:1, 6:1, 7:7, 13; 9:14). First, the phrase is transformed into a question, and then a standard Pauline form of emphatic denial *me genoito!* (by no means) is added[25]: "Do I myself then as a slave serve with my mind the law of God but with the flesh the law of sin? [By no means.]" Campbell includes a note setting forth MacKnight's reasoning:[26] "Translated in this manner, interrogatively, the passage contains a strong denial, that the person spoken of, after being delivered from the body of this death, any longer serves, as formerly, with the mind only, the law of God, and with the flesh the law of sin in his members, whereas, translated as in our English Bible [KJV] ... it represents the delivered person as still continuing in that very slavery to sin ..." As it stands, according to MacKnight, the KJV rendering of verse 25 is "utterly wrong, and even dangerous." Yet in the 1832 revised edition Campbell dropped this reading in favor of one much closer to the KJV: "Wherefore, then, indeed, I myself serve, with my mind, the law of God; but with the flesh, the law of sin."

That Smith was not interested in correcting the SCB in light of the best available manuscript evidence of his day is demonstrated on a larger scale at those points where the JST adopts readings from the SCB which were even then widely recognized as inferior. This becomes immediately apparent, for example, in reference to the most familiar disputed texts: the longer ending of Mark 16:9-20,[27] the woman taken in adultery (John 8:1-11),[28] the replacement of "tree" with "book" (Rev 22:19),[29] and–by far the most debated biblical verse in Smith's day–1 John 5:7, the so-called *comma Johanneum.*[30] All of these were known to Smith's contemporaries.

This is *not* to say Smith did not intend to restore the Bible to its original condition, which I believe he did, only that in doing so he did not pay attention to the work of scholars. Perhaps their efforts were beyond him. The nearest we come to seeing this in JST Romans 7 is in verses 18b = 19b, where the JST takes over from the SCB a reading based on the inferior *oux eurisko.* The best manuscripts have simply *ou* here, which makes for an abrupt termination.[31] At a relatively early stage in the history of the manuscript tradition *oux eurisko* was introduced as a stylistic improvement. The shorter and more difficult reading had been adopted by Mill, Griesbach, and Lachmann. Still it is not at all certain that this textual decision had trickled down to the circles in which Smith lived and moved. Campbell's Bible, for example, while resorting to Griesbach on several occasions, still prefers *oux eurisko:* "Indeed to incline lies near me; but to work out what is excellent, *I do not find* near me" (italics mine). Even Charles Hodge, while noting the variant, insisted in 1835 that the "common text is retained by most editors on the authority of the great majority of MSS. versions and fathers."[32]

## ROMANS 7 IN EARLY NINETEENTH-CENTURY AMERICA

Interpretation of Romans 7 in the first decades of the nineteenth century was closely linked to the lively debated issue of the extent of human depravity and the nature and existence of original sin. The Old-Calvinist interpretation–which would have been the time-honored one in America,[33] and at this time was most ardently defended at Princeton Seminary–read the chapter in a way consistent with the reformed doctrine of total depravity, as set out in the classical reformed statements such as the Westminster Confession (VI, 2, 4); the Canons of Dort (III-IV, Art. 4, 6; and "Rejection of Errors," Par. 4); the Belgic Confession (Art. XIV); and the Heidelberg Catechism (Lord's Day III). The corruption of the unregenerate is so complete that it is not possible to describe them with phrases like "I delight in the law of God after the inner man" (Rom 7:22) or "I consent to God's law" (Rom 7:16). Therefore the struggle described in 7:14-25, by a simple process of elimination, *has to* reflect Christian experience. Once this is admitted, it further follows that, even after regeneration, indwelling sin remains a real and constant problem in the Christian life. Thus, Princeton's Charles Hodge who, without doubt would have been the most representative defender of the Old-Calvinist view, remarks in his 1835 commentary:[34] "Paul merely asserts that the believer is, and ever remains in this life, imperfectly sanctified; that sin continues to dwell within him; that he never comes up to the full requisitions of the law, however anxiously he may desire it. Often as he subdues one spiritual foe, another rises in a different form; so that he cannot do the things that he would; that is, cannot be perfectly conformed in heart and life to the image of God."[35] So intense was this tension for Paul as he wrote Romans 7 that, as Matthew Henry's popular commentary said, it was "as if he had a dead body tied to him, which he must have carried about with him."[36]

This dark vision of human nature, however, did not strike a sympathetic cord with the self-confident temper of the newly formed nation, in which even the religious outlook was, to use Nathan Hatch's apt term, quickly becoming "democratized."[37] On most fronts the general attitude was one of self-reliance and confidence, even over confidence, in human potential.[38] In addition, the Old Calvinism had begun for many to take on, if not the sinister appearance of a tyrannical clerical elite, at least the near ridiculous appearance of high-flying irrelevance. Nowhere is this more symbolically portrayed, and perhaps with more historical significance, than in Charles Finney's refusal to study at Princeton on the ground "that I would not put myself under such an influence as they had been under. I was confident that they had been wrongly educated and were not ministers that met my ideal of what a minister of Christ should be."[39] It was in some part due to this shift in temper that the second dominant view, the Methodist-Revivalist interpretation, would increase in importance as the century progressed.

The famous 24 May 1738 entry in Wesley's *Journal,* where he tells how his heart was "strangely warmed" while listening to Luther's *Preface to the Epistle of the Romans* at Aldersgate Street, already contains the understanding of Romans 7 which was to become standard in Methodism. All his prior religious experience is described there in terms of Romans 7:14-25:

> 9. All the time I was at Savannah I was thus beating the air. Being ignorant of the righteousness of Christ ... I sought to establish my own righteousness, and so labored in the fire all my days. I was now properly *under the law.* I knew that *the* law of God was *spiritual; I consented to it that it was good.* Yea, *I delighted in it after the inner man.* Yet was I *carnal, sold under sin.* Every day was I constrained to cry out, *What I do, I allow not: for what I would, I do not; but what I hate, that I do* ... I find ... the law in my members, warring against the law of my mind and still bringing me into captivity to the law of sin.
> 10. In this state I was indeed fighting continually, but not conquering. Before I had willingly served sin; now it was unwillingly, but I still served it.

The "I" of Romans 7:14-25, then, is not a Christian but one who is yet "under law," for whom the religious life is one of almost continual frustration. By applying the passage to himself, Wesley reveals his belief that it does not describe an experience unique to Jews–such a view had been championed by the English Unitarian John Taylor–but rather, as he says in another place, to "the state of all those, Jews and Gentiles, who *saw* and *felt* the wickedness both of their hearts and lives, and groaned to be delivered from it."[40] Essentially the same view is given later in Wesley's *Explanatory Notes on the New Testament* (1754). Except there, perhaps only because the explanation is more pointed, Wesley gives the whole chapter from verses 7-25 a developmental pitch. For verse 7 he comments: "The character here assumed is that of a man, first ignorant of the law, then under it and sincerely, but ineffectually, striving to serve God". By verse 24 the "struggle is now come to the height; and the man, finding there is no help in himself, begins almost unawares to pray, *Who shall deliver me?*" At the very end of the chapter, he "is now utterly weary of his bondage, and upon the brink of liberty." The liberty itself only comes in 8:1. In reading the chapter as a dramatic narrative Wesley reveals his close dependence on the Pietist Johann Albrecht Bengel's *Gnomon Novi Testamenti* (1742).[41]

Of equal importance for our period is Adam Clarke's *Commentary,* which presents the same view in greater depth. *Clarke's Commentary,* not to mention Clarke himself, was immensely popular in America. And this in spite of its disproportionate size (six large volumes for both Testaments). As we have already related, Emma Smith's uncle Lewis seems to have owned a set. Clarke's position on Romans 7 was essentially that of Wesley, though set forward with greater erudition. (Even the great German F. A. G. Tholuck thought fit to familiarize himself with Clarke's remarks on the chapter, and he quotes from them in his own 1824 commentary on Romans).[42] Also Clarke does not bring in from Wesley and Bengel the desire to read the chapter as a dramatic narrative. Rather he grounds the argument in the contrasting affirmations of verses 5 and 6, which are then understood as expanded upon in 7:7-25 and 8:1-11 respectively.[43]

This view gained a new impetus beyond the boundaries of Methodism in the influential Moses Stuart, professor at Andover from 1812. The importance of Moses Stuart to early nineteenth-century American Christianity is hard to overestimate. He is viewed as one of the key figures in the resurgence of critical biblical scholarship in America and a great defender of the Orthodox cause against Unitarianism. As a student of Yale's Timothy Dwight, Stuart was closely tied to the "moderate Calvinism" of New Divinity circles, and was thus able to provide a way for those circles to entertain an understanding of Romans 7 that previously might have been viewed with suspicion because of its connection with Methodism and Unitarianism.[44]

When tracing lines of dependence, therefore, for the interpretation of Romans 7 as held by the later perfectionists of Oberlin College and by John Humphrey Noyes and his Oneida Community, we are lead first back to Stuart rather than Methodism. In 1831 Noyes learned this position under Stuart himself at Andover[45] as did Oberlin's future president, Asa Mahan, a few years earlier.[46] So even though Stuart's commentary on Romans did not actually appear until 1832, his interpretation of Romans 7 had already been exercising wide influence through his students.[47] Despite the difference of confessional context, Stuart's arguments are not essentially different from Clarke's. Again the contrast between 7:5 and 6 is seen painted largely in 7:7-25 and 8:1-11 (or 17), thus limiting the entire discussion of Romans 7:7-25 to those yet under law.[48] Indeed, insists Stuart, the language of 7:14-25 could not possibly refer to Christian experience since "if Christians, who are of course under grace and are dead to the law (6:14. 7:6), are actually in the state here represented, then would it follow, that neither grace nor law hinders them from being the servants of sin."[49]

Closer to Joseph Smith's circle, Alexander Campbell championed his own version of this view according to which the "I" had a more generalized symbolic reference to Israel, Paul "in his own person represents the Jew from the days of Abraham down to his own conversion." In the 1827 *Christian Baptist,* Campbell paraphrases several key passages in the chapter.[50] Israel was "alive without law" (v. 9) in the days of the patriarchs before the law of Moses had been given. At that time "I [=Israel] never felt myself subject to death, for where no law is there is no transgression." But with the coming of the commandment from Sinai, sin "revived or came to life, and ... death was inflicted upon us Jews in a way of which there was no example before the promulgation of the law ..." In verse 14 the law is called "spiritual" because it "has respect not only to the outward actions, but in some of its precepts reaches to the thoughts." In contrast, the "I" is called "carnal" because "the people, of which I am one, to whom that law was given, were a fleshly people enslaved to appetite." "[I]t was not," Campbell goes on to say for verses 22-23, "owing to any defect in the law, nor in my perceptions and approbation of it mentally, but in the inclinations and propensities to which a human being in this present state is unavoidably subjected—that I failed in finding happiness, peace, or comfort under the law." As to the question whether JST Romans 7 clearly depends on the Campbell Bible, the answer is: it does not.

## THE JOSEPH SMITH TRANSLATION AND ROMANS 7

Joseph Smith's rendering of Romans 7 appears to be motivated by two concerns: (1) finding a solution that strikes a balance between the two dominant interpretations of his day, and (2) furnishing a "biblical basis" for his own restorationist program in relation to the idea of Christianity as a renewed and, therefore, a better kind of law-keeping, and (perhaps) the legitimation of "polygamy."

With the Old-Calvinist interpreters, Smith sets as the overall temporal horizon of verses 14-25 the apostle's *present* Christian experience. Yet at the same time he tempered those statements deemed by Methodist-Revivalist interpreters to reflect sub-Christian sentiments of regular spiritual frustration and defeat; placing at least some of these in the past. This is evident at a number of points, most obviously at 7:14 itself: "For we know that the {~~law~~} COMMANDMENT is spiritual; but WHEN I WAS UNDER THE LAW,] I {~~am~~} [WAS YET] carnal, sold under sin." Smith further makes the chapter refer not to one law but to two: (1) the Mosaic law, which the "I" used to be under (e.g., vv. 6, 14, 21 = 23), and (2) the "commandment of Christ," which the "I" is now under as a Christian (vv. 9, 14, 23 = 24). This "commandment of Christ" is imprinted on the mind of the believer, and it is against it that the indwelling sinful principle is at war (v. 23 = 25). The cry of wretchedness (v. 24 = 26) has to do not with the ongoing state of the "I"—as was the case in *both* contemporary prevailing interpretations—but with the condition of a Christian who fails for whatever reason to subdue indwelling sin.

Also more in line with Old-Calvinist than the Methodist-Revivalist interpretaters is Smith's not making the chapter turn, in any sense, on a radical change of nature within the regenerated believer; i.e., there is no hint of latent perfectionism.[51] Instead the old law/restored law contrast is pivotal. The basis for this is Smith's idea that the Mosaic law had been intentionally made deficient by God. According to JST

Exodus, after the original set of tablets of the law had been broken in anger by Moses (Ex. 32:19), a second set was prepared and God again wrote. But this time, Smith tells us, the Lord left out certain essential matters originally included in the first set: "[B]ut it shall not be according to the first, for I will take away the priesthood out of their midst: therefore my holy order, and the ordinances thereof, shall not go before them ... But I will give unto them the law of a carnal commandment ... " (34:1-2; also JST Deut. 10:1-2). The phrase "law of a carnal commandment," was imported from the KJV Hebrews 7:16.[52] The law then is inadequate for salvation not because it is "weakened by the flesh," as Paul would have it (Rom. 8:1), but because it had been made defective by God. The new law is better and more effective because it is a restored law, while the old "law of a carnal commandment" was part of an inferior "preparatory gospel" (D&C 34:26; 1835 ed. IV:4).

The same old law/restored law distinction is reflected at a number of points in JST Romans where the issue of the relation of the law and salvation is being discussed. Thus in 4:5 the SCB's "him that worketh not, but believeth" is changed in NT MS 2 to "him that {~~worketh~~} SEEKETH not TO BE JUSTIFIED BY THE LAW OF WORKS, but believeth"; and in 4:6 "righteousness without works" is changed to "righteousness without THE LAW OF works."[53] The "law of works" in each case appears to be synonymous with the "law according to a carnal commandment." This same understanding continues into JST Romans 7. Interestingly, however, it is not the law of Moses, the "law of a carnal commandment," that strikes the "I" of Romans 7 dead. Rather this occurs in relation to the "commandment of Christ." Throughout the chapter the instrumentality of the law in the death of the "I" is played down and the blame laid exclusively at the feet of sin:

> (5) ... the motions of sins, which were {~~by~~} NOT ACCORDING TO the law, did work in our members, to bring forth fruit unto death.
> (10) And WHEN I BELIEVED NOT the commandment OF CHRIST WHICH CAME, which >was ordained< to life, I found {~~to be~~} IT CONDEMNED ME unto death.
> (11) FOR sin, taking occasion, {/~~by~~/} DENYED the commandment, AND deceived me, and by it {~~slew me~~} I WAS SLAIN.[54]

The last two verses quoted reveal that the "I" dies because it has been tricked by sin into not *believing* the commandment of Christ.

Also intriguing in light of the overall restorational focus of the chapter is verse 19 (=JST vv. 20-21): "For the good that I would HAVE DONE WHEN UNDER THE LAW, I FIND NOT TO BE GOOD; THEREFORE] I do IT not: (JST 21) but the evil which I would not DO UNDER THE LAW, I FIND TO BE GOOD; that, I do."

Certain behavior, previously considered evil, has now under the restoration become acceptable. But what behavior does Smith have in mind? Certainly this might be nothing more than a general reference to the comparative level of freedom enjoyed under the new law of Christ. But the language seems too strong for this. There is some evidence, in fact, that the reference may be to a more specific concern: providing a theological justification for the reintroduction of polygamy. Perhaps a clue is to be found in possible psychological self-legitimation implied in the next verse (20 = 22). When he does the "evil" which he formerly would not do, "it is no more <that> I [SEEK TO <\> do {~~it~~} [W]RONG, but TO SUBDUE sin that dwelleth in me."

Significantly, the same basic argument appears a full decade later in an 1842 letter to Sidney Rigdon's unmarried daughter, Nancy. A day or two after an attempt at winning her as one of his plural wives was rebuffed, Smith dictated a letter, apparently intended to weaken her resolve by insinuating that her resistance amounted to disobedience to God's law. His arguments echo significantly the language of the JST rendition of Romans 7:19-20 (= JST 20-22): "That which is wrong under one circumstance, may be, and often is, right under another ... Whatever God requires is right, no matter what it is ... even things which might be considered abominable to all who understand the order of Heaven only in part, but which, in reality, were right, because God gave and sanctioned by special revelation."[55] It seems especially fitting that a consideration of Smith's changing sexual standards and practices should come to mind in the context where the old "law of a carnal commandment" is being contrasted with the restored "commandment of Christ." Needless to say, explicit reference to what remained a secret practice until after Smith's death would not have yet been possible. Especially in a work slated for public consumption like the JST. If this understanding of the JST rendering of Romans 7:19-20 (= 20-22) is correct, then it represents one of the earliest justifications of polygamy from the hand of Smith.[56]

Although the revelation permitting plural marriage (D&C 132 in LDS editions) was not given until 12 April 1843, it is now widely recognized that even long before that time Smith's sexual activities exceeded the limits laid down by it (most notably in his taking of married women as plural wives[57]). Allegations of sexual impropriety had dogged Smith's heels from the earliest days of the church. Our interest in this regard is limited to the period around the time Smith was involved in the production of the JST. In 1834, an affidavit by Emma Smith's cousin, Levi Lewis, referred to a remark by Martin Harris five years previous that "he [Harris] did not blame Smith for his attempt to seduce Eliza Winters &c."[58] The year 1832 (especially important as that in which Smith produced JST Romans 7) was particularly eventful in this regard. Since these facts are known and have been investigated, only a brief review, drawing primarily from Richard Van Wagoner's *Mormon Polygamy: A History*, will be necessary. On 24 March 1832 Smith was tarred and feathered, according to one account, for seducing Nancy Marinda Johnson, in whose father's house he was residing. A certain Eli, identified (apparently erroneously) as Nancy's brother, is said to have called for Smith's castration.[59] Later testimony also mentions liaisons in this year between Joseph and two servant girls employed in the Smith household: one named Miss Hill, and the other unnamed.[60] Another name coming down to us from roughly this period is Vienna Jacques.[61] Emma Smith spent much of 1832 pregnant with Joseph Smith III (b. 6 November 1832).

Later evidence further suggests that Smith was already at this time trying to hammer out a theological basis for an eventual turn to open polygamy. Joseph B. Noble, a close friend of the Mormon leader, later related that Smith had become convinced of the legitimacy of polygamy "while ... engaged in the work of translation of the Scriptures."[62] Orson Pratt, noted Mormon missionary and apostle, also pointed to early 1832 as the time when Smith told certain individuals that "the principle of taking more wives than one is a true principle, but the time had not yet come for it to be practiced."[63]

Four points, then, suggest that JST Romans 7 may reflect this same concern: (1) the parallel argumentation in the letter to Nancy Rigdon ten years later;[64] (2) the evidence implying that Smith was involved in various extramarital liaisons in that year, behavior that could be described as "evil which I would not DO UNDER THE LAW";[65] (3) the later testimony of friends pointing on the one hand to 1832 and on the other to the time of the production of the JST as when Smith began to formulate his reasons for an eventual return to open polygamy; and (4) the overall restorational focus of JST Romans 7 itself.

## CONCLUSION

Joseph Smith's rendition of Romans 7 offers little in terms of real insight into Paul's meaning, and Smith's "restorations" bring us no closer to the form of the text as it "came from the pen of the original writers." Still it provides an interesting window to understanding the passage as it was debated in the early decades of the nineteenth century and to the Mormon prophet himself; his developing teaching and character, and his methods and motives for producing the JST. Whatever else might be said, one of the secrets of Smith's success was his ability to focus the attention of followers around some revelational project; thereby keeping the sense of eschatological expectation high. The first such project, of course, was the Book of Mormon. The JST project followed quickly in June 1830, only two months after the organization of the church. Romans 7 provided a special opportunity in this regard. Not only was Smith able to rule authoritatively in a passage that had been debated for centuries (with the inevitable consequence of increasing his prestige in the eyes of his followers) but at the same time he was able to use the occasion to create a "biblical basis" for his own restorationist program through the "clarification" of obscurities in this difficult chapter.[66]

### *NOTES*

1. Robert J. Matthews, *"A Plainer Translation": Joseph Smith's Translation of the Bible: A History and Commentary* (Provo, UT: Brigham Young University Press, 1975), 56.

2. For a detailed account of the manuscript history of the JST, see ibid., 55-81. The SCB and the various manuscripts of the JST are currently housed in the archives of the Reorganized Church of Jesus Christ of Latter Day Saints, Independence, Missouri.

3. SCB: but //JST: for (v. 2); *so* long as//*only as* long as (v. 2); where-

fore//nevertheless (v. 12); law//commandment (v. 14) (but see n32); but what//for that which (v. 15); it//sin (v. 17 = 18); that//which (v. 17 = 18); it//wrong (v. 20 = 22); but//and now (v. 23 = 24).

4. Slew *me*//I was slain (v. 11); the law *is* holy//the law *to be* holy (v. 12); I *am* carnal//I *was yet* carnal (v. 14); evil *is* with me//evil *was* with me (v. 21 = 23).

5. Even (v. 4); to be (v. 10); how (v. 18 = 19). The only point where modern editions of the JST differ in Romans 7 from the changes indicated by Smith is in the retention of the "even" at Romans 7:4.

6. Belief in the Bible's corruption was common in early nineteenth-century America. In 1804, for example, Thomas Jefferson, then president of the United States, spent a few evenings clipping and pasting two KJVs with a view toward "Abstracting what is really his [Jesus'] from the rubbish in which it is buried, easily distinguished by it's luster from the dross of his biographers, and as separable from that as a diamond from the dung hill" (Dickenson W. Adams, ed., *Jefferson's Extracts from the Gospels: "The Philosophy of Jesus" and "The Life And Morals of Jesus,"* in *Papers of Thomas Jefferson*, 2d. Series [Princeton, NJ: Princeton University Press, 1983], 388). Similarly, Thomas Paine, in his *Age of Reason* (1794; P. S. Foner, ed., *The Complete Writings of Thomas Paine*, 2 vols. [New York: Citadel, 1969], 472-73), remarked: "It is a matter altogether of uncertainty to us whether such of the writings as now appear under the name of the Old and New Testaments are in the same state in which those collectors say they found them, or whether they added, altered, abridged or dressed them up." Lucy Mack Smith reported that in 1803 Asael Smith, grandfather of Mormonism's founder, heard that his son (Joseph Smith, Sr.) was interested in Methodism and so, "came to the door one day and threw Tom Paine's *Age of Reason* into the house and angrily bade him read that until he believed it" (Jerald and Sandra Tanner, *Mormonism–Shadow or Reality?* 4th ed. [Salt Lake City: Utah Lighthouse Ministry, 1982], 373; Richard L. Anderson, *Joseph Smith's New England Heritage* [Salt Lake City: Deseret Book, 1971], 207).

7. This confirms for a specific passage the general contention of Kevin L. Barney ("The Joseph Smith Translation and Ancient Texts of the Bible," *Dialogue: A Journal of Mormon Thought* 19 [Fall 1986]: 87) that "the JST is almost entirely comprised of additions to the KJV" (see also Robert J. Matthews, "Joseph Smith Translation of the Bible (JST)," in *Encyclopedia of Mormonism*, 5 vols., ed. Daniel H. Ludlow [New York: Macmillan, 1992], 2:764). Barney's otherwise excellent study is flawed in its assumption that it "was not a common practice to compare textual variants until the middle and late nineteenth century" (87). This, as will become plain, is incorrect. Thus, for example, in the first passage Barney discusses (Matt. 5:22) he has some trouble explaining why the JST agrees together with ancient manuscripts against the KJV in deleting "without a cause." Barney would have been able to make his case more pointedly for this passage had he been aware that such variants were

known and discussed in Smith's day–and not only among scholars. So the popular *Clarke's Commentary* (Adam Clarke, *New Testament ... With Commentary ... A New Edition with the Author's Final Corrections* [New York: Carlton & Porter, n.d. [1832?], 1:712), for example, which Smith appears to have known (see n19), remarks: "*[W]ithout a cause,* is wanting in the famous *Vatican* MS. and two others, the *Ethiopic,* latter *Arabic, Saxon, Vulgate,* two copies of the old *Itala, J. Martyr, Ptolemeus, Origen, Tertullian,* and by all the ancient copies quoted by *St. Jerome.* It was probably a marginal gloss originally, which in the process of time crept into the text."

8. On 16 February 1832, Joseph Smith and Sidney Rigdon were modifying John 5:29 (D&C 76; 1835 ed., XCI). They continued their work until 20 March and picked up again in June to carry on throughout the summer and winter. On 2 February 1833 the project was declared complete. H. Michael Marquardt has suggested that Romans 7 may have been modified "during February or early March 1832" (letter to the writer, 4 Sept. 1991), but it may have been slightly later in the year.

9. Similary, in the Book of Mormon an angel tells Nephi in a *vaticinium ex eventu* of a time when the Bible will fall into the hands of a "great and abominable church" and, as a result, there will be, "many plain and precious things taken away" from it (1 Ne. 13:28). For a recent discussion of the types of changes made by Smith, see Philip L. Barlow, "Joseph Smith's Revision of the Bible: Fraudulent, Pathologic, or Prophetic?" *Harvard Theological Review* 83 (1990): 54-60.

10. That Smith depends in his modifications on the English rather than the Greek Bible is especially clear in cases where they make sense in English but are impossible in Greek. For example, Romans 1:11, in which the KJV has Paul wanting to see the Romans so as to "impart unto you some spiritual gift, to the end ye may be established," Smith changes to read: "impart unto you some spiritual gift, </> THAT {~~ye~~} IT may be established IN YOU <to the end>." By repositioning "to the end," Smith changes the meaning by moving but not altering the words. In the KJV the phrase "to the end" serves as a simple purpose clause: "to the end that" = *in order that.* The underlying Greek likewise is a purpose clause composed of *hina* + subjunctive. If this phrase were moved to the end of the sentence in Greek, it would not yield the meaning Smith wants. In order to arrive at that, something like *eos telous* (1 Cor. 1:8), *eis telos* (Matt. 10:22, 24:13; Mark 13:13) or *achri telous* (Heb. 6:11; Rev. 2:26) would be required.

11. For example, Richard P. Howard, "Some Observations on Joseph Smith, Jr.'s Revision of Romans 3:21-8:31," privately circulated, 1975; Barney; and Stan Larson, "The Sermon on the Mount: What Its Textual Transformation Discloses Concerning the Historicity of the Book of Mormon," *Trinity Journal* 7 (1986): 39.

12. See R. J. Matthews in Monte S. Nyman and Robert Millet, eds., *The Joseph Smith Translation* (Provo, UT: BYU Religious Studies Center, 1985), 286.

13. See Barlow, 57; also Barney, 85-86; Howard, 4-5; and Dale E. Luffman, "The Roman Letter: An Occasion to Reflect on 'Joseph Smith's New Translation of the Bible,'" in Maurice L. Draper, ed., *Restoration Studies III* (Independence, MO: Herald House, 1986), 198-99.

14. Howard, 4; Scott H. Faulring, ed., *An American Prophet's Record: The Diaries and Journals of Joseph Smith* (Salt Lake City: Signature Books in association with Smith Research Associates), 1989.

15. Barlow, 57.

16. B. M. Metzger, *A Textual Commentary on the Greek New Testament*, cor. ed. (New York: United Bible Societies, 1975), 514.

17. A few manuscripts read *tou thanatou* (e.g., D, F, G).

18. Wesley's *Explanatory Notes*, a work of premier authority among American Methodists, rendered the passage: "But now we are freed from the law, being dead unto that whereby we were held."

Joseph Smith's early interest in Methodism is well known from his account of the 1824 Lane and Stockton Revival at Palmyra (Smith's incorrect date is 1820): "My father's family was proselyted to the Presbyterian faith" but "my mind became somewhat partial to the Methodist sect, and I felt some desire to become united with them" (JS-H 1:7, Pearl of Great Price; 1851 ed., 37; Dean C. Jessee, ed., *The Papers of Joseph Smith* (Salt Lake City: Deseret Book, 1989). Smith goes on to say in the same context, however, that he was kept from joining the Methodists or any other sect by a vision: "I was answered that I must join none of them, for they were all wrong, and the personage who addressed me said that all their creeds were an abomination in his sight; that those professors were all corrupt ..." (JS-H 1:19, Pearl of Great Price; 1851 ed., 38). Nevertheless, according to Emma Smith's cousins Joseph and Heil Lewis, Smith later took steps to become a member of the Methodist church in 1828 at Harmony, Pennsylvania (*Amboy Journal*, 30 Apr., 21 May, 11 June, 2 July, 1879; cf. L. K. Newell and V. T. Avery, *Mormon Enigma: Emma Hale Smith* [Garden City, NY: Doubleday, 1984], 25, 314n2).

19. Clarke includes a marginal reading that had been present in the KJV from 1611: "Or, *being dead to that*" (2:79). The SCB did not include this marginal reading. Perhaps Smith had another KJV that did. In any case, regarding Smith's knowledge of *Clarke's Commentary*, H. Michael Marquardt provided the following reference to remarks by Smith's wife's uncle, Rev. Nathaniel C. Lewis, as reported in the *Methodist Quarterly Review* (Jan. 1843): 113: "[W]hen the story came out about the 'gold plates,' and the 'great spectacles,' he (Lewis) asked Joe if any one but himself could translate other languages into English by the aid of his miraculous spectacles? On being answered in the affirmative, he proposed to Joe to let him make the experiment upon some of the strange languages he found in Clarke's Commentary,

and stated to him if it was even so, and the experiment proved successful, he would then believe the story about the gold plates. But at this proposition Joe was much offended, and never undertook to convert 'uncle Lewis' afterward."

20. Alexander Campbell, *The Sacred Writings of the Apostles and Evangelists of Jesus Christ, Commonly Styled the New Testament: Translated from the Original Greek, by George Campbell, James MacKnight, and Philip Doddridge, Doctors of the Church of Scotland* (Buffaloe, VA: Printed and Published by Alexander Campbell, 1826, 1828). Late in 1832 Campbell, in response to six years of public reaction, issued a third revised and enlarged edition. In this he reflects even more clearly the correct reading *apothanontes:* "But now having died *with Christ*, we are released from the law." This edition was issued later in the same year that Smith "translated" Romans 7 (the copyright was entered on 6 August 1832 and Campbell's preface carries the date 10 October 1832).

21. C. E. B. Cranfield, *Commentary in the Epistle of Romans (International Critical Commentary)*, 2 vols. (Edinburgh: T. & T. Clark, 1975), 1:368.

22. Venema's suggestion is better since, in moving all of verse 25b, rather than only the latter half, as Smith did, he retains Paul's "in the mind"/"in the flesh" contrast.

23. Rudolf Bultmann, "Glossen im Römerbrief," *Theologische Literaturzeitung* 72 (1972): col. 198; Franz J. Leenhardt, *The Epistle of Romans: A Commentary*, trans. H. Knight (London: Lutterworth, 1961), 195 and 200; John Ziesler, *Paul's Letter to the Romans* (London: SMC / London, Philadelphia: Trinity, 1989), 199.

24. Matthew Black, *Romans (New Century Commentary)*, 2d. ed. (Grand Rapids, MI: Eerdmans, 1989), 102; James Moffatt, *The New Testament: A New Translation* (New York: Hodder & Stoughton/George H. Doran [1913]), 194: C. H. Dodd, *The Epistle of Paul to the Romans (Moffatt New Testament Commentary)* (London: Hodder & Stoughton, 1932), 114-15; J. Müller, "Zwei Marginalien im Brief des Paulus an die Römer," *Zeitschrift fur die neutestamentliche Wissenschaft* (1941): 249-54.

25. In the diatribe "a speaker or writer makes use of an imaginary interlocutor to ask questions of or raise objections to the arguments or affirmations that are made. These responses are frequently stupid and are then summarily rejected by the speaker or writer ..." (Abraham J. Malherbe, "*Me Genoito* in the Diatribe and Paul," *Paul and the Popular Philosophers* [Minneapolis: Fortress Press, 1989], 23-25, esp. 25). The standard older work on Paul's use of the diatribe is by Rudolf Bultmann (*Der Stil der paulinischen Predigt und die kynisch-stoische Diatribe. FRLANT 13* [Göttingen: Vandenhoeck & Ruprecht, 1910]); more recently, see Stanley Stowers (*The Diatribe and Paul's Letter to the Romans. SBLDS 57* [Chico, CA: Scholars Press, 1981]).

26. Campbell, appen. xxv; 1828, 425.

27. See, for example, Clarke, 1:343. The language of the passage is echoed

further in D&C 24:13 (1835 ed., IX:6 = Book of Commandments 25:23) where it is put into the mouth of God.

28. Clarke, 1:576.

29. This error developed only in the Latin manuscript tradition from an apparent confusion between the original Latin *ligno* and *libro* in some Vulgate manuscripts. This occurred because of (1) a similarity in appearance or sound of the two words, (2) a conscious assimilation to Revelation 3:5, 13:8, and 20:15, or (3) an accidental assimilation to the word *libro* which occurs three other times in the immediate context. Erasmus, lacking a complete Greek manuscript of the Apocalypse when hastily preparing his edition of the Greek New Testament, made do by translating Revelation 22:16-19 from the Latin Vulgate into Greek. This situation was noted, for example, in two review articles in the *North American Review,* a journal which Mormon historian D. Michael Quinn says was "frequently advertised for sale in the Palmyra area" (*Early Mormonism and the Magic World View* [Salt Lake City: Signature Books, 1987], 174). The first, by James Diman Green, appeared in October 1822 (see 465-66), and the second, by John Gordon Palfry, in July 1830 (see 267). The location of Erasmus's Apocalypse manuscript was not at that time known, but has since been rediscovered. Still, as Green remarked, Erasmus had acknowledged Revelation 22:19 "to have been made in this manner; though it is evident that the whole of the *six* last verses had no better origin ..."

30. The controversy over this classic trinitarian text raged throughout Smith's lifetime, largely in connection with the Unitarian controversy. Joseph Steven Buckminster, popular Unitarian preacher and Boston minister, remarked that among the small number of "wilful interpolations" into the Greek text, "1 John, V. 7, is by far the most notorious, and most universally acknowledged and reprobated" (Joseph Stevens Buckminster, "Abstract of Interesting Facts Relating to the New Testament," *Monthly Anthology and Boston Review,* Dec. 1808, 639). It would be impossible to offer anything like a comprehensive list of relevant contemporary literature. Closest to home, Smith's copy of Thomas Hartwell Horne's *Introduction* (currently in possession of the RLDS church) devoted no less than thirty-one pages to the issue (Thomas Hartwell Horne, *An Introduction to the Critical Study and Knowledge of the Holy Scriptures,* 4 vols. 4th ed. [Philadelphia: E. Littell, 1825], 4:435-66). (On the fly-leaf of the first volume Joseph Smith's name is written in pencil along with "Kirtland, Ohio, 1834.") *Clarke's Commentary* also included "Observations on the Text of the Three Divine Witnesses" at the end of its treatment of 1 John. Alexander Campbell (*The Christian Baptist* 5 [1827]: 363-64) spoke forcefully against the authenticity of the passage, preferring instead to "literally translate the Greek text of Griesbach, which reading is moreover approved and confirmed by Michaelis, and other great critics and collators of ancient MSS." At the time Campbell wrote, John David Michaelis's *Einleitung in die gottlichen Schriften des Neuen Bundes* (1750) was widely available in America in

Herbert Marsh's English translation of the 1788 fourth edition (1802), which included an extensive "Dissertation on 1 John V. 7" by John Michael Michaelis, *Introduction to the New Testament,* 4 vols., 2d. ed., trans. Herbert Marsh (London: F. and C. Rivington, 1802 [orig. Eng. ed. 1793], 4:412-41); see also William H. Hunt, "Authenticity of 1 Jn 5:7, 8," *Literary and Theological Review* 2 (1835): 141-48. The 1840 edition of Horne's *Introduction,* finally, includes a forty-eight-entry annotated bibliography of "Treatises on the Genuineness of the Disputed Clauses in 1 John v. 7, 8."

31. Metzger, 514. The UBS committee gave the reading only a C rating. Yet *ou* is not only supported by the earliest and best manuscripts (for example, A, B, C) and had made its way into all forms of the Coptic version, but it is also supported by the principle *lectio difficilior lectio potior* (the more difficult reading is to be preferred). In other words in this instance it is easier to imagine someone transforming a sentence in order to correct awkward style than to envision someone changing perfectly good style and making it awkward for no apparent reason.

32. Charles Hodge, *A Commentary on the Epistle to the Romans Designed for Students of the English Bible* (Philadelphia: Grigg & Elliot, 1835), 290.

33. See, for example, the poem of Anne Bradstreet (d. 1672) about the two sisters Flesh and Spirit ("The Flesh and the Spirit," in Harrison T. Meserole, ed., *Seventeenth-Century American Poetry* [New York: W. W. Norton, 1968], 20-22) and Jonathan Edwards's *Original Sin* (*Original Sin [The Great Christian Doctrine of Original Sin defended; Evidences of its Truth Produced ... Containing, in Particular, a Reply to the Objections and Arguings of Dr. John Taylor ...],* ed. Clyde A. Holbrook [New Haven, CT: Yale University 1970 (1758)], 304-305). David Brainerd's diary frequently contains the missionary's dispairing cry of wretchedness, patterned after Romans 7:24 "O Wretched man ..." (Jonathan Edwards, *The Life of David Brainerd* [New Haven, CT: Yale University Press, 1985 (Orig. 1749)], 100, 108, 109, 123, 181, cf. 186). In the early part of the nineteenth century, Unitarian William E. Channing described the Calvinist view as follows in his "The Moral Argument Against Calvinism": "Calvinism teaches that, in consequence of Adam's sin in eating the forbidden fruit, God brings into life all his posterity with a nature wholly corrupt, so that they are utterly indisposed, disabled, and made opposite to all that is spiritually good, and wholly inclined to all evil, and that continually" (*The Works of William E. Channing, D.D.* [Boston: American Unitarian Association, 1890], 461).

34. This same year also brought forth a commentary on Romans by the controversial New-School Presbyterian, Albert Barnes. It was felt by many within the Presbyterian fold that Barnes had departed in serious ways from the Westminster Confession in a number of key doctrinal areas, including original sin. Charles Hodge reviewed this commentary in his *Biblical Repertory* (7 [1835]: 285-340). And, while much was said that was critical, still Hodge was

"happy to report that the view of the latter part of the seventh chapter is in accordance with the *ordinary interpretation* of Calvinistic interpreters" (318); i.e., it was understood to refer to an exclusively Christian experience. This same understanding was retained by Barnes in subsequent editions (e.g., Albert Barnes, *Notes Explanitory and Practical on the Epistle to the Romans: Designed for Bible Classes and Sunday Schools,* 9th ed. [New York: Harper, 1869], 153-4).

Charles Hodge also treats Romans 7 elsewhere (e.g., *The Way of Life* [Grand Rapids, MI: Baker, 1977 (Orig. 1841)], 58, 110-15; *Conference Papers* [New York: Charles Scribner's Sons, 1879], 93-4; *Systematic Theology* [New York: Charles Scribner's Sons, 1872], III, 247). The same understanding of Romans 7 is also seen, for example, in the works of the great Southern Presbyterian theologian Robert L. Dabney (*Lectures in Systematic Theology* [Grand Rapids, MI: Zondervan, 1972 (Orig., 1878)], I, 193; 1972, 675).

Finally, Charles G. Finney later in the century wrote: "One opinion that has extensively prevailed, and still prevails, is that the latter part of the chapter is an epitome of Christian experience ... The only other interpretation given is that which prevailed in the first centuries, and which is still generally adopted on the continent of Europe, as well as by a considerable number of writers in England and in America, that this passage describes the experience of a sinner under conviction, who was acting under the motives of the law, and not yet brought to the experience of the gospel. In this country, the most prevalent opinion is that of the seventh chapter of Romans delineates the experience of a Christian" (Finney, "Legal Experience," in Louis Parkhurst, Jr., *Principles of Victory* [Minneapolis: Bethany, 1981], 87-108 [originally *Lectures to Professing Christians* (1880), 320-38]).

35. Hodge, *Romans*, 299.

36. Matthew Henry, *A Commentary on the Holy Bible ... with Practical Remarks and Observations,* 6 vols. (London: Ward, Lock, Boden, n.d. [Orig. ed. 1707-12]), 6:960. Henry's commentary was being published in America by 1816, first at Philadelphia. Concerning the authorship of the Romans section of the final volume of Matthew Henry, an anonymous article in Nathaniel Taylor's *Quarterly Christian Spectator* (2 [1830]: 283) remarked: "Dr. Watts, in his copy of the Exposition, upon a blank leaf at the beginning of the last volume, wrote the following statement:–'The Rev. Mr. Matthew Henry, before his death had made some small preperations for the last volume. The Epistle of Romans indeed, was explained so largely by his own hand, that it needed only the labor of epitomizing ...'" This epitomizing was done by Mr. John Evans.

37. Nathan O. Hatch, *The Democratization of American Christianity* (New Haven, CT: Yale University Press, 1989).

38. As exemplified in Ralph Waldo Emerson's famous 1841 essay, "Self-Reliance" (Robert E. Spiller et al., eds. *The Collected Works of Ralph Waldo*

*Emerson* [Cambridge, MA: Belknap Press of Harvard University, 1971-87], 2:27-51) and his mentor, William Ellery Channing's 1838 "Self-Culture" (Channing, 12-36) and his *The Perfect Life,* a series of twelve discourses put together by Channing's nephew after his death (ibid., 925-1020).

39. Charles G. Finney, *The Memoirs of Rev. Charles G. Finney: Written by Himself* (New York: A. S. Barnes, 1876), 45-46.

40. John Wesley, *The Doctrine of Original Sin, According to Scripture, Reason, and Experience: In Answer to Dr. Taylor* (New-York: J. Soule and T. Mason, 1817 [orig. 1756]), 145-46.

41. In the "Preface," Wesley declares that "Many of his [Bengel's] excellent notes I have therefore translated; many more I have abridged ..." In his notes on Romans 7, Wesley follows Bengel closely, often almost word for word.

42. Friedrich August Tholuck, *Exposition of St. Paul's Epistle to the Romans: With Extracts from the Exegetical Works of the Fathers and Reformers,* trans. Robert Menzies (Philadelphia: Sorin and Ball, 1844), 210-11. Princeton's Charles Hodge chalked up Tholuck's approbatory quotation of Clarke to "a moment of forgetfulness" on the part of the great man (Hodge, *Romans,* 199).

43. Clarke, 2:77-89.

44. This same view was also set forth by the English Unitarian John Taylor (d. 1761) in his *The Scripture-Doctrine of Original Sin Proposed to Free and Candid Examination* (London: for the author by J. Wilson, 1740), 214. The importance of Taylor's work is seen in the fact that it drew fire from both John Wesley (145-46, on Rom. 7) *and* Jonathan Edwards (304-305 and 331-32n9, on Rom. 7).

45. John H. Noyes, *"The Way of Holiness." A Series of Papers Formerly Published in The Perfectionist at New Haven* (Putney VT: J. H. Noyes & Co., 1838), i: "The author was taught by Prof. Stuart, that the seventh chapter of Romans is *not* a description of Christian experience"; John H. Noyes, *Salvation From Sin, The End of Christian Faith* (Oneida, NY: The Oneida Community, 1876), 21-3; Ethelbert D. Warfield et al., eds., *The Works of Benjamin B. Warfield,* 10 vols. (New York: Oxford University Press, 1932), 8:254. A full paraphrase of Romans 7:7-25 was also published by John H. Noyes, "Paul Not Carnal. Exposition of Romans vii 7-25," *The Perfectionist* 1 (20 Oct. 1834): 11-12; also in *"Way of Holiness,"* 37-64 and *The Berean: A Manual for the Help of Those Who Seek the Faith of the Primitive Church* (Putney, VT: Published at the Office of the Spiritual Magazine, 1847), 188-99. Consistent with his Princetonian background B. B. Warfield, the great chronicler of Perfectionism, speaks contemptuously of the adoption of Stuart's view. At Andover, we are told, Mahan "learned at least to deal with the seventh chapter of Romans so that it would interpose no obstacle to his later theories" (8:43). And of the Oneida Perfectionists, Warfield comments that "Of course Noyes begins by setting aside Rom. VII. 14ff" (8:320).

46. Warfield, 8:43; Asa Mahan, *Autobiography: Intellectual, Moral, and Spiritual* (London: T. Woolmer, 1882), 346-47.

47. For other examples of this view from Oberlin, see Samuel D. Cochran, "Chalmers on Romans," *Oberlin Quarterly Review,* 1846, 18-24; and Finney, in Parkhurst, 87-108.

48. Moses Stuart, *Commentary to the Epistle to the Romans with a Translation and Various Excurus* (Andover: Flagg & Gould, 1832), 283.

49. Ibid., 556. The uniqueness of Stuart's view to American Calvinism of all stripes is reflected in the fact that he is the only example Hodge cites in support of there being "distinguished writers of England and our own country" who held it (Hodge, *Romans*, 297). Similarly, Stuart himself, when listing supporters for his own position, includes no Americans (Stuart, 561).

50. Campbell, 424-25.

51. Both Smith's previous interest and familiarity with Methodism and Sidney Rigdon's former association with Campbell would naturally incline these two participants in JST Romans 7 to understand verses 14-25 as describing pre-Christian experience. Because of these prior influences it becomes striking that Smith would understand at least some of these verses to describe present Christian rather than past pre-Christian experience. In the minds of Methodist-Revivalist interpreters, as we have seen, the dire wretchedness of the man of Romans 7:14-25 is scarcely an acceptable description of the Christian life. Smith feels sympathy with this objection and so makes some of the darker statements in the chapter refer to the pre-Christian past. Had Smith really had no intention of balancing the two dominant views of his day, we should not have expected him to make the primary reference of the passage the canonical author's present Christian experience as the Old-Calvinist interpreters did.

52. Further reference to it was also inserted by Smith after John 1:17: "For the law [of Moses] was after a carnal commandment, to the administration of death; but the gospel was after the power of an endless life ..." Dependence on Hebrews 7:16 is obvious because of the reference to the "power of an endless life." This process of transporting verses and terminology from one book to another is further proof of the view of Richard P. Howard (4) and others that the JST is not a restoration of the ancient text. Further discussion of the "law of the carnal commandment" also appears under the dates 22 and 23 September 1832 (D&C 84:23-8; 1835 ed. IV, 4).

53. NT MS 2, folio 4, p. 123; also Rom. 4:2.

54. The apparent motive behind changing the voice of the SCB's "slew" from active to passive ("was slain") was to transfer the reference of the preceding pronoun "it" from *the law* to *sin.*

55. John C. Bennett, *The History of the Saints; Or An Exposé of Joe Smith And Mormonism* (Boston: Leland & Whiting, 1842), 243-45; also Jessee.

56. The only earlier example mentioned in standard treatments comes

from the Book of Mormon itself. Though the Book of Mormon adopts a clear anti-polygamous stance (e.g., Jacob 1:15, 2:23-35, 3:5; Mosiah 11:2, 4, 14; Ether 10:5), in one instance a comment appears which, in light of later developments, may have been intended to leave the door open to the eventual introduction of polygamy. The passage begins with a standard renunciation of the practice: "Wherefore, my brethren, hear me, and hearken to the word of the Lord: For there shall not any man among you have save it be one wife; and concubines he shall have none" (Jacob 2:27). Yet, a few lines later he says: "For *if I will,* saith the Lord of Hosts, raise up seed unto me, *I will command my people: otherwise,* they shall hearken unto these things" (italics mine; see Lawrence Foster, *Religion and Sexuality: Three American Communal Experiments of the Nineteenth Century* [New York: Oxford University Press, 1981], 132-33).

57. The polygamy revelation specified that plural wives are to be taken from among virgins: "[I]f any man espouse a virgin, and desire to espouse another, and the first give her consent; and if he espouse the second, and they are virgins, and have vowed to no other man, then he is justified; he cannot commit adultery ..." (*Deseret News, Extra,* 14 Sept. 1852, 27; reprinted in Foster, 254, and D&C 132:61). Examples of married women Smith is thought to have pursued include Prescinda (Mrs. Norman) Buell; Sarah (Mrs. John) Cleveland; Mrs. Durfee; Mrs. Robert D. Foster; Sally (Mrs. Samuel) Gulley; Clarissa (Mrs. Levi) Hancock; Lucinda (Mrs. George W.) Harris; Zina (Mrs. Henry) Jacobs; Sarah (Mrs. Hiram) Kimball; Jane (Mrs. William) Law; Mary (Mrs. Adam) Lightner; Fanny (Mrs. Roswell) Murray; Sarah (Mrs. Orson) Pratt; Mary (Mrs. Parley) Pratt; Ruth (Mrs. Edward) Sayers: and Patty (Mrs. David) Sessions. John C. Bennett (1842, 256) also mentions an as yet unidentified Mrs. A**** S****. See further Todd Compton, *In Sacred Loneliness: The Plural Wives of Joseph Smith* (Salt Lake City: Signature Books, 1997).

58. Eber D. Howe, *Mormonsim Unvailed, or a Faithful Account of the Singular Imposition and Delusion, From Its Rise to the Present Time* (Painesville, OH: Published by the author, 1834), 268. Lewis also claimed to have "heard them both [Joseph Smith and Martin Harris] say, adultery was no crime."

59. Fawn M. Brodie, *No Man Knows My History: The Life of Joseph Smith,* 2d. ed. rev. (New York: Knopf, 1971), 119. But see the reservations of Richard S. Van Wagoner (*Mormon Polygamy: A History,* 2d ed. [Salt Lake City: Signature Books, 1989], 13n4). That John Johnson had no son Eli is not enough to dismiss this account entirely. Reference is also made to the apparent involvement of an Eli in Smith's own version of the incident (William Mulder and A. Russell Mortensen, eds., *Among the Mormons* [New York: Knopf, 1969], 67).

60. Van Wagoner, 4-5.

61. Ibid., 4.

62. Ibid., 3.

63. Ibid., 3.

64. Though to be sure it could also be argued that this case represents a

specific *application* of the principle previously presented in JST Romans 7; a principle which may have originated under different circumstances and with a different original point of reference.

65. This could not be said, however, of polygamy proper since that *was* tolerated under the law of Moses. This points up the difficulty of trying to describe Smith's activities prior to the revelation of April 1843 as "early examples of polygamy." This use of the word is really anachronistic.

66. Romans 7 is the most heavily reworked chapter in the whole of JST Romans.

# 14. "The Lord Said, Thy Wife Is a Very Fair Woman to Look Upon": The Book of Abraham, Secrets, and Lying for the Lord

*Susan Staker*

SECRETS FUNCTIONED AS A WARRANT OF AUTHORITY, WHICH BRIGHAM Young used to win for himself and the Quorum of the Twelve Joseph Smith's mantle of leadership during the succession contest following Smith's murder in the summer of 1844.[1] Young and those who followed him to Utah were determined that Smith's legacy of secret teachings in Nauvoo, Illinois, would continue. These secret teachings included plural marriage, temple rituals including the endowment and second anointing, and political Kingdom of God. Generally those who refused to follow Young, especially those gathering around the Reorganized Church of Jesus Christ of Latter Day Saints in the 1860s, wished instead to distance themselves from the secret teachings of Nauvoo and to see them as foreign to the economy of Smith's religious imagination.

More recently Nauvoo's secret teachings have been used as a warrant of authority by some concerned about the status of women in today's LDS church. In this vein, for example, some scholars have argued that Smith gave women a priesthood in Nauvoo's secret rituals. They trace in the twentieth-century a diminution of the spiritual and institutional privileges accorded by Smith to women in Nauvoo.[2]

Certainly it is true that a transformation in the institutional fortunes of women comes into view in Nauvoo, beginning in the spring of 1842. The institutional structures of the LDS church developed during the Kirtland, Ohio, period were thoroughly homosocial–men among men. Women (along with children) were included only in the rituals of baptism and "sacrament." Only one revelation in the 1835 Doctrine and Covenants was addressed to a woman. Men were the ones ordained to positions within the increasingly elaborate hierarchy of power. Only men were counted for purposes of attendance in the early conferences of the church. Only men participated in the washing and anointing rituals associated with the dedication of the House of the Lord in Kirtland in the spring of 1836.

It was in Nauvoo that women (distinguished finally from children) participated in their own organization, the Female Relief Society. Overseeing these meetings, Joseph Smith explicitly licensed the women to heal the sick and demonstrate other gifts of the spirit. And it was in Nauvoo that women were included for the first time in sacred rituals beyond baptism and the sacrament. In Nauvoo's secret rituals of the temple endowment and second anointing, both men and women were confirmed in the glorious prospect of becoming kings and queens, priests and priestesses, gods and goddesses.

However, despite such demonstrable distance between Kirtland and Nauvoo, it is unwise to bring our twentieth-century wishes for an egalitarian structure between men and women to our interrogations of Mormon history. The historical record cannot bear the weight of our desires. Nauvoo's innovations for women were inextricably linked to a more general institutional turn towards secrecy. And this turn toward secrecy occurred within a cultural landscape articulated around a dense labyrinth of secrets, especially secrets about plural marriage. Within this context, Smith's institutional innovations in Nauvoo seem more designed to contain and control the unruly energies and voices of the women than to enable them, to inscribe them safely within a hierarchy of male privilege and power.

One suggestive window onto a landscape of secrecy like that of Nauvoo in the spring of 1842 and onto the position of a woman within such an ambiguous landscape can be found in a portion of the Book of Abraham which Joseph Smith published and apparently translated during March 1842–the story of Abraham disguising his wife as his sister. The revisions made to the King James version of this story significantly restructure the relations which obtain among God, Abraham, and Sarah, and arguably make of the incident a narrative about lying for the Lord.[3] In Joseph Smith's Book of Abraham, God commands the husband to keep secrets and to lie and then the husband commands his wife. This is not what happens in the Bible account.

The Book of Abraham was published for the first time in the 1 March and 15 March 1842 issues (numbers 9 and 10 of volume 3) of Nauvoo's *Times and Seasons*. The 1 March issue included the following notice attributed to "Joseph": "This paper commences my editorial career, I alone stand for it, and shall do for all papers having my signature henceforward."[4] The notice that Smith was now editor of the *Times and Seasons* would have in itself made the 1 March issue noteworthy. This was the first time that Smith had publicly assumed such direct control and responsibility for a Mormon newspaper. Until then the only publications which had been accorded such a direct seal of authority from Smith had been the Book of Mormon in 1830 and the first edition of the Doctrine and Covenants in 1835.[5]

The authority lent by Smith's signature only underscored the dramatic nature of the first two issues of his editorship.[6] The 1 March issue was headlined with a strange woodcut copied from the Egyptian papyri Smith had acquired in Kirtland in the summer of 1835. These woodcuts were followed with the portion of the Book of Abraham Smith had translated during the fall and winter of 1835-36 (in current editions of the Pearl of Great Price, Abr. 1-2:18).[7]

The 15 March issue began with the second (and what would be the final) installment from the Book of Abraham and followed with additional woodcuts.[8] Smith's diary suggests that he translated and revised this second installment of the Book of Abraham for the *Times and Seasons* on 8-9 March–after the first installment went to press (Abr. 2:19-5:21). The 1842 date for the second installment seems confirmed by surviving manuscript evidence, as well.[9] By 19 March Wilford Woodruff, who was working at the paper, recorded in his journal that they were typesetting the section translated the week before: "Spent the day in the printing Office. We struck off about 500 No of the 10

No 3 vole of Times & Seasons which contained the portion of the Book of Abraham that gave his account of Kolob, Oliblish, God sitting upon his Throne The Earth, other planets & many great & glorious things as revealed to Abraham through the power of the priesthood. The truths of the Book of Abraham are truly edifying great & glorious which are among the rich treasures that are revealed unto us in the last days."[10]

Woodruff's diary does not mention the incident about Abraham disguising his wife as his sister which begins the 15 March installment. Certainly this incident on first glance seems at some distance from the grand cosmology dominating this second installment–the geography of heaven, a council in heaven, the creation of the earth. Perhaps it is the seemingly disconnected status of the fragment which in the end recommends it as important. It could so easily have been left out, have escaped Smith's attention as it escapes Woodruff's.[11]

When Smith suspended work on the Book of Abraham in 1836, he was dictating Abraham's autobiography, which follows in substantive ways Abraham's life in the King James Bible. When Smith returns to the manuscript in 1842, he includes only a fragment of the one incident from Abraham's life found at Genesis 12:10-20. The Bible's biography of Abraham stretches through thirteen more chapters. Smith's decision to include only this fragment suggests that it somehow spoke to him as he returned to his work on the Egyptian project. Perhaps he saw the outlines of Nauvoo's own tangled topography in the narrative landscape drawn by this story in Genesis.[12]

This incident occurs before the covenant so Abraham and Sarah are still known as Abram and Sarai. The story in the Bible begins: "And there was famine in the land: and Abram went down into Egypt to sojourn there; for the famine was grievous in the land. And it came to pass, when he was come near to enter into Egypt, that he said unto Sarai his wife, Behold now, I know that thou art a fair woman to look upon: Therefore it shall come to pass when the Egyptians shall see thee, that they shall say, This is his wife: and they will kill me, but they will save thee alive. Say, I pray thee, thou art my sister; that it may be well with me for thy sake; and my soul shall live because of thee."[13]

It is Abram's idea to keep Sarai's status as his wife secret in order to protect himself from the consequences of anticipated male rivalry. Certainly this strategy works most immediately to his advantage.

Pharaoh takes Abram's beautiful "sister" into his household, presumably as his wife or concubine, and rewards her "brother" Abram for the exchange by giving him "sheep, and oxen, and he asses, and men servants, and she asses, and camels." Abram seems quite happy with the spoils of this rather traditional sounding marriage bargain–an exchange of wealth, an alliance of sorts made outside one's group by exchanging a woman. But Abram seems not to have considered the long-term consequences of his bargain. How will he retrieve his wife/"sister"?

Only at this point in the Bible story does God intervene: "And the Lord plagued Pharaoh and his house with great plagues because of Sarai Abram's wife. And Pharaoh called Abram, and said, What is this that thou hast done unto me? why didst thou not tell me that she was thy wife? Why saidst thou, She is my sister? so I might have taken her to me to wife: now therefore behold thy wife, take her, and go thy way." And so Abram and Sarai are banished from Egypt.

As in Nauvoo, this world is complicated by secrets and confusions surrounding marriage customs and taboos.There is potential for violence in this world where marital status is uncertain, where men may become rivals unawares and in ignorance transgress boundaries long guarded by convention and tradition. Lying and disguise recommend themselves as strategies of defense and survival in this world. But these defenses in turn contribute to the disordering and blurring of those boundaries and differences which constitute the traditional social order.

In the Bible Abram centers the narrative on the problem of male desire and proposes the scheme requiring secrecy and lying. The character aligned most closely with Abram is Pharaoh. Abram predicts the Pharaoh's response to Sarai, confirming the ubiquity and solidarity of male desire. This solidarity is underscored and formalized through the literal exchange of Sarai. The solidarity of Abram and the Pharaoh is further underscored through the formal presentation of their characters in the Bible. Both men are given direct speech, which provides some access to individual motives.

In contrast, the two remaining characters in the story, the Lord and Sarai, are presented entirely in third person. Neither of them speaks. As a result their individualized responses to the situation tend to be effaced. This formal parallel may suggest an alliance of sorts between them. Certainly it is possible to read God's interventions as speaking for Sarai's interests. God gets her out of Pharaoh's household. (Though it is also possible to imagine that Sarai was just fine in Egypt.)

Still the formal distinctions between God and Sarai are just as telling. The woman is an object of desire and of exchange within the story, she is allowed no independent action. In contrast, God acts, sending the plagues on Pharaoh. Although his motives remain unnarrated, his actions bring him down on the side of conventional taboos and boundaries concerning marriage and desire which Abram has knowingly obscured and the Pharaoh unknowingly transgressed.[14]

The Book of Abraham revisions to this incident do not really vanquish problems of disorder and violence which threaten the world of the narrative. But Smith's revisions do shift the blame and restructure key relationships–between God and man, between men and women.

Here is the entire incident as it appears in the 15 March 1842 number of the *Times and Seasons*: "15. And I, Abraham, journeyed, going on still towards the South; and there was a continuation of a famine in the Land, and I Abraham concluded to go down into Egypt, to sojourn there, for the famine became very grievous. And it came to pass when I was come near to enter into Egypt, the Lord said unto me, behold, Sarai, thy wife, is a very fair woman to look upon, therefore it shall come to pass when the Egyptians see her, they will say she is his wife; and they will kill you, but they will save her alive; therefore see that ye do on this wise, let her say unto the Egyptians, she is thy sister, and thy soul shall live. And it came to pass that I, Abraham, told Sarai, my wife, all that the Lord had said unto me; therefore say unto them, I pray thee, thou art my sister, that it may be well with me for thy sake, and my soul shall live because of thee."

Smith's revisions transpose the story from third-person narrative to first-person autobiography. The source of narration in the King James Bible is mysterious, impersonal, unsituated. Its authority comes from its magisterial aura, its distance able to narrate even God creating the world. One of the consistent impulses organizing Smith's New Translation of the Bible, begun in 1830, was to situate the magisterial, impersonal narration of the King James Bible within the frame of human history. Thus the first installment of the New Translation

(Moses 1, in PGP), dictated in June 1830, provides a frame story for the Bible. God appears face to face to Moses, shows him a vision of the earth's creation, and commands him to transcribe what he sees and hears. Moses, in effect, takes dictation from God. Thus the beginning line of the King James Bible, "In the beginning God created the heaven and the earth," becomes in Smith's New Translation, "Yea, in the beginning I created the heaven, and the earth upon which thou standest."

Smith's further changes to Genesis in 1830 reveal that Moses had additional textual resources as well, since God's prophets and seers, beginning with Adam, kept written records of their interactions with God, a "book of remembrance":[15] sacred stories narrated within a frame circumscribed by personal experience and memory (Moses 2-3; 6-7).[16]

There was already ample precedent then for Abraham's autobiography, begun in 1835-36. The Book of Abraham is situated on this New Translation terrain of "remembrance," Abraham recounting his own personal experiences with God. One of the defining characteristics of an autobiographical account is that it is retrospective, a product of memory. One of the sure signs of memory can be seen in the first words of Smith's revision: "I, Abraham." At the time he is living through the story, he is not yet known by the name God will later give him but is known rather as Abram. In calling himself Abraham, he inserts retrospectively the position and authority of his final and proper name before God into the confines of the earlier story.

What is striking, of course, is that Abraham adopts a different naming practice for his wife. She remains Sarai in the text. This dissymmetry of proper names marks the story as preeminently the product of male memory. She too will receive a proper name from God. But no trace of her new name, Sarah, makes it into the confines of Abraham's story.

If Sarai appears in the Bible as most closely parallel to God–at least in formal qualities of narration–this is not so in the Book of Abraham. Through Smith's revisions, God and Abraham become allies. And Sarai is left the character most at a distance from God.[17]

The alliance between God and Abraham in Smith's revisions depends on a shift in responsibility or blame and in the locus of agency and action within the story. Whereas in the Bible, Abram assumes responsibility for the scheme to pass off Sarai as his sister rather than his wife, in Smith's version God assumes the responsibility for this scheme. One of the consistent strategies of Smith's New Translation of the King James Bible in the decade leading up to his 1842 revisions of this Genesis incident for the Book of Abraham was to restructure blame and agency within biblical narrative. Often such restructuring involved relieving God of responsibility for actions which have come to seem discomfiting and even suspect to modern sensibilities.[18]

It is against the background of such common moves in Smith's New Translation that Smith's 1842 revisions to Abraham's story come rather sharply into relief. Rather than absolving heaven of blame, these revisions have God assume responsibility formally meted to an earthling. In the Bible God enters rather late in a plot set in motion by Abram. Now God initiates the plot. In the Bible God is silent. Now he introduces the topos of male desire: the fair female as the object of the male gaze. "Behold, Sarai, thy wife, is a very fair woman to look upon," Abraham remembers God saying. In the wake of God's new voice and new agency, guarding against the consequences of male desire becomes a matter of sacred secrecy, of lying for the Lord.

God's new centrality to the story results in a radical restructuring of the relationship between heaven and earth. This restructuring of relations installs the God character at the apex of an unambiguous hierarchy of order: God speaks to the man who speaks to the woman who does not speak.[19] In the Bible a distance is maintained between the schemes of the men (Abraham and Pharaoh) and the violent resistance of God, between the human order and the divine. In Smith's revision the boundaries between heaven and earth blur as God implicates himself in the messiest of human affairs, secrets and lies involving male desire and transgressed marital taboos.

At the same time, Abraham's prestige is enhanced through his alliance with God. He is no longer Pharaoh's double so much as God's. It is God and Abraham who see that Sarai is fair, who conspire together. And with God in charge, Abraham cannot be faulted for any complications in the wake of God's secrets. On this matter, we must, of course, take Abraham's word. For the new narration of the story means that Abraham becomes the only available channel to God. Not only does he speak God's words to the woman but more globally the autobiographical text of "I, Abraham," stands as the necessary mediator of all God's words. Gods words are now accessible only through Abraham's words.

If Smith's revisions make God and Abraham more alike, they do not so enhance Sarai's position. Rather the dissymmetry in the names—Abraham and Sarai—in the end reveals itself as a fitting sign for more general dissymmetries which the narrative revisions only exacerbate. Certainly Sarai's position in the Bible is hardly enviable. But at least the third-person form of narration made of her an independent character and paralleled her most closely with the character of God. In the Book of Abraham, in contrast, the woman not only has no voice and no action, but she no longer appears as an independent character. Now her very existence is consistently mediated either by the speech of the man or the speech of God. God speaks to Abraham but not to her. Instead Abraham relays to her what God has said. Through this chain of speech, a clear hierarchy is erected with God at the top and woman at the bottom. Her link to God can only be forged through obedience to the man.

In fact, it is possible to argue that her presence is erased from the Book of Abraham altogether. The narrative breaks off precisely at the point Sarai would make her entrance as an independent character into the story. The Bible story had made clear the dangerous communication between erotic desire, secrecy, and violence. Truncating the story means that many of the knottiest problems pressing against a world threatened by the blurring of boundaries in matters of desire and marriage are left hanging. The potentially dangerous consequences of secrets and lies are effaced from Smith's version of the story.

Perhaps the most intriguing set of questions is left by the erasure of the woman and any trace of her "remembrance" in this book of male memory. Certainly the Book of Sarai would remember to ask the obvious question left hanging by the Book of Abraham: What about the woman? In the Bible it is God's resistance to Abram's scheme which unmasks Abram's secrets and his lying and gets Sarai out of Egypt. Since in the Book of Abraham the plan of lying and disguise is now God's plan, one can only wonder with a good deal of concern about Sarai's end? What will happen if she obeys the chain of command and enters Pharaoh's household?

In the Bible story, of course, the woman demonstrates her submission to the structure of male desire. She obeys Abram and goes into Pharaoh's household. But in Smith's version, it should be pointed out, her ultimate submission, her obedience, no longer only to her husband but now through him to God, is left unnarrated and thus uncertain. There is, perhaps, even a certain imploring quality in Abraham's address to Sarai: "Say unto them, I pray thee." What does Sarai reply?

The story of Abraham and Sarai in the 1842 portion of the Book of Abraham may leave such knotty questions in suspense. But the men and women living in Nauvoo's tangled landscape of secrets had no such luxury. They were being asked to lie for the Lord about matters of marriage and convention and to live in the wake of such volatile secrets.[20]

Certainly by the spring and summer of 1842, when he was dictating this story, Smith was a man whose secrets transgressed the boundaries of traditional marriage conventions and taboos. He had married over a dozen secret wives, at least nine already married to living husbands. And he was turned down by other married women. In some cases Smith was pressing his marriage proposals on women without knowledge of the husbands (even apostle husbands on missions).[21] Further neither Smith's first wife, Emma, nor his brother Hyrum were privy to these secrets. But Smith had introduced a number of close associates, especially in the Quorum of Twelve, to his secrets. And some of these allies, including Brigham Young and Heber C. Kimball, were with Smith's help themselves taking secret wives.

Not surprisingly this was a time of high anxiety in Nauvoo, with the city's circuits of gossip pressing against the limits of secrecy and discretion. Arguably the period between March and May 1842 comes at the cusp of densest secrecy. For in late May 1842 Smith's marital secrets would be dragged onto a public stage as a vicious scandal erupted around Smith's falling out with close associate and initiate to many secrets, John C. Bennett–Nauvoo's mayor and the church's assistant president. This period of dense but threatened secrecy coincides with a flurry of institutional strategies of containment. During the three-month period before this break and crisis, Smith not only becomes editor of the newspaper and publishes the Book of Abraham but also organizes the Masonic Lodge, organizes the Female Relief Society, receives a revelation about the political Kingdom of God, and institutes the "endowment," a ritual which among other things swears adherents to secrecy. By the time of Smith's death two years later, these innovations would reveal themselves as the beginnings of a whole institutional superstructure to protect and pass on secrets, as the foundation for the ambitious theocracy, the Kingdom of God, which Smith's followers in Nauvoo's secrets would pursue to the borders of the twentieth century.

That initiates in the May 1842 "endowment" saw the new ritual as crucially about secrets and safety (the same concerns highlighted by the Abraham story) can be seen in a letter written a month later by Heber C. Kimball, one of the first nine initiates, all men, to a fellow apostle: "Brother Joseph feels as well as I Ever see him. one reason is he has got a Small company that he feels safe in thare hands. and that is not all. he can open his bosom to and feel him Self safe."[22] Clearly Kimball sees secrecy and safety closely intertwined in this new ritual. Kimball would later preach, "You have received your endowments. What is it for? To learn you to hold your tongues."[23]

During this same period, Smith was also making it clear to the women that he saw their fortunes intimately connected with whether or not he found them similarly able to hold their tongues and adhere to a code of sacred secrets. "The tongue is an unruly member," he told them during a meeting of the Female Relief Society that spring, "hold your tongues about things of no moment, a little tale will set the world on fire."[24] Smith's words and actions in the spring of 1842 suggest that he intended to initiate women as well as the men into the company of safe confidants created by the endowment ritual. In the service of this goal, he moved to bend the new women's organization to the ends of sacred secrecy.

But Smith's efforts to this end met with little success in the spring of 1842. No women received the endowment for another full year, when the select company of men *and* women known as the Quorum of the Anointed finally came into existence. The women would have to wait until 1843 for Smith to win from his wife Emma her submission, however briefly, to his word that God's words required her obedience to the secrets and difficulties of plural marriage.

The fortunes of women in the institutional structures of early Mormonism were thus inextricably tied to the fortunes of Mormonism's first couple in negotiating the complications and dangers of Nauvoo's marital secrets. The women of Nauvoo were caught in the middle of their struggle. On the one side was Joseph, pressing for their hands in marriage, for promises not to tell, for help in soliciting other wives. On the other was Emma, enlisting them to prove the rumors against Joseph false, rumors which from personal involvement they often knew were true. This struggle becomes the immediate context for Smith's institutional innovations for women in Nauvoo.

About half of the women attending the first, 17 March, meeting of the Relief Society and chosen by Emma to serve as leaders in the new Relief Society organization were already or would very soon become secret wives of her husband Joseph (or in one case a daughter would become the wife, in another the woman refused).[25] Additional secret wives of Joseph and also some of his associates as well as other women privy to at least some of the secrets of plural marriage attended the founding meetings of the association during the spring. These women were required by Smith to keep their marriages secret from Emma, to lie for the Lord and for him. Matters got particularly complicated in the meetings of the new Relief Society organization during the spring, when Emma began using her position as "Elect Lady" and "presidentess" of the society to track down and squelch rumors multiplying on the circuits of Nauvoo's gossip about her husband and his closest associates.

The case of Clarissa Marvel provides a view into the complexity of life in Nauvoo's culture of secrecy. Emma seized her opportunity to launch a campaign against rumors at the second meeting of the Relief Society on 24 March 1842, a meeting Smith did not attend. Emma asked the women for a plan to bring young Clarissa Marvel "to repentance" and accused the girl of "scandalous falsehoods on the character of Prest. Joseph Smith without the least provocation." "I presume that most of [you] know more about Clarissa Marvel than I," Emma told the women. Unfortunately for Emma, this statement would prove to be more than true. One of the few who would publicly defend Clarissa at the meeting was Emma's sister-in-law, Agnes M. Coolbrith Smith, recent widow of Joseph's brother Don Carlos. The irony of Agnes's defense for Clarissa was that the circulating "scandalous falsehoods" concerned Smith's actions towards Agnes. And there was more fire than smoke in these rumors. For Smith seems already to have married his brother's widow by the date of this meeting.[26]

Emma was not ready to give up. At the third meeting a week later, after her husband left the room, Emma again brought up Clarissa's case. Finally Sarah Cleveland, Emma's counselor in the new organization, moved that Elizabeth Durfee and Elizabeth Allred should investigate. Not only Sarah Cleveland but also Elizabeth Durfee were among the women Smith married in the spring of 1842. Sarah Cleveland was fifty-three, Elizabeth Durfee fifty. Elizabeth Allred was also apparently privy to Smith's secrets about plural marriage. In fact these fifty-or-so women, "Mothers in Israel" as they were sometimes termed, were employed by Smith in making his approach to other women about plural marriage. For example, Sarah Cleveland would act on behalf of Joseph and Eliza R. Snow, Emma's secretary in the organization, when they secretly married in late June. Not surprisingly, Elizabeth Durfee resisted her appointment to the committee. Still within three days this incident was more or less concluded when Clarissa was induced to sign a carefully worded statement: "This is to certify that I never have at any time or place, seen or heard any things improper or unvirtuous in the conduct or conversation of either President Smith or Mrs. Agnes Smith. I also certify that I never have reported any thing derogatory to the character of either of them."[27]

Smith had come to this third meeting of the Female Relief Society with strategies for containing and diffusing the dangers of the situation. In effect, he outlined to the women what could be possible for their society if they could prove themselves worthy to keep God's and his prophet's secrets: "Pres. Joseph Smith arose–spoke of the organization of the society. ... Proposed that the society go into a close examination of every candidate–that they were going too fast–that the society should grow up by degrees; should commence with a few individuals–thus have a select society of the virtuous. ... All must act in concert or nothing can be done, that the society should move according to the ancient Priesthood, hence there should be a select society, separate from all the evils of the world, choice, virtuous and holy. Said he was going to make of this society a kingdom of priests as in Enoch's day–as in Paul's day."[28]

Smith had spent the morning before this third meeting helping to prepare a letter for the Relief Society, a letter about Nauvoo's secrets. Evidence suggests this letter was read to the women that day–probably after Smith's provocative remarks, probably by Emma.

The letter explicitly worries that the women are "not sufficiently skill'd in Masonry as to keep a secret" and then begins teasing into view preconditions for the women's select society. It first warns the women against "unprincipled men" who are claiming authority from Joseph to "debauch the innocent." Do not believe them, Smith's letter tells the women: "we do not want any one to believe *any thing* as coming from us contrary to the old established morals & virtues & scriptural laws, regulating the habits, customs & conduct of society; and all persons pretending to be authorized by us, or having any permit, or sanction, from us, are & will be, *liars & base impostors* & you are authorized on the very first intimation of the kind to denounce them as such, & shun them as the lying ... serpent, whether they are prophet, seers, or revelators Patriarchs, twelve Apostles, Elders, Priests, Mayor, Generals, City councillors, Aldermen, Marshalls, Police, Lord Mayors or the Devil they are alike culpable & shall be damned for such evil practices; and if you yourselves adhere to anything of the kind, you also shall be damned."[29] One can only imagine the accents of her voice if Emma read this letter to the women.

The letter concludes: "Let this Epistle be had as a private matter in your Society, and then we shall learn whether you are good masons." Smith's letter then is not only about Nauvoo's secrets, but it is also set up as a test of whether the women can keep secrets. Presumably if the contents of the letter make it onto the circuits of Nauvoo's gossip, then the women have failed the test. But if they hold their tongues, they will reveal themselves as a select society moving after the pattern of the ancient priesthood.

This letter is circumspect about naming names—still keeps them secret. But within weeks of this letter, John C. Bennett went public with his sensational version of events in Nauvoo—highly elaborated, often fanciful, but with insider information about Smith's secret wives. Charges and counter charges flew in local newspapers all summer. Bennett printed his account, first in the newspapers during the summer, then in a book-length exposé in the fall. A young girl named Martha Brotherton, who apparently had been sought in marriage by Brigham Young with both Heber C. Kimball's and Smith's help, printed hers. Also stories about Smith soliciting and being rebuffed by Sydney Rigdon's daughter, Nancy, and Orson Pratt's wife, Sarah, were making their way along gossip's circuits into the public conversation, helped by Bennett. For example, Bennett had printed in a local newspaper the letter written by Smith to Nancy Rigdon at the time she refused his proposal in April. Smith's words to Nancy might easily have been Abraham's words to Sarai: "That which is wrong under one circumstance, may be and often is, right under another. ... This is the principle on which the government of heaven is conducted–by revelation adapted to the circumstances in which the children of the kingdom are placed. Whatever God requires is right, no matter what it is, although we may not see the reason thereof till long after the events transpire." During the summer Smith and Pratt broke over Smith's proposal to Pratt's wife. In defense Smith set out in the newspapers (with "affidavits" sworn to the "truth") to do what he had warned he would do in his letter to the women in March–shun and destroy those who "lied"–or in other words those who disclosed Nauvoo's secrets.[30]

The state of affairs in Nauvoo by August 1842 can be measured in a poem appearing in a Nauvoo newspaper authored by Eliza R. Snow, Emma's counselor and friend, Joseph's secret wife. In the poem she describes an angel looking down on Nauvoo's "vague scenery":

> He'd be apt to conclude from the medley of things:
> We've got into a jumble of late–
> A deep intricate puzzle, a tangle of strings,
> That no possible scheme can make straight.
>
> Tell me, what will it be, and O, where will it end?
> Say, if you have permission to tell:
> Is there any fixed point unto which prospects tend?
> Does a focus belong to pell mell?
> From the midst of confusion can harmony flow?
> Or can peace from distraction come forth?
> From out of corruption, integrity grow?
> Or can vice unto virtue give birth?
>
> Will the righteous come forth with their garments unstained?
> With their hearts unpolluted with sin?

And then the final two lines of Eliza's poem after she has been driven to question whether even the righteous can escape Nauvoo with their garments unstained and their hearts unpolluted with sin:

> *O yes; Zion, thy honor will still be sustained,*
> *And the glory of God usher'd in.*[31]

These final two lines are literally underlined in the typography of the printed poem. Within the context made by the poem itself, this abrupt move from the tangle of the personal and the immediate to the clarity of the abstraction "Zion" and from the deeply troubled and elaborated questioning to a forced, militant declaration advertises itself as an act of will, of wish. Certainly the questions and pain in this poem's voice survive beyond its quick, happy ending.

This anguished voice also echoes back to the story of Abraham and Sarai which Smith left hanging in suspense in the March 1842 installment of the Book of Abraham. I have focused my observations here on the difficulties for women in Nauvoo's tangled landscape of secrets and lies in the spring and summer of 1842 precisely because it was the woman's story which was effaced by the Book of Abraham's revisions of the King James Bible's incident. Within this context, Eliza Snow's poem can serve as the prologue for a woman's "book of remembrance" for Nauvoo. (And within this context we are left wishing as well for the words of a Book of Sarai.)

Nauvoo's secrets, the foundation on which the Mormon church has been erected, are inextricably linked then with Nauvoo's lies. Or with what Smith's revisions to the story of Abraham and Sarai frame as God's lies. However we students of Mormonism and Joseph Smith write our books of remembrance for Nauvoo, we must squarely face this enduring legacy.

*NOTES*

1. For a discussion of the importance of Nauvoo's secrets in the succession struggle, see D. Michael Quinn, *The Mormon Hierarchy: Origins of Power* (Salt Lake City: Signature Books, 1994), 143-46; also Andrew F. Ehat, "Joseph Smith's Introduction of the Temple Ordinances and the Mormon Succession Questions," M.A. thesis, Brigham Young University, 1982.

2. See in particular, D. Michael Quinn, "Mormon Women Have Had the Priesthood Since 1843," in *Women and Authority: Re-emerging Mormon Feminism*, ed. Maxine Hanks (Salt Lake City: Signature Books, 1992), 365-410; Margaret and Paul Toscano, *Strangers in Paradox: Explorations in Mormon Theology* (Salt Lake City: Signature Books, 1990); also Margaret Toscano, "Put On Your Strength O Daughters of Zion: Claiming Priesthood and Knowing the Mother, in *Women and Authority*, 411-38. Hanks's volume collects a number of essays which argue for a more egalitarian nineteenth-century model based primarily on the secret teachings of Smith in Nauvoo between 1842 and 1844.

3. For the broader context of this theme in Mormon history, see B. Carmon Hardy, "Lying for the Lord: An Essay," Appendix I in *Solemn Covenant: The Mormon Polygamous Passage* (Urbana: University of Illinois Press, 1992), 363-88.

4. With this notice, Smith assumed editorship of the paper from Ebenezer Robinson. In today's parlance, Smith's assumption of the editorship might be characterized as something of a "hostile takeover," made in the name of the Quorum of the Twelve.

Before the takeover, Smith had already been realigning the structure of power in Nauvoo as the apostles began returning from their successful missions, particularly in the British Isles. It was among this group that Smith would find his most loyal allies in the secrets of Nauvoo. Pressing against the limits of the 1835 revelation which had organized the Quorum of the Twelve as a "travelling high council" with authority as missionaries away from the church's center, Smith had begun rewarding these successful missionaries with a domestic base of operations by installing them in the governing councils of Nauvoo, the church's center stake, and in supervisory roles in the building of the temple and the Nauvoo House, only just begun.

The *Times and Seasons* had begun in Nauvoo as a joint, largely independent venture of Smith's brother, Don Carlos Smith, and his partner, Ebenezer Robinson, who had salvaged the church printing press hidden in the mud during the final violent days of the Mormons in Missouri. Don Carlos had died in 1841 just as members of the Twelve were beginning to return to Nauvoo. Robinson later recalled, long after he left the church, that he was "greatly surprised" when on 28 January 1842 Smith received a revelation which informed Robinson that it was God's "will" to have the Twelve "take in hand the Editorial department of the *Times and Seasons*." Three days later on 3 and 4 February, Smith and his associates in the Twelve completed the takeover of Robinson's business and, according to Robinson, evicted him and his family from the premises. See Ebenezer Robinson, *The Return* 2 (Oct. 1890): 324, 325; see also Scott G. Kenney, ed., *Wilford Woodruff's Journal*, 9 vols. (Midvale, UT: Signature Books, 1983-85), 2: 153 (3 and 4 Feb. 1842); Dean C. Jessee, ed., *The Papers of Joseph Smith*, Vol. 2, Journal 1832-42 (Salt Lake City: Deseret Book Co., 1992), 356-57, 361, 362.

It is intriguing to note that in 1844, Smith would become concerned that

Robinson's wife, Angeline, was reporting to Emma about Smith's activities. Joseph Lee Robinson, brother of Ebenezer, wrote in his journal that his brother's wife "had some time before this watched Brother Joseph the Prophet, had seen him go into some house that she had reported to sister Emma." For a discussion of this incident, see Linda King Newell and Valeen Tippetts Avery, *Mormon Enigma: Emma Hale Smith* (Garden City, NY: Doubleday & Co., Inc., 1984), 177-78. Nancy Hyde, whom Smith by revelation had housed with the Robinsons in December 1841, would become one of Smith's secret wives. Also Smith and his associates in the Twelve would come in the spring of 1842 to use the printing office as the focus of a variety of secret meetings associated with plural marriage. One can only wonder if, already in 1842, Smith was concerned about the watching eyes and the unruly tongue of Ebenezer Robinson's wife.

5. In those cases Smith had closely supervised work on the volumes. And both of these volumes had been elevated to the status of scripture, God's voice, before coming off the press. See D&C 18 (June 1829) which discusses the status of the Book of Mormon text. In the case of the 1835 Doctrine and Covenants, it was officially received in an August 1835 meeting, before the book itself was off the press.

6. The excitement which the appearance of this document must have occasioned in Nauvoo is suggested by Wilford Woodruff in his journal for 19 February 1842: "The Lord is Blessing Joseph with Power to reveal the mysteries of the kingdom of God; to translate through the urim & Thummim Ancient records & Hyeroglyphics as old as Abraham or Adam, which causes our hearts to burn within us while we behold their glorious truths opened unto us.

"Joseph the Seer has presented us some of the Book of Abraham which was written by his own hand but hid from the knowledge of man for the last four thousand years but has now come to light through the mercy of God. Joseph has had these records in his possession for several years but has never presented them before the world in the english language untill now. But he is now about to publish it to the world or parts of it by publishing it in the Times & Seasons, for Joseph the Seer is now the Editor of that paper. ...

"I have had the privilege this day of assisting in setting the TIPE for printing the first peace of the BOOK OF ABRAHAM that is to be presented to the inhabitants of the EARTH in the LAST DAYS." See Kenney, *Woodruff's Journal*, 2:154-56 (19 Feb. 1842).

7. Manuscripts which can be dated to 1835 through such techniques as handwriting analysis of the scribes (W. W. Phelps and Warren Parrish) exist for Abraham 1 through 2:18. A manuscript in the hand of Willard Richards also has survived for this first installment and portions of the second. Richards was serving as Smith's scribe in the spring of 1842. There is a natural break at Abraham 2:18 in the Richards manuscript; the writing ends part way down

the page and does not continue on. The rest of the pages (13 of the total 14) continue down to the bottom. The Richards manuscript seems to have been a printer's manuscript since certain revisions in this manuscript solve problems in the 1835 manuscripts, and these changes in Richards's manuscript appear in the 1842 *Times and Seasons*. Taken together, this evidence supports the scenario I am sketching here–that the portion of the Book of Abraham dating from 1835-36 is found in Abraham 1-2:18.

8. In 1842 it was not intended that this would be the final installment of the Book of Abraham. Smith had written the following long version of the short announcement which finally appeared announcing Smith's editorship: "A considerable quantity of the matter in the last paper was in type before the establishment came into my hands.–Some of which went to press without my review or knowledge and a multiplicity of business while entering on the additional care of the editorial department of the *Times and Seasons* must be my apology for what is past.–

"In future I design to furnish much original matter which will be found of inestimable advantage to the saints,–& all who desire a knowledge of the kingdom of God,–and as it is not practicable to bring forth the new translation of the Scriptures & various records of ancient date & great worth to this generation in the usual form by books I shall permit specimens of the same in the Times & Seasons as fast as time and space will admit,–so that the honest in heart may be cheered and comforted and go on their way rejoicing,–as their suls become expossed.–& their understanding enlightened by a knowledge of God's work through the fathers in former days as well as what He is about to do in latter days to fulfill the words of the fathers.–

"In the present no. will be found the commencement of the Records discovered in Egypt some time since as penned by the hand of Father Abraham which I shall outline to translate & publish as fast as possible till the whole is completed and as the saints have long been anxious to obtain a copy of these records those [who] are now taking this Times & Seasons will confer a special favor on their brethren who do not take the paper by informing them that they can now obtain their hearts."

A year later, when John Taylor took over editorship of the *Times and Seasons*, he would again reiterate plans to continue publishing additional material from the Book of Abraham: "We would respectfully announce to those of our subscribers, (and there are a good many of them) who commenced their subscriptions for the *Times and Seasons* at the time when brother Joseph took the editorial department, that the term for which they subscribed for is nearly at a close: most of those commenced at the seventh and eighth numbers; at the time when the translations from the Book of Abraham commenced. This is the sixth number, which only leaves four weeks until the time that they subscribed for, will be fulfilled.

"We have given this timely notice that our friends may prepare themselves. We would further state that we had the promise of Br. Joseph, to furnish us with further extracts from the Book of Abraham. These with other articles that we expect from his pen, the continuation of his history, and the resources that we have of obtaining interesting matter; together with our humble endeavors, we trust will make the paper sufficiently interesting."

Both of these documents are quoted in H. Donl Peterson, *The Story of the Book of Abraham: Mummies, Manuscripts, and Mormonism* (Salt Lake City: Deseret Book, 1995), 150, 153; quoting from Joseph Smith Collection, "Letters of 1842," LDS archives, Historical Department, Church of Jesus Christ of Latter-day Saints, Salt Lake City, Utah; and John Taylor, "Notice," *Times and Seasons* 4 (1 Feb. 1843): 95.

9. According to the 8 March entry of Smith's journal: "Commence Translating from the Book of Abraham, for the 10 No of the Times and Seasons–and was engaged at his office day & evening." According to the 9 March entry: "Examining copy for the Times & Seasons ... in the morning. in the afternoon continued the Translation of the Book of Abraham ... & continued translating & revising & Reading letters in the evening." See Jessee, *Papers of Joseph Smith,* 2:366, 367.

I am indebted to Ed Ashment for bringing to my attention the point at which Smith began working on the Book of Abraham in 1842. Abraham 2: 19-25 (the Abraham/Sarai incident) is absent from all extant manuscript copies. The manuscripts which date from 1835 break off at 2:18. And the Richards manuscript has a natural break after 2:18 as well. All extant manuscript evidence thus argues for an 1842 date for this passage. (Portions of the second installment, beginning with 3:18, have also survived in Richards's hand. The extant version begins at page 7, suggesting that Richards began again at page one with 2:19.)

10. Kenney, *Woodruff's Journal,* 2:159 (19 Mar. 1842). Both the 1 and 15 March issues came out after the printed dates.

11. A number of contemporary scholars have noted the passage. See, for example, Dan Vogel, "'Prophet Puzzle' Revised," in this compilation. Vogel writes: "Thus in excusing Abraham, Smith introduced the more troubling proposition that God is sometimes the author of deception. This assertion would have undoubtedly outraged not only [Adam] Clarke but orthodox believers generally, that is, had they been paying sufficient attention to Smith's teachings. It was nevertheless a concept that fit comfortably with Smith's personal and private theology."

Stephen Ricks notes the same passage and addresses the importance of God assuming responsibility for the incident: "In Abraham 2, the dynamics of the situation are changed dramatically, since here it is God who commanded Abraham to have Sarah claim that she is his sister. ... of primary obedience to God's commands." Although Ricks does not address an 1842 context for Smith's work on this passage, he does turn to a letter written in the spring of 1842: Smith's letter in response to Nancy Rigdon's refusal of Smith's proposal of marriage: "In a letter to Nancy Rigdon, Joseph Smith emphasized the primacy of obedience to God: 'That which is wrong under one circumstance, may be and often is, right under another. ... Whatever God requires is right, no matter what it is, although we may not see the reason thereof till long after events transpire.'" See Stephen D. Ricks, "The Early Ministry of Abraham (Abraham 1 and 2)," in *Studies in Scripture*, Volume Two: The Pearl of Great Price, ed. Robert L. Millet and Kent P. Jackson (Salt Lake City: Randall Book Co., 1985), 221-22.

See also Hugh Nibley, "The Sacrifice of Sarah," *Improvement Era*, Apr. 1970, 79-95. This is Part 11 in the series "A New Look at the Pearl of Great Price." Nibley focuses in particular on the version of the Sarah and Abraham story which appears in the Genesis Apocryphon.

In this version of the story, Sarah is let go from Egypt when Abraham heals the Pharaoh through the laying on of hands (82). In his reading of the Book of Abraham version of the story, Nibley emphasizes the fact that God commands Abraham. But Nibley insists that "no one commands Sarah–the whole thing is left up to her as a matter of free choice. ... throughout the story every crucial decision rests with Sarah and Sarah alone. Why do we say that no one commands Sarah? God commanded Abraham to propose a course of action to Sarah, but Abraham did not command Sarah–he asked her humbly for a personal favor." Nibley's interpretation relies heavily on the phrasing of the language "I pray thee," for example. However, in the end Nibley relies on a distinction between the "law of God" and the "law of her husband" which seems somewhat at odds with this notion of request and free choice: "Abraham is abiding by the law of God; the whole question now is, *Will Sarah abide by the law of her husband?* And she proved that she would, even if necessary at the risk of her life. It was as great a sacrifice as Abraham's and Isaac's, and of the same type" (89; italics in original). Interestingly, Nibley does not note that there is no proof in the Book of Abraham that Sarah proves she will abide the law. Nor does Nibley provide a reference for how he knows that she does.

12. The place of the character Abraham within the economy of Smith's religious imagination can be focused by comparing the function of Abraham with another biblical figure who is consistently important to Smith. In fact, the two characters are, as I have already hinted, evoked as doubles of sorts within Smith's texts: Moses and Abraham. Both are seer characters in the sense described in the Book of Mormon, those who become channels for God's secrets and God's power and in particular are given the guardianship of God's sacred records, old and new. Both see God face to face and view the wonders of his creation. Abraham begins the House of Israel, receives promise of the land. Moses reconfirms and reconstitutes the House of Israel, leading them again to the same promised land.

Moses assumes a prominent place in the first text Smith dictates in 1829, the Book of Mormon. Near the end of his work on that book, Smith dictates a passage which reveals him as a "choice seer" and a latter-day Moses. Moses assumes a recurring and important role in the series of texts dictated by Smith between 1830 and 1835 which gradually work their way to the elaborate structure of male priesthood which Smith foregrounds and codifies through his organization and revision of key revelations for the 1835 edition of the Doctrine and Covenants. Arguably then the character Moses comes to stand as one prominent sign or pointer to the homosocial structures which I have begun by suggesting characterized the institutional structuring of the church through the Kirtland period. Women appear at the beginning of Moses's story in the King James Bible but are conspicuously absent thereafter, and in fact Moses is traditionally known more for the ambiguities of his own family life rather than for its exemplary nature. He is known not in conjunction with a wife but with his brother Aaron (another key figure used in working through the male priesthood story).

Abraham does not have the prominence Moses does in Smith's text during the Kirtland period. But he does begin to appear, always within the same crucial context, as a sign or pointer towards those imaginative spaces where Smith during the Kirtland period is beginning to consider the position of women and of families in the larger cosmic scheme of things. Certainly Abraham's story in King James Genesis is a story about God's place in human matters of sexuality and fertility. In the larger story of Abraham, God takes to himself the control of marriage and family. Abraham's penis is the first to be circumcised as the sign of God's covenant with Israel.

A number of scholars of Mormon history have suggested that it was while Smith was working on Abraham's story in his New Translation of King James Genesis that he first received a revelation commanding a system of plural marriage patterned on the marriage system of Abraham (and Isaac and Jacob, the "Patriarchs"). It is true that Abraham is prominently featured in the revelation on plural marriage—or "eternal" or "celestial" marriage as it came to be known—as it was dictated in 1843. There are no substantive revisions to the story of Abraham in Smith's New Translation of the King James Bible as they have been preserved. (This means that there are no substantive revisions in the New Translation to the incident Smith used to begin his 1842 translation for the Book of Abraham.) For a discussion of Kirtland polygamy, see Danel W. Bachman, "New Light on an Old Hypothesis: The Ohio Origins of the Revelation on Eternal Marriage," *Journal of Mormon History* 5 (1978): 19-32.

However, there is a revelation allowing for the possibility of plural marriage which reportedly dates from July 1831 during the period when Smith was off and on working on his New Translation. Abraham's name (along with Enoch) is evoked in this revelation as the ancient prophets they should emulate when seeking "new doctrine." And evidence has survived that Smith may well have been involved with plural marriages as early as Kirtland. For a copy of this revelation, see Fred C. Collier, comp., *Unpublished Revelations of the Prophets and Presidents of the Church of Jesus Christ of Latter Day Saints,* Vol. 1 (Salt Lake City: Collier's Publishing Co., 1979), 57-58.

Even in 1842, when Smith already has a dozen or so secret wives, and 1843, when he finally tries to win his wife Emma and his brother Hyrum to the practice, plural marriage is never directly spoken about in public and only makes its way into the public conversation along the circuits of gossip or in coded or encrypted discourse. By 1843 in Nauvoo the names of the patriarchs, of Abraham, Isaac, and Jacob, will have become signs within the coded discourse of insiders to Nauvoo's secret practice of plural marriage.

It is striking within this context that already in Kirtland the name of Abraham consistently points to matters of biology and inheritance and family which are necessarily intertwined with human fertility and sexuality. The name of Abraham and the patriarchs thus becomes a token of Smith's explorations beginning in 1832 of an inherited or biological "patriarchal" priesthood. The first installment of the Book of Abraham dating from Smith's work on the Egyptian papyri in 1835-35 would have reminded readers of these explorations, for it is preoccupied with priesthood lineage and inheritance (and inheritance not only of God's sacred secrets but also of Satan's evil secrets as well).

When Smith for the first time begins performing marriages in Kirtland's not-yet-completed House of the Lord in the fall and winter of 1835-36 and is at the same time first working on the Book of Abraham, even though these are not yet "plural marriages" (although one bride has not been divorced from her first husband), Smith recurrently promises to the brides and grooms "the blessings of Abraham Isaac and Jacob" (See Jessee, *Papers of Joseph Smith,* 2:138, 154). This practice emphasizes the more general sense in which the character Abraham is associated with Smith's addresses to a range of concerns associated with family. In 1835, for example, Smith, who is at the time painfully concerned about the eternal status of his dead brother Alvin, receives a vision of Abraham, Alvin, Noah, and others in the celestial kingdom. (This vision now appears in D&C 137.)

This vision was occasioned by Smith's receiving the ordinances of washing and anointing which were performed for him and others of the First Presidency on 21 January 1836 in preparation for the dedication of the House of the Lord in the spring. Smith was anointed by his father who "sealed upon me the blessings of Moses to lead Israel in the latter days, even as moses led him in days of old, –also the blessings of Abraham Isaac and Jacob" (see Jessee, *Papers of Joseph Smith,* 2:154-59). And during the dedication of the House of the Lord on 3 April 1836, as it is recorded in current editions of the Doctrine and Covenants, "Elias appeared, and committed the dispensation of the gospel of Abraham, saying that in us and our seed all generations after us should be blessed" (D&C 110:12). The events of Nauvoo, or more specifically the secret events of Nauvoo, would make painfully clear what exactly was involved for the men and women of the church in this "gospel of Abraham."

13. I am taking the liberty of collapsing the verses of the King James Bible into paragraph form; I am adding or deleting no words, phrases, punctuation, and so on. I take this liberty in order to facilitate a comparison between the King James version of the incident and the version as printed in the 15 March 1842 issue of the *Times and Seasons*. There the entire Abraham and Sarai incident appears as paragraph number fifteen.

14. Still Abram is not punished for his trickery. He gets back his wife, thanks to God, and it seems that he gets to keep "all that he had" from Pharaoh as well. Pharaoh is punished, though he points out this seems rather unfair since Abram was the one who lied.

The Lord's violent intervention in the narrative reveals that ultimately Abram and the Pharaoh are more rivals than allies. The alliance was a cover based on a trick or ruse. In this the narrative makes clear the dynamics of what in common parlance has been called the love triangle. Within the triangular relationship of erotic desire–two men desiring the same woman–the most charged pole of relationship links the two men. Desiring the same woman, the men in effect become mirror doubles of each other, identical but opposite. Within this triangle the woman, the object of desire, becomes relatively insignificant. Prestige for the object of desire is conferred largely through connection to and exchange between the two men. The rivalry between them adds the threat of violence to the volatile mix. In the end then there is inescapable communication between violence and desire and secrecy in this world. Secrecy and deception become tokens in the struggle for supremacy between the rivals. Abram's secret installs him in a position of power. God's violent intervention in effect reveals Abram's secret and its revelation issues in a reversal of the power relation.

Theorist René Girard has explored the love triangle at length as "mimetic desire." See especially Girard, *Deceit, Desire, & The Novel: Self and Other in Literary Structure*, trans. Yvonne Freccero (Baltimore, MD: Johns Hopkins University Press, 1965); original 1961. Also Girard, *Violence and the Sacred*, trans. Patrick Gregory (Baltimore, MD: Johns Hopkins University Press, 1977 (original 1972), especially chap. 6, "From Mimetic Desire to the Monstrous Double," 143-68. Especially helpful to my own work has been that of Eve Kosofsky Sedgwick, who builds at length on Girard's notion of triangular desire. See especially her *Between Men: English Literature and Male Homosocial Desire* (New York: Columbia University Press, 1985), especially chap. 1, "Gender Asymmetry and Erotic Triangles," 21-27. See also Naomi Schor, *Breaking the Chain: Women, Theory, and French Realist Fiction* (New York: Columbia University Press, 1985), 78-89; Mieke Bal, *Death and Dissymmetry: The Politics of Coherence in the Book of Judges* (Chicago: University of Chicago Press, 1988), 95-127.

15. See Moses 6: 5-8. It is important to note that the term "priesthood" was added to this passage while Smith was revising his work on this passage 1833. It does not appear in the manuscript he dictated in late 1830. In 1830 the Mormon notion of priesthood had not yet been elaborated but would be by 1833. For a discussion of the development of the notion of priesthood, see Quinn, *Origins of Power*, 1-38; Gregory A. Prince, *Power From On High: The Development of Mormon Priesthood* (Salt Lake City: Signature Books, 1995), esp. 1-45.

16. This consistent impulse to situate the narration of sacred stories within a frame circumscribed by personal experience and memory, which from the beginning organizes Smith's New Translation of the King James Bible, already builds on the narrative practice of the Book of Mormon, which Smith dictated in the spring and summer of 1829. In 1829 (a year after the loss of the first 116 pages of manuscript) Smith began dictating the new Book of Mormon manuscript with the section dramatized as Mormon's summary or "abridgment" of Nephite history. The situatedness of Mormon's abridgment is dramatized from time to time with asides from Mormon interpolated into the third-person history. Such first-person interpolations into a third-person text are even more characteristic of the summary of Jaredite history made by Mormon's son, Moroni. Smith's dictation of the Book of Mormon gives way in its final third to first-person narrative–first the letters and sermons of Mormon and Moroni and finally the first-person autobiographies of Nephi and his immediate ancestors. A precedent for the first person accounts in the "book of remembrance" (for Enoch's story, and finally for Abraham's) is in fact embedded in the final section of first person accounts in the Book of Mormon (at 2 Nephi 3). Lehi on his deathbed quotes to his son Joseph from an ancient fragment dramatized as coming from Joseph of Egypt (this fragment looks forward to Smith's own textual calling in the last days as a "choice seer," a latter-day Moses).

17. In considering God as a "character" in the story, I am indebted to the work of Mieke Bal: "The position of most feminist biblical scholars is based on a hierarchy of speakers. Trible, in spite of her critique of male behavior toward female characters, maintains a positive view of the Bible based on an attempt to exonerate Yahweh from the scandal caused by male characters. Even if all narrative agents treat women horribly, the voice of the deity is often invoked to save the ideological tenor of the overall text. Narrative theory does not accommodate such a view. It places the divine character on the same level, as a character that is, as the other characters. ... If truth there is, it lies in the structure of positions and roles, the distribution of power they display"; Bal, *Death and Dissymmetry*, 33-34.

Another useful book in this context is Jack Miles, *A Biography of God* (New York: Vintage Books, 1996). Miles describes the development of the God character as a textual construct in the Hebrew Bible. According to Miles,

"Knowledge of God as a literary character neither precludes nor requires belief in God, and it is this kind of knowledge that the book before you attempts to mediate" (4).

18. This impulse to absolve God from any blame for ambiguous events can be seen, for example in Smith's revisions in the fall and winter of 1830-31 to the Bible stories of Cain and of Noah. Smith's New Translation of Cain's story adds the character of Satan and an elaborate conspiracy of evil to the plot in order to explain and justify God's rejecting Cain's offering and cursing his posterity. Similarly in Smith's New Translation of Genesis, it is Noah who repents that "the Lord had made man on the earth" rather than the Lord repenting his creation as in King James (see Moses 5, 8).

This same impulse to shift any ambiguous culpability away from God can be seen a year later in 1832 as Smith revises Moses's story in Exodus (these revisions do not make their way into the Pearl of Great Price). In the King James story, God hardens Pharaoh's heart, has unrestrained fits of anger. (For example, JST Ex. 4:21, 7;3, 7:13, 9:12, 10:1, 10:20, 11:10, 14:4, 14:8, 14:17; also JST 4:24-26, 9:17). In Smith's New Translation, Pharaoh hardens his own heart, Moses is the one who loses it. In one striking example, the King James language "the Lord repented of the evil which he thought to do unto his people" becomes in Smith's New Translation "And the Lord said unto Moses, if they will repent of the evil which they have done, I will spare them" (JST Ex. 32:14).

19. It can be argued that Smith enhances the prestige and power of God within his version of the narrative and emphasizes hierarchy in the structuring of relations through the mechanism of what René Girard calls "mimetic desire." Rather than a triangle consisting of Abraham, Pharaoh, and Sarah, Smith's version focuses on a triangle consisting of God, Abraham, and Sarah. Girard chooses the term "mimetic desire" because it emphasizes the importance of "imitation" in structuring gender relations. In mimetic or "imitative" desire a disciple chooses an object of desire largely because he wishes to follow his model. The choice of object is only secondary. In other words the notion of "mimesis" or repetition, re-presentation, imitation, has embedded within its structure a hierarchy, a dissymetrical relation of power. Mimetic desire then is as much about the distribution of power and prestige as it is about desire and the structuring of gender relations. Joseph's triangle of relations drawn in his revision of the King James story provides on one level then an absolutely prototypical example of Girard's mimetic desire. Sarai's prestige within Joseph's version of the story begins with God's declaration–not that of Abraham or of Pharaoh–that Sarai is "fair," that she is a natural object of male desire. Within this context of mimetic desire, God's preeminence comes because he is figured as the model and Abraham the disciple within a triangle of desire.

20. On 19 December 1841, only three months before he translated this

installment for the Book of Abraham, Smith broached the subject of sacred secrets to a group of trusted associates in his home. Revelation, access to God's secrets, Smith told them, depends on the ability to keep secrets, especially the secrets of God's prophet. Wilford Woodruff wrote of the evening in his journal: "Joseph the Seer arose ... & said, 'if we kept the commandments of God we should bring forth fruit & be the friends of God & know what our Lord did, 'Some say Joseph is a fallen Prophet because he does not bring forth more of the word of the Lord' 'Why does he not do it' are we able to receive it No (says he) not one in this room. ... The reason we do not have the secrets of the Lord revealed unto us is because we do not keep them but reveal them, we do not keep our own secrets but reveal our difficulties to the world even to our enemies then how would we keep the secrets of the Lord Joseph says I can keep a secret till dooms day." "Friend" is the word Smith uses to describe the nearness of the relation which might obtain between God and man. Becoming a friend of the prophet is made the first step in becoming God's friend. Specifically keeping the prophet's secrets proves worthiness to receive God's. Smith is the prophet because he knows how to keep a secret. The December 1841 sermon is circumspect in speaking about the exact nature of the prophet's secrets, but the March 1842 Book of Abraham story is more open about the nature of a prophet's secrets. Here God and Abraham are close allies, in the parlance of the December sermon, "friends," in secrets–and lies–about trespasses of marital taboos and conventions, matters of gender and desire. See Kenney, *Woodruff Journals*, 2:142-43 (19 Dec. 1841).

21. For discussions of polygamy in Nauvoo, see Richard S. Van Wagoner, *Mormon Polygamy: A History* (Salt Lake City: Signature Books, 1989); George D. Smith, "Nauvoo Roots of Mormon Polygamy, 1841-46: A Preliminary Demographic Report," *Dialogue: A Journal of Mormon Thought* 27 (Spring 1994): 1-72; Todd Compton, "A Trajectory of Plurality: An Overview of Joseph Smith's Thirty-Three Plural Wives," *Dialogue: A Journal of Mormon Thought* 29 (Summer 1996): 1-40. Also the first chapter of Carmon Hardy's study of Utah polygamy provides an excellent short introduction to Smith's practice: "The Principle Commenced," in Hardy, *Solemn Covenant*. See also Lawrence Foster, *Religion and Sexuality: The Shakers, the Mormons, and the Oneida Community* (Urbana: University of Illinois Press, 1984; paperback of Oxford University Press, 1981).

Wives of apostles included Sarah Pratt, wife of Orson Pratt, and Nancy Hyde, wife of Orson Hyde. See Compton, "Trajectory of Plurality," 2. For discussions of the Sarah Pratt story, see in particular Richard S. Van Wagoner, "Sarah Pratt: The Shaping of an Apostate," *Dialogue: A Journal of Mormon Thought* 18 (Fall 1985): 67-83; Gary James Bergera, "Seniority in the Twelve: The 1875 Realignment of Orson Pratt," *Journal of Mormon History* 18 (Spring 1992): 19-58.

Smith's wives who were already married (Compton's and Smith's dates):

Lucinda Pendeleton Morgan Harris (C, 1838?; S, 1842); Zina Diantha Huntington Jacobs (C&S, 27 Oct. 1841); Prescendia Lathrop Huntington Buell (C&S, 11 Dec. 1841); Sylvia Sessions Lyon (C, 8 Feb. 1842; S, 1844); Mary Elizabeth Rollins Lightner (C, Feb. 1842; S, 17 Jan. 1842); Patty Bartlett Sessions (C&S, 9 Mar. 1842, Patty is mother of Sylvia); Marinda Nancy Johnson Hyde (C&S, Apr. 1842); Elizabeth Davis Goldsmith Brackenbury Durfee (C, before June 1842; S, 1842); Sarah Kingsley Howe Cleveland (C, before 29 June 1842; S, 1842); and Elvira Annie Cowles Holmes (C, 1 June 1843; S, 1842). Evidence suggests that Smith also asked for the hands of the following women who were married (see Compton for discussion of these women, 7-8): Sarah Melissa Granger Kimball; Mary Ann Angell Young (wife of Brigham Young); Jane Silverthorne Law (wife of William Law); Sarah Bates Pratt (wife of Orson Pratt); Leonora Cannon Taylor (wife of John Taylor). Accounts suggest he also asked Mrs. William Smith (wife of his brother; he married the widow of his brother Don Carlos) and Mrs. Robert D. Foster.

22. Heber C. Kimball to Parley P. Pratt, 17 June 1842, LDS archives. I have silently added minimal punctuation to the letter in order to help reading; spelling and capitalization remain unchanged.

23. Heber C. Kimball, 2 Aug. 1857, *Journal of Discourses*, 26 vols. (Liverpool, Eng.: Latter-day Saints Booksellers' Depot, 1855-86), 5:134.

24. Andrew F. Ehat and Lyndon Cook, *The Words of Joseph Smith* (Provo, UT: Religious Studies Center, Brigham Young University, 1980), 120-21; minutes of 26 May meeting.

25. For an overview of early Relief Society meetings and for a discussion of Emma Smith and plural marriage, see Newell and Avery, *Mormon Enigma*, esp. chaps. 7-9.

Sarah M. Kimball, who initiated the organization of a woman's group, was already married but received a proposal from Smith. She declined. See Compton, "Trajectory of Plurality," 7; for an interesting incident demonstrating tension between Smith and Sarah Kimball's husband, see Jessee, *Papers of Joseph Smith*, 2:384.

Among the twenty women who attended the first 17 March meeting of the Relief Society were at least seven women whom Joseph Smith had already approached about marrying him or would approach. These included the officers of the new organization: Emma's first counselor, Sarah M. Cleveland; her treasurer, Elvira A. Cowles; her secretary, Eliza R. Snow. Smith married the daughter of Emma's second counselor, Elizabeth Whitney. Other wives, soon-to-be wives, or attempted wives of Smith among the original twenty members included: Martha Knight, soon-to-be-widow of Bishop Vinson Knight, Desdemona Fullmer, Sarah M. Kimball, and Nancy Rigdon. The original twenty members also included Nancy's sister Athalia, whom gossip had connected to Smith in Kirtland, and also Leonara Taylor, wife of John Taylor. Some time during these months, Smith had tested the Taylors by asking for, receiving, and then not following up on John Taylor's permission to marry Leonara. For the dates of these marriages, see Compton, "Trajectory of Plurality," 2-3; Smith, "Nauvoo Polygamy," 60-61. Compton lists 1843 for the date of Smith's marriages to Cowles and Fuller. These dates come from retrospective affidavits rather than contemporary indications. In the case of Cowles, at least one source suggests that the marriage may have occurred in 1842. The following are both Compton's and Smith's dates for these marriages (Compton's dates are the more conservative): Sarah Cleveland (C, before 29 June 1842; S, 1842); Eliza Roxcy Snow (C&S, 29 June 1842); Sarah Whitney, daughter of Elizabeth Whitney (C&S, 27 July 1842); Martha Knight (C&S, Aug. 1842); Desdemona Fullmer (C, July 1843; S, 1842).

According to minutes, the following women attended the 17 March meeting: "Mrs. Emma Smith, Mrs. Sarah M. Cleveland, Phebe Ann Hawkes, Elizabeth Jones, Sophia Packard, Philindia Merrick [Myrick], Martha Knights [Knight], Desdemona Fulmer [Fullmer], Elizabeth Ann Whitney, Leonara Taylor, Bathsheba W. Smith, Phebe M. Wheeler, Elvira A. Coles [Cowles], Margaret A. Cook, Athalia Robinson, Sarah M. Kimball, Eliza R. Snow, Sophia Robinson, Nancy Rigdon, and Sophia R. Marks." See Jill Mulvay Derr, Janath Russel Cannon, and Maureen Ursenbach Beecher, *Women of Covenant: The Story of Relief Society* (Salt Lake City: Deseret Book Co., 1992).

26. Compton, "Trajectory of Plurality," 33-34.

27. For a discussion of this meeting, see Newell and Avery, *Mormon Enigma*, 109-10. See also 326n9 for discussion of the term "Mother in Israel" and documentation of the activities of these older women in contacting prospective plural wives for Joseph Smith.

28. Ehat and Cook, *Words of Joseph Smith*, 110.

29. The scenario presented here is my best reconstruction of what seems to have occurred. However, there are uncertainties about when the letter was read and also about who read the letter. Also questions about whether this third meeting occurred on 30 March or 31 March. The minutes record a 30 March date for the meeting. Smith's journal records a 31 March date for the meeting. Since the first and second meetings occurred on 17 March and 24 March, it is likely that the third meeting occurred a week later on 31 March.

There is no mention of the reading of the letter in the minutes kept of the 30 March (?) meeting. A copy of the letter read was inserted in the minutes at 28 September 1842 with the following notation: "The following Epistle was read before the Society early after its organization but was not forwarded to be recorded; the Secretary not being present at the time of its reading else it would have appeared in its proper place."

Smith's diary entry for 31 March 1842, kept by Willard Richards, reads: "In council at his office with Elders Young. Taylor &c. & wrote an Epistle to the Female Relief Society and spoke to the Society in the afternoon"; Jessee, *Papers of Joseph Smith*, 2:374. This entry would seem to indicate that the letter was composed that day expressly for the meeting occurring later in the day. Van Wagoner, *Mormon Polygamy*, indicates 30 March; the text of Newell and Avery, *Mormon Enigma*, says 28 April (111) but a note indicates 30 March (326). The letter is also discussed by Kent L. Walgren, "James Adams, Early Springfield Mormon and Freemason," *Journal of the Illinois State Historical Society* 75:2 (Summer 1982): 131-32. All three sources indicate that Emma read the letter. A transcribed copy of the Nauvoo meetings of the Relief Society can be found in the Linda Newell Papers, Special Collections, Marriott Library, University of Utah, Salt Lake City.

30. Martha Brotherton's account was first printed in the 15 July 1842 *St. Louis Bulletin*. John C. Bennett began publish his account of Nauvoo by July in the *Sangamo Journal*. He would also publish various contemporary documents during the summer–such as the controversial letter written by Smith to Nancy Rigdon and the "affidavits" against Sarah Pratt and others–in the same paper. He would collect his account and various documents into his book published in September: John C. Bennett, *The History of the Saints; Or, An Exposé of Joe Smith and Mormonism* (Boston: Leland & Whiting, 1842). Various answering documents from Smith and his followers appeared in the *Times and Seasons* and also the *Wasp* during the summer. For an overview, see Van Wagoner, *Mormon Polygamy*, esp. chap. three, "Protecting the Lord's Anointed," 29-40. For a copy of the Nancy Rigdon letter and discussion of its authenticity, see Dean C. Jessee, comp., *The Personal Writings of Joseph Smith* (Salt Lake City: Deseret Book, 1984), 506-509.

31. *Wasp*, 20 Aug. 1842.

# 15.

# Knowing Brother Joseph Again: The Book of Abraham and Joseph Smith as Translator

*Karl C. Sandberg*

*No man knows my history.*—Joseph Smith

*Millions shall know Brother Joseph again.*—Mormon hymn

THE ORIGINAL PROBLEM PROMPTING THIS ESSAY OCCURRED improbably more than thirty years ago as I was sifting through the four *in folio* volumes of Pierre Bayle's 1697 *Dictionnaire historique et critique* in search of something else and came upon his articles on biblical personages. Bayle, a Huguenot refugee and Calvinist controversialist writing in Holland from 1680 to 1704, was one of the most erudite men of his time and had apparently encountered the Hebrew Cabala and the rabbinical tradition during his exile in Rotterdam. Here in his article on Abraham was information with a familiar ring: Sarah was Abraham's niece; Abraham was exceptionally well educated, was an astronomer, and opposed the idolatrous religions among which he was raised; he was therefore persecuted, and his life was threatened by idolaters; and a book about Abraham existed anciently that gave an account of the creation.

All of this information was familiar because it was also found in the Book of Abraham (Joseph Smith's rendition of ancient papyri, begun in 1835 and published in 1842), but it was not found in Genesis. What could account for Pierre Bayle's dictionary in the Book of Abraham, or vice versa?

The problem took another turn when Joseph Smith's papyri, which had been missing and presumed lost for eighty to ninety years, resurfaced in 1967 and were examined and translated by Egyptologists. One fragment of papyrus was identified as the ostensible source of the Book of Abraham, but it bore no relationship to the Book of Abraham either in content or subject matter.[1] This discovery raised more questions: What is the Book of Abraham, and what is to become of the concept of Joseph as translator?

The issue was complicated further by a more careful reading of the text of the Book of Abraham itself. It contains some information about Abraham found in Genesis and some information contained in extra-biblical sources but not in Genesis. The most significant parts of the book, however, the concepts that make it one of the prime source documents of Mormon theology, are original, with no apparent source in any previous document or tradition. Yet the text exists, and Joseph produced it. All this might lead us to ask: What went on in Joseph's mind when he produced the Book of Abraham? What kind of person was he? What kind of religion did he launch? And what did Joseph mean when he said, "No man knows my history"? The problem became that of "knowing Brother Joseph again."

Ezra Pound's verse from *The Ballad of the Goodly Fere* might appropriately be applied: "Oh, they'll not get him in a book,/ Though they write it cunningly,/ No mouse of the scrolls was the goodly fere/ But a man o' men was he."

Before we can have any hope of getting Joseph Smith into a book or, more specifically, understanding the religion which grew out of his revelations, many more pieces must be put into place. One key piece is the concept of "translation" as he understood and practiced it. Understanding this process and, in particular, the role of stones, symbols, and documents in it will enable us to see the turn of his mind, which cast the character of Mormonism with its paradoxes of the rational and the revelatory, of the intelligible and the numinous, and ultimately of the institutional and the individual.

This argument has several strands, which will have to be developed separately.

## I

A new look at Joseph might begin by trying to see him as he saw himself, from the inside out.

On 6 April 1830, at the inception of the Mormon church, a revelation given through Joseph Smith instructed him that in the record to be kept in the new church, he, Joseph, should be called "a seer, a translator, a prophet, an apostle of Jesus Christ" (D&C 21:1). In 1835, in the description and definition of the offices of the two priesthoods, the presiding high priest of the church is characterized as being "a seer, a revelator, a translator, and a prophet" (D&C 107:92). On 19 January 1841, three years before Joseph's death, his brother Hyrum was designated as "a prophet, and a seer, and a revelator unto my church, as well as my servant Joseph" (D&C 124:94), but to Joseph it was given "to be a presiding elder over all my church, to be a translator, a revelator, a seer, and a prophet" (v. 125). It seems clear that Joseph consistently thought of himself as a translator and did not think of himself as a seer or a prophet separate and apart from his role as a translator. It is perhaps significant that neither of the two major biographers of Joseph Smith (Fawn Brodie's *No Man Knows My History* and Donna Hill's *Joseph Smith: The First Mormon*) assign great importance to this unusual self-perception.

What is translation? Translation as ordinarily practiced in our time and culture starts with a document in language A and ends with the creation of a document in language B. The language in document A will work on the levels of denotation, connotation, register, and discourse as determined by the culture in which it was produced. Translation, then, is a process of understanding the document in language A and finding the words and the structures in language B that express the document's denotations, connotations, register, and discourse in culture B. For a translation to be completely accurate, the reading of the document in language A must be so exact that it excludes all possible meanings but one, and the rendition into document B must be correspondingly exact. The ideal translation is the slave of the original, adding nothing and taking nothing away.[2]

The check on the accuracy and adequacy of the translation is always rational and consists of rereading document A to see how appropriately and adequately the entire content and range of expression of A is re-expressed in B. Translation does not require a special gift; it can be performed by anyone with a knowledge of two languages and can always be checked by anyone who knows both languages.

Joseph Smith did not think of translation in these terms. We can save ourselves much rumination if we accept at the outset that Joseph Smith never did document-to-document translation based on a knowledge of two languages, except as an exercise in his Hebrew class in the winter of 1835-36. Several major articles have appeared in the past two decades detailing the historical circumstances of Joseph Smith translations, and all solidly establish that many times during the translation of the Book of Mormon he was not even looking at the gold plates. Doctrine and Covenants 7 comes from a parchment hidden up by John the Revelator and "translated" by Joseph and Oliver through the Urim and Thummim without the parchment being physically present. When Joseph translated the Old and New Testaments, he made no claim to be consulting Greek or Hebrew manuscripts–he simply revised the substance.[3] Only the Book of Abraham has an original document to compare with the translation, and the original and the translation show no relationship to each other.

The fact is that Joseph Smith and those of his time and milieu used the term "translation" in a way far different from any in use today. (The contrast between Joseph Smith's culture of the 1830s and our own can be seen in some measure by the immense disparity in the use of the term.) Michael Quinn points out, for example, that even in encyclopedias of the 1830s Egyptian "characters" and hieroglyphics (compare the "reformed Egyptian" of the Book of Mormon) were thought to be occult symbols to be deciphered or interpreted by an arcane art now entirely lost.[4] The word "translation" itself needs to be translated from one culture into another.

How then did Joseph Smith himself understand the term "translation"? Here we are not in doubt, for the Book of Mormon speaks very directly about translation, and the process is not one familiar to the Translation Department in the LDS Church Office Building today. When the brother of Jared is commanded to write the things that he has seen and heard and to seal up the record in a language that others, coming later, will not be able to "interpret," he is also commanded to hide up two stones he has received, stones which "shall magnify to the eyes of men these things which ye shall write" (Ether 3:21-28, 4:5).

A more detailed account appears in Mosiah 8:5-19, where King Limhi asks Ammon if he can "interpret languages." An exploring party has come across records kept on metallic plates by a people that has since disappeared, and the king wants to know the cause of their destruction. Ammon says that he cannot interpret but that he knows someone who can, a man who "can look, and translate all records that are of ancient date; and it is a gift from God." The aids this man uses are "called interpreters, and no man can look in them except he be commanded, lest he should look for that which he ought not and he should perish. And whosoever is commanded to look in them, the same is called a seer" (v. 13).

When the king exclaims that a seer is greater than a prophet, Ammon explains that a seer is indeed a prophet and also a revelator, because "a seer can know of things which are past, and also of things which are to come, and by them shall all things be revealed, or rather, shall secret things be made manifest, and hidden things shall come to light, and things which are not known shall be made known by them, and also things shall be made known which otherwise could not be made known" (v. 17). The interpreters were, in fact, prepared for the specific purpose of "unfolding all such mysteries to the children of men" (v. 19). These interpreters are elsewhere identified as stones (Mosiah 28:13).

In a subsequent passage, Alma instructs his son Helaman to preserve the twenty-four plates because they contain the record of the secret works and abominations and wickedness of the people that had been destroyed and to preserve the interpreters along with them. The record will be read in effect by a stone, which "shall shine forth in darkness unto light" (Alma 37:23) and by which the Lord will "bring to light all their secrets and abominations, unto every nation that shall hereafter possess the land" (v. 25). The one who has this high gift of God is called a "seer," and by virtue of this gift, the greatest of all possible gifts of God, is also a "revelator" and a "prophet" (Mosiah 8:16).

Translation, as understood in the Book of Mormon, is the gift of seeing hidden things, both good and evil, and making unknown things known. It is carried out or made possible through the use of physical objects stones which enable the user to see what is hidden and thus to describe it and bring it to light. Translator is synonymous with seer. The capacity of revelator and the status of prophet derive from seership.

When the seer translates, he does not go from document to document, because part or all of the original document has been lost or is in an unknown language. He must go back to the original source of the document, to God, and get the reading from him. Translation thus derives from a keenly perceived connection with the numinous, and through this connection come statements that we call revelation. Here the term "numinous" calls for some clarification.

The concepts of the empirical, the rational, and the intelligible, to which the numinous stands in contrast, are easily understood. We know a thing when we can measure it, or when our uncertainty about it is reduced to zero, or when we can see it in relation to other known things. When we speak of the numinous, however, we are talking about the stuff of religious or creative experiences, about forces that are experienced as real but that remain unseen. They engage, entice, attract, illuminate, or move us to act but cannot be measured or analyzed. We may be gripped by them, moved by them, lifted up or cast down by them, but however much we try to encompass them by thought, something always escapes. They are experienced as indefinitely large and ultimately mysterious. They cannot be delimited except to say that they are as large as the stove, the table, the cupboard, and quite a bit more besides. In the realm of religion they manifest themselves in the experiences of conversion or of mysticism, as William James, for example, so clearly and abundantly describes in his classic *The Varieties of Religious Experience.* In modern psychiatry these experiences are tapped by deep analysis. They might be referred to, as in Jungian psychology, in terms such as the "anima" or the "shadow" or the "unconscious."[5] Nonetheless, no description of the forces of the numinous or unconscious is ever more than partial. Experience with them is real but subjective. If, then, the experience of the numinous is subjective and cannot be observed directly, how much can we say about the translation process Joseph went through? How did he do it?

We can start by just looking. Had we been present in the room at the time as practicing empiricists, we would have said Joseph was translating with stones. William Smith, Joseph's brother, in 1891 told of having seen the "interpreters"–two stones set in a bow–and having looked into them. For William they did not work, because translation was a gift, one he did not have.[6] It was these two stones that Joseph used to produce at least part of the first 116 manuscript pages of the Book of Mormon, the pages Martin Harris lost. When Joseph started to translate again, he did not use the interpreters, but a stone he had found while digging a well in 1822. When Joseph translated, he put the stone in his hat, put his face far enough into the hat to exclude light, and then dictated. This same stone was the medium through which he received a number of revelations through 1829, some of which were published in the Book of Commandments in 1833. On a number of occasions, the plates were not physically present or, if they were, Joseph did not look at them as he translated.[7]

But we can recognize the shortfall in empirical observation when we want to add, "Yes, but how did he really do it?" For we have to say either that something else was going on inside Joseph that we do not get at by observation, or that the stones possessed some causal quality (they were "magic spectacles"), or that the book (in the case of the Book of Mormon) does not exist.

We can take a step closer to understanding Joseph Smith's mind and spirit by looking at his translation process from two different but complementary perspectives.

The first is that of Jungian psychology. It is fair to say that no figure of the twentieth century has done more than Jung (1875-1962) to describe the breadth and sound the depths of the human unconscious. How does that which is latent and formless within an individual emerge and take on a form? The way that the analyst or the individual makes contact with the deep well of the unconscious is often through the medium of a concrete object. Jung gives the example of one of his analysands who had taken a long train ride in Russia. "Though he did not know the language and could not even decipher Cyrillic script, he found himself musing over the strange letters in which the railway notices were written, and he fell into a reverie in which he imagined all sorts of meanings for them."

The incident was revealing for Jung in that it showed him that one could reach the center of the psyche "from any point on the compass.

One could begin with Cyrillic letters, from meditations upon a crystal ball, a prayer wheel, a modern painting, or even a casual conversation about some trivial event."[8] Or, we might add, a stone. And it is informative to learn that in Joseph's milieu stones were often used as means of locating lost objects,[9] but it is even more informative to note that Jung and his associates, in describing psychic phenomena empirically in Africa, in North and South America, and in Asia, conclude that stones have been and are a universally recurrent means of contact with the divine power.[10] Joseph's translation process by a stone was strange but, from a more universal vantage point, not altogether unusual.

The second perspective comes from comparing the self-description that poets, musicians, mathematicians, inventors, and painters have given of the creative process they have experienced with the self-description that Joseph gives of his translation process. The two kinds of experiences turn out to be remarkably similar.

In an introductory essay to an anthology of accounts of artistic and scientific creation, Brewster Ghiselen describes the recurring patterns that can be observed in the creative process. It begins with an awareness that something has gone wrong which needs to be set right. The artist first experiences an extreme dissatisfaction with the existing order of his or her inner world. Some problem or experience has troubled the waters, perhaps bringing with it a sense of unrealized potential or an initial "commerce with disorder."[11] Time is out of joint. The creative power, an extension of the life force, overreaches and finishes breaking down the established order and then reorganizes it out of the "surging chaos of the unexpressed."[12] The finished product often includes items not found originally.

The process also appears to be spontaneous and automatic, as a seemingly independent force guides the work. Mozart often found appearing in his mind whole musical ideas, which he then worked into their orchestrated form. When he wrote them down, he appeared to be taking dictation from the muse.[13] Picasso, walking through the forest of Fontainebleau, might have had an "indigestion of greenness,"[14] which he would have to resolve into a form and later translate into a painting that appeared to take shape spontaneously on the canvas. "At the beginning of each painting," says Picasso, "there is someone who works with me. Toward the end I have the impression of having worked without a collaborator."[15] The mathematician Poincaré had the experience during a sleepless night of seeing all of his ideas about the solution of a particular problem "colliding" and working themselves out to a solution, which he had only to write down the next morning, he himself serving, as it were, as scribe to his ideas.[16] And Max Ernst describes his own creative experiences as resembling the poet who is "writing at the dictation of something that makes itself articulate within him." Just so, "the artist's role is to gather together and then give out that which makes itself visible within him."[17] The artist no less than the prophet is a seer.

This same process was at work with Joseph Smith. After a long period of indeterminacy during his adolescence caused by the status of his family and the tensions and divisions in the family over religion, the contentions and uncertainties with regard to religion among the churches, and the anxiety over his personal follies and shortcomings (JS-H 2:5-10),[18] the elements of his experience came together in something greater than the sum of its parts. Certainly he experienced a gestation period of deep and earnest thought that he later associated with revelation: "The things of God are of deep import; and time, and experience, and careful and ponderous and solemn thoughts can only find them out. Thy mind, O man! if thou wilt lead a soul to salvation, must stretch as high as the utmost heavens, and search into and contemplate the darkest abyss, and the broad expanse of eternity—thou must commune with God."[19] For Joseph also, the experience of revelation, a gift that could be cultivated by anybody, was sudden and illuminating. It was the feeling of "pure intelligence flowing into you, it may give you sudden strokes of ideas ... you may grow into the principle of revelation."[20]

What was the role of the stone in this process? We may surmise that for Joseph the stone was a catalyst—because of his belief in the stone and his attunement to the world of the numinous, or the unconscious, where unseen powers moved, collided, contended, danced, and held their revels, the stone became the means of concentrating his psychic energies and giving them form. When the translation of the Book of Mormon began, it appeared to be automatic, even given by dictation, as Oliver Cowdery describes it: "These were days never to be forgotten—to sit under the sound of a voice dictated by the inspiration of heaven, awakened the utmost gratitude of his bosom! Day after day I continued, uninterrupted to write from his mouth, as he translated with the Urim and Thummim, or, as the Nephites would have said, 'Interpreters,' the history or record called the 'Book of Mormon.'"[21]

But let us recognize that having said this much we still have not said the essential. We cannot say precisely how we got the theory of relativity, or the *Ninth Symphony,* or the Koran, or such recent claimants of divine revelation as the *Urantia Book* or the *Course in Miracles.*[22] The stone, and indeed all experiences with the numinous and the creative, remain a scandal to the analytical mind.

But as important as the stones are for understanding Joseph as seer, they are even more important for understanding Mormonism because of two unexpected results which derived from them, for we inevitably ask whether any check exists on this kind of subjective translation, which seemingly plucks the new book out of the air. What will keep the translator from simply making up what he wants? What will keep the reader or believer, in Jonathan Swift's phrase in his "Tale of a Tub," from "the possession of being well deceived, the calm and serene state of being a fool among knaves"? It was in natural response to this question that one of the paradoxes of Mormonism appeared. We would be making a gross error in interpreting Joseph and Mormonism if we did not recognize that the stones, those seeming instruments of the magical world, brought with them the dichotomous elements of institutional authority and of rationalism.

The institutional test came early as egalitarian revelations threatened the cohesion of the community of Saints in late 1830 and early 1831. Hiram Page, a brother-in-law to David Whitmer and one of the eight witnesses of the Book of Mormon, also had a seer stone and received revelations with it concerning the building up of Zion. Joseph had a revelation in September 1830 saying that "No one shall be appointed to receive commandments and revelations in this church, except my servant Joseph Smith, Jun., ... For all things must be done in order, and by common consent in the church, and by the prayer of faith" (D&C 28:2, 13). In other words, revelation was to be subjected to an institutional test. The ideas of common consent and the prayer of faith provided for the participation of individual members in ratifying revelations, but the burden of the message was that any individual revelation was subject to established institutional authority.

The test by individual reason, however, had come even earlier.

While on the one hand the process of translation appeared to be entirely subjective and automatic to some of those surrounding Joseph (all their lives David Whitmer and Martin Harris believed Joseph saw English words under the unknown characters when he looked into the stone), Oliver Cowdery had the opposite experience. Assisting Joseph as a scribe, Oliver believed so much in the marvelous process of translation that he wanted to translate, too, apparently assuming the process to be automatic. When he tried and failed, it was explained to him that translation is also a process of studying the subject out in one's own mind, getting an idea, and having an inward confirmation (D&C 9:7-9). Significantly, Lucy Mack Smith remembered Joseph as being the least bookish of her children but the one most inclined to "meditation and deep study."[23] The process of translation involves the intellect, and the end result is propositional and rational.

In May 1831 another revelation came to Joseph giving him the key for discerning which revelations came from God and which did not: "He that preacheth and he that receiveth, understand one another, and both are edified and rejoice together. And that which doth not edify is not of God, and is darkness. That which is of God is light; and he that receiveth light, and continueth in God, receiveth more light; and that light groweth brighter and brighter until the perfect day" (D&C 50:22-24). The same test is also implied within the Book of Mormon in Alma 32. The test of the goodness of the seed, the word, is whether it sprouts, grows, and brings forth increase.

The test of revelation and of translation is understanding and intelligibility, the congruence of "hidden things made known" with a growing body of understanding, coupled with a pragmatic confirmation of their goodness or futility in one's life. Revelation and translation depend upon the understanding and experience, and thus upon the reason, of the recipient for their verification.

This invitation to reason and learning quickly broadened. Whereas the Book of Mormon had been offered to the world almost as an act of defiance–the sealed book that the learned could not read[24]–in another eighteen months revelation would enjoin the Saints to seek out and read the best books that the learned could read (D&C 88:77-80, 118-19). Both divine and human enlightenment tasted good and were seen as being served from the same abundant table.

The spirit of this commandment was fulfilled in the *Messenger and*

*Advocate* (published in Kirtland, Ohio, from 1834 to 1837), which included not only doctrinal discussions but articles on such topics as Roman history, and in the School of the Prophets, where some forty participants gathered to "teach each other diligently" and even engaged a learned Jew, a professor Joshua Seixas, to teach them Hebrew. This growing stream of Mormonism culminated in the 13th Article of Faith, which states that all truth from whatever source is a part of the religion, to be sought out and possessed.

What can we conclude, then, about translation as Joseph knew it? The word "translation" comes to embody and express the central tension in Mormonism. In the Joseph Smith experience with translation, the primary contact was not with the contents of a document but with the mind of the seer, which determines what the document should say. The seer is the one who makes contact with the deep, mysterious, and powerfully moving parts of the soul or historical milieu and sees into them in such a way as to transform them, to give them form, and to bring them to light, so that they may be examined, analyzed, and tested experientially. The "seer" brings the numinous into the realm of the intelligible, where its content becomes authoritative but at the same time subject to analysis and examination, and may be—must be—tested by reason and experience (without the process of its production necessarily being understood). The tension between the rationalism of the Enlightenment and the supernaturalism of the frontier milieu, which Richard Bushman describes,[25] appears to be only one aspect of the deeper paradox and tension within Joseph Smith himself, a condition that remained constant in him throughout his life and in the church he founded through the present time. Mormonism is a two-winged bird whose wings do not always flap in unison.

## II

We can move still closer to understanding Joseph by seeing another paradox of his personality, expressed by the respective roles of stones and symbols in his mental processes. As we come to see the role of symbols, we can begin to see the structure of Joseph's individual works and the progressions in his work as a whole. In seeing the structure of his works, we can see the progressions of his mind, and we thus obtain an indispensable key for understanding him and his work.

To reiterate, the stone[26] represented and was a means of Joseph's direct contact with the numinous. As a child of his times, he held to the efficacy of the stone in the process of translation: it made known what was hidden. In the early 1830s, while translating (revising) the New Testament, he came upon John 1:42, which in the King James version reads, "And when Jesus beheld him, he said, Thou art Simon the son of Jona: thou shalt be called Cephas, which is by interpretation, a stone." Joseph rendered the verse: "And when Jesus beheld him, he said, Thou art Simon, the son of Jona, thou shalt be called Cephas, which is, by interpretation, a seer, a stone."[27]

In the Book of Abraham, produced between 1835 and 1842, we learn that it was through the Urim and Thummim that Abraham gained his ideas of the heavens, the planets, and the eternity of intelligences (Abr. 3:1, 4). In 1843 Joseph declared, "The place where God resides is a great Urim and Thummim. This earth, in its sanctified and immortal state, will be made like unto crystal and will be a Urim and Thummim to the inhabitants who dwell thereon, whereby all things pertaining to an inferior kingdom, and all kingdoms of a lower order, will be manifest to those who dwell on it; and the earth will be Christ's. Then the white stone mentioned in Revelation 2:17, will become a Urim and Thummim to each individual who receives one, whereby things pertaining to a higher order of kingdoms will be made known" (D&C 130:8-10). Although Joseph stopped using the seer stone sometime early in 1830 and gave it to Oliver Cowdery, he apparently possessed several similar stones throughout his life.[28]

Nonetheless, as Joseph came into contact with book learning, symbols (going from the visible to the intelligible) came to play an increasingly important role in his revelations and appear to have had an even more pervasive influence on the form, content, and production of his revelations than stones had.

Jung's notion of symbols is especially appropriate: "Man, as we realize if we reflect a moment, never perceives anything fully or comprehends anything completely ... [therefore] we constantly use symbolic terms to represent concepts that we cannot define or fully comprehend." A word or anything immediate or visible is symbolic "when it implies something more than its obvious and immediate meaning. It has a wider 'unconscious' aspect that is never precisely defined or fully explained. Nor can one hope to define or explain it. As the mind explores the symbol, it is led to ideas that lie beyond the grasp of reason."[29] People are generators of symbols, and symbols are generators of ideas.

In his essay article "A Mormon Midrash? LDS Creation Narratives Reconsidered," Anthony Hutchinson associated the Mormon creation narratives of the Book of Moses and the Book of Abraham with the literary form of midrash, interpreting an original text by translating, embellishing, or adding to it.[30] The relationship of symbols to the creative process shows how a midrash might be produced.

If we examine the texts produced by Joseph Smith, a common pattern emerges. First, there is a symbol: a fact, an image, or an experience that expresses a sense of a mystery, or something that has been lost or hidden. At the same time, the symbol becomes a catalyst, pointing to something beyond itself with a hint, idea, or suggestion from which Joseph leaps to ideas and whole systems that emerge entire and new, bypassing a pedestrian plodding from premises to conclusions. The symbol thus sets loose a flood of information, ideas, and connections that go far beyond the initial question and end by establishing a new cosmic context. Joseph's translations are thus never slave to an original document; they always start with a symbol and add something that was not there before. The new revelation becomes another metaphor, the starting point for yet another revelation. In this process, we see another dimension of the idea of "continuing revelation" and another fundamental characteristic of Joseph's mind.

Michael Quinn describes in great detail the symbols of the magical or arcane in Joseph's milieu and with which Joseph was familiar.[31] I find no evidence that they moved Joseph to produce much text. Symbols of a different order, on the other hand, did move his mind powerfully and resulted in the primary revelations shaping later Mormon theology. Two of several such symbols[32] can be cited from Joseph Smith's translation of Genesis, undertaken sometime in 1830 and finished by 1833.[33]

The first was the figure of Enoch. Prior to December 1830, as Joseph said later, "much conjecture and conversation frequently occurred among the saints concerning the books mentioned, and referred to in various places of the Old and New Testament, which were nowhere to be found. The common remark was, they were *lost books*; but it seems the apostolic churches had some of these writings, as Jude mentions or quotes the prophecy of Enoch, the seventh from Adam. To the joy of the flock ... did the Lord reveal the following doings of olden times from the prophecy of Enoch."[34]

It is not impossible that Joseph had heard of a translation of the lost Book of Enoch—one had been available since 1821[35]—but what is significant is the way in which he responded to the symbol. The one verse in Jude becomes sixty-nine verses in Genesis 7 of the Inspired Revision or Moses 7 in The Pearl of Great Price, expressing new and large ideas about the nature of Zion and the character of God, as Enoch walks and talks with God and sees in panoramic vision the end of the world and God's judgments.

Enoch, having grown prominent as a symbol in Joseph's mind, in turn appears to have led to another symbol, Melchizedek, who in turn becomes the generator of new ideas about the priesthood. When Joseph began his revision of Genesis and came to the account of Abraham offering tithes to Melchizedek, Melchizedek and the priesthood he held were associated with Enoch and described in terms that do not occur in any of Joseph's previous revelations. We learn that Melchizedek was a man of faith who as a child feared God, stopped the mouths of lions, and quenched the violence of fire. "And thus, having been approved of God he was ordained an high priest after the order of the covenant which God made with Enoch. ... For God having sworn unto Enoch and unto his seed with an oath by himself, that everyone being ordained after this order and calling should have power, by faith, to break mountains, to divide the seas, to dry up waters, to turn them out of their course; to put at defiance the armies of the nations, to divide the earth, to break every band, to stand in the presence of God" (JST, Gen. 14:26, 27, 30, 31).

We are already here far beyond any concept of priesthood elaborated in the Book of Mormon, where the role of priesthood is seen simply as the performance of rituals and ordinances. We are well on our way toward D&C 84 and D&C 132, where the priesthood is seen as the key to knowledge and the channel of power and increase. (Joseph Smith said several times that he had restored the fullness of the church, the priesthood, or the gospel, but the character of revelation was such that the fullness never got full—there was always something else to be added.[36] Joseph's translation of Genesis was really part of the gathering theological flood in Joseph's mind that was sweeping through and changing everything, including the political and social order.)

To these two examples we can add D&C 76, dated 16 February 1832. Joseph and Sidney were working on translating the Gospel of John—again without recourse to Greek texts—and again Joseph sensed that "many important points touching the salvation of man had been taken from the Bible, or lost before it was compiled."[37] Again, he appealed directly to God, the original source—"this caused us to marvel, for it was given to us of the Spirit" (v. 18)—and the result, again, was a new cosmic context in which the recipients of celestial glory "are priests of the Most High, after the order of Melchizedek, which was after the order of Enoch, which was after the order of the Only Begotten Son" (v. 58). Those who come into the celestial kingdom are those who "have come to an innumerable company of angels, to the general assembly and church of Enoch, and of the Firstborn" (v. 67). The symbols of Enoch and Melchizedek have become part of a larger cosmic order, much more elaborate than in the Book of Mormon but still considerably less elaborate and comprehensive than in D&C 132.

The next great symbol in Joseph's development was Abraham.

III

The Book of Abraham, begun in 1835 and published in the *Times and Seasons* in 1842, stands at midpoint among the source documents for the elaboration of Mormon theology. There is, in fact, a clear progression in the expansion of the concepts of the nature of God, humans, priesthood, and salvation from the Book of Mormon (1829) through Joseph Smith's translation-revision of the Bible (1830-33), D&C 84 and 88 (1832), the Book of Abraham (mostly 1835-36), and D&C 121 (1839) to D&C 132, the temple ceremony, and the King Follett discourse (1842-44). Among Joseph Smith's revelations, the Book of Abraham serves as a prime source for the doctrines of the premortal existence of human spirits and the plurality of Gods, stands as a halfway house in the movement toward plural marriage, and marks a stage in the development of statements about priesthood as the key to the power and knowledge of God.

In 1835 a Michael Chandler exhibited in Kirtland some Egyptian mummies and papyri, which members of the church bought from him. Joseph Smith said, "I began the translation of some of the characters or hieroglyphics [of these papyri], and much to our joy found that one of the rolls contained the writings of Abraham, another the writings of Joseph of Egypt—a more full account of which will appear in its place, as I proceed to examine or unfold them."[38] In the current LDS edition of the Book of Abraham, the book is presented as "a Translation of some ancient Records, that have fallen into our hands from the catacombs of Egypt.—The writings of Abraham while he was in Egypt, called the Book of Abraham, written by his own hand, upon papyrus."

Since resurfacing in 1967, having been missing and presumed lost for some eighty to ninety years, the papyri have been examined and translated by Egyptologists. As previously indicated, the fragment of papyrus identified by some as the ostensible source of the Book of Abraham bears no relationship to the Book of Abraham either in content or subject matter.[39] On the other hand, LDS Egyptologist Edward Ashment has suggested that it is not certain that Joseph Smith considered he had gotten the Book of Abraham from the papyri—he may have "received a revelation comprising the Book of Abraham [and] tried to match his revealed text with the *snsn* text in an effort to decipher Egyptian hieroglyphics."[40] In either case, there is a problem. Either Joseph's translation is in error, or there is no translation as we currently use the term.

Let us explore the latter possibility. The Book of Abraham does not fit with modern ideas about translation. It is not a document-to-document translation; Joseph got it wrong about the papyri having been written by the hand of Abraham. The English text nonetheless fits precisely with the pattern of translation as the restoring of things lost or the unfolding of things not known. The production of the book involves symbols that moved Joseph's mind to a vastly greater cosmic context.

The first stimulus seems to be the expanding ideas of Abraham and the priesthood, which derive from Joseph's previous revelations. The second stimulus is his contact with Hebrew, which by powerful coincidence Joseph began studying during the winter of 1835-36, shortly after he became deeply engrossed in the Egyptian papyri. The third stimulus is extra-biblical lore about Abraham, which Joseph encountered at about this same time.

Joseph's encounter with Hebrew has been carefully studied by Louis Zucker,[41] who describes the circumstances of the class, the qualifications of Professor Seixas, and the effect that Hebrew had on Joseph's thinking and revelations, especially on his revelation of the Book of Abraham. The presence of Hebrew words in the text (for example, the names of the sun, moon, stars, and firmament) can easily be accounted for by referring to Professor Seixas's grammar book. (These Hebrew terms are not important for adding ideas to the book, but they are important for showing that Joseph's mind was occupied with Hebrew.)

Not so easily explained is something quite different and more significant: other Hebrew words are used and carried far beyond their bare meaning into the elaboration of a new concept. The word *gnolaum* for example, is a noun form that may also be used as an adverb; but it is used by Joseph as an adjective in elaborating a doctrine of the premortal existence of spirits: "Yet these two spirits ... shall have no beginning ... no end, for they are *gnolaum*, or eternal" (Abr. 3: 18). The word *Elohim*, which is a plural form consistently interpreted as a singular by Jewish commentators, becomes the springboard for a polytheistic theology in chapters 4, 5, and 6, departing from the strict monotheism of the Book of Moses and of Abraham 1, 2, and 3. Zucker then gives a very insightful comment: "It has not been my intention to imply that Joseph Smith's free-handling of Hebrew grammar and the language of the Hebrew Bible shows ineptitude. ... I simply do not think he wanted to appear before the world as a meticulous Hebraist. He used the Hebrew as he chose, as an artist, inside his frame of reference, in accordance with his taste, according to the effect he wanted to produce, as a foundation for theological innovations."[42] In a more recent essay, Michael Walton makes the same points and emphasizes the influence of Joseph's Hebrew studies on the syntax and key words of the Book of Abraham.[43] Joseph worked as an artist, taking familiar material and transmuting it into something new and larger. Translation, then, is transmutation.

The third stimulus working in Joseph's mind was the extra-biblical information on Abraham. The problem initially prompting this essay, that of establishing a link between Joseph Smith and this material, was solved bit by bit but turned out to have only secondary significance. Joseph had access to information about Abraham through three identifiable sources: two learned Jews (Joshua Seixas and Alexander Neibaur) and Josephus, with whose writings, especially the *Antiquities of the Jews*, he was almost certainly familiar.

Joshua Seixas, the teacher engaged to teach a ten-week course of Hebrew at the School of the Prophets in Kirtland, was a learned and devout Jew, as evidenced by his authorship of a manual of Hebrew grammar to "promote the best of all studies, the study of the Bible."[44] It has sometimes come as a surprise to Bible-bound Christians that all the extant information about Abraham was not included in Genesis but has always been available to anyone learned in the rabbinical schools and traditions (as Joshua Seixas certainly was), since these traditions form an intrinsic part of the Jewish study of the scriptures.

We know from Professor Zucker's article that on at least one occasion (6 March 1836), Joseph went alone for instruction in Hebrew[45] and that on two other occasions (7 and 8 March), the "first class" translated chapters 17 and 22 of Genesis, both of which deal with Abraham.[46] It is not unlikely that the Jewish professor had occasion before, during, or after these sessions to mention or describe other information about Abraham.

Another possible source of information about Hebrew traditions was Alexander Neibaur, the first Jewish convert to Mormonism. He had studied in a Jewish rabbinical seminary and was familiar with Jewish philosophers and commentators. He settled in Nauvoo, Illinois, in 1841, became friends with Joseph, and was close enough to him to become a sometime German tutor to him. The Book of Abraham appeared in *Times and Seasons* in the spring of 1842, after Neibaur's arrival.

A more immediate and demonstrable source is Flavius Josephus (A.D. 37-ca. 100) in whose writings the same lore appears. His *Antiquities* was translated into English in 1737, and a copy of the 1794 edition was in Joseph Smith's hometown library;[47] but we need not speculate about a direct link. As we skim over the pages of the *Messenger and Advocate* for December 1835, whom do we find quoted at length by Oliver Cowdery but ... Josephus![48] And the reference is to the part of the *Antiquities* corresponding to Genesis. We cannot escape the conclusion that Josephus was read and talked about in

Kirtland in 1835. And since Josephus lays out this extra-biblical lore in such matter-of-fact detail and abundance, it seems reasonable to assume that Joseph Smith's already keen sense that much in the scriptures had been lost and needed to be restored may have been quickened, even to restoring more than was in Josephus.

Having said that much and having established the strong likelihood that Joseph did encounter the learning of the rabbinical tradition, we still have not explained the Book of Abraham, for its most striking characteristics are not in what is familiar, but in what transforms and transcends the familiar to the point of becoming original. The Book of Abraham is, in fact, an elaboration of the idea of priesthood as the key to knowledge, passing through Joseph's new learning, and ending with a new picture of the cosmos.

Abraham 1:26-27 has most often been read as a statement of the relative status of the white and black races, but in the context of the whole chapter these verses seem to be more a statement about the superiority of Abraham's priesthood, with its knowledge and keys to knowledge, compared to the learning of the Egyptians. Abraham is first portrayed as a seeker after knowledge, and his attainment of great learning is connected in a novel way with his "appointment unto the Priesthood" (vv. 2-4). The learning of the Egyptians, as recounted in the rabbinical tradition, is reflected in the Book of Abraham in Pharaoh's having received "the blessings of the earth, with the blessings of wisdom." But the superiority of Abraham and of the priesthood emerges as Pharaoh is cursed as to the priesthood (v. 26), which also accounts for the idolatrous imitation of the priesthood among the Egyptians (vv. 6-27). That this cursing was not merely a manifestation of nineteenth-century racism is shown by the fact that Pharaoh, who was cursed as to the priesthood, is depicted in facsimile 3 as being white.

Again, in Josephus, the study of astronomy causes Abraham to become the first monotheist. In the Book of Abraham, Abraham's study of astronomy leads to the vision of the heavens (given through the Urim and Thummim!), and from there Joseph takes us to a discussion of the eternity and therefore the premortal existence of spirits or intelligences, the purpose of earthly existence, the appointment of a redeemer and the revolt in heaven, and the creation of the earth and its life forms by a multiplicity of gods under the direction of one supreme God.

The Book of Abraham, in sum, reflects Joseph's first contact with substantive learning outside of the strictly biblical tradition in the study of Hebrew and the rabbinical tradition that attends it. This learning seems to have acted on his mind, along with his fascination with the papyri and mummies, in the same way that symbols and seer stones previously had. It served as a catalyst to "the gift of seeing" in the quantum leaps of revelation. The Book of Abraham is not the product of a document-to-document translation, but it fits exactly with the pattern of the seer-as-translator, unfolding what was hidden and expanding the symbol to the larger concept. For its authenticity the book depends not on a previous document but rather on its own internal merits.

We can feel the tug of the tide carrying us forward to 1842 and Joseph's encounter with the symbols of Masonry, likewise transformed and carried to new meanings, and the further symbol of Abraham as the polygamous patriarch, ending with the transformation of humans into eternally increasing and creating gods. However, we must leave these latter themes undeveloped and must recognize as well that the themes we have examined are susceptible to deeper probing and analysis (for example, the process of Joseph's translations, which might be clarified still more by Jungian views on the relationship between symbols and creativity). We must conclude with a statement of the premises and conclusions of this essay and their implications for Mormon belief and for new biographical light on Joseph Smith.

The first implication concerns the nature of revelation.

The tidying up of Mormonism over the past century or so has resulted in two views of revelation. One sees revelation as divine dictation to which a passive recipient makes no contribution, perhaps pausing even in mid-revelation to ask, "Would you mind spelling that word?" The recipient may be changed by the revelation, but the revelation is not limited by the culture nor changed by the life experiences of the recipient–it arrives pure and unsullied, as with a letter brought by a postman. David Whitmer had such an idea of the translation process of the Book of Mormon, believing Joseph saw letters and whole words through the seer stone and then simply dictated them to the scribe.[49] According to this view, as revelations are collected, their parts are interchangeable and their authority is equal: a verse from 1 Samuel 11 is just as valuable and binding as a verse from the Doctrine and Covenants or the Sermon on the Mount.

Such finalized revelation is a precondition to the construction of a dogmatic theology, one that can give definitive answers and cast the last stone. A dogmatic theology is a closed system. The first item on its agenda is authority, and the practical focus it yields for the religious life is obedience to this authority.

In the other view, the revelator is a prism shaped by his or her culture and life experiences. The light of the revelation is changed by the recipient, whose effort, study, and contribution are indispensable. The revelation reflects and in important ways is limited by the cultural context of the recipient, even while transcending it in others. The parts of the revelation are all valuable but not interchangeable. A later revelation may even contradict an earlier one, while each retains its parcel of truth. The revelation is always continuing and progressive, never fixed and final, and always partial.

In 1835, for example, had we asked for an absolute and final answer to the question of the number of personages in the godhead, the Lectures on Faith would have told us, "Two."[50] In 1843 we would have been told, "Three" (D&C 130: 22-23). In 1832, had we wanted to know what God was like, we would have been told that he was omnipotent and omniscient, and that he had always been that way.[51] In 1844, had we been present at the King Follett funeral discourse, we would have heard that God was once a man.[52] We should therefore expect that a continuing revelation may well modify previous revelations and that one day we will see in a wider context everything that we now believe.

This kind of continuing and partial revelation, which includes all of Joseph's translations, does not allow the construction of a dogmatic theology. This kind of revelation can vitalize, but not finalize. The theology derived from it serves as point of reference, as something to think with, but the system remains open, and the first item on the religious agenda is the responsibility of the individual to choose what is important in the living of his or her life. The focus of the religious life is on individual initiative.

The second implication of the views in this essay derives from the first and relates directly to authority-based belief. The earliest anti-

Mormon writers assumed that if they could link the Book of Mormon to a previous document (such as the Spalding manuscript), they could demolish the book's credibility. Pro-Mormon writers have assumed that if they could link the book with a previous document (such as the golden plates), the authority of the book would be established. Similarly, anti-Mormon writers have assumed that by severing the Book of Abraham from the papyri, they have settled the authority question, and some pro-Mormon writers have twisted every possible way to avoid those implications. In either case, the question ends up with a binary mode of thought: either Joseph Smith was an infallible spokesman for God, or he was a fraud.

The mischief with this binary mode is twofold. First, it leaves unsettled the question of how the document, even if authentic, becomes an authority. If the original manuscript of the Gospel of Mark, written in Mark's own handwriting, were discovered in a cave in upper Egypt, we would still have to resolve the question, for example, of whether Mark mistook epilepsy for demonic possession; we would still have to say why we believe that Mark got it right.

Second, the binary mode insulates us from, and in many cases causes us to miss, the contact with primary religious questions. To the extent that I base my life on an authority *out there*, the authority becomes responsible for me. As that authority diminishes, I must perforce take more responsibility myself.

With the more detailed descriptions we now have of the production of the Book of Mormon and the Book of Abraham, the immediate and primary link of the resulting texts is with the mind of the seer and not with a document, and the question changes complexion. Maintaining an authority-based faith becomes more and more difficult. Ultimately, I believe, both books must stand or fall on their own intrinsic worth, on the religious value of their content, as do the Koran, the *Bagavahd-Gita,* the *Urantia Book,* and the *Course in Miracles.* In William James's phrase, they must be judged by their fruits, not their roots, and individual responsibility in judging them then becomes total. No book becomes an authority by its origins, and all books become authorities to the extent, and only to the extent, of their yeast.

Could it be different? The Book of Mormon itself claims that it will be authenticated experientially and pragmatically, or at least that is how I understand Alma 32 and Moroni 10:4-5. The same test must also be applied to the Book of Abraham, as should the test enjoined since the beginning of Mormonism with regard to any supposed revelation: that which is light continues to increase in light, in congruence with a growing body of understanding. In the very terms of Mormon revelation, then, the translation or revelation cannot become an authority until it is completed and ratified in the mind and experience of the recipient.

As for "knowing Brother Joseph again," any new biography of Joseph Smith ought to include an account of how his mind worked, at least to the extent that it can be known through the texts he produced. Much of the current intellectual energy of Mormonism is being spent on establishing context, and, while context is indispensable and will require us to think in new ways, it will nonetheless miss the essential quality in Joseph until it is joined with text, which shows what he did with his context.

In addition, if we wish to understand Joseph Smith better, we should think of him as a complex man embodying a number of paradoxes. Richard Cummings has described the many facets of "literal mindedness" as the quintessential Mormon way, rooting life in a very narrow and particular spot;[53] but the genius of Mormonism, as expressed in the belief in a continuing revelation and in the 13th Article of Faith, has nonetheless been to go beyond the literal and to accept no limit as permanent. In this paradox, Mormonism continues to mirror its first prophet, for Joseph Smith manifested a curious literal mindedness throughout his life, all the while reacting powerfully to symbols, which always carried him beyond the immediate and the literal. A reductionist view, that he was "nothing but ...," will miss this essential quality.

When we think of him as a translator, we should think of him as a seer, one who sees into the powerfully moving, unseen forces of the soul and the rest of the cosmos to give these forces form. The resulting translation becomes authoritative only as reason completes this retrieval from the unknown by finding light and coherence in it and by confirming it in practice. Thus, since its inception, Mormonism has embodied a dialectic and has been shaped by this tension between the revelatory and the rational and pragmatic. To be a Latter-day Saint aware of beginnings is to be left with the individual task of making sure that all of the foregoing gets translated correctly.

*NOTES*

1. Grant S. Heward and Jerald Tanner, "The Source of the Book of Abraham Identified," *Dialogue: A Journal of Mormon Thought* 3 (Summer 1968): 93-98; Richard A. Parker, trans., "The Book of Breathings (Fragment 1, the Sensen Text, with Restorations from Louvre Papyrus 3284)," *Dialogue: A Journal of Mormon Thought* 3 (Summer 1968): 98-99.

2. A translation in this sense is seldom more than approximate. Matthew Arnold maintained that no one had ever adequately translated Homer–one translator may have captured his swiftness but not his nobility; another may have captured his nobility but not his plainness. On the other hand, Fitzgerald's translation of Omar Khayam into English is accounted by many who know both languages to exceed the quality of the poetry in the original, and Fitzgerald, not Omar Khayam, is credited as the poet of the *Rubyiat*.

3. See Richard Van Wagoner and Steven Walker, "Joseph Smith: 'The Gift of Seeing,'" *Dialogue: A Journal of Mormon Thought* 15 (Summer 1982): 48-68, reprinted in the present compilation; Blake T. Ostler, "The Book of Mormon as a Modern Expansion of an Ancient Source," *Dialogue: A Journal of Mormon Thought* 20 (Spring 1987): 66-123; James E. Lancaster, "The Method of Translation of the Book of Mormon," *The John Whitmer Historical Association Journal* 3 (1983): 51-61; Edward H. Ashment, "The Book of Mormon–A Literal Translation?" *Sunstone* 5 (Mar.-Apr. 1980): 10-14; and Stephen D. Ricks, "Joseph Smith's Means and Methods of Translating the Book of Mormon," Preliminary Report (Provo, UT: FARMS, 1984).

4. D. Michael Quinn, *Early Mormonism and the Magic World View* (Salt Lake City: Signature Books, 1987), 151-52.

5. Carl G. Jung, M. L. von Franz, Joseph L. Henderson, Jolande Jacobi, and Aniela Jaffe, *Man and His Symbols* (New York: Dell Publishing Co., 1964), 72-73, 88.

6. Ostler, 103.

7. Detailed descriptions of the translation process appear in Van Wagoner and Walker, 50-55; Ostler, 103-105; Lancaster, 52-56; Ashment, 11-13; and Ricks, 1-6.

8. Jung et al., 11.

9. When the report went around the countryside that Joseph was on the trail of hidden plates of gold, many of the local citizenry believed in the plates' existence as much as Joseph did and, according to the account of Lucy Mack Smith, sent some sixty miles for a conjuror to come and help them locate the plates. Joseph was nonetheless able to forestall them because he carried the Urim and Thummim around with him, and they warned him when the plates were in danger (Lucy Mack Smith, *Biographical Sketches of Joseph Smith the Prophet and His Progenitors for Many Generations*[Liverpool, Eng.: published by S. W. Richards for Orson Pratt, 1853], 102-104).

In another example, after Joseph had obtained the plates and had hidden them temporarily in a box in the cooper's shed, "a young woman by the name of Chase, sister to Willard Chase, found a green glass, through which she could see many wonderful things, and among her great discoveries she said she saw the precise place where 'Joe Smith kept his gold bible hid.'" Evidently the glass worked just fine, for the mob went to the exact place she indicated, tore up the floor, and found the box in which she had seen the plates. Fortunately, Joseph had had an intimation of danger and had removed the plates from the box, hidden them in another place, and had replaced the box as before (ibid., 108-109).

For David Whitmer the stone even became the test of the authenticity of revelations–it was after Joseph stopped using the stone and started to give revelations by his own mouth that he began to trust in the arm of flesh and to drift into error (David Whitmer, *An Address to All Believers in Christ* [1887; reprint, Salt Lake City: Modern Microfilm, 1984], 12).

10. M. L. von Franz, "The Process of Individuation," in *Man and His Symbols*, ed. Carl G. Jung (New York: Dell Publishing Co., 1964), 227.

11. Brewster Ghiselen, *The Creative Process* (New York: New American Library, 1952), 12, 13.

12. Ibid., 14.

13. Ibid., 44-45.

14. Ibid., 59.

15. Ibid., 57.

16. Ibid., 16.

17. Ibid., 65.

18. C. Jess Groesbeck, "The Smiths and Their Dreams and Visions," *Sunstone* 12 (Mar. 1988): 22-29.

19. In Joseph Fielding Smith, ed., *Teachings of the Prophet Joseph Smith* (Salt Lake City: Deseret Book, 1976), 137.

20. Ibid., 151.

21. In *Times and Seasons* 2 (1 Nov. 1840): 201.

22. The *Urantia Book*, published by the Urantia Foundation (Chicago, 1955) is a history of the past and future of this planet (Urantia), with a life of Jesus, the whole being given by a corps of revelators appointed to this purpose. *A Course in Miracles*, published by The Foundation for Inner Peace in 1975, was dictated by an inner voice to its author, or recipient.

23. L. M. Smith, 84.

24. Whitmer, 11-12.

25. Richard L. Bushman, *Joseph Smith and the Beginnings of Mormonism* (Urbana: University of Illinois Press, 1984), 7-8, 71-72.

26. The term "Urim and Thummim" apparently did not appear in any publication before 1833, when W. W. Phelps associated the stones or interpreters with the Old Testament practice of inquiring of the Lord through

Urim and Thummim (Van Wagoner and Walker, 61). The reference to translation by the Urim and Thummim in D&C 10:1 differs from the same revelation in the 1833 Book of Commandments. D&C 17, where the term is used, was not published until 1835.

27. F. Henry Edwards, "Introduction," in *Joseph Smith's "New Translation" of the Bible* (Independence, MO: Herald Publishing Co., 1970), 23.

28. Van Wagoner and Walker, 59-61; Quinn, 195-204. I must mention in passing that the notion of the seer and the use of physical objects as prompts to or media of inspiration were not restricted to the "magical world view" or the burned-over district of the American frontier. In the age of Romantic inspiration, when William Blake was having his mystical visions and Swedenborg in the manner of a seer was laying bare the correspondence of the natural and spiritual orders, characters in Balzac novels expatiated freely on phrenology, Goethe composed poetry while holding the skull of Schiller, and Victor Hugo, the poet-seer, consulted the spiritualistic mediums on the island of Jersey. The rationalism of the Enlightenment was never totally dominant.

29. Jung et al. The Jungian paradigm with its concepts of the unconscious, the animus and anima, the shadow, and individuation offers rich possibilities for understanding Joseph which are beyond the scope of this present essay.

30. Anthony A. Hutchinson, "A Mormon Midrash? LDS Creation Narratives Reconsidered," *Dialogue: A Journal of Mormon Thought* 21 (Winter 1988): 11-74.

31. Quinn, 97-111.

32. A more complete study of Joseph before 1830 would have to include the symbols of Israel, including the lost ten tribes, of Zion, and of the curse (which figures so prominently in the Book of Mormon and the Book of Moses). A study of Joseph in Nauvoo would have to include the symbols of Masonry.

33. Edwards, 15.

34. In ibid., 8.

35. Quinn, 172.

36. David John Buerger, "'The Fullness of the Priesthood': The Second Anointing in Latter-day Saint Theology and Practice," *Dialogue: A Journal of Mormon Thought* 16 (Spring 1983): 22, 24.

37. *History of the Church of Jesus Christ of Latter-day Saints*, 7 vols. (Salt Lake City: Deseret News, 1902), 1:245; hereafter HC.

38. Ibid., 2:235-36.

39. Heward and Tanner, 93-98; Parker, 98-99.

40. Edward H. Ashment, "The Book of Abraham Facsimiles: A Reappraisal," *Sunstone* 4 (Dec. 1979): 44.

41. Louis Zucker, "Joseph Smith as a Student of Hebrew," *Dialogue: A Journal of Mormon Thought* 3 (Summer 1968): 41-55.

42. Ibid., 51-53.

43. Michael T. Walton, "Professor Seixas, the Hebrew Bible, and the Book of Abraham," *Sunstone* 6 (Mar.-Apr. 1981): 41-43.

44. Zucker, 6.

45. Ibid., 46.

46. Ibid., 47.

47. Quinn, 263.

48. Oliver Cowdery, "Egyptian Mummies–Ancient Records," *Messenger and Advocate* 2 (Dec. 1835): 234.

49. Whitmer, 12.

50. "Lectures on Faith," in *Joseph Smith Begins His Work*, vol. 2, ed. Wilford C. Wood (Salt Lake City: by the author, 1963), 55.

51. Ibid., 37-38.

52. J. F. Smith, 345.

53. Richard J. Cummings, "Quintessential Mormonism: Literal-mindedness as a Way of Life," *Dialogue: A Journal of Mormon Thought* 15 (Winter 1982): 93-102.

# Epilogue: The King Follett Discourse, Excerpts

*Joseph Smith*

THERE ARE BUT VERY FEW BEINGS IN THE WORLD WHO UNDERSTAND rightly the character of God. If men do not comprehend the character of God, they do not comprehend their own character. They cannot comprehend anything that is past or that which is to come; they do not know–they do not understand their own relationship to God. The world knows and comprehends but little more than the brute beast. If a man knows nothing more than to eat, drink, sleep, arise, and not any more, and does not comprehend what any of the designs of Jehovah are, what better is he than the beast, for it comprehends the same things–it eats, drinks, sleeps, comprehends the present and knows nothing more about God or His existence. This is as much as we know unless we are able to comprehend by the inspiration of Almighty God. And how are we to do it by any other way? ...

Here then is eternal life–to know the only wise and true God. You have got to learn how to make yourselves Gods in order to save yourselves and be kings and priests to God, the same as all Gods have done–by going from a small capacity to a great capacity, from a small degree to another, from grace to grace, until the resurrection of the dead from exaltation to exaltation–till you are able to sit in everlasting burnings and everlasting power and glory as those who have gone before, sit enthroned. I want you to know that God in the last days, while certain individuals are proclaiming His name, is not trifling with you nor me. ...

It is plain beyond comprehension and you thus learn that these are some of the first principles of the Gospel, about which so much has been said. When you climb a ladder, you must begin at the bottom rung. You have got to find the beginning of the history and go on until you have learned the last principle of the Gospel. It will be a great while after the grave before you learn to understand the last, for it is a great thing to learn salvation beyond the grave and it is not all to be comprehended in this world. ...

I advise all to be careful what you do. Stay, all that hear. Do not give way. Don't make any hasty moves. You may be saved, or you may by and by find out that someone has laid a snare for you and you have been deceived. Be cautious: await. If a spirit of bitterness is in you, don't be in haste. When you find a spirit that wants bloodshed–murder–the same is not of God, but is of the devil. Say you, "That man is a sinner;" well, if he repents, he shall be forgiven. Out of the abundance of the heart, man speaks. The man that tells you words of life is the man that can save you. The best men bring forth the best works. I warn you against all evil characters who sin against the Holy Ghost; for there is no redemption for them in this world nor in the world to come. ...

You don't know me–you never will. You never knew my heart. No man knows my history. I cannot do it. I shall never undertake it. I don't blame you for not believing my history. If I had not experienced what I have, I could not have believed it myself. I never did harm any man since I have been born in the world. My voice is always for peace. I cannot lie down until my work is finished. I never think evil nor think anything to the harm of my fellowman. When I am called at the trump and weighed in the balance, you will know me then. I add no more. God bless you. Amen.

–Excerpted from Stan Larson, ed., "The King Follett Discourse: A Newly Amalgamated Text," *BYU Studies* 18 (Winter 1978)

# CONTRIBUTORS

THOMAS G. ALEXANDER is Lemuel Hardison Redd, Jr., Professor of Western American History at Brigham Young University, Provo, Utah, and the author of, among other books and essays, *Mormonism in Transition: A History of the Latter-day Saints, 1890-1930.* "The Place of Joseph Smith in the Development of American Religion: A Historiographical Inquiry" first appeared in *Journal of Mormon History* 5 (1978): 3-17.

ROBERT D. ANDERSON, M.D., is a semi-retired psychiatrist in Bellevue, Washington. He became interested in applied psychoanalysis during studies with the Seattle Psychoanalytic Institute, and wondered what results might occur in a psychological examination of the Book of Mormon. His full-length psychobiography of Joseph Smith is forthcoming from Signature Books, Salt Lake City, Utah. "Toward an Introduction to a Psychobiography of Joseph Smith" first appeared in *Dialogue: A Journal of Mormon Thought* 27 (Fall 1994): 249-72.

GARY JAMES BERGERA is associate publisher of Signature Books, Inc., and immediate past managing editor of *Dialogue: A Journal of Mormon Thought.* "Joseph Smith and the Hazards of Charismatic Leadership" first appeared in *Journal of the John Whitmer Historical Association* 6 (1986): 33-42.

NEWELL G. BRINGHURST is Instructor of History and Political Science at College of the Sequoias in Visalia, California. Involved in an ambivalent twenty-eight-year relationship with Mormon studies, he is currently president-elect of the Mormon History Association and the author of three books and some thirty articles. His latest book, *Altered Lives: Fawn McKay Brodie and the Craft of Modern Biography*, is forthcoming from the University of Oklahoma Press. "Joseph Smith, the Mormons, and Antebellum Reform–A Closer Look" first appeared in *John Whitmer Historical Association Journal* 14 (1994): 73-91.

RICHARD L. BUSHMAN holds three degrees from Harvard University. He has taught at Brigham Young University, Boston University, the University of Delaware, and Columbia University, where he currently is Gouverneur Morris Professor of History. His many books include *Joseph Smith and the Beginnings of Mormonism* (1984) and *The Refinement of America: Persons, Houses, Cities* (1992). He is presently working on a full-life biography of Joseph Smith. "Joseph Smith as Translator" is published here for the first time.

EUGENE ENGLAND is professor emeritus of English at Brigham Young University, Provo, Utah, and the author of, most recently, *Making Peace: Personal Essays*. "How Joseph Smith Resolved the Dilemmas of American Romanticism" is published here for the first time.

LAWRENCE FOSTER is a professor of American history at Georgia Tech in Atlanta and author of *Religion and Sexuality*, which won the Mormon History Association's Best Book Award. His second book, *Women, Family, and Utopia*, discusses Mormon women's reactions to plural marriage and explores the changing role of Mormon women. "The Psychology of Religious Genius: Joseph Smith and the Origin of New Religious Movements" first appeared in *Dialogue: A Journal of Mormon Thought* 26 (Winter 1993): 1-22.

RONALD V. HUGGINS has a Th.D. in New Testament from the Toronto School of Theology, University of Toronto. His essays have appeared in a number of scholarly journals, including the *Journal of Biblical Literature*, *Novum Testamentum*, the *Revue de Qumran*, and *Dialogue: A Journal of Mormon Thought*. He currently resides in Spokane, Washington. "Joseph Smith's 'Inspired Translation' of Romans 7" first appeared in *Dialogue: A Journal of Mormon Thought* 26 (Winter 1993): 159-82.

LANCE S. OWENS is a physician and clinical professor at the University of Utah, Salt Lake City. He received a 1994 best article award from the Mormon History Association for his essay "Joseph Smith and Kabbalah: The Occult Connection." "Joseph Smith: America's Hermetic Prophet" first appeared in *Gnosis Magazine*, Spring 1995, 56-64.

KARL C. SANDBERG is DeWitt Wallace Professor Emeritus of French and Humanities at Macalester College in St. Paul, Minnesota. He has taught at Duke University, the University of Arizona, the University of Minnesota, the University of Colorado, and Brigham Young University. "Knowing Brother Joseph Again: The Book of Abraham and Joseph Smith as Translator" first appeared in *Dialogue: A Journal of Mormon Thought* 22 (Winter 1989): 17-37.

JAN SHIPPS, professor emeritus of religious studies and history at Indiana University-Purdue University, Indianapolis, is the author of *Mormonism: The Story of a New Religious Tradition.* "The Prophet Puzzle: Suggestions Leading toward a More Comprehensive Interpretation of Joseph Smith" first appeared in *Journal of Mormon History* 1 (1974): 2-20.

SUSAN STAKER, past managing editor of *Sunstone* magazine, lives in Portola Valley, California, and is Editorial Manager, User Education, for Adobe Systems Incorporated in San Jose. "'The Lord Said, Thy Wife Is a Very Fair Woman to Look Upon': The Book of Abraham, Secrets, and Lying for the Lord" is published here for the first time.

ALAN TAYLOR is a professor of history at the University of California at Davis. He is the author of *Liberty Men and Great Proprietors: The Revolutionary Settlement on the Maine Frontier, 1760-1820* (Chapel Hill: University of North Carolina Press, 1990) and *William Cooper's Town: Power and Persuasion on the Frontier of the Early American Republic* (New York: Alfred A. Knopf, 1995). The latter won the Beveridge, Bancroft, and Pulitzer prizes in American history. "Recovering the Context of Joseph Smith's Treasure Seeking" first appeared, in a slightly different form, in *Dialogue: A Journal of Mormon Thought* 19 (Winter 1986): 18-28.

RICHARD S. VAN WAGONER, a clinical audiologist practicing in Salt Lake City, Utah, is the co-author of *A Book of Mormons,* and author of *Mormon Polygamy: A History, Lehi: Portraits of a Utah Town,* and *Sidney Rigdon: A Portrait of Religious Excess.* "Joseph Smith: 'The Gift of Seeing'" (co-authored with Steven C. Walker) first appeared, in slightly different form, in *Dialogue: A Journal of Mormon Thought* 15 (Summer 1982): 49-68.

DAN VOGEL is the author of *Indian Origins and the Book of Mormon* and *Religious Seekers and the Advent of Mormonism,* as well as the editor of the multi-volume *Early Mormon Documents.* "'The Prophet Puzzle' Revisited" first appeared in *Dialogue: A Journal of Mormon Thought* 31 (Fall 1998): 125-40. He lives in Westerville, Ohio, with his wife Margie and is currently working on a biography of Joseph Smith's early life and teachings.

STEVEN C. WALKER (Ph.D., English, Harvard University) is a professor of English at Brigham Young University, Provo, Utah, where he teaches Victorian and modern British literature as well as courses on the Bible as literature and Christian fantasy. "Joseph Smith: 'The Gift of Seeing'" (co-authored with Richard S. Van Wagoner) first appeared, in slightly different form, in *Dialogue: A Journal of Mormon Thought* 15 (Summer 1982): 49-68.